Desktop Publishing:

Producing Professional Publications

By Benedict Kruse

Illustrations prepared on desktop computers by

John L. Banner

Foreword by

Kamiran Badrkhan

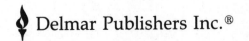 Delmar Publishers Inc.®

NOTICE TO THE READER

Workstation courtesy of Computer Professionals, Albany, New York
Photo by Mike Gallitelli/METROLAND PHOTO

Delmar Staff

Production Editor: Eleanor Isenhart

Associate Editor: Jay Whitney
Design Coordinator: Susan C. Mathews

Editing Manager: Gerry East
Production Coordinator: Linda Helfrich

For information, address Delmar Publishers Inc.,
2 Computer Drive West, Box 15-015,
Albany, New York 12212

COPYRIGHT © 1989
By DELMAR PUBLISHERS INC.

Printed in the United States of America
Published simultaneously in Canada
by Nelson Canada
A Division of International Thomson Limited

10 9 8 7 6 5 4 3 2 1

Library of Congress Cataloging-in-Publication Data
Kruse, Benedict.
    Desktop publishing : producing professional publications / by
Benedict Kruse ; illustrations prepared on desktop computers by John
L. Banner ; foreword by Kamiran Badrkhan.
        p.   cm
    Includes index.
    ISBN 0-8273-3619-5 (pbk.).   ISBN 0-8273-3620-9 (instructor's
guide)
    1. Desktop publishing.   I. Title.
Z286.D47K8   1989
686.2'2—dc19   88-28565
                                                              CIP

Contents

Foreword xi

Preface xiii

1. Documentation and Publishing as an Industry 1

Editorial Budget   1
A Trade and Its Marks   2
   The World of Movable Type   3
   Printing as a Process   4
Letterpress Printing   6
Lithography: From Art Form to Information Medium   7
Xerography: Printing Electronically   8
   The Laser Printer   9
Creating Images to Be Printed   9
Type Itself   13
The Computerized Desktop   15
   Role of Computer Technology   15
   Role of Television Technology   16
   Role of Communications Technology   17
The Makeup Desk   18
The Composing Room   18

2. The Publishing Process 19

Editorial Budget   19
Finding a Common Denominator   20
What Is a Process and Why Is Publishing a Process?   20
Writing a Manuscript   21
Copy Editing   23
Production Editing   23
Capturing Text   25
Typesetting   26
Illustrating   26
Proofreading   26
Designing and Laying out Pages   27
Making up Pages   28
Printing and Binding   29

Marketing and Distribution   35
Managing the Process   36
Perspective   36
The Makeup Desk   36
The Composing Room   36

3. Desktop Publishing: Tools and End Products 37

Editorial Budget   37
Computer Equipment: Components and Operations   38
    Input Components   38
    Processing Components   42
    Output Components   47
    Storage Components   49
Computer Software: Linking Users and Their Tools   52
    System Software   52
    Application Software   54
Software Access: Menus and Icons   56
Ancillaries and Auxiliaries   57
Matching Systems and Applications   59
The Makeup Desk   60
The Composing Room   60

4. Manuscript Preparation 61

Editorial Budget   61
Manuscript Sources   62
    In-House Authorship   63
    External Authorship   63
    Coordination Tips   63
The Manuscript Development Process   68
Text Capture   69
    Starting Work   69
    Word Wrap Feature   70
    Saving Text   70
    Typesetting Codes   71
    Proportional Spacing Decisions   71
Review and Revision   72
    Inserting New Text   72
    Deleting Text   72
    Moving or Copying Text   73
    Relative Efficiency of Electronic Methods   74
Release to Typesetting   74
Format   74
Proof   76
Release for Makeup   76
The Makeup Desk   77
The Composing Room   77

5. Text-Only Publications 78

Editorial Budget   78
Text-Based Documents   79
    Reports   79
    Requests for Proposal   79
    Proposals and Bids   80

Contracts or Other Legal Documents   80
Newsletters and Bulletins   81
Manuals and Books   83
Design Checklist   87
Borders and "White Space"   87
Typeface Selection   89
Line Width   89
Type Size and Leading   96
Running Heads   96
Folios   96
Overall Page Layout   99
Top and Bottom Alignment   99
Production Techniques   104
Budgeting and Managing Projects   104
Scope the Job   104
Schedule the Work   105
Set Budgets and Monitor Costs   105
The Makeup Desk   106
The Composing Room   106

6. Line Illustration Techniques **107**

Editorial Budget   107
What Is Line Art?   108
Role and Uses of Line Art in Publications   108
Line Art Preparation Software Tools   108
Drawing a Line   108
Creating a Rectangle   110
Special Effects   110
Stock Art   115
Line Art as a Layout Element   116
Illustrating Text   116
Building Visual Interest   116
Generated Line Art   116
Line Art Example: Organization Chart   118
Line Art Example: Flowchart   120
Line Art Example: Electronic Diagram   122
Line Art Example: Floor Plan   122
Line Art Example: Publication Logo   124
Scanner Input   126
Positioning Photographs   127
Using Illustrations   128
The Makeup Desk   130
The Composing Room   130

7. Manuals and Illustrated Reports **131**

Editorial Budget   131
Types of Reports   132
Characteristics and Formats   132
Some Special Situations   132
Types of Illustrations   132
Special Line Art Possibilities   132
Roles for Photos   134
Design Principles   136

Layout and Production   137
  Copy Fitting   137
  Positioning Illustrations   138
  Sketching Layouts   138
  Dummying   139
Using Page Makeup Software   140
  About PageMaker   141
  Using PageMaker   143
Page Makeup Tools Are Flexible   150
The Makeup Desk   151
The Composing Room   151

8. Presentation Graphics and Principles of Color Reproduction 152

Editorial Budget   152
Challenge and Opportunity   153
Some Basics on Audio-Visual Presentations   153
  Management Briefings   153
  Information and Instruction Sessions   154
Role of Desktop Publishing   155
Color and Computers   155
  Color Boards and Monitors   156
  Slide Attachments   156
  Plotters   157
  Color Cartridges in Laser Printers   157
  Output Format   158
  Hand Coloring   159
  Use of an Office Copier   159
Designing in Color   160
  Primary Colors   160
  Balance and Control   162
  Type in Color   163
Integrating Graphics into a Presentation   163
The Makeup Desk   164
The Composing Room   164

9. Marketing Support Publications 165

Editorial Budget   165
The Impact of Desktop Publishing   166
Types of Market-Support Publications   167
  Brochures   167
  Catalogs   167
  Product Information Sheets   168
  Price Lists   170
  Capabilities and Facilities Descriptions   170
Design Principles   170
Design Techniques   172
  The Grid Approach   172
Production Considerations   174
  Page Makeup Software   174
  Preparing for Color Printing   176
The Makeup Desk   181
The Composing Room   181

10. Newsletters 182

Editorial Budget 182
The Newsletter Medium 183
Types of Newsletters 183
    Profit-Making Newsletters 183
    Nonprofit Newsletters 185
    Sponsored Newsletters 187
Design and Layout Considerations 187
    Column Formats 188
    Logo and Masthead 194
    Mailing Indicia 194
Production Concerns 197
    Text Capture and Page Makeup 197
    Copy Checking 198
    Binding 198
    Distribution 200
    Scheduling 200
The Makeup Desk 201
The Composing Room 201

11. Magazines and Journals 202

Editorial Budget 202
The Media 203
Types of Publications 203
    News and Weekly Magazines 203
    Feature-Oriented Magazines 203
    Business Magazines 203
    Professional Magazines and Journals 203
    Sponsored Magazines 204
Media Characteristics 204
    Formats 204
    Cover Options 205
    The Advertising-Circulation Connection 205
    Layout 205
    Color 205
    Photography 206
Design and Layout Emphasis 206
    Placing Advertisements 206
    Identify a Role for Your Computer 206
    High-Resolution Output 207
    Photo Selection and Placement 208
Production Concerns 210
The Makeup Desk 212
The Composing Room 212

12. Newspapers 213

Editorial Budget 213
The Medium 214
    Paper Stock 214
    Printing Production 214
    Page Size 215
    Publication Schedule 215

Circulation   216
Use of Computers   216
Publishing Functions   218
Copy Sources and Handling   218
Advertising Copy   220
The Makeup Function   222
Production Concerns and Techniques   227
Computer Work Stations   228
Pasteup Techniques   228
Special Typography to Match Makeup   229
Circulation Documentation   229
The Makeup Desk   230
The Composing Room   230

13. Books **231**

Editorial Budget   231
The Book Business   232
Book Industry Segments   232
The Nature of Book Production   234
Common Production Requirements   234
Manuscript Development   234
Production Scheduling: A Special Challenge   235
Marketing Challenges   235
Textbook Marketing   235
Trade Book Marketing   236
Book Development   236
Manuscript Submission   236
Developmental Editing   237
Copy Editing   237
Production Editing   237
Design and Layout   237
Typesetting and Mechanicals   238
Indexing   240
The Makeup Desk   241
The Composing Room   241

14. Setting up a Production Facility **242**

Editorial Budget   242
Joining the Club   243
Analysis, Not Paralysis   243
Define Desired Results   244
Identify Sources or Inputs   244
Define Processing Requirements   245
Determine Needs for Storage and File Handling   246
Specify Equipment and Software Requirements   247
Desktop Publishing Equipment: A Technology in Transition   247
Hardware/Software Decision Criteria   248
The Computer   248
Disk Storage   249
Printer   252
Publishing Software   252
Electronic Typesetting   254
Networking   254

Provide for Human Factors   255
    Ergonomic Factors   255
Desktop Publishing Trends   257
    Increased Hardware Capabilities   259
    More Sophisticated Software   259
    Coordination Between Desktop and Larger Publishing Systems   259
    Advances in Printing Technology   261
The Makeup Desk   262
The Composing Room   262

Appendix A: Software Tools for Desktop Publishing 263

Appendix B: Layout Forms 269

Glossary 277

Index 287

Copyright/ Trademark Notice

The items listed below, which are mentioned in this book, are covered by copyright and/or trademark protection.

Adobe Systems, Inc.
Aldus Corporation
Aldus PageMaker
Allied Merganthaler
Apple Corporation
Apple LaserWriter
Apple LaserWriter Plus
Apple Macintosh
Apple Macintosh Plus
Apple Macintosh SE
Apple Macintosh 2
Compaq
EPSF
Hayes
IBM
IBM MT/ST
IBM OS/2
IBM PC
IBM PC DOS
IBM PS/2
Linotronic 100

Linotronic 300
Linotype
MacDraw
MacDraw II
MacDraft
MacLink
MacLink Plus
MacPaint
Merganthaler
Microsoft Word
MS DOS
MultiMate
PageMaker
PICT
PostScript
SuperPaint
TIFF
Ventura Publisher
WordPerfect
WordStar
Xerox Corporation

Foreword

Books like this one are encouraging to encounter for professionals involved in occupational education. Few books of this caliber exist. At least, I have encountered precious few in more than a decade of experience as a classroom teacher and administrator in the field of occupational education. This experience has helped me to establish a clear picture of the expectations faced by professionals in occupational education:

The business community wants job-ready graduates from its secondary and post-secondary educational institutions.

To impart practical, employable skills to our students, we educators need effective tools. Among other requirements, we need texts that reflect real-world experiences and methods—materials that prepare students to move into the job market without being surprised by the vast differences between their educational preparation and the realities they encounter.

Desktop Publishing: Producing Professional Publications is the kind of instructional tool that is needed by occupational educators. The book is timely: It is available at a time when the discipline of desktop publishing is experiencing rapid acceptance and growth.

Desktop Publishing is a superior instructional tool—for several reasons. For one thing, the book is written at a level that can be understood and assimilated by students who seek careers in commercial art, publication production, and journalism. Another important feature is that the book has real-world relevance. Benedict Kruse has a lifetime (more than 40 years) of professional writing and publishing experience. His background shows within this book.

The content of this work is far more than a digest of theoretical presentations and advertising claims made by manufacturers and software suppliers. Benedict Kruse *does* desktop publishing. His explanations help students learn to produce professional publications—and to acquire the background needed for employability.

Over and above the practicality of the content of this book is a solid pedagogical structure that is based upon the author's extensive experience in curriculum design and development and in the preparation of materials to impart learning. I have served on committees for which he provided staff support and guidance. Benedict Kruse is a doer—as a writer, consultant, and publication developer. He is committed to building capabilities for economic survival within that segment of the population that is shortchanged economically and culturally. This book has been written to bring his years of experience into the classroom of any instructor who seeks to equip students with a working capability in desktop publishing.

Kamiran Badrkhan, PhD

Associate Dean, Occupational Education

Long Beach City College

Long Beach, CA

Preface

WHERE THIS BOOK IS COMING FROM

The microcomputer is, first and foremost, a tool— one designed to help people to solve problems and to perform better on existing jobs. *Desktop Publishing: Producing Professional Publications* is organized and written from this vantage point.

For the author of this book, the first sentence above is both a goal and a commitment. The statement that the microcomputer is a tool means, of course, that the users of that tool are people. Further, it is assumed that the people who seek to learn how to use microcomputers are motivated, that they want to do a better job of solving problems and to be more productive on the job. For situations in which microcomputers are to be applied to create publications, the users are writers, editors, and publication production people. The problems to be solved and the performances to be delivered involve creating a wide range of different types of publications.

The point: A knowledge and capability in the area of publishing are basic requirements. These prerequisites must be in place before any tool— no matter how powerful— can be applied.

Therefore, this book is, first and throughout, about publishing in its many forms and aspects. Publishing is the context. Within that context, this book moves, with much-needed clarity and depth, to help the reader/learner understand uses and values of desktop computers in publishing.

This book is intended to help establish basic knowledge and to serve as a basis for the building of skills in publication production generally and in desktop publishing specifically. Therefore, the book is of potential value to any student or professional interested in the production side of publishing.

TARGET AUDIENCE

Specific individuals who should find this book helpful include:

- Journalism students can master most of the skills of makeup and production required to qualify for jobs in electronic newsrooms.

- Students interested in technical writing and/or business communication can gain practical knowledge in designing and producing publications to meet needs of audiences.

- Students interested in graphic arts can benefit from the instruction provided in use of desktop computers as illustration and publication-development tools.

- Persons in editorial and/or publication-production positions can use this book to establish the knowledge needed to update their skills. For both employed and entry-level people, this book should hold important keys for both employment and advancement.

Learn From the Ground Up

This book, remember, is based on the premise that the computer is a tool for people. Therefore, its content is designed to eliminate any and all apprehensions about computers. The point is made strongly that computers are not complex; they are simple. To stress the ease with which people can master computers, computers are described in terms of their limitations. The simple capabilities of computers, once understood, make it easy to master them as tools. The initial explanations about computers and their role in publishing puts the reader/learner at ease— regardless of whether or not the individual has had previous exposure to computers and their use.

The point: This book can be used by anyone with an interest in publishing and the role of computers in creating publications. There are no prerequisites. This single work is the basis for a complete learning experience.

SPECIAL FEATURES

By design, this book combines theoretical information and hands-on practice to help establish threshold-level application and employment skills in desktop publishing. Early chapters introduce broad, general concepts. Then, a series of specific chapters cover skills in typesetting, illustration, and publication layout. These are followed by chapters on specific kinds of publications.

Within each chapter, there are a series of learning tools. At the beginning of the chapter is a section called **Editorial Budget.** This title is derived from the practice on newspapers and magazines of preparing content summaries for each issue. The budgets become tools for deciding priorities and placements for stories and for layout of entire issues.

Technical and industry terminology is introduced as relevant throughout the book. As each new term is used for the first time, it is printed in **bold italics** for emphasis. The term is defined in context within the text. As an additional learning aid, the term also is included and defined in a box entitled **Desktop Jargon** that appears on most right-hand pages within the book.

At the end of each chapter, two kinds of assignments are provided. These are designed to impart practical experience in use of desktop publishing. **The Makeup Desk** assignments deal with the selection of editorial content and the design of publications. **The Composing Room** provides assignments related directly to the use

of desktop computers for the creation of publications.

Finally, an Appendix provides an extensive list, with descriptions, of current software available for the Apple Macintosh and IBM PC or compatible that can be used for desktop publishing. Company names and addresses are given for convenience in obtaining further information.

INSTRUCTOR'S GUIDE

An Instructor's Guide that accompanies and supplements this text provides extensive, coordinated pedagogical materials. For each chapter in the text, the Instructor's Guide includes the following:

- A set of **Lecture Notes** presenting a concise outline of each chapter is designed to assist in class presentations.
- A set of **Pedagogical Hints** offers material, some of which goes beyond the literal content of the text, that can be stressed in lectures or class discussions.
- For each chapter, a set of **Supplementary Projects** is provided as the basis for special or extra student assignments.
- For each chapter, a set of **Multiple Choice** and a separate set of **True-False** questions are provided.

In addition to these materials on each chapter, the Instructor's Guide contains a set of **transparency masters** that can be used to assist in class presentations.

CONTENT ORGANIZATION WITHIN THIS TEXT

This book begins, in Chapter 1, with a general introduction to publishing as an industry. The chapter includes a brief history of printing and publishing that provides a framework within which to describe and discuss the role of each of the major composition and reproduction processes. The review starts with Johann Gutenberg and progresses through letterpress, offset, and xerographic reproduction to computerized systems generally and desktop publishing methods specifically.

Chapter 2 introduces the concept that publishing is a process that involves a series of steps. The steps that begin with the writing of a manuscript and culminate with printing, binding, and distribution then are identified and described. The discussion is generic. But specific strengths and contributions of desktop publishing methods are identified within the overall context of a continuous process.

With an overview of the publishing process as a framework, Chapter 3 proceeds to review the **Tools and End Products** of desktop publishing. This chapter features a description of what computers are and how they work. Emphasis is on the simplicity of computer functions. The idea is to establish that computers are so simple and fundamental that they can be mastered readily—just as is done with any other occupationally oriented tool.

The chief role of most publications is to package and present textual information. Therefore, manuscript preparation is the starting point in the development of most publications. The steps in manuscript preparation and the use of desktop computers for this function are covered in Chapter 4.

Once a student has mastered the word processing and typesetting tools covered in Chapter 4, he or she is ready to produce rudimentary documents that consist entirely of text. Chapter 5 describes, step by step, how some publications, such as simple reports and legal documents, can be produced entirely through use of word processing and typesetting software that run on desktop computers.

To go beyond creation of publications that contain text only, students need to know how illustrations are prepared on desktop systems. Tools and techniques for preparation of line illustrations on desktop computers are covered in Chapter 6. In a series of examples, students are shown how a number of different types of line art can be created with basic drafting software. Included are an organization chart, a flowchart, an electronic circuit diagram, a floor plan for a building, and a logo for a hypothetic publication. This chapter also covers the use of photographs to illustrate publications.

The logical next step is for students to learn how to combine illustrations and text into different types of publications. Chapter 7 begins this learning experience by discussing principles of production for manuals and illustrated reports. The basic design and layout skills for publication planning also are covered. These include copy fitting, positioning of illustrations, preparation of preliminary layout sketches, and dummying of publications. Students also are carried through a demonstration of computerized page makeup through use of PageMaker software.

In Chapter 8, students learn about presentation graphics. The main outputs of desktop computers used for presentation graphics are overhead transparencies and slides. Descriptions of the work involved provide an opportunity to impart some basic training in desktop publishing capabilities for generating color images and end products. In the process, the chapter includes a basic review of the nature and characteristics of color. Color imaging through both additive and subtractive primary colors is described. Practical hints for adding color to presentation graphics include descriptions on use of slide makers, color plotters, and color toner cartridges on laser printers.

The next class of publications, covered in Chapter 9, provides support for the marketing of a company's products. The techniques described apply to production of such publications as brochures, catalogs, product information sheets, price lists, and capabilities/facilities descriptions. The chapter goes into further depth on the use of design grids.

A major output from desktop publishing systems is newsletters, covered in Chapter 10. Topics include types of newsletters, design features, and special production concerns.

Chapter 11 deals with the application of desktop publishing techniques to magazines and journals. Emphasis is placed heavily on the special production techniques that apply to these media.

Use of desktop techniques for newspaper production is covered in Chapter 12. The content of this chapter establishes the relationships between the large computer systems used on major papers and the extensive use of desktop computers on weeklies and small dailies. The chapter explains that the page size of newspapers discourages on-line makeup with desktop computers. Therefore, the principles and methods of pasteup are reviewed.

Chapter 13 deals with books. Given the capabilities of new pagemaking software packages, books have become good candidates for desktop computer production. The chapter reviews the book business as an industry and identifies the special requirements associated with book production.

Chapter 14 wraps the presentation with a review of how to set up a desktop publishing facility and what to expect in near-future developments.

SOURCES AND ACKNOWLEDGMENTS

The presentation sequence and content described above are based on realistic, pioneering experience in computerized publishing generally and desktop publishing specifically. The author is vice president and creative director of *information/education (i/e)*, a company that specializes in development services for books and other learning materials.

The staff at i/e has been writing and editing publications through computerized methods since 1979. During 1979, i/e commissioned development of proprietary software that was used to transmit manuscript from its offices to a commercial typesetting facility. Since 1980, it has been standard to set type for complete books in as little as one week. Desktop publishing techniques have been in use since 1985. Currently, desktop computers are used in the production of some 3,000 to 4,000 book pages each year.

This book reflects the extensive experience that has been accumulated by i/e and its staff. As noted on the title page, all of the line illustrations for this book were prepared by John L Banner, i/e's art director. The text also reflects the knowledge and experience of other members of the i/e team. In particular, this book was made possible through the knowledge, support, and direct supervisory efforts of Bettijune Kruse, president of i/e. Production and content contributions also were made by staff members Vivian McDougal and Douglas Lathrop.

As befits a book on desktop publishing, this book went together under an expedited schedule.

The manuscript was written in less than three months and production was handled in about 60 days. This turnaround would have been impossible without the vision and support of Jay Whitney, the book's sponsoring editor at Delmar Publishers Inc. Jay had the foresight and imagination to recognize the value of a book that imparted publishing knowledge in addition to providing guidance in operation of desktop publishing computers. He coordinated manuscript development and review and provided guidance for a review and revision process that added greatly to the quality of the final product.

Essential contributions came from the reviewers who kept up with the expedited schedule for development of this book and made important contributions to its content and structure. The author is delighted to single out and recognize the efforts of two outstanding reviewers:

- Elaine Schmittke, Assistant Professor at Nassau Community College
- Dr. Jean W. Vining, Houston Community College System.

Finally, significant contributions were made by Dr. Kamiran Badrkhan, Associate Dean, Occupational Education, Long Beach City College. He helped review the content and pedagogical concepts that went into the initial design of the book. He validated the author's judgment about the approach to be taken. Then, he contributed the Foreword that precedes this Preface.

Documentation and Publishing as an Industry

1

Editorial Budget

*For newspapers and other periodicals, a **budget** generally is a series of summaries of the articles or stories ready for use. In this book, each chapter begins with a budget. The budget alerts you to the topics to be covered. The importance of each topic to your knowledge of desktop publishing also is explained.*

❑ **Movable type** was introduced during the 1450s. This invention started an information explosion. Modern printing became possible.

❑ **Letterpress** was the dominant method of printing for some 500 years. Letterpress printing transfers impressions directly to paper from metal type.

❑ **Lithography,** or **offset printing,** has replaced letterpress as the main printing technique. Original images are transferred, or offset, from a plate to a rubber blanket. The image on paper comes from the rubber blanket.

❑ **Xerography** combines the technologies of printing and electronics. Electricity magnetizes a metallic surface. Light demagnetizes areas where there is no image. The image attracts a magnetic material that forms an image, which is transferred to paper.

❑ **Writing** of text to be printed can be aided by use of computers. The text created by writers is processed by computers to create type.

❑ **Typefaces** are images that represent letters, numbers, and symbols. Many hundreds of faces are available to help make printing attractive. These fall into two broad categories, **serif** (Roman) and **san-serif** (Gothic).

❑ **Desktop publishing** encompasses a complete system for creating printed materials. A number of modern technologies are used, including computing, television, and communications. A complete publishing system can be assembled on a desktop.

A TRADE AND ITS MARKS

It was introduction time at a typical social gathering. People were telling each other, in a friendly way, what they did for a living. A burly fellow of medium height took his turn. He turned to a man who already had been identified as an editor of newspapers and magazines.

"I guess you can tell I'm an old-time printer," the burly gentleman said. He raised his left hand to expose a finger that had its first joint missing.

As trademarks go, missing fingers are not especially prideful. But this identification did have a ring of truth. For hundreds of years, printing was done from metal type and metal image masters called *cuts*. The metal pieces from which printing was done were assembled into forms to hold them in place for printing. Before the forms could be put together, the metal pieces had to be trimmed on open-blade saws. The odds were against the working printers. Sooner or later, something would hang up in the saw and whack off a fingertip. If a printer managed to escape the saw, other risks waited. The printer stood a good chance of having a finger crushed. This happened if a metal type form fell on the finger.

Metal type and related machinery are all but gone. Today, the great majority of printing masters are generated by computers. Printing impressions pour forth from computer-controlled presses. The main dangers are gone. Printers no longer have to handle heavy forms of metal type. These forms could weigh up to 100 pounds each in work areas like those shown in **Figure 1-1.**

Fortunately, the heritage of *hot-metal printing* includes more than maimed hands. Many terms and practices of hot-metal printing still are used in the modern, computerized world

Figure 1-1. Hot-metal typesetting could be difficult and dangerous. Type was locked into heavy forms. The work could be strenuous.

of publishing. For example, in the days of hot-metal printing, workers and their jobs were described in interesting ways. One of these involved the job of dealing with type that had been used for a printing job. Used type was remelted and cast again. When a printing job was done, it was customary to *pie,* or break up, the used type forms. The type to be remelted was dropped into a *hell box.* This container got its name from the flames and heat of the melting process. In charge of the hell box and the re-melting of type metal was a young apprentice. He was known as a *printer's devil.*

These methods are gone. But the goals of printing and publishing professionals remain the same. This book is about computer techniques that lead to published works. The end products that result take in any reading materials that people use for work or pleasure. Examples include business documents, newsletters, magazines, technical manuals, and even books like this one. In this modern world of computer technology, many of the terms and principles still used come from the days of hot-metal printing.

The World of Movable Type

Johann Gutenberg invented movable type during the 1450s. His methods were refined and mechanized over many years. But there was comparatively little change in basic concepts for more than five centuries. **Figure 1-2** is a replica from a page of Gutenberg's Bible.

Hot metal is all but gone. But the history of hot-metal printing still lives. One heritage of Gutenberg's invention is mass literacy. Before 1450, language communication was mainly oral, or spoken. Information was spread from place to place largely by troubadors. As they traveled, they paused to recite poems and sing ballads about news and gossip of the day. Few people had the power of the written word. Books were scarce because they had to be hand-printed, letter by letter. Most printed documents were religious or royal (proclamations of rulers).

Even though literacy was limited, demand for printed materials grew rapidly. Reading, back then, was largely for religion or entertainment. Books were too expensive for common people. Also, people who worked didn't have the time to read books. However, the ability to read represented power. People recognized this and

Figure 1-2. Movable type led to mass literacy. This page is a reproduction of the Gutenberg Bible, the first book set with movable type.

wanted to learn to read. Gutenberg gave them their chance by increasing the number of books available. Printing also lowered the cost of books. Gutenberg's idea was to capture all the letters and numbers used in printing in a series of little metal molds. Hot metal was poured into these molds. Later, after the molds cooled, small strips of metal a little more than an inch high could be removed. At the end of each was a letter,

 ## DESKTOP JARGON

cut Metal plate for letterpress printing of pictures.

hot-metal printing Letterpress printing. Done from metal type.

pie To break up a form of metal type.

hell box Container for discarded type.

printer's devil Apprentice in charge of hell box.

number, or symbol. Groups of these strips were assembled side by side in a metal holder. They were locked in place to form a **reverse-reading** text. Reverse reading means simply that the letters were backwards from their normal, **right-reading** impressions.

The idea: Assemble sequences of metal letters into a holding mechanism. Press them against a sheet of paper. Remove the paper and, as if by magic, you have a finished document. The word **press** itself was borrowed from another industry—winemaking. To create impressions on paper, Gutenberg adapted a pressure-operated device used to squeeze juice from grapes. The squeezing machine was called a press. Gutenberg used the same name. A holding device that contained type and engravings showing pictures was placed on the bed of a wine press. The surface of the type was inked and a piece of paper was laid on top. When the press handle was cranked, the pressure transferred the image to a single sheet of paper. An early, hand-operated printing press is illustrated in **Figure 1-3.**

It turned out that Gutenberg really had something. During the last half of the fifteenth century, more than 10 million pages were printed on the new presses. The power of ideas had gained a powerful delivery system. Martin Luther and others relied on the printed word to build followings for new interpretations of religious tenets. Poetry flourished.

In England, the works of a popular playwright named Shakespeare were immortalized when they were printed in the 1620s. During the seventeenth and eighteenth centuries, the novel evolved, thanks to the ability to print thousands of copies. By the late eighteenth and early nineteenth centuries, automatic presses were run by steam engines. These presses provided the capacity that led to publishing of **periodicals.** A periodical is a printed document, a publication, that is issued regularly, at set time periods. Included are newspapers and magazines. Since then, newspapers and magazines have become major media for distributing information.

For more than four centuries, printing was based on use of individually cast letters that were assembled by hand. Typesetting remained a slow, manual process until the 1890s. Things changed when Ottmar Mergenthaler invented a machine he called the Linotype. Mergenthaler's breakthrough mechanized Gutenberg's technology. Typecasting molds, called **mats,** were stored in a magazine controlled by a keyboard. When keys were pressed, mats were brought together in a group. Mergenthaler's machine then cast a full line of type at a time. The name, Linotype, comes from the ability to cast complete lines. A linecasting machine is illustrated in **Figure 1-4.**

Printing as a Process

Note, even from this brief narrative, that, as it became mechanized, printing became a **process.** The printing process, any process for that matter, consists of a series of steps. These steps are followed in sequence to produce a planned result.

Initially, printing was a one-step, craft procedure. A scribe copied one manuscript to create another—by hand. Later, pages were gathered and bound into books, also one item at a time.

Figure 1-3. The first printing devices were adapted from presses that were used to squeeze grapes. Printing presses were hand operated for about four centuries.
Courtesy of Smithsonian Institution, Photo No. 17539-B.

Figure 1-4. A major breakthrough in typesetting came with the invention of the Linotype, a machine that could cast entire lines in a single operation. This is a typical linecasting unit.

With mechanization, the process broke down into a series of steps. One person, at a Linotype machine, would create type from an original text. A separate person, called a *compositor,* would assemble type for printing. This involved arranging type on a work surface called a *stone.* The stone got its name from the fact that slate rock was used. The assembled type was locked into a metal form, called a *chase.* The chase was a frame that held the type and cuts in place during printing. Actual printing then took place in a separate step.

Setting and composing type was an exact business that required precise measurements. Through the years, a system of measurement evolved in the printing industry. This system has carried forward into present-day computer composition. The basis for printing measurement was based on the sizes of metal type molds. To this day, measurements still are quoted in *ems.* An em, in printing measure, is the width of an uppercase "M" in any given typeface. When most type was the same size, the width of the em became standard—six to the inch.

Through the years, six-to-the-inch measurements became standards for printing and business machines. Eventually, the term em became variable according to type size. In its place, the term, *pica,* was used to represent one-sixth of an inch. To break down type sizes

 DESKTOP JARGON

reverse reading Backwards image, such as metal type for transfer to paper.

right reading Type or printing master with type that reads correctly.

press Printing device.

periodical Publication produced on a regular schedule.

mat Mold for casting of metal type on Linotype machine.

process Series of steps followed in sequence to produce planned result.

compositor Person who makes up pages of type and illustrations for printing.

stone Work surface for making up hot metal forms.

chase Form used to lock up metal type.

em Unit of measure equal to capital letter M in font being used.

pica Unit of measure equal to one-sixth of an inch.

Figure 1-5. This is a pica rule used to measure type sizes in picas and points.

precisely according to height, the pica was divided into 12 parts. This followed the measurement system under which a foot was broken into 12 inches. One-twelfth of a pica is known as a *point.* **Figure 1-5** shows a printer's ruler that includes these units of measure. In summary:

- One inch equals six picas.
- One pica equals 12 points.
- One inch also equals 72 points.

You have just mastered a measuring system you may use for desktop publishing.

LETTERPRESS PRINTING

Within the overall printing process, separate technologies evolved for typesetting (composition) and printing. The technique for producing printed impressions directly from type and image cuts is known as *letterpress.*

Letterpress remained the main printing method until a gradual technological transition began in the 1940s. Letterpress also is known as *direct-image printing.* This is because impressions are generated directly from type.

High-speed letterpress printing is done on rotary presses. A rotary press produces images from round cylinders. This is different from "flatbed printing," in which the impressions come directly from type locked in a chase. Rotary presses can print on continuous rolls of paper. This is many times faster than feeding individual sheets for flatbed printing.

In rotary letterpress printing, a mold is made from the type chase. This mold is used in a metal casting process to create a half-round plate. In turn, the plate is locked onto a rotating press unit. Most large-circulation newspapers were printed by rotary letterpress techniques until the 1960s. These rotary units were able to produce between 80,000 and 100,000 complete

Figure 1-6. For many years, high-speed printing was done on rotary letterpress units from metal cylinders.

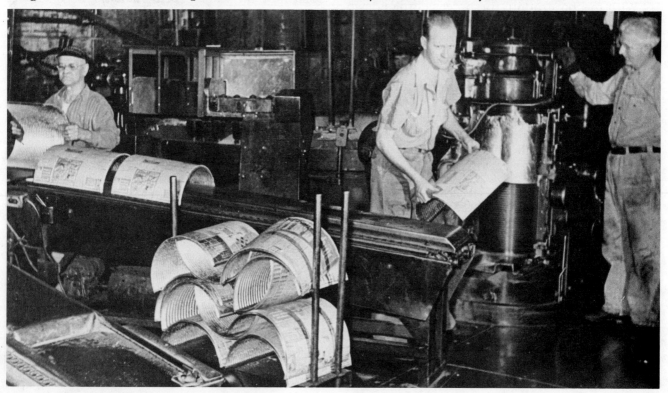

newspapers per hour. **Figure 1-6** shows part of a rotary letterpress operation.

LITHOGRAPHY: FROM ART FORM TO INFORMATION MEDIUM

An alternate printing method that has become dominant recently is known as *offset printing* or *lithography.* Offset lithography is based on a simple chemical principle: Oil and water don't mix. Master impressions are formed with a waxy material that attracts greasy inks and repels water.

The term, offset, derives from the fact that there is no direct impression from printing master to paper. Instead, the image is transferred from the printing master to a *blanket.* This is usually a roller of smooth rubber. The rubber surface will accept the impression from a grease-based ink. Of course, the grease repels the water used to wash the blanket between impressions. The image that appears on paper comes from the blanket rather than from the printing master. **Figure 1-7** contains drawings that illustrate the letterpress and offset reproduction methods.

Figure 1-7. These drawings show the letterpress (bottom) and offset (top) printing processes.

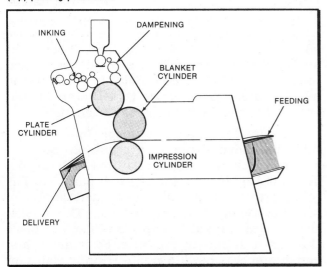

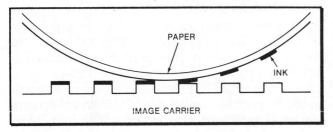

Lithography originated as an art technique, one that is still used. A skilled artist draws on a smooth surface with a special lithographic crayon. The crayon is a waxy material that will hold a grease-based ink and repel water. Traditionally, lithographic originals were created on smooth-surfaced stones. An advantage of lithographic printmaking was that the artist could create a right-reading original. By comparison, other printmaking art techniques, such as etching, required that the artist create reverse-reading masters. This was more difficult.

To make artistic prints, the surface of the stone was covered with a grease-based ink. The ink adhered to the crayon markings only. The stone was washed to remove any unwanted residue of ink. The image then was passed through the press on the first of two operations. This transferred the image to a rubber blanket. In a second operation, the image was transferred from the blanket to paper.

Lithography gained commercial printing potential through use of photography. Under the *photo offset* process, an original image is created as a starting point. The original can be typeset, typewritten, or handwritten. This original is photographed to create a *negative.* On negative film, dark and light values of images are reversed. That is, black type is clear or white on a negative. White background is solid black, as shown in **Figure 1-8.**

Under photo-offset techniques, negatives are used to create printing plates. The plates are

 DESKTOP JARGON

point Unit of measure equal to one seventy-second of an inch.

letterpress Method of printing from metal type.

direct-image printing Letterpress; printing from metal type.

offset printing Method of printing through transfer of image to rubber blanket, then to paper.

lithography Offset printing through transfer of images.

blanket Image transfer unit in offset printing.

photo offset Offset printing using photographic platemaking.

negative Photographic image in which black and white values are reversed.

Figure 1-8. Offset platemaking is done from negative lithographic film. Note how the light and dark values of the image are reversed. Photo by Benedict Kruse.

made of metal or plastic and are coated with a photographic material called a **photo resist.** A resist is a material that forms an image that will attract grease and repel water. The negative is placed in close contact with a photosensitive plate and exposed to light. When the image is developed, the clear area is removed. The image is reproduced in the resist material. On an offset press, ink sticks to the resist and is transferred to a rubber blanket. The image then is transferred to paper from the blanket.

In general, offset printing is a high-quality reproduction process. Offset presses do a better job than letterpress equipment of producing clear images of type and illustrations. However, an offset publication is three full image **generations** removed from the original art. First, a film negative is made. Then, a printing plate is created. Finally, an image is printed on rubber and transferred to paper. No matter how careful the printer may be, some detail and image quality always is lost. Therefore, as a future desktop publisher, it is good for you to be aware of printing processes. In particular, you should know what these processes do to the materials you create.

Offset printing makes preparation of printing masters more convenient than composition of metal type. In a sense, the convenience of offset methods is the basis for this book. The need to cast type in hot metal was eliminated. Whole new technologies of **cold-type composition** and **photocomposition** were developed. Desktop publishing is a recent innovation in this branch of technology. That is, desktop computers produce cold-type composition. The point: Improved printing makes it easier to prepare the materials to be printed.

XEROGRAPHY: PRINTING ELECTRONICALLY

Printing and publishing are a process. This process takes in a number of steps. These steps include preparation of words and pictures to be reproduced, preparing image masters such as plates, printing, and distribution of end products. During the electronic age, some of these steps have been combined through use of electronic techniques.

The technology that bridges this gap is **xerography.** This technology has revolutionized many office and publishing procedures. Xerography was developed during the 1920s by Dr. Chester F. Carlson, a scientist with the Batelle Memorial Institute. The principle: Certain metals, such as selenium, become light sensitive when an electrical field is applied. When light strikes the surface of the electrically sensitized material, the magnetic field is lost in the affected area. This means that the areas that were not struck by light remain magnetized.

Xerography uses this principle by applying a material called **toner** to a sensitized surface. Toner is a plasticized material that adheres to a series of tiny ferrous (iron-based) particles. The toner forms an image on the magnetized area of the electrically-charged surface. The image, then, is transferred to paper and fixed in place through heat and/or pressure. For many years, xerography was used to create printing plates for office-sized offset presses.

A major breakthrough for communication through printed images occurred in 1959. The Xerox Corporation introduced an automatic copying machine based on xerographic principles. Xerox introduced a machine that could produce printed copies directly from an original image of type and illustrations. The image was created at relatively high speeds, on plain paper. The need for platemaking was eliminated. Copies were made directly from the original documents. The convenience of xerography was accepted enthusiastically. Within a short time, xerographic reproduction became a multi-billion-dollar industry. A drawing of the xerographic process is presented in **Figure 1-9.**

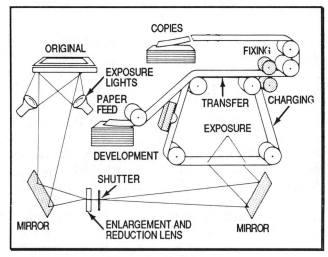

Figure 1-9. This drawing shows the xerographic reproduction process.

The Laser Printer

Since 1959, xerographic processing has jumped ahead in rapid strides. One of the big innovations has been the development of the *laser printer.* Laser printers now are an integral part of most desktop publishing installations. A laser uses xerography in a special way. A normal xerographic copier creates an image by sensing the light and dark values of an original document. On a laser printer, the images are originated within a computer. The image values then are transferred to a laser, or concentrated light beam. The laser beam moves back and forth over the xerographic drum to form the image, which is transferred to paper. The quality of laser-printer outputs from units like the one shown in **Figure 1-10** now approaches that of some offset presses.

CREATING IMAGES TO BE PRINTED

It has been the more than 500 years since the invention of movable type. Through all these years, the basic purpose of printing has not changed: People have ideas and information to communicate. Publishing and printing are the

Figure 1-10. Laser printers like the one shown here produce images under direct control of computers. Speeds approach those of small offset presses.
Courtesy of Datagraphix, Inc.

ways to get the job done. The need to communicate ideas and information has led to development of a multibillion-dollar industry.

For hundreds of years, technology played little or no role in the preparation of messages to be communicated. Until the very late years of the nineteenth century, people drew pictures and wrote manuscripts by hand. Handwriting was the only method available. In the 1880s, people who bore the ancient and honorable title of *scrivener* made a profession of handwriting

DESKTOP JARGON

photo resist Photographic material used to make offset plates.

generation Reference to number of times a photo image has been copied.

cold-type composition Typesetting directly onto paper through strike-on or photographic methods.

photocomposition Typesetting with photographic methods.

xerography Electrostatic method of image reproduction.

toner Image-forming substance in xerographic printing.

laser printer Xerographic printer that uses beam of light to register images on xerographic drum.

scrivener Artisan who created handwritten documents.

documents. These documents ranged from business correspondence to government pronouncements. Handwritten manuscripts were the source documents for typesetting and printing. Scriveners did their work chiefly with hand-sharpened feather quills undoubtedly taken from large numbers of unwilling birds. That was the state of a technology that was shaken to its roots in the last decade of the nineteenth century.

One invention that altered business documentation and publishing was the typewriter. A major shock resulted when typewriters were introduced into business offices. Established and proud scriveners would have nothing to do with these demonic devices. To deal with the problem, businesses began to hire women to operate the new typewriters. These new employees were identified by the same name as their machines. That is, the first women who worked in American offices were called "typewriters." **Figure 1-11** shows a typewriter of this time period.

Figure 1-11. Machines for typing and computation were introduced into offices during the latter part of the nineteenth century. Courtesy of The National Archives.

Introduction of the typewriter also helped to speed up the development of text to be published. Once the keyboard was mastered, proficient typists could generate text rapidly. Through the years, it became common to find typists who could operate at speeds above 100 words per minute. By comparison, handwriting generally takes place at speeds somewhere below 20 words per minute.

Over a period of several decades, the basic typewriter keyboard was adapted to a series of more advanced text-writing machines. The typewriter itself was electrified during the 1920s. Later, typesetting capabilities were added through machines that generated documents that looked like typesetting. Also, paper tapes with punched holes were used to record, or "capture," text entered into a keyboard. The tape then could be used to retype text on automatic typewriters. As computers came into wide use, electronic methods were used to increase typing production. Typewriters were equipped to record information on and read text from magnetic tape and magnetic cards. **Figure 1-12** shows a tape-operated typewriter. Then, computer-type memories were added.

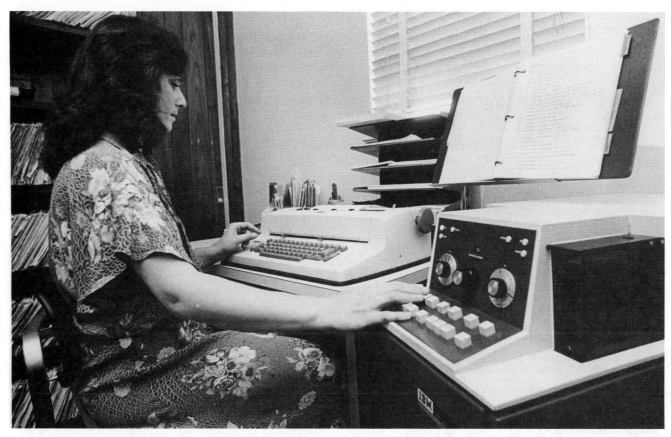

Figure 1-12. Automated typing was made possible in the 1960s with machines that recorded and read text through use of magnetic tape.

Finally, type composition was done electronically through use of computers. At first, it took a relatively large computer to handle typesetting. One major job for which computer typesetting was applied was newspaper publishing. Several technologies were combined to make electronic publishing possible. During the 1960s, the printing industry was able to deliver offset presses that could generate papers at letterpress speeds— 80,000 per hour and above. Cold-type composition rapidly replaced hot-metal methods. During the same time span, computers gained the capacity to handle text writing, editing, and typesetting for large daily papers. **Figure 1-13** shows computer terminals in use in a large newspaper office.

Phototypesetting devices added to computers had capacities in the range of 10,000 lines per minute. A typesetter could format and output a full page of classified advertising in about two minutes. Information could be fed automatically into large computers operated by newspapers. Millions of words of text were captured directly from the wires of news services. Many

thousands of additional words of text were entered by reporters, editors, and advertising personnel.

In the newspaper business, electronic typesetting proved highly profitable. A large paper might have 100 or more Linotype operators capturing text. If reporters and wire services entered the text directly, the entire process of manual typesetting was eliminated. The savings easily equalled the millions of dollars it cost to install large computer systems.

Initially, type was set in strips, or *galleys,* that were pasted on art boards for newspaper platemaking, as illustrated in **Figure 1-14.** That was the technology of the late 1960s and 1970s. By the late 1970s, new equipment made it possible to eliminate the need to prepare galleys and paste up type. Complete composition, including the positioning of photos and ads, could be done on computer terminals. Some systems provided full-color capabilities.

 DESKTOP JARGON

galley Trial impression, or proof, from type.

Figure 1-13. Major newspapers led the way in use of computers for writing, editing, and typesetting. Computer work stations now are commonplace in newsrooms.
Photo by Benedict Kruse.

Then, during the 1980s, the technology for computerized typesetting was introduced to small computers. The small desktop computers were, themselves, new on the market. Grad-

Figure 1-14. One way to prepare pages for offset printing is to paste galleys of type onto boards, as is being done in this photo.
Photo by Benedict Kruse.

ually, the small computers gained enough power to handle typesetting and publishing jobs. As they did, techniques were developed to put them to work as writing and publishing tools.

The key was in the increased power that was made available in small computers. To illustrate, the computers that controlled the first moon shots in the 1960s occupied large rooms and required special air conditioning. These mammoth computers supported calculations through memories with capacities for 64,000 (64K) characters of data. Today, desktop microcomputers with memory capacities of four million characters and even more are commonplace. Price tags for complete systems have dropped from millions of dollars to thousands. **Figure 1-15** shows a modern microcomputer.

As small computers gained large capacities, both typesetting and graphics capabilities became available. The term, graphics, refers to the ability of a computer to develop and process images, or pictures.

Graphics processing had started on big systems during the 1970s. Early uses were for control of manufacturing equipment. These large systems also were used to develop engineering plans for buildings and aircraft. As microcomputers gained capacity, these capabilities also gravitated downward. For desktop publishers, graphics processing systems have

Figure 1-15. Modern microcomputers like this one provide complete processing and output capabilities on desktops.
Courtesy of IBM.

introduced capabilities to create complex drawings directly on computer displays. Desktop computer users then can capture these drawings for inclusion in publications.

TYPE ITSELF

When you compose messages designed to be read, delivery of your messages is through the human eye (and mind). What the eye sees is a stylized set of characters. These characters represent an alphabet, numbers, symbols, words, sentences, and paragraphs. Large, constantly increasing amounts of information have been published and read, sometimes by eyes that showed signs of strain. Thus, the easier type is to read, the more successful a publication can expect to be. Making type easier to read has been a continuing challenge. Through the centuries, designers have come up with hundreds of formats intended to make type more attractive and more readable.

Out of these attempts, several principles have emerged. Awareness of these principles and their application can be of major value in designing and developing publications through desktop techniques. One principle for conveying messages through use of type lies in the function performed. Specifically, there are differences between messages aimed at attracting your attention and those that convey detailed information.

Think of a newspaper or magazine. Each publication contains a series of stories or articles. The text of these articles tends to be in type that is small in size and set in close-packed lines. Usually, newspaper type is organized into a series of columns. If this text were all there was, not many newspapers or magazines would be read. Massive pages of text set in the same type are dull in appearance and tedious as reading matter. So, to make pages more interesting to view, the text type generally is broken up by headlines. The headlines provide visual focal points for the reader's eye. Also, the information in the text becomes more digestable when the key information is summarized in headlines. Many newspapers break up text even further through the use of subheadings within the stories.

To make their pages look more interesting, most publications use different *headline* and *text,* or *body,* type formats. The format that imparts a different appearance to type is called a *face,* or *typeface.* Headline typefaces invariably are bold, or dark. They stand out from the overall, gray appearances of line after line of body type. Text faces, in turn, are designed to ease the job of reading a lot of information.

Design techniques used to make typefaces attractive and readable fall into two broad formatting categories:

- Serif
- San-serif.

A *serif* is a short, light horizontal line placed at the end of the straight lines of letters. Faces that have these lines are identified by a name that reaches way back into history: *Roman.* As the name implies, the concept for this type design feature dates back more than 15 centuries, to the Romans.

The other major class of typefaces uses straight lines and simple circles to form letters. This kind of type is known as *san-serif.* Based on their historic origins, san-serif styles are known as *Gothic* faces. This dates the design concepts to a more recent time than Roman faces: the Middle Ages. Examples of serif and san-serif faces are shown in **Figure 1-16.**

Most publications that use a lot of text— including newspapers, magazines, and books— use serif (Roman) faces for body type. The serifs tend to ease the movement of the reader's eye across a line of type. This is important for publications that use a lot of text.

Figure 1-16. Roman typefaces have serifs to lead the eye across printed lines. Gothic typefaces have no serifs and are considered to present a crisp, clean appearance.

Roman Text Face
Gothic Heading Face

Some advertisements and a few publications use Gothic type for text. Usually, this practice is confined to short segments of text. Use of Roman typefaces for text has been going on for centuries. Readers have been conditioned to use of serif faces for text. There are publication designers who feel that the stark appearance of Gothic faces provides a different, modern look. You— along with all of the world's publishers, editors, and readers— are entitled to your own conclusions. The purpose here is to acquaint you with the principles that have been applied.

Publication headlines tend to use Gothic faces to establish a contrast between text and headings. However, many publications use a contrasting serif face to achieve the same result.

Also, reader attention can be called to headlines or elements within text through use of different styles of the same typeface. One technique is to use a darker image, or version, of a face. Darkened typefaces are called *bold.* Bold versions of typefaces sometimes come in different degrees. Examples include *demibold* (slightly darker than the basic face) or *ultrabold* (superdark).

Another way to attract the eye and emphasize text content is through use of *italic* typefaces. An italic face slants from left to right. The idea of italicizing type is to establish easy identification and emphasis. As an example, the key terms in this book are printed in "bold italic" to help you locate and identify them. Also, use of bold italic helps to create visual interest. The interest is achieved by breaking up the gray appearance of entire pages of Roman-style body type. **Figure 1-17** provides examples of these varying typefaces.

Figure 1-17. This set of specimens demonstrates the comparative appearances of standard, boldface, italic, and bold italic images.

This is standard text in a face known as "Bookman."

This is italic text in a face known as "Bookman."

This is boldface text in a face known as "Bookman."

This is boldface italic text in a face known as "Bookman."

As indicated, these principles of design and readability of typefaces have evolved over centuries. They apply regardless of how the type you read was created.

THE COMPUTERIZED DESKTOP

A desktop publishing system uses a number of capabilities borrowed from three industries:

- Computing
- Television
- Communications.

Role of Computer Technology

A **computer,** basically, is a series of electronic switches supported by magnetic recording capabilities. The power of the computer stems from the electronic speeds at which it operates: Electronic signals are carried at speeds of approximately 186,000 miles per second. Therefore, a computer can perform its operations at rates of hundreds of thousands per second. These operations are simple. Computer processing capabilities are limited to basic addition and to comparison of two values.

The value of explaining computer operations in a book on desktop publishing: You will be using computers. Therefore, it is important to recognize that computers are simple and easy to work with. There is nothing really awesome about a computer once you understand how it works.

A computer has a series of electrical switching circuits. The setting of the switches controls the combination of electrical values. Current passes through electrical circuits to perform the addition or comparison functions to which computers are limited. Note that the only arithmetic a computer performs is addition. If subtraction is needed, the electrical values are set to negative. Subtraction on a computer is negative addition. Multiplication is repeated addition. Division is repeated negative addition.

Computer **logic,** or "intelligence," comes from simple comparisons of values. A computer can tell if one value is equal to, less than, or greater than another. Processing steps can be selected or altered on the basis of comparisons. The power of computers lies in the fact that a lot of simple tasks can be performed in extremely short time spans. A single addition operation, for example, takes only a few millionths of a second on a desktop unit. Supercomputers can handle these functions at rates of up to 80 million operations per second.

Selection and sequencing of instructions to be performed are done under control of **programs.** A program is a sequence of instructions that the computer stores internally, to be retrieved and followed as necessary. Programs and information to be processed are stored in electronic memory. A memory consists of a series of electronic switches that can be set by the computer to represent information. The computer can retrieve signals from memory and translate them into letters and numbers. In addition, computers record information magnetically on **storage** devices. The method used is similar to the operation of audio or video cassette recorders. The configuration of a typical microcomputer system is shown in **Figure 1-18.**

DESKTOP JARGON

headline Unit of type that titles a story or article.

text Series of words that presents information.

body Portion of publication that contains informational text.

face, typeface Images that present letters, numbers, and symbols.

serif Horizontal lines added to type characters for design and readability.

Roman Style of type that uses serifs.

san-serif Style of type with no serifs.

Gothic Style of type with no serifs.

bold Type face with dark image.

demibold Typeface with medium-dark image.

ultrabold Typeface with extra-dark image.

italic Typeface with characters that slant from left to right.

computer Electronic device that processes and stores information. Can set type.

logic Computer capability; compares two items and acts on results of comparison.

program Set of instructions that directs computer operation.

storage Computer capability to record and retrieve information.

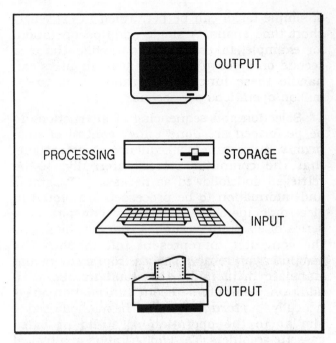

Figure 1-18. This diagram shows the parts of a microcomputer and the working relationships among components.

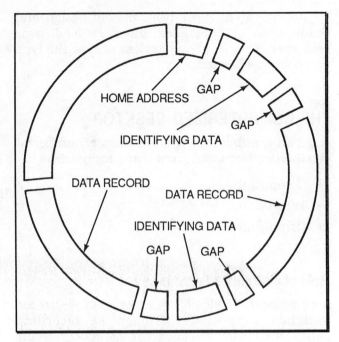

Figure 1-19. This diagram shows the pattern followed for recording information on magnetic disk devices.

To be of value, computers must be able to communicate with people. Necessary operations include *input* and *output.* Input is the entry of information. This can be done by people who use keyboards or from recorded information that is stored by magnetic devices. To demonstrate, **Figure 1-19** is a diagram showing how information is recorded on the surface of a magnetic disk. Output is generated by the computer and can take several forms. Outputs can be recorded on magnetic media, displayed on video tubes (as described below), or can be printed on paper.

Desktop publishing is achieved through use of special programs. These programs cause computers to accept instructions from key-boards or picture-generating devices. Outputs can be in the form of images on paper that are ready for offset printing. Output also can be directly to film that can be used to make offset plates. The point: Desktop publishing encompasses the full processes of image creation and reproduction. These processes used to require multiple operations on different equipment, usually by a number of people. This is one reason why a person out to master desktop publishing should understand the full process of publishing and printing.

Role of Television Technology

To produce typeface and graphic (pictorial) outputs under computer control, your equipment must be able to generate electronic images. In this function, a desktop publishing system uses the same basic technology as television. Desktop publishing systems generate signals that are similar to those that come from a television camera.

Consider what happens in a television camera. Like any camera, the TV system has a lens that senses an image. This image is focused upon a light-sensitive surface within the camera. In a TV system, the image is sensed on the face of an electronic tube. The function of the tube is to translate the image into a continuing, or linear, series of electronic signals.

To do this, the imaging tube has a device that scans the image on the face of the tube with an electron beam. The beam senses light and dark (as well as color) values in the image and converts these values to electronic signals. Along each scan line, there are hundreds of points at which light, dark, and color values are sensed. The scan pattern of a video display is illustrated in **Figure 1-20.**

A desktop publishing display is formed in essentially the same way as a television signal. A major difference is that the signals originate through computer processing rather than through a camera and lens. Some desktop publishing devices actually are able to scan images from TV cameras or directly from docu-

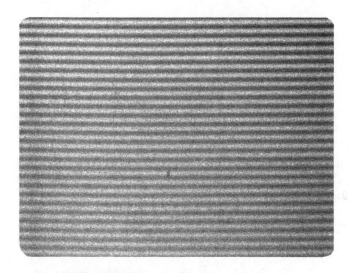

Figure 1-20. This photo shows the scan pattern followed in presenting images on video screens.

a desktop publishing system begin with a keyboard or graphics device such as a **mouse.** Also linked into the same system are the computer itself and devices that generate displays, and operate output units. To form each of these links, the computer generates signals that turn the individual units on or off— or that trigger operations. Communication capabilities, in other words, link the basic technologies to produce the results you need. The communication links within a desktop publishing system are illustrated in **Figure 1-21.**

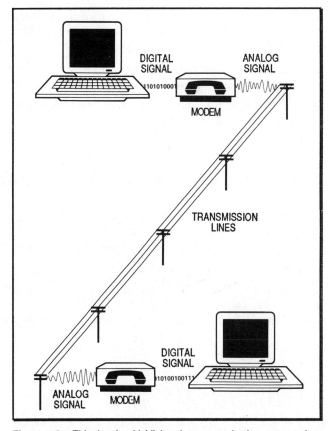

Figure 1-21. This drawing highlights the communication patterns that exist to support operation of a microcomputer system used for desktop publishing.

ments. In those instances, the image information is stored within the computer just as though it had been created from input devices. The computer still generates image-forming signals from stored information.

To round out its capability, the desktop publishing system needs a way to record and reproduce its generated images. This is done through xerographic laser printers or through laser outputs that record information on photographic film.

Role of Communications Technology

Desktop publishing is carried out through use of a **system.** In computer terminology, a system is an assembly of equipment, programs, people, procedures, and materials. These elements of a system function together to produce desired results. In desktop publishing, elements of a system include:

• One or more computers
• A series of programs to run the computer and process words and pictures
• A printing device
• A series of procedures that instruct people in creating publications

To make a desktop publishing system work, it is necessary to have a means of linking the required devices so that they can communicate with one another. The communication links in

 DESKTOP JARGON

input Entry of data or instructions into computer.

output Results delivered by computers for use by people or machines.

system, computer Combination of equipment and programs to process, store, and retrieve information.

mouse Device that permits use and control of computer.

This has been a brief tour of the technologies involved in desktop publishing and their contributions to creation of printed documents. The chapter that follows takes a closer look at the human side of publishing. The steps and procedures followed by people who develop messages and deliver them through desktop publishing systems are reviewed.

THE MAKEUP DESK

On newspapers and other periodicals, the makeup desk is the place where publications are organized and designed. Within this book, a section at the end of each chapter will have reviews and exercises designed to help extend your knowledge and skills in this area.

1. Examine a number of publications, including newspapers, magazines, or books. From this, find and bring to class two or more different Roman and three Gothic typefaces. These can be actual publications or xerographic copies.

2. Of the samples you find, identify the Roman and the Gothic face for which you find the design most pleasing. Explain what you like about each of the faces you consider best.

3. Of the samples you find, identify the Roman and the Gothic face that you find least attractive. Explain your reasons.

THE COMPOSING ROOM

On newspapers and other periodicals, the composing room is where final production takes place. **The Composing Room** *section at the end of each chapter of this book contains review materials and assignments designed to help hone your skills in this area.*

1. Prepare a report on the development and importance of desktop publishing. In addition to the information in this chapter, you can read articles or other books in your school library. In your report, emphasize the role of small computers in developing new methods for creating quality publications. If possible, prepare the text of your report on a computer.

The Publishing Process

2

Editorial Budget

❑ **Each publication is unique.** You must adapt general principles of desktop publishing to specific publications on which you work.

❑ **Publishing is a process.** The process has a series of steps. These steps are followed one after another to develop a publication.

❑ A **manuscript** is a starting point for a publication. This is the basic text, or reading matter, to be presented.

❑ **Copy editing** requires a detailed review of the manuscript. The manuscript is changed or corrected to meet the needs of a publication's readers.

❑ **Production editing** prepares a manuscript for typesetting and preparation of printing masters.

❑ **Text capture** is the first step in typesetting under a desktop publishing system. Capturing translates the text into a form that can be handled by a computer.

❑ **Typesetting** formats the text in a desired typeface.

❑ **Illustration preparation** enhances and supports the text. Line illustrations (drawings and tables) can be prepared on desktop systems more precisely and economically than by hand.

❑ **Proofreading** is a quality control step. A proofreader checks text for accuracy and style.

❑ **Design and layout** organize content of a publication for reader appeal.

❑ **Page makeup** assembles the final pages in a form ready for printing.

❑ **Printing and binding** are reproduction and manufacturing steps. These operations generate the final, published product.

❑ **Marketing and distribution** deliver published products to their target audiences.

❑ **Production management** is necessary to coordinate schedules and to monitor actual development of a publication.

19

FINDING A COMMON DENOMINATOR

Publications are individual. No two publications are exactly alike. Even a periodical contains differences from one issue to another. This is true despite the fact that the same designs and layouts are used in each issue.

The differences among publications reflect the kinds of people involved. Writers, artists, editors, and other publishing professionals are creative people. They go into publishing because of the opportunities to be different and original. Differences among publications result from the creativity of the people who develop them.

Though they are different, all publications also must have certain things in common. Publication development is a job. To do the job, it is necessary to follow certain standards. These standards are necessary because publications are developed through use of certain, common equipment. For example, everyone has to follow the same rules to set type on a computer. Standards also must be followed to print a document on a press. To become a desktop publisher, you must learn about and develop skills in these standard operations.

The discussion that follows covers the basic steps in the overall, standard process of publishing. As a basis for describing the process, a common example is used: this book. This book has been produced through desktop publishing methods. Therefore, it can be used to demonstrate desktop publishing. In addition, the book provides information that will help you to build your skills as a desktop publisher.

WHAT IS A PROCESS AND WHY IS PUBLISHING A PROCESS?

A process is a series of steps that are followed in sequence to deliver a planned or known result. Processes are used for many purposes. There are processes for manufacturing, decision making, driving a car, and developing publications. Regardless of its purpose, each process has a set of common parts, or requirements. These parts include people, procedures, equipment, and materials.

People are the key. It takes the talent and understanding of people to use a process such as desktop publishing. Equipment makes desktop publishing possible. Procedures are designed to control use of the equipment. And materials include the paper, ink, and other supplies from which publications are created.

Coordinating these parts of a process can be a complicated job. Complex jobs are handled best by breaking them down into a series of known steps, or tasks. Notice the term "complex." A job that is complex can include elements that are unknown and unpredictable. For example: Will all of the stories in a budget fit into the pages available? Can the manuscript and illustrations for a book fit into 320 pages?

Process methods provide a proven way to deal with unknowns. Consider what happened in 1960: President John F. Kennedy committed the United States to putting a man on the moon. The voyage was to take place before the end of the decade. At that time, the idea of space exploration was loaded with unknowns. Planning a trip to the moon was not exactly like taking a bus ride. It was impossible to anticipate all of the problems. To be handled successfully, the job had to be broken down into a series of manageable parts. Separate teams were set up to handle such jobs as guidance, navigation, thrust, and rocket design. Other specialists went to work on spacecraft design, life support, radiation shielding, and reentry. The parts were developed individually and assembled into a system that worked. **Figure 2-1** shows the end result of a process approach to project management.

Figure 2-1. Each successful space mission represents completion of a step-by-step process management technique similar to those used in the publishing process covered here.
Courtesy of Finley Holiday Films.

The same type of thinking works in the development of a publication. To do desktop publishing, you should be familiar with the basic process involved. The steps in a process that applies to all publications are identified and described in the remainder of this chapter. The flowchart in **Figure 2-2** diagrams this sequence of steps.

Figure 2-2. This flowchart identifies the steps in the publishing process covered in this chapter and shows the relationship among them.

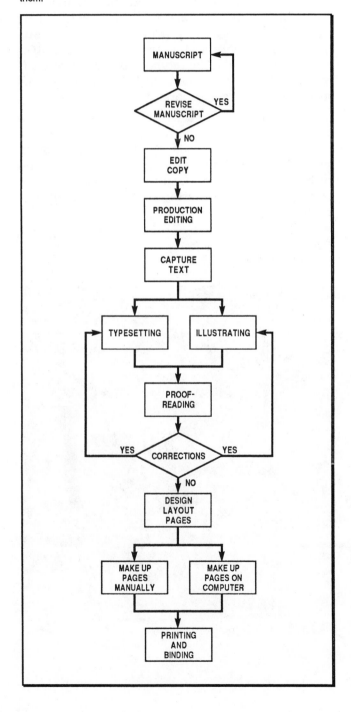

WRITING A MANUSCRIPT

A *manuscript* is the text of a publication in its initial, or "raw," state. A manuscript consists of a text—words, numbers, and symbols. Before computers were used by writers, all manuscripts were typed or written on paper. Use of computers has led to development of what has been called an *electronic manuscript.* The text of an electronic manuscript still consists of words, numbers, and symbols. But they are recorded on computer files and may be printed on paper by computers. In almost all cases, the manuscript is the raw material to be packaged within a publication. That is, the manuscript is the message a publication is to deliver.

Before computers became publishing tools, writing had no direct connection with the steps in production of a publication. Editing and production procedures for most publications didn't begin until the manuscript was written. Newspapers and news magazines were exceptions. These publications also led the way in creating the techniques you will use on desktop computers. News demands urgency. At newspapers, procedures were needed to coordinate the steps of writing, editing, typesetting, and printing into tight schedules. On large newspapers, it was standard to be able to get an important story into print quickly. Newspapers usually could set type and get a story into print in as little as 30 minutes.

Newspapers needed many pieces of equipment and skilled people to deliver these results. Today's desktop publishing methods make this kind of capability available to anyone. Computers have become valuable tools for both writing and typesetting. Today's computers and programs can do the whole job. Writers can use computers to produce basic manuscripts. Then computers can accept the same text. Quickly, the computers can set type and may even be able to prepare entire pages of publications.

The point: Before anything else can happen, a manuscript to be published must be captured. Capturing makes the manuscript available

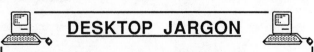

DESKTOP JARGON

manuscript The text of a publication in an initial, or intermediate, state.

electronic manuscript Text or manuscript stored on computer media.

within the electronic files of a desktop publishing computer. Today, therefore, it makes sense to write the original manuscript on a desktop computer. It is possible to do the whole job on a single computer. Or, it is possible to write the manuscript on a separate computer. Then, the text can be transferred to a desktop publishing unit. That, incidentally, is the way this book was produced. Methods for preparing manuscripts on computers are covered in a later chapter.

For this book, the manuscript was written on an IBM PC (personal computer) and other units that were technically compatible. The term "compatible" means that two or more units of equipment can be used interchangeably for the same job. The author used PC equipment partly because they were old friends. The shop in which this book was written has used desktop computers since 1979. This was long before desktop publishing methods were available. In this situation, it was attractive to keep using in-place PC equipment. After all, the computers were paid for. However, as explained in a later chapter, there also are technical reasons why PC tools have been retained. **Figure 2-3** shows a typical desktop computer work station suitable for publication production.

Manuscript preparation on computers is an established technique on its own. Desktop computers have replaced typewriters in many business offices. This use of computers is known as *word processing.* Benefits from word processing have been great enough to pay for millions of personal computers. These computers are in place and ready for use within desktop publishing systems. The benefits that have led to purchase of these computers include the ability to edit manuscripts electronically and to print out typed copies quickly and automatically. Before a book can go into production, a manuscript typically must be revised an average of three or four times. When manuscripts were typewritten, 400 to 500 pages had to be retyped completely at each revision. Then, each new draft had to be proofread and corrected by hand.

Computer-assisted writing makes it easier to go from manuscript creation to typesetting. Once the manuscript for this book was released for production, the text was transferred to a desktop publishing system. Complete chapters were transferred and formatted in type in a matter of hours.

Figure 2-3. This is a typical desktop work station suitable for publication production.
Courtesy of Apple Computer, Inc.

Figure 2-4. This is a typical newspaper copy desk. Photo by Benedict Kruse.

COPY EDITING

The job of **copy editing** takes place after a complete manuscript— or part of a large manuscript— has been created, or **drafted.** A draft is a version of a manuscript that is in work. The copy editor is responsible for polishing the text in preparation for publication. One task is to read the text, or **copy,** to be sure the content is clear and understandable. In publishing, a manuscript frequently is referred to as "copy."

The need for copy editing is universal. Even experienced writers create sentences that are hard to understand. The copy editor is responsible for assuring that the ideas and information in the manuscript are clear. Also, the copy editor has responsibility for language **style.** Style involves the way language is used. Elements of style include grammar, common usage, punctuation, capitalization, and paragraphing.

At newspapers, editing is done at copy desks like the one in **Figure 2-4.** Today, most copy editing is done on computer terminals. However, for reference, **Figure 2-5** shows a page of copy that has been edited by hand.

Traditionally, copy editing has been done on typed manuscripts. Increasingly, this job is being done directly on computers. Each technique— direct **on-line** editing and the pencil-and-paper method— has its own place and value. To edit work you do yourself, on-line editing is superior and faster. It is far faster to make entries through a keyboard than with a pencil. However, if you are editing the work of another writer, it can be valuable to mark a typed manuscript. In this way, all changes are visible and apparent. Communication between editor and writer is enhanced.

In any case, the end result should be a manuscript that is ready for publication. This manuscript can be on paper, in computer storage, or both.

PRODUCTION EDITING

The production editor marks the manuscript with codes to identify the type formats to be used in headings and body text. Production editing also provides a quality control opportunity. The editor can find and correct any spelling, typographical, or usage errors prior to typesetting.

 DESKTOP JARGON

word processing Use of computer hardware and software to generate text.

copy editing Review of manuscript to correct errors and language usage.

draft An initial or interim version of a manuscript.

copy Term for text or manuscript.

style Standard for use of language.

on-line Direct operation of a computer by a user to create or modify files.

Desktop Publishing – Chapter 2 – Release Draft v. 3 (09/13/88)   5

Traditi̟nally, copy editing has been done on manuscripts that were typed. [handwritten: O; typed; ☉; strikethrough on "that were typed."]

Increasingly, this job is being done directly on computers. Each

technique--direct ^on-line^ editing the pencil-and-paper method--has its own [handwritten: and]

place and value. To edit work you do yourself, on-line editing is superior and

faster. It is far faster to make entries through a keyboard than with a

pencil. However, if you are editing the work of other writer, it can be [handwritten: an^]

valuable to mark a typed manuscript. In this way, all changes are visible and

apparent. Communication between editor and writer are enhanced. [handwritten: is (strikethrough on "are")]

In any case, the end result should be a manuscript that is ready for

publication. This manuscript can be on paper, in computer storage, or both.

PRODUCTION EDITING

The production editor marks the manuscript with codes to identify the type

formats to be used in headings and body text. Production editing also provides

Figure 2-5. This manuscript page illustrates manual copy editing methods.

Sometimes, *production editing* can be included in the copy editing step. This often is the case for periodicals produced under tight schedules. There may be time for a single editing only. Also, periodicals tend to have standardized production specifications. In these cases, production editing is part of other working steps.

Under desktop techniques, production-editing functions often can be included within the work of manuscript preparation or copy editing. In producing this book, for example, the author included typesetting control codes in the original manuscript. Copies of the manuscript then were circulated to a selected group of technicians and educators for review. Copy editing then included revisions suggested by reviewers, as well as conventional editing. At the same time, the experienced editor also checked the typesetting codes that had been incorporated into the manuscript.

A point worth stressing: Desktop publishing is more "forgiving" than traditional typesetting methods. Corrections can be made more conveniently and at lower costs than with conventional techniques. One reason is that the complete process is controlled within a single organization. Another lies in the simplicity of modifying text on desktop publishing computers. Therefore, production editing is less critical under a desktop publishing system. To aid communication and control in the production of this book, the author included descriptions of essential illustrations within the manuscript. As shown in **Figure 2-6,** these notes helped guide the work of designers and project managers.

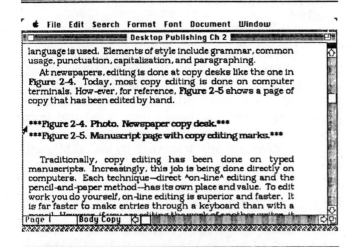

Figure 2-6. This illustration shows the method used for identifying illustrations for this book.

CAPTURING TEXT

The term **capture** describes the process of converting an original, or source, document into a computer-readable form. If a manuscript is produced on paper, it may be necessary to perform the capture function manually, through a keyboard.

In some situations, capture may be automated with **optical character recognition (OCR)** techniques. Text is printed in special characters like those shown in **Figure 2-7.** Typed or printed pages are fed into a reading device called a **scanner.** The text is sensed and entered into computer files automatically.

A separate step to capture text may be unnecessary or minor under desktop publishing techniques. If a manuscript is written on a computer, the capture process may be unnecessary or highly simplified. The writer may use a computer set up for desktop publishing. If so, the manuscript, after it has been edited, is ready for typesetting with no further preparation.

As another option, a manuscript may be prepared on an IBM PC or compatible system that doesn't match the publishing computer. If so, a communication link may be used to transfer text between computers. To illustrate, the text for this book was transferred from a PC to an Apple Macintosh Plus through use of a program called Maclink Plus. A screen display presenting the options and controls for this operation is shown in **Figure 2-8.** The manuscript for an entire book the size of this one can be transferred in a few hours.

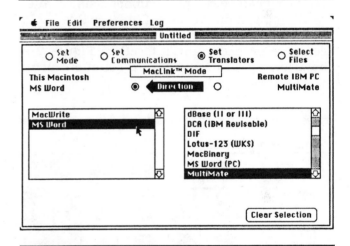

Figure 2-8. This screen display controls the transfer of manuscript from an IBM PC to a Macintosh Plus.

Figure 2-7. This is a sample of an OCR font.

ABCDEFGHIJKLM
NOPQRSTUVWXYZ
1234567890

DESKTOP JARGON

production editing Final review and correction of manuscript in preparation for production.

capture Process for entry of text into a computer in machine-readable format.

optical character recognition (OCR) Method of reading printed text directly into a computer through use of special equipment.

scanner Device that reads text or images from paper directly into a computer.

TYPESETTING

When text is stored electronically in a desktop computer, it is in raw form. That is, the text consists of magnetic codes that identify letters, numbers, and symbols. These files generally can be displayed on a video screen in a format that people can read. They also can be printed in a typewriter-like format.

To transform text into professional-looking type, additional programs and processing are needed. These programs enable the user to select type *fonts,* to mix fonts within a publication, and to make up pages. A type font is another term for typeface. Each font includes letters, numbers, and symbols that follow a specific design.

If you are familiar with word processing on microcomputers, be prepared to deal with far more detail as you move into typesetting. Word processing can be completed under a single, integrated application package. Consider this book. More than a dozen different application packages were needed to put it together. **Figure 2-9** shows an application software selection menu used for this project.

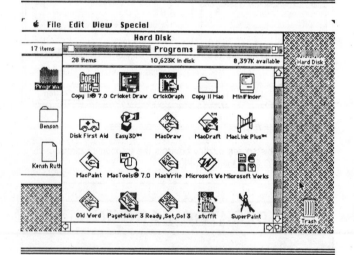

Figure 2-9. A large number of application programs must be mastered to set type and assemble a publication like this book.

The point: Typesetting and other tasks connected with desktop publishing are not simple. A desktop computer is more complex than a microcomputer set up to handle word processing alone. But the payoffs in personal satisfaction and financial savings can be substantial.

Cost savings can be dramatic. In 1979, the shop where this book was produced established a telephone link from its word processing computers to a computer typesetting service. Through the years, efficiencies accumulated. Typesetting costs averaged about one-third less than industry standards. Desktop techniques reduced these already-low costs by an additional one-third.

ILLUSTRATING

At the same shop, large volumes of line art are generated. Included are statistical tables, technical drawings, flowcharts, organization charts, and other diagrams. In this situation, economies in preparation of artwork were sufficient to pay for the desktop publishing equipment. Costs for preparing typical drawings and diagrams were reduced by 30 to 40 percent.

The artist who uses a desktop computer as an illustration tool works with a display that identifies a series of lines, shapes, and patterns. Under program control, these elements are combined quickly into illustrations. For example, to draw a line, the mouse is clicked to select the thickness of line. Then, the mouse is clicked and held down at the point where the line is to start. Next the mouse is moved so the cursor is at the point where the line is to end. When the mouse is released, the line is positioned on the screen.

Similar techniques generate images in the forms of squares, rectangles, circles, or other shapes. The basic display for an electronic drafting program, with an illustration in work, is shown in **Figure 2-10**. As necessary, it also is possible to place keyboard-entered type in illustrations.

Completed illustrations are stored as electronic files and can be combined with text files in finished publications.

PROOFREADING

Proofreading is a quality control measure. During proofreading, the typeset text is read carefully to find and correct errors. The effort put into proofreading reflects a publisher's pride in the products to be delivered.

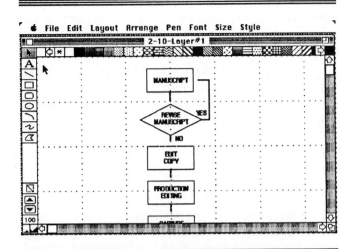

Figure 2-10. This display provides drawing tools and a desktop space for use in preparing line illustrations.

Consider: There may be hundreds of thousands of opportunities for error in a publication such as a textbook or a large magazine. The manuscript or articles presented for publication may have an overall length of 125,000 to 150,000 words. This means that the text to be typeset contains more than a half-million characters. Any one of these can be incorrect. Also likely, any two or three may be transposed or placed in the wrong order.

Typesetting errors are hard to detect. People naturally tend to read text for meaning. Dropped or misprinted letters are easy to miss. A proofreader must concentrate on detail. It takes special training and discipline to look at pages of type one word at a time, then to check each word letter by letter for accuracy. This detailing represents only part of a proofreader's job, which also includes:

- Check the type being proofed against the original, or source, manuscript. Be sure no text has been dropped or added.

- Find and fix any and all typographical errors. **Computers are not infallible.** The proofreader must recognize this and must learn to be a professional skeptic.

- Even if type matches a source manuscript, find and correct errors in spelling, grammar, and usage.

Proofreading, in short, is a last chance to assure or upgrade the quality of a publication. An

Figure 2-11. This is a galley proof that has been read and corrected.

example of text that has been proofread is shown in **Figure 2-11.**

DESIGNING AND LAYING OUT PAGES

The **design** and **layout** functions actually span several of the steps in the publishing process. Design involves selection of the elements that affect appearance. Included are typefaces and the overall organization of type and illustrations on pages. Layout is the positioning of actual text, illustrations, and any other elements to conform to the design.

To illustrate how the design job is spread over several steps in the publishing process, consider selection of typefaces. This step, obviously, must be completed before typesetting takes place. Even before that, the appearance of the publication determines the length and style of the manuscript.

The nature of the design and layout steps varies widely for individual publications. Periodicals, including newsletters, magazines, and newspapers, tend to have established

DESKTOP JARGON

font A typeface. Set of characters that conforms to a specific design.

proofreading Quality control procedure for reading and correcting errors in typesetting.

design Specification covering use of type, illustrations, and other elements in a publication.

layout Placement of publication elements to conform to design.

formats. Typefaces and layout styles are pre-selected. For other publications, such as books, design may begin from scratch for each project.

Layout, however, cannot begin until the *elements* of a publication and their space requirements are known. In a publishing sense, an element is any unit of type, illustration, or decoration. One way to lay out a publication is to prepare a *dummy.* A dummy is a layout that shows where type and other elements fit on a publication page. A dummy can be developed to varying degrees. One kind is a rough sketch that shows positions of elements marked on a form that represents the page size. Another approach is to paste all type in place and show positions for illustrations.

If the publication will require a table of contents and/or an index, the dummy can be used to prepare them. As production continues, the dummy serves as a basis for *pasteup.* During pasteup, type is positioned on *boards,* or heavy sheets of paper, for reproduction. **Figure 2-12** shows a dummy being prepared, In **Figure 2-13**, a dummy is being used as a guide for pasteup.

Use of *page makeup* software within a desktop publishing system can eliminate both dummying and pasteup. Design and layout can be combined into a single, electronic page make-up step. This technique is covered in the section that follows.

MAKING UP PAGES

Finished pages ready for printing are called *mechanicals.* This is another old-time printing term. Its origin comes from the days when metal

Figure 2-12. In this photo, a rough dummy for a newspaper page is being drawn on specially printed forms.
Photo by Benedict Kruse.

on a display screen. Type and illustrations can be fit within the boundaries displayed on the screen. Type, illustrations, and other elements can be called up from electronic files and fitted into pages. Pages then can be printed in camera-ready form through use of a laser printer or phototypesetter. These devices and their uses are described in a later chapter. To demonstrate how the system works, however, **Figure 2-14** shows a screen display for two pages of this book.

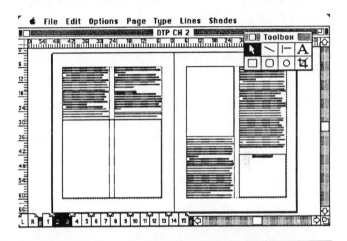

Figure 2-13. In this newspaper composing room, mechanicals are being prepared to conform to a dummy. Photo by Benedict Kruse.

Figure 2-14. This screen display shows, in miniature, two pages of this book prepared through electronic page makeup.

pieces were assembled and locked into mechanical forms. Today, a mechanical is a reproduction master that is used to create offset printing plates.

As indicated before, one way to make up pages is through pasteup. Type and illustrations are pasted on white sheets of heavy paper (or lightweight cardboard). This method meets the need to provide *camera-ready* mechanicals for platemaking. Some desktop publishers consider pasteup techniques to be obsolete. Experience has taught the author that it is best to hold on to all available tools. Don't discard anything that can work for you. For some jobs—and for some people—dummying and pasteup still have their place. In particular, manual dummying is a sure, safe method for publications with complex designs.

Electronic page makeup also has advantages. One is that it doesn't take a trained artist to handle electronic page makeup. Page makeup software can be used to create page layout forms

PRINTING AND BINDING

Most publication printing is done by the photo offset method. To create lithographic printing

 DESKTOP JARGON

element A unit of type or an illustration to be included in a publication.

dummy Layout that designates placement of elements in a publication.

pasteup Placement of publication elements on a carrier sheet from which plate-making film will be shot.

board Carrier sheet used in pasteup.

page makeup software Set of programs that permits organizing publication elements into pages.

mechanical or **camera-ready mechanical** Finished pasteup from which plate-making film can be shot.

plates, pasteup boards or laser printouts are photographed by large cameras. This produces sheets of film with full-page images of type and line art. **Figure 2-15** shows a litho camera. In **Figure 2-16,** a camera operator is examining a sheet of litho film.

In most instances, separate negatives must be shot for photographs or textured drawings. Reproduction of photographs presents a special problem. This stems from the fact that a printing press applies ink evenly over an entire image area. This means the press itself can't vary shades of gray or intensities of colors.

To show shades of gray or tone values, a process known as *halftone* reproduction is used. Halftone images are formed by a series of dots. An enlarged section of a halftone image is shown in **Figure 2-17.** The dots reproduce points of black (or colored) inks in different densities throughout an image area. Thus, when you see a

printed photograph, you are looking at a series of dots of different intensity. Different dot patterns are used for printing on different papers. For example, newspaper reproduction typically uses halftone screens that establish dot patterns of 65 to 85 dots per inch (DPI). Magazines and books generally are printed on higher quality paper. Photo reproductions generally are in dot patterns of 133 or 150 per inch. For publications of really top quality, dot patterns of 200 to 300 per inch may be used.

The density of dots in reproduction masters also may be referred to as "lines." This term, like so many used in graphic arts, stems from old-time printing practices and terms. To create dot patterns photographically, a halftone screen is placed between the original photo or other art element and the film. Originally, the dot patterns were represented by spaces between fine, criss-crossing lines that were etched on glass. So, measures were given in lines per inch. Computers operate differently. They establish patterns in terms of rows of dots. Thus, the computer-related term *dots per inch (DPI)* is the equivalent of *lines per inch.*

Figure 2-15. Lithographic process cameras are large enough to shoot multiple publication pages.
Photo by Benedict Kruse.

Figure 2-16. This photo shows a technician examining sheets of
platemaking film.
Photo by Benedict Kruse.

Figure 2-17. This is an enlarged section of a halftone negative
showing the reproduction dot pattern.

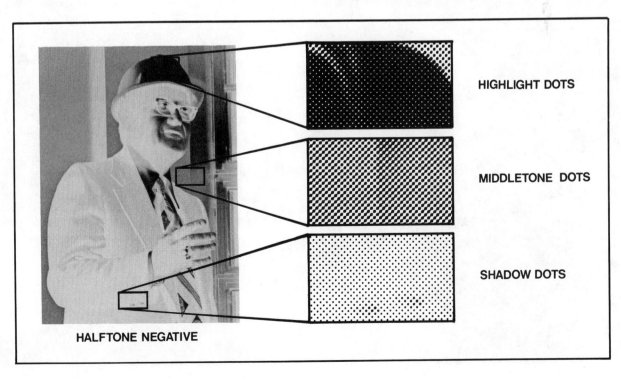

HIGHLIGHT DOTS

MIDDLETONE DOTS

SHADOW DOTS

HALFTONE NEGATIVE

To create offset plates, halftone and line images must be brought together. This is done through a procedure known as *stripping.* Within the graphic arts industry, a stripper is a specialist who integrates film elements in preparation for platemaking.

The stripper works at a table with a brightly lighted glass surface. A master layout form known as a *template* is mounted on the glass. Film images of the type and photos are positioned over the template. These film elements then are attached to goldenrod-colored sheets. Windows are cut in the goldenrod carrier sheets so that the film is exposed for reproduction onto printing plates. Separate goldenrod sheets, or *flats,* are stripped for halftone and line film. The line flat has halftone areas blocked out.

The matching of line and halftone film elements during stripping is known as *registration.* That is, the elements contained on different flats must match to within a few thousandths of an inch. To achieve this tight registration, strippers use a *pin-register* system that is standard in the printing industry. Bars containing a series of round pins are mounted on the stripping table. Holes are punched into film and flats to match the registration pins. **Figure 2-18** shows a stripper at work.

When all of the flats have been stripped, they are used to *burn* offset printing plates. The reference to burning comes from the fact that the resist material that coats the plate is exposed to light to form the image. The photo-resist material repels water and attracts ink during printing. During burning, the stripped film is placed against the offset plate and exposed under a high-intensity, ultra-violet light. Chemicals then are used to develop the photographic image and to prepare the surface of the plate for printing. This step includes developing the photographic image and *etching* the surface of the plate. Etching cleans away all non-image areas. Ink adheres to the developed photographic resist but is not picked up by the etched areas. Platemaking is illustrated in **Figure 2-19.**

Plates are mounted on printing cylinders and the press is adjusted to register printed images. Offset presses deliver either printed sheets or folded *signatures.* A signature is a printed unit that has been folded for use in a publication. If printing is done on sheets, the sheets must be folded into signatures on separate machines. Signatures generally are produced as

Figure 2-18. A stripper is preparing film for platemaking. Courtesy of Eastman Kodak Company.

Figure 2-19. Lithographic film is exposed in special devices to create offset plates.
Photo by Benedict Kruse.

parts of magazines and books. **Figure 2-20** shows a web press in operation.

Binding is a process that assembles signatures into finished publications. During

Figure 2-20. This photo shows an offset web press that operates newspapers at high speeds for large volume jobs.
Courtesy of Griffin Printing & Lithographic Co., Inc.

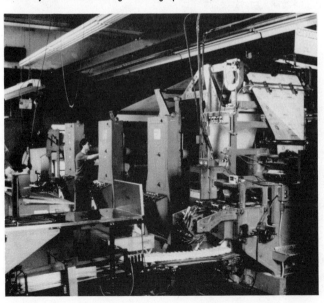

DESKTOP JARGON

halftone Dot pattern used to reproduce photos and other continuous-tone illustrations.

dots per inch (DPI) Measure of the number of halftone dots per linear inch.

lines per inch Each line in a row of halftone dots. *See also* dots per inch.

stripping Organization and positioning of film for platemaking.

template A guide used in placement of film during stripping.

flat A carrier sheet into which platemaking film elements have been positioned.

registration Positioning of image elements to close tolerance for preparation of lithographic plates.

pin register A method of registering film elements for preparation of lithographic plates.

burn Exposure of light-sensitive lithographic plates through negative images.

etching Processing of lithographic plates to remove unused light-sensitive coating.

signature A printed unit that has been folded for use in a publication.

binding The assembly of signatures into a finished publication, including the affixing of covers if necessary.

binding, signatures are **gathered** into proper sequence and are glued or **stitched** to hold the signatures together. When signatures are glued together, the process is known as **perfect binding.** The matched signatures are held together under pressure and a plasticized material is applied to the bound end of the publication, called the **spine.**

Stitching can be done either through sewing or stapling of multiple signatures to hold them in place. The sewing process is exactly as it sounds. A special sewing machine applies stitches with a strong cord. Many textbooks, particularly those used in secondary schools, use sewn bindings. You can identify a sewn binding by looking at the top and/or bottom of the bound book. The corded threads are tied in a neat row at the top and/or bottom of the book.

Stapling is a method of stitching under which staples are driven into the paper to hold pages together. The staples can be applied in place of sewing to hold multiple signatures on top of each other. A more common use of staples in binding is for **saddle stitching.** This method generally is used for magazines or booklets with 100 pages or less. Under saddle stitching methods, publications are printed in one signature or have multiple signatures nested inside one another. There is no spine, only a "saddle" at the crease where the pages come together. Staples are driven through this crease point to hold pages together. Saddle stitching contrasts with spine-type binding, which is described as **side stitching.**

Still another method is **comb binding.** This method uses a plastic holder inserted into holes punched in the paper. Comb binding can be done with desktop machines as shown in **Figure 2-21.**

A publication may have one of several types of covers, as shown in **Figure 2-22.** **Self-covered** publications, including many magazines, have cover material printed on front and back pages. There is no differentiation between the type of

Figure 2-21. This machine does comb binding. Courtesy of General Binding Corporation.

Figure 2-22. The publications in this photo include books with soft and hard covers and self-covered magazines. Note the different bindings that are represented.
Courtesy of Griffin Printing & Lithograph Co., Inc.

paper or material used for the cover and the pages of the publication itself.

A *soft cover* is printed on a cardboard-like material that generally is heavier than the pages of the publication. This cover wraps around the assembled signatures and has the same dimensions as the publication itself.

Hard cover or *case bound* books have rigid covers created by enclosing sheets of heavy, rigid cardboard in a printed wrapper. The printed cover generally is of a flexible, durable material, such as cloth or plastic sheeting. Hard covers are used for books or special reports. These covers generally are slightly larger in dimension than the body of the publications they enclose, or encase.

Either just before or after covers are affixed, the publication goes through a *trim* operation. The trimming process gives the finished publication even, smooth sides. Without trimming, the outside edges of a publication would be uneven and rough. This results from the thickness of multiple pages that make up a signature. The outside will have shorter widths than those at the center. Untrimmed edges can cause severe paper cuts as readers run their fingers along the edges. Trimming is performed with a large,

powerful set of knives that even the margins of the finished product. Hard-covered books are trimmed before the covers are applied. Self-covered and soft-covered publications are trimmed after binding is complete. Magazines and newspapers usually are trimmed on the press.

MARKETING AND DISTRIBUTION

Every publication is intended to be read. Therefore, arrangements must be made to deliver finished products to readers. In some instances, publication subscriptions are sold to readers. Thus, distribution is to paying customers. Other publications are distributed without cost to readers. In any case, the publishing job isn't done until publications are in the hands of their intended readers.

This book is about development and production of publications through desktop methods.

 DESKTOP JARGON

gather Bringing together signatures during binding.

stitch Any method of joining signatures during binding.

perfect binding Method of joining signatures through use of a plastic coating material.

spine The edge of a publication at which signatures are joined.

saddle stitching The joining of signatures by driving staples into the folded edge of the signatures.

side stitching The joining of printed signatures through use of staples or stitches at the edges of signatures.

comb binding Method for joining pages with plastic holders.

self-covered Description of publication on which the cover content is printed on the same paper as the body pages.

soft cover A cover printed in flexible material.

hard cover A rigid cover for a publication, usually formed by encasing heavy cardboard.

case bound A hard-cover publication made by encasing cardboard within a printed exterior material.

trim The cutting away of uneven edges of a publication on a press or during binding.

Therefore, no detailing is presented about marketing techniques or distribution methods. However, marketing goals should guide the efforts of writers, editors, artists, and others. As a desktop publisher, it is part of your job to focus on the needs and interests of your readers.

MANAGING THE PROCESS

Developing a publication is a process that follows a planned sequence of steps to deliver a specific result. At every step, knowledgeable people must plan for, coordinate, and monitor the work to be done. When things go wrong—and they will—knowledgeable people must be on hand to identify and solve problems.

This book is about production. Therefore, there is no great detailing of management processes. However, for each stage, management considerations are covered.

PERSPECTIVE

The idea of this chapter has been to establish a framework, or perspective, for the knowledge and skills you will develop as a desktop publisher. Your next logical step is to take hold of the basics, to learn about the equipment and programs used to perform desktop publishing. This overview is provided in the chapter that follows.

THE MAKEUP DESK

1. Examine at least three publications, including at least one periodical. For one publication, identify the type elements that must be designed. Be sure to include all page headings, page numbers, each kind of heading or headline, body type, and special treatments within the body of the text.

2. For at least one publication, suggest a different arrangement of these elements—a modification in makeup that would make the publication more pleasing to you.

THE COMPOSING ROOM

1. Secure a magnifying glass or device that can be used to examine halftone reproductions in periodicals. Look at areas of photographs with different tone values. Describe the dot patterns that you observe.

Desktop Publishing: Tools and End Products

Editorial Budget

❏ **Each computer system** is unique and is assembled to support a specific user job. However, all computers include a series of devices that perform certain basic functions: input, processing, output, and storage. Computers are controlled by sets of instructions, programs, that are known as software. The equipment, collectively, is known as hardware.

❏ **Input** is done through keyboards entry, communication with other systems, a mouse, graphics tablets, and scanners.

❏ **Processing** is done in a central processing unit (CPU) that consists of a control unit, an arithmetic logic unit, and a main memory. These devices function together to process data. Further processing also may be done by a graphics card included as part of the computer's circuitry.

❏ **Graphics displays and outputs** are generated in two ways. Pixel graphics treat each point on the screen as an individual picture element. Vector graphics establish reference points that are connected with lines or shapes.

❏ **Computer outputs** are generated on displays, printers, or plotters, or are transmitted directly to communication channels. For desktop publishing, laser printers or computer typesetting devices often are used.

❏ **Information files** that support desktop publishing systems are maintained on disk or tape drives. Recording can be on magnetic or light-sensitive media.

❏ **Computers are controlled** by two kinds of software: system and application. System software controls equipment. Application software controls processing of user jobs.

❏ **Application software** for desktop publishing systems includes special packages for word processing, drafting, painting, and page makeup.

❏ **Access to software and information files** can be gained through use of menus, icons, or direct commands.

❏ **Ancillary and auxiliary items** often are needed to complete a desktop publishing work station. Items that can help make a user more comfortable and/or efficient include furniture, lighting, mouse, glare screens, large monitors, and supplementary processor cards. The idea is to match each system to the needs of the user.

COMPUTER EQUIPMENT: COMPONENTS AND OPERATIONS

A computer is a system because it is made up of a series of coordinated parts, or components. The parts of computer systems are identified and described in this chapter. Each computer system is unique—different from others. However, each functional computer system will have certain kinds of components. These components are classified according to function:

- Input
- Processing
- Output
- Storage.

Use of all of these functions requires programs that accept and execute instructions from human operators. Collectively, all of the programs that enable you to use a computer are known as *software.* Be aware that a computer is a collection of machinery that does nothing on its own. To produce work, a computer must be loaded with a number of software elements and must be directed in its operation by a person who follows established procedures.

Computer operation involves both equipment elements, or *hardware,* and software. The sections that follow describe hardware components and their functions first. The software dimension is covered immediately afterward.

The diagram in **Figure 3-1** shows the relationships of the four functions of a computer system.

Figure 3-1. This diagram shows the relationships among the parts of a computer system.

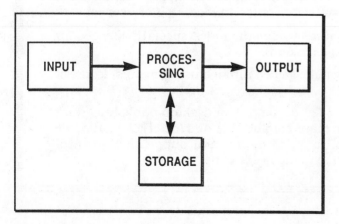

Input Components

Input components are tools with which people— computer *users*—enter information and instructions. Computers used for desktop publishing require separate kinds of tools for entry of text and graphics (pictorial information). Some of the more common and valuable input tools are identified and described below.

Text input with keyboards. Almost all publications produced with desktop computer tools include text. In turn, just about all text included within published documents originates through keyboard input. Desktop computers include keyboards with alphabetic and numeric keys. Computer keyboard layouts are like those of standard typewriters. The keyboards of most desktop computers also have additional keys to control functions of the computer itself.

To illustrate, all computer keyboards must have keys that control movement of the *cursor.* The cursor is a blinking line or block that appears on the computer's display. The cursor indicates the point at which the next keyboard entry is to be made. To control input, it is necessary to be able to move the cursor up and down, left and right. Most keyboards, like those shown in the accompanying illustrations, have cursor movement keys identified by arrows. The arrows point in the direction in which the cursor moves.

Other function keys control such operations as deletion or insertion of portions of text. Further descriptions of text input are provided in a later chapter on word processing and text formatting. Keyboards for IBM PC and Macintosh Plus computers are shown in **Figure 3-2.**

Operating features—more specifically their "feel" and ease of use—vary among keyboards. Each user should test keyboards and select according to operating comfort. For example, the IBM PC keyboard has a unique, crisp touch. This is caused by devices within each key mechanism that produce clicking sounds. Each time a key is depressed, a corresponding click is heard. For high-speed text entry, the clicks can help an operator to match keystrokes to the entries being made. Other keyboards have softer, flowing touch sensations. Some users feel these are faster and easier to use.

In the real world, you may not have a choice in keyboards available to you. If you do, try two

Figure 3-2. Keyboard layouts for (top) IBM PC compatible and (bottom) Macintosh Plus computers are shown here. Note the resemblance to typewriter keyboards and also the availability of special "function" keys.
(Top) Courtesy of Micro Switch, Division of Honeywell, Inc.
(Bottom) Courtesy of Apple Computer, Inc.

or more to determine which is most comfortable. If you are buying a new computer, you may be able to select the keyboard you want without extra cost. Even if you are working on an existing computer, remember that keyboards can be attached in seconds. It may be worthwhile to spend $100 or so to get a keyboard that is comfortable for you.

Text input through communication links. Input to a desktop system can be through a *modem,* a

DESKTOP JARGON

software All of the programs that enable you to use a computer, including those that operate the system and control individual jobs.

hardware All units of computer equipment.

user Person who uses computers or the information they generate.

cursor Blinking line or block that indicates the point on a screen at which the next keyboard entry is to be made.

modem A device that enables computers to communicate over telephone lines.

communications device. Modem is an acronym for the functions **modulate** and **demodulate.** These are the steps followed in communication among computers.

To send a message, the computer modulates the signal. This converts signals from the on-off pulses of computer language to the tones of communication carriers. Signals carried over telephone circuits are the same as those that transmit voices. Modulation converts the signals for transmission. Demodulation, then, converts signals back into the language of the receiving computer.

Through modems and public communication networks, computers can send and receive signals from other computers. Transmissions can be from across a building or across oceans; distance is no factor. Thus, any writer or editor, working on any computer system, can provide direct input to a desktop publishing system. A display that can be used to control text transmission is shown in **Figure 3-3.**

Figure 3-4. A mouse is used for graphics input on the Macintosh system shown here.
Courtesy of Apple Computer, Inc.

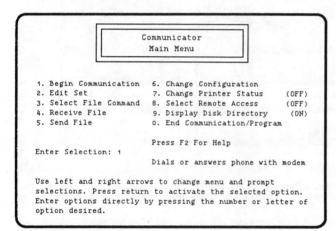

Figure 3-3. This screen display can be used to control transmission over telephone lines. The software dials telephone numbers automatically.

Graphics input with a mouse. Graphics input records images within a computer system. Entry of imaged information is only one of a number of functions that can be performed with a mouse. Others include program selection and function control for individual software packages. These vital capabilities are covered later in this chapter. A Macintosh system with a mouse is shown in **Figure 3-4.**

For graphics input, a mouse depends upon its ability to move a cursor rapidly to any point on a screen display. The user then enters signals that activate processing operations. Thus, the mouse can be used to select shapes, lines, forms, or tones to be captured. Then the mouse can be positioned to create desired images.

For example, to form a rectangle, the mouse is used to select this shape from the menu. The operator clicks the mouse to indicate the function to be performed. Then, the mouse is clicked at a point where one corner of the rectangle will be located. When the operator moves the mouse, the corresponding movement of the cursor causes the software to form an image of a rectangle.

Figure 3-5 contains a series of screen images that show the process of drawing a rectangle. Similar capabilities are available for circles, ellipses, and other shapes. Also, under some graphics programs, the mouse can be used to draw images on a display screen.

Graphics input through a tablet. A **graphics tablet** like the one shown in **Figure 3-6** permits a user to input images by drawing on a metal surface. The drawing is done with a pencil-like instrument called a **stylus.** As the stylus is moved across the surface of the tablet, its

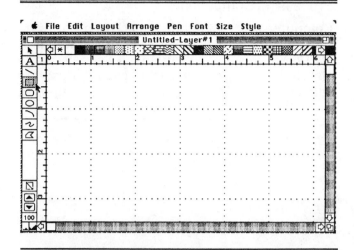

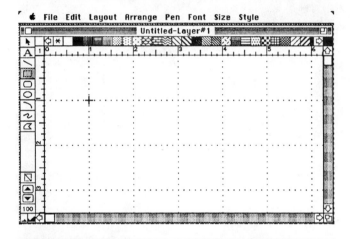

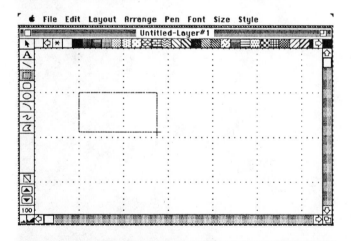

Figure 3-5. These screen images show, in three steps, the sequence followed to draw a rectangle. First, (top) the user selects the shape to be drawn. Next, middle, the starting point for placement of the shape is selected. Then, (bottom) the mouse is dragged to the final position and clicked and the rectangle appears.

Figure 3-6. A graphic table generates input from images drawn on a metal surface.
Courtesy of GTCO Corporation.

positions are tracked by sensors beneath the surface. Impulses from these sensors are converted to images.

The tablet also can be used to trace images into a desktop system. A picture is placed over the surface of the tablet and traced with the stylus. Software also is available that makes it possible to call upon a menu display of lines, tones, and shapes by touching positions on the tablet. Images are generated in the same manner as covered in the description of the mouse.

DESKTOP JARGON

modulate Conversion from computer code to communication code for transmission over telephone lines.

demodulate Conversion of transmitted signals from communication code back to computer code.

graphics tablet Device that permits a user to input images by drawing on a metal surface.

stylus Device for drawing. Can input graphic images from tablet. Also, a pen-like device used for drawing output images on plotter.

Graphics input through a scanner. Images also can be entered electronically through use of a **scanner.** This is a device that passes a beam of intense light over the surface of a sheet of paper that contains an image. The tone values of points along the path traced by the light are converted to electronic signals. These are recorded in the computer and reflected in a display. The scanned image also is stored within a computer. Then, it can be included within publications through transfer from storage. A text scanner is shown in **Figure 3-7.**

Processing Components

Computer processing takes place in a hardware component known as the **central processing unit (CPU).** You also may hear this device referred to simply as a **processor.** CPU capabilities vary widely in size and capacity. For example, a

Figure 3-7. This document scanner automatically converts text on paper into ASCII-coded data for storage, display, or communication by word-processing systems.
Courtesy of DEST Corporation.

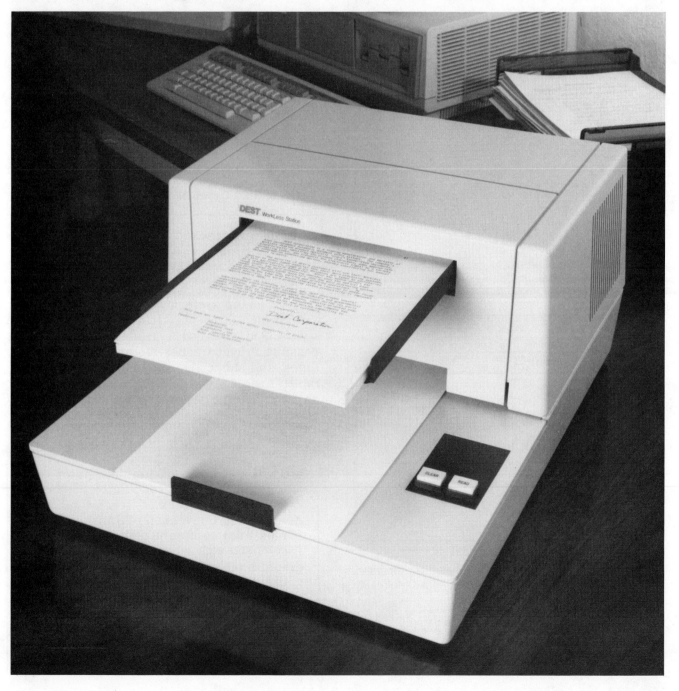

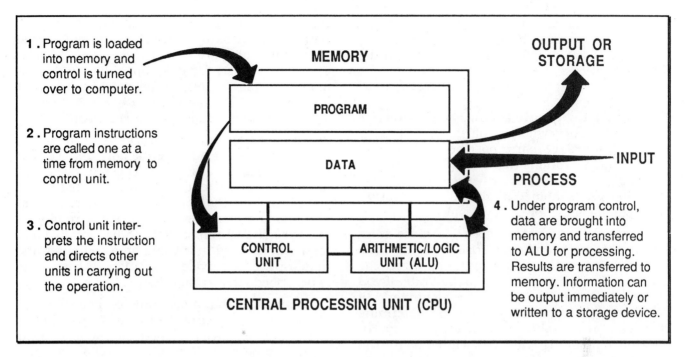

1. Program is loaded into memory and control is turned over to computer.

2. Program instructions are called one at a time from memory to control unit.

3. Control unit interprets the instruction and directs other units in carrying out the operation.

MEMORY

PROGRAM

DATA

OUTPUT OR STORAGE

INPUT

PROCESS

CONTROL UNIT

ARITHMETIC/LOGIC UNIT (ALU)

CENTRAL PROCESSING UNIT (CPU)

4. Under program control, data are brought into memory and transferred to ALU for processing. Results are transferred to memory. Information can be output immediately or written to a storage device.

Figure 3-8. This diagram shows the parts of a central processing unit and the connections that link them.

typical desktop computer may have a capacity to process between two and eight *million instructions per second (MIPS)*. By contrast, massive supercomputers can handle up to 80 MIPS, with greater capacities on the way. Regardless of size, however, virtually all CPUs consist of three major parts:

- Control unit
- Arithmetic logic unit (ALU)
- Memory.

These three elements, or components, are included in all computers. They are identified and their functional connections are shown in the diagram in **Figure 3-8.** In addition, a special, optional hardware unit is needed in computers that process graphics images. This *graphics card,* or *graphics processor,* also is covered later in discussions of processing components.

Control unit. The *control unit* is the hub of the entire system. It is the point at which instructions are received and dispatched to devices that will carry them out. Part of the function of the control unit includes communication with the other components.

Realize that the operations controlled are small and simple. Codes represent such basic operations as ADD, SUBTRACT, COMPARE, MOVE, READ, and WRITE. These increments of

programs that process data are so small that they are called *primitives.* Together, all of the primitives make up an *instruction set* that defines a computer's processing capabilities.

 DESKTOP JARGON

scanner Device that inputs graphics by passing a beam of intense light over the surface of a sheet of paper that contains an image.

central processing unit (CPU) Device within a computer that performs processing and control functions.

processor Another term for central processing unit.

million instructions per second (MIPS) Measure of computer processing speed.

graphics card or **graphics processor** Circuit card added to microcomputer to process and display images.

control unit Device within a CPU that controls input, output, and internal communication for execution of program instructions.

primitive A basic instruction that can be executed by a computer.

instruction set A set of primitives that can be executed by a computer.

Each instruction or data item to be processed by a computer passes through the control unit. Instructions are decoded and dispatched to the assigned device.

Arithmetic logic unit (ALU). The *arithmetic logic unit (ALU)* is where actual computing takes place. ALU circuits carry out the addition and comparison operations that *transform* data into information. That is, raw values input to a computer are combined or altered in the ALU to give them meaning for use by people.

Remember: The ALU does no more than simple arithmetic and comparison. On the basis of comparisons, the control unit can direct the course of further processing. To illustrate: If you worked 45 hours last week, the computer will compare that number with 40 and determine that you are qualified for overtime pay. In desktop publishing, the ALU will compare the identifier for a typeface you specify with stored names. This causes the system to set your manuscript in that face.

Memory. A good way to visualize the function of *memory,* or *main memory,* is to think of it as a reservoir. Memory holds the segments of programs and the units of information that are to be processed or output to other devices. For this reason, memory also is known as *primary storage.* Storage in memory is temporary. Programs and information are moved to memory only when they are needed for processing. Items are held only as long as they are needed to complete processing and to be transferred out.

Because of the transitory nature of its operation, main memory often is likened to a "scratchpad." One of the reasons for the existence of this scratchpad function is that main memory operates at high speeds. Recall that a processor handles millions of instructions per second. Therefore, memory has to be able to store and retrieve information items in a few millionths of a second. This kind of support is not available with other storage devices. Main memory is many hundreds of times faster than magnetic storage units.

To achieve the needed speed, most modern memories are built from high-performance microchips. Individual chips typically store up to 256,000 (256K) points, or *bits,* of information. Eight bits of data make up one *byte,* or character

represented by a letter, number, or symbol. Within your desktop computer, arrays (groups) of memory chips are mounted on circuit boards. Computers used for desktop publishing commonly provide capacity for between one and four million bytes, or characters. **Figure 3-9** shows an array of microchips on a circuit board.

In addition to temporary main memory, most computers also have memory devices that provide permanent storage. These devices generally are special chips that can be read by a computer. But the computer cannot record information on these devices, known as *read-only memory (ROM)* chips. ROM chips usually store instructions used in turning on a computer and preparing it for service. Operation of these units is described later in this chapter.

Remember that a computer is a series of devices with no power of their own. To use a computer, it is necessary to enter instructions in the form of programs. Typically, a ROM unit provides the instructions necessary to get a computer started. When the power is turned on, the programs in the ROM chip are read. These cause the computer to test its own circuits to make sure the equipment is operational. Then the instructions stored in ROM cause the computer to read in the programs needed to begin operations.

This approach to starting up a computer is called *booting* the system. The term is derived from the design under which programs are loaded. Loading begins with a series of modules that check out the equipment and prepare it for use. Because the process begins from a blank, inoperative start, it is called *bootstrapping.* Booting simply is short for bootstrapping. ROM devices initiate the booting procedure.

Graphics processor. The great majority of computers are designed to process information in the form of characters—letters, numbers, and symbols. A typical desktop computer handles a set of 128K or 256K characters. The ability to generate these characters is incorporated in standard hardware and/or software.

A desktop computer's video screen typically displays character patterns with 80 positions of width and 24 lines of depth. This means that a character display generally has a total capacity of 1,920 positions. Each time you strike a key, the entire display on your screen is generated from scratch. However, the electronic cycle time

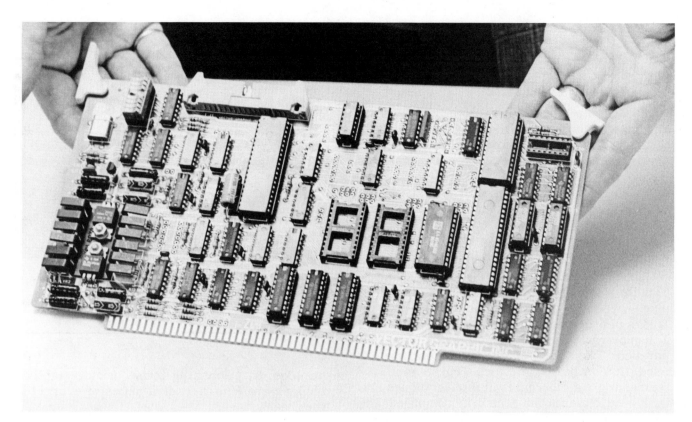

Figure 3-9. Computer processors and memories are formed from arrays of microchips on circuit boards. The microchips are contained in "packages" mounted on the board.

is so fast that the human eye does not observe the regeneration process.

When a desktop computer requires graphics capabilities, a separate circuit board generally is placed in the processor component. This, in effect, is a *coprocessor* that works alongside the regular processor. The graphics card takes over the role of generating displays on your video screen.

Graphics displays are formed differently from character displays. A graphics card provides the capability to treat the entire video screen as a series of tiny, individual points. The image on a computer screen is formed in the same general way as the picture on your TV tube. That is, an electron beam (a series of electron beams for color) scans the inside face of the tube in a pattern of lines and points.

A typical scan pattern includes 525 horizontal lines along the face of the screen. This scan pattern is shown in Figure 1-20. On each of these lines, there are 525 (sometimes more) points at which image information is displayed.

DESKTOP JARGON

arithmetic logic unit (ALU) Device within the CPU that performs arithmetic calculations and comparison operations.

transform To convert data to information through processing.

memory or **main memory** Part of CPU that stores and retrieves program segments and data to support processing.

primary storage Another name for main memory.

bit A single binary position used to establish value or meaning for information handled by a computer.

byte A group of eight binary bits that represents a letter, number, or symbol within a computer code.

read-only memory (ROM) A device that stores data that can be read only; computer cannot alter content of this memory unit.

bootstrapping or **booting** Procedure that prepares computer for service from a "cold," or unused, start.

coprocessor An auxiliary device used to enhance a computer's processing capacity.

In video terms, each point, which may be either in an on or off state, is called a *pixel.* This means that a graphics display contains at least 275,625 individual imaging points—as compared with 1,920 for a character display.

To compare these figures, consider that each character occupies eight bits of information. Memory and storage required for each pixel display screen is up to 34,400 characters. This means that a screenload of graphics information requires more than 17 times as much memory and storage as a character display. Also, it takes the computer at least 17 times as long to produce and display a graphics image as a character display.

These comparisons are based on an assumption that each type of display—character and pixel—occupies every position on the screen. This is not the case. The time needed to generate a display varies with the amount of information handled. Two types of display-generation are used in computer graphics. These methods represent great differences in the techniques and time requirements for generating displays. The methods are:

• Vector graphics
• Pixel graphics.

Vector graphics. A *vector* is a line or a shape whose position and size can be determined mathematically. In video displays, *vector graphcs* are lines or shapes that can be defined through identification of points on a screen. The vector programs generate the lines, curves, or other shapes.

The procedure is the same as for drawing a line. The user clicks the mouse to select a shape. Then the mouse is clicked at the starting point on the screen. As the mouse is moved, or dragged, the shape expands. When the mouse is released, the shape is positioned on the screen. Examples of this drawing technique are shown in **Figure 3-10.**

In terms of storage and processing requirements, vector graphics are economical. Information is stored mathematically. Mathematical notations represent the screen positions and shapes. This is much more efficient than pixel techniques, described next.

Pixel graphics. Pixel graphics techniques generate a different kind of image from vector

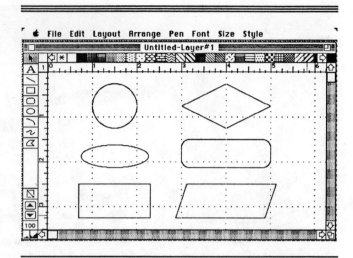

Figure 3-10. This display demonstrates the kinds of images that can be created with vector graphics techniques.

graphics. In publishing terms, vector graphics displays are *line art,* or a series of connected lines.

Pixel graphics displays show *tones* or image values that can be represented by connected points of light and dark. The image generation process follows the same general procedure as for the halftone reproduction methods described earlier. That is, each pixel in the image area has a black or white value. In composite, the image presents tone values. In some instances, the tones may be solid color (black or other color) or solid white. Because each point within a pixel image is represented as one bit of data, this kind of graphics display also is called *bit mapped.*

Each point in an image area represents a unit of information. So, creation of pixel images requires a lot more processing and storage than vector images or character displays. If your desktop publishing system requires a capability for pixel graphics, comparatively large memory and storage capabilities are needed. Your graphics requirements represent a major factor in the configuration and cost of your desktop publishing system.

If your computer has a graphics coprocessor, all of your displays, including ordinary text, are generated through graphics techniques. This means that functions such as keyboard input and text editing may be somewhat slower than on a character-oriented system. Input speed is one reason why the shop that produced this book uses separate computers for text and graphics jobs.

In addition to being more efficient for the handling of text, this arrangement also saves money. Manuscript writing takes most of the time involved in book development. By separating the functions, it becomes possible to prepare manuscripts on a machine that costs $600 or less. By comparison, computers with desktop publishing capabilities now cost three to twelve times as much.

Output Components

The term *output* refers to any means of organizing and generating information from computers for use by people. In general, there are four kinds of devices that meet output needs:

- Displays
- Printers
- Plotters
- Communication channels.

Displays. A *display* is a temporary means of showing information to a user. The most common name for a microcomputer display unit is a *cathode ray tube (CRT).* An alternate name is *video display terminal (VDT).* Under either name, these devices employ the same underlying technology used for TV pictures. The main difference is that signals are generated by computer outputs, not from video cameras. VDT work stations can have single-color (*monochrome*) displays or full-color picture tubes. The display unit also is called a *monitor.*

Computer displays also can be in *matrix* format, to be viewed as a series of points of light. These are used for specialized purposes, such as scoreboards. Other display outputs can use projection equipment for presentation on large screens. For your purposes, the main display output will remain the VDT screen.

Printers. A wide range of *printers* is available. All printers deliver computer outputs, or *printouts,* on paper. These can be used by people who don't work directly on computers. Many types of printers are available. The two used most commonly with desktop systems are laser and phototypesetting units.

To produce outputs that are acceptable for printing reproduction, most desktop systems use a xerographic laser printer. The most common type of laser printer in current use generates images at 300 dots per inch. However, newer models can produce images at up to 1,200 dots per inch.

Another method for achieving camera-ready output for printing is to link the desktop system with a phototypesetting machine. Outputs range from 1,250 to 2,500 dots per inch and are produced on photographic paper.

Many desktop publishing systems generate rough, preliminary outputs on *dot matrix*

DESKTOP JARGON

pixel Point on a display screen at which image-forming data can be presented.

vector A line or a shape whose position and size can be determined mathematically.

vector graphics Lines or shapes that can be defined through identification of points on a display screen.

line art Images formed with solid lines.

tone Image value that can be represented by shades of gray or shaded color values.

bit map A method of image formation through pixel values. Bit mapping assigns value to each bit, or point, in an image area.

output Any means of organizing and generating information from computers for use by people.

display A temporary form of computer ouput, such as a video tube or scoreboard.

cathode ray tube (CRT) or **video display terminal (VDT)** Display device used within a computer work station.

monochrome Reference to a computer display that presents information in a single color.

monitor Computer display device.

matrix Display formed by highlighting a series of positioned dots or point values.

printer A device that imprints character impressions on paper under computer control.

printout A document generated by a device connected to a computer.

dot matrix printer An output device that imprints images in a matrix format (a set arrangement of rows and columns).

printers. These are devices that form images by striking an inked ribbon and transferring the image to paper. A dot matrix printer generally is used to form characters as a combination of imprinted dots. Graphics outputs also can be achieved by using the dot printing elements to replicate the dot patterns of a graphics display. These outputs often are useful for a preliminary look at work in progress. However, dot matrix outputs are not satisfactory for printing reproduction.

Plotters. A *plotter* is a device that draws pictures under computer control. The vector values in a line image are translated by special software. These values are used to drive a drawing mechanism that includes a stylus. In this case, the stylus is a pen-like writing instrument. The stylus writes on a sheet of paper or drafting film. The effect is to draw pictures.

This method, though available, generally is not used with desktop publishing systems because the same graphic images can be generated on laser printers. One exception would be the generation of overhead transparency slides in color. Plotters would represent an inexpensive method for producing full-color outputs. A plotter is shown in **Figure 3-11.**

Communication channels. Most microcomputers include *input/output (I/O) ports.* These are connectors that can transmit signals from a computer to other devices or to telephone communication lines.

One use for a communication channel is to move information from the processor to other components of the computer system. For example, displays and printers are linked to the CPU by internal communication channels. Also, communication links are necessary for use of *secondary storage* units. The role and functions of storage devices are covered in the next section.

Figure 3-11. The stylus in the upper-right corner of this flat-bed plotter writes on paper to produce the picture. Courtesy of Hewlett-Packard Company.

Communication over telephone lines or other channels is handled through modem devices. These are covered earlier in the discussion on input.

Storage Components

Storage devices are the places where information can be stored permanently and retrieved as needed. In the early days of computer applications, storage was used largely to house software and information for individual jobs. With experience, people began to realize that information managed by computer systems had tremendous value in itself. Today, information resources created and managed by computers are considered to be the most important assets of computerized systems. The size and scope of storage capabilities of a modern computer system are illustrated in **Figure 3-12.**

For desktop publishing systems, storage devices play key roles. For one thing, a desktop publishing system is software-intensive. That is, it takes many software elements to implement a desktop system. Therefore, it takes large storage capacities to maintain needed software.

Figure 3-12. The ability to store and retrieve massive amounts of information is one of the key capabilities of modern computer systems. These disk files supports publication of a daily newspaper. Photo by Benedict Kruse.

The other major requirement is for storage of the text and graphics files used to create the publications themselves. Two major types of storage devices are used with desktop systems:

- Disk
- Tape.

 DESKTOP JARGON

plotter An output device that draws pictures through use of a stylus.

input/output (I/O) ports A computer communications channel.

secondary storage Reference to device that stores and retrieves information for support of a computer system. Storage is long-term or permanent.

Disk storage. A *disk* used for information storage is a round platter that spins at high speeds. Information is recorded on and "read" from the surface of a disk by a *read/write head.* This is a device that records encoded information, usually in the form of magnetic spots. In some cases, recording and reading are done through small holes burned into the surface of a disk by a laser beam.

The read/write head is positioned just above a recording *track* of a disk that spins beneath it. All information is recorded in circular paths, or tracks, that are aligned around the central hub of the disk. Depending on the type of disk used, there may be between 40 and 400 tracks on a single disk surface. The read/write head may move back and forth over the surface of the disk for track selection. On high-performance units, there may be a separate head positioned above each recording track.

On magnetic disk devices, recording is done by magnetizing or demagnetizing specific spots along each track. On laser disk devices, the intense light beam burns small holes in a plastic-coated surface. These holes then are read as codes by another beam that reads the information.

Storage to support a desktop publishing system uses two kinds of disk devices: *diskettes* and *hard disks.* Diskettes, which are flexible, also are called *floppy disks,* or just "floppies."

Hard disks are attached permanently to a computer system. They consist of rigid metal platters that are coated with magnetic material. Hard disks provide high capacities and comparatively rapid access speeds. Each disk holds much more information than a diskette. In addition, rotation speeds are 10 times as fast, making possible faster access. Because of these features, hard disks are valuable for the storage and use of desktop publishing software. Individual hard disk drives have capacities for between 10 and 300 *megabytes,* or millions of bytes.

Diskettes are flexible plastic disks that are coated with magnetic materials. Diskettes are not mounted permanently on a computer system. They are inserted individually to load software or information files, as shown in **Figure 3-13.** Diskettes can be used to record information that also is stored on hard disk. The idea is to provide separate, "backup" copies of software programs and information files. These backups can be called upon in case of a malfunction of the hard disk. Capacities for

Figure 3-13. This photo shows a diskette being inserted into the drive of a microcomputer.

individual diskettes range from 360,000 bytes to 1.2 megabytes.

All laser disks use metal bases with plastic coating. Many hard disks—both magnetic and laser—use platters that are removable from the drive. Many other magnetic hard disk units are sealed permanently to keep out dust and moisture. These sealed units are known as *Winchester disks.* **Figure 3-14** shows one of these units.

Tape storage. Limited use is made of *tape storage* devices within desktop publishing systems. The magnetic tape used in computers resembles the material used for audio and videocassette recording. The main difference is that information is encoded in the bit patterns of a computer system.

The major use for tape devices is to create backup copies of information and software files. Special tape units marketed for this purpose are relatively low in cost and can operate at comparatively high speeds. A unit of this type is illustrated in **Figure 3-15.** The idea: Once a day, the content of a hard disk is copied to a high-capacity tape cassette. The operation takes only a few minutes. If the content of a hard disk device is destroyed accidentally, the tape can be used to recreate files.

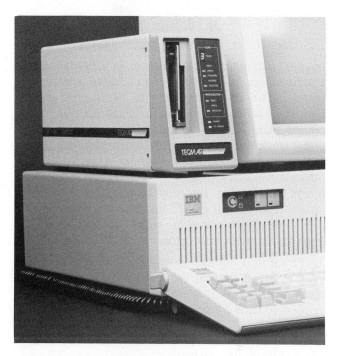

Figure 3-15. Information content stored on hard disk files can be protected by using units like the one shown to create backup copies. Courtesy of Martin Marietta Data Systems.

Figure 3-14. This photo shows the interior of a Winchester disk drive.
Courtesy of Ampex Corporation.

 DESKTOP JARGON

disk A platter used for secondary storage of programs and information. May be coated for magnetic or laser recording.

read/write head A device that records and retrieves data from magnetic media, including tapes and disks.

track A circular path around the surface of a disk platter that is used for recording and reading of data.

diskette, floppy disk, or **floppy** Terms for recording media used with microcomputers, small acetate disks with magnetic coating.

hard disk Recording platter with a rigid metal or plastic base.

megabyte Measure for one million bytes.

Winchester disk A type of hermetically sealed hard disk used with microcomputers.

tape storage Method of secondary storage using magnetic tape.

COMPUTER SOFTWARE: LINKING USERS AND THEIR TOOLS

To perform work, a computer needs operating instructions in the form of programs written by people. The first programs to be loaded in the booting process come from ROM chips. These instructions check out all of the equipment in the computer system. For example, the ROM instructions cause the computer to write blanks into all memory positions. Then, the computer reads back the entries to verify that each location is working. Similarly, the ROM causes the central processor to send out signals to be sure disk drives and printers are connected.

Once the checkout is complete, the control unit reads a disk drive from which other software is loaded. Two categories of software are needed to make a computer operational:

- System software
- Application software.

The term *system software* takes in all programs that control operation of the computer itself. By contrast, *application software* describes programs that control the processing of user jobs. In combination, system and application software are designed to deliver services to computer users.

When computers were introduced initially, all programs were devoted to running applications. The work of controlling computer equipment was left to human operators. This meant that, for every job, it was necessary for people to handle computer setup. Human operators had to set the switches, ready the printers, and enter all of the information needed for processing. Under these procedures, computers spent most of their time out of service, undergoing setup.

Gradually, computer scientists devised programs that could take over these burdens. Today,

virtually all computers have operating systems that control the equipment and make the computer available directly to users. The layers of software that support user access and control over computers are illustrated in **Figure 3-16.**

System Software

Several types of programs are provided to control operation of the computer. In addition to controlling the computer equipment, system software also provides routine support for most user applications. The major types of system software needed for desktop publishing are identified and described as follows.

The operating system. When *operating system (O/S)* software was developed, the terms *monitor* and *supervisor* often described the functions performed. Some technicians still identify monitor and supervisor programs as components of operating systems. As these names suggest, the software monitors the operating status of a computer. Operating systems also supervise the execution of work.

To illustrate the value and support provided by O/S software, think through the interaction you enjoy with a desktop computer. Before you boot a system, you insert a diskette containing the operating system software. If your computer has a hard disk, the operating system already is available. The ROM program will find the O/S package and load its main program, the COMMAND module, into memory.

The COMMAND module contains the instructions necessary to enable a user to take control of the computer. With the COMMAND module in place, you can load any jobs on which

Figure 3-16. This diagram demonstrates that users access and control modern computers with the aid of multiple layers of software.

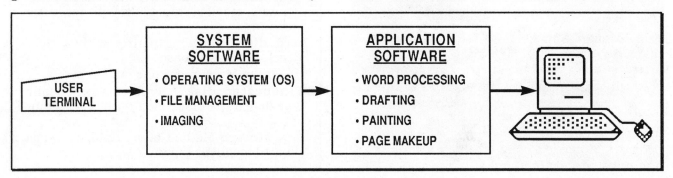

you want to work. Also, you can cause the computer to copy files from one disk to another or to print the content of a file onto paper. The COMMAND module also controls the communication capabilities of a computer. I/O programs within the COMMAND module enable the computer to read entries you make from a keyboard. The COMMAND program also enables you to generate and maintain the displays on your video screen.

In addition to the COMMAND module, the operating system also has a series of *utilities.* These are programs that perform necessary services required by all users. For example, O/S utilities enable users to *format* diskettes or hard disks in preparation for use. Formatting is a procedure under which the computer creates, electronically, the tracks for writing and retrieving information. Another utility causes the computer to display the directory of files stored on disk devices. Other utilities make it possible to copy files from one disk to another.

When applications are being run, the operating system provides the support needed to create and record information files. That is, the operating system controls recording of information onto disks or other storage devices. Then, the O/S makes notes in a directory to indicate the storage locations occupied by files. All this is done without effort by the user.

In short, the operating system provides the support you need to take control of a computer. You can do this without getting involved in operating details. Without an operating system, each user would have to assign memory and storage locations for all files. It also would be necessary to load special programs to handle input and output. With an operating system in place, your computer becomes *user friendly.* This term describes the ability of software to direct hardware operation to make it easier for people to use computers.

File management and database software. A main reason for use of computers is for gathering, organizing, and managing information resources. As indicated, the operating system has capabilities for managing the use of storage devices. This includes the assignment of recording space and the retrieval of recorded items. But people still need a way to collect information and make it meaningful.

A basic collection of usable information, either in text or graphic form, is called a *file.* Thus, each illustration prepared under graphics software might consist of a separate file. Similarly, each letter, memo, magazine article, or book chapter may be set up as a separate text file. Records required for business operations also must be organized into files. Examples include information on customers and on products.

As operations become more complex, a user job may require references to multiple files. For example, assume you are producing a newsletter on a desktop publishing system. You might use nine different files containing stories to be published and seven files with line illustrations. Similarly, a business may have files with information on customers, products, payroll, and others. Together, multiple files that are to be used in coordination are called a *database.* A software package used to coordinate management of the multiple files is known as a *database management system (DBMS).* To support desk-

 DESKTOP JARGON

system software Sets of programs that operate the computer and make processing available to users and their applications.

application software Programs that process user applications.

operating system (O/S) software A set of programs that controls operation of a computer; a unit of system software.

monitor A function of system software that checks the computer's operating status.

supervisor A function of system software that directs computer operations.

utilities System software routines that provide standard support functions, such as sorting, copying files, etc.

format Function that prepares magnetic media for use.

user friendly Term that indicates relative ease of use for a computer.

file A set of related records processed as a unit.

database Group of files that are to be used in coordination and permit access to individual data items.

database management system (DBMS) Software package used to coordinate management of the multiple files and to collect and access data at the item level.

top publishing, an extensive capability for file and/or database management is needed.

Imaging software. This portion of system software controls the generation of camera-ready outputs to a laser printer or typesetter. Laser printers generate images as a series of dots. The most popular laser printers currently in use form images with patterns of 300 dots per inch. This density of dot patterns is greater than the resolution possible on current display screens. For example, the Macintosh Plus displays have patterns of 72 dots per inch (DPI). Imaging software converts the text and illustration files stored within computers to the density pattern needed to generate output.

The most popular imaging software package currently in use is PostScript, a product of Adobe Systems, Inc., Mountain View, California. The PostScript program is stored in the laser printer of a desktop system. The program converts the 72 DPI patterns of the computer display to the 300 DPI patterns of the laser printer. The version of PostScript used with the Apple LaserWriter occupies a full megabyte of memory. Versions available with typesetting machines can generate outputs with patterns of 1,250 and 2,500 DPI. These systems require a special processor to control outputs.

The point: To generate outputs for desktop publishing, special system-level software tools are needed.

To illustrate: This text used system and application software that occupied more than 10 megabytes of storage. When the system was installed initially, the availability of a 20 megabyte hard disk seemed like an infinite capacity. Experience has shown, however, that the hard disk becomes loaded very quickly. Inactive files must be purged every few months.

Application Software

A desktop publishing system needs a number of application programs or application "packages." These are used to set type, create illustrations, and combine type and illustrations to generate complete publication pages. The major categories of application software and their uses are described next.

Word (text) processing software. Millions of desks in business and government organizations now hold microcomputers as replacements for typewriters. This transition was sparked and supported by the availability of word processing software.

Until the mid-1980s, most business documents were typed individually on typewriters. A typical document, such as a letter, had to be edited, revised, and retyped completely each time a change was made. From four to seven retypings might be needed before a letter was ready for mailing. Word processing software made the generation of business documents faster, easier, and less costly.

The breakthrough came with programs that made it possible to create, store, and revise text in computer memories. These capabilities posed a special challenge. Computers were designed to store and process data. In this sense, data consist of a series of short items that can be handled uniformly. To illustrate, think of an employee file used to process payrolls. Standard information items can be formatted for employee number, name, street address, city, state, ZIP code, date of employment, position held, pay rate, and many other items. In handling data files, computers can allocate spaces for items of fixed length. This information can be stored and retrieved efficiently.

By contrast, documents use text files. Text is built from words. No two people say the same thing in the same way. Files vary in length. There is no uniformity. For this reason, it can be difficult to mix data and text files on the same computer system. Word processing software was designed to handle this job with minimum strain on the computer system and in close coordination with O/S software. With diskette storage, files of documents could be stored compactly. Diskettes even could be included in the file folders where paper documents were stored.

With word processing software, retyping of documents became simple and inexpensive. The text file for the document was edited under control of word processing software. Then the entire document could be printed out at any time with automatic accuracy and at high speeds.

Word processing application packages are basic ingredients for desktop publishing systems. Within each desktop publishing system, there will be at least one word processing application package, often more. These programs prepare the text for publication. The most popular programs also have the ability to format text into finished, publication-ready typefaces. In addition, advanced word processing packages introduced recently can format text into complete, publication-ready pages. Some of these packages even have the ability to integrate illustrations within the text. A menu that shows some of the features of a typical word processing program is shown in **Figure 3-17.**

Drafting software. *Drafting software* is used to create line drawings on a desktop publishing system. Each drafting package provides a display that enables a user to choose from among a variety of lines and shapes. These options are used to create vector-type illustrations. **Figure 3-18** shows a display screen that controls use of a drafting program. To appreciate the value of drafting application packages, consider that savings on line drawings alone were sufficient to pay for the equipment on which this book was produced.

Painting software. Pixel illustrations are created with **paint** programs. The display that supports use of a paint program generally provides a **palette** that presents a selection of lines, tone values, patterns, and possibly colors. These are available for creation of illustrations that can be described as "artistic." Painting software

supports use of either a tablet or a mouse. Skilled artists can achieve results with painting software that qualify for exhibition in art galleries. A display for a typical paint program is shown in **Figure 3-19.**

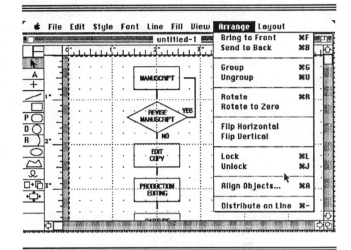

Figure 3-18. This screen display shows the tools available with a drafting software package.

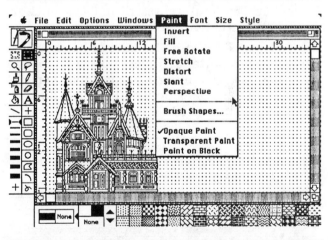

Figure 3-19. This screen display shows the palette and other tools available with a painting software package.

Figure 3-17. This screen display shows a menu of a popular word processing program to illustrate some available options.

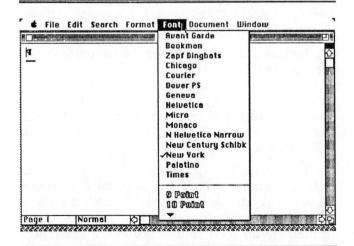

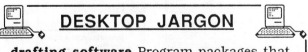

DESKTOP JARGON

drafting software Program packages that support preparation of line drawings.

paint software Program packages that support preparation of art with tone values.

palette Specialized tone and line selection menu provided with paint software.

Page makeup software. *Page makeup* packages make it possible to perform a kind of "electronic pasteup" on computer screens. With these application programs, the user can create and display the layout for a publication. Text and graphics files then can be "imported" from storage and positioned on the outlines of the pages, as shown in **Figure 3-20.** As pages are made up electronically, they can be stored. Then, the pages can be reused, revised, and output as reproduction masters.

Printouts of made-up pages are, in many systems, the end products of desktop publishing applications.

SOFTWARE ACCESS: MENUS AND ICONS

When a desktop publishing system is assembled fully, its stored files can include:

- A dozen or more system software packages
- A dozen or more application packages
- Fifty to 100 text and graphics files.

These files, in total, represent millions of characters of instructions and information.

To be useful, these files have to be organized and, more important, understood well enough for easy use. Operating systems, file management packages, and application programs all provide techniques for cataloging files within

Figure 3-20. This screen image shows a display of a two-page spread created under control of page makeup software.

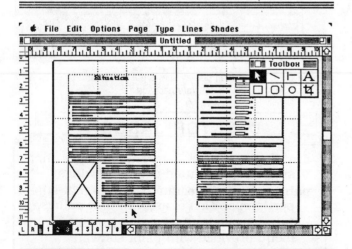

computer systems. These catalogs and the displays they produce hold the keys to finding the tools and information you need.

User access to software packages and information files can be handled in two ways: use of a *menu* or through commands. A menu, simply, is a list or a display that lets the user know what selections are available. A command is an instruction to the system that is entered through a keyboard by a user. A command identifies the program or file to be acted upon. Each command also specifies a primitive function to be performed. Typical commands might include a functional instruction such as LIST, PRINT, or COPY. Each command would include the name of the information file that is to be used.

Most systems permit you to use either menu or command methods interchangeably. Generally, an inexperienced user works with menus until a system is thoroughly familiar. Then, to save time, commands are used to speed up operations. Remember that the techniques are interchangeable. However, the examples in this book are based on use of menus. This technique is easier for people just getting started in desktop publishing.

Within a desktop publishing system, users encounter multiple levels of menus. These multiple levels are said to form a *hierarchy.* Generally, the first level a user encounters is the operating system. Within each operating system is a collection of software tools, or *modules.* Other system software packages, including file maintenance and imaging programs, generally can be accessed through menus. Access also may be possible through entry of commands while the computer is under control of the operating system. Most application packages also will be identified and will be accessible through a menu devoted to major software items.

Menus are lists of items. Menu options can be selected either through keyboard entries or with a mouse. For keyboard selection, a number or letter is entered that corresponds with a menu listing. Once the selection is made, the choice is activated by pressing the RETURN (also called ENTER) key.

If a mouse is used, the menus will consist of sets of *icons.* An icon is a pictorial representation. For example, information documents or files typically are stored within *folders* represented by an icon that looks like a file folder. Selection, generally, is by using the mouse to *click* on the icon that represents the desired choice. Clicking occurs when the cursor has been moved to make a selection and the mouse button is pressed.

To summarize: To use a desktop publishing system, you need software tools. You also have to understand the capabilities of your software tools. In addition, you should be familiar with the information files (documents) stored within your system. This knowledge will enable you to select items from the software files and database as you create publications.

ANCILLARIES AND AUXILIARIES

Desktop publishers receive a seemingly endless stream of mail that offers system accessories and additions. Depending on your outlook, these mailings can make your life more interesting or far more complex. The best bet: Keep an open mind. At least some accessory and/or ancillary equipment and/or software will be needed to use your desktop publishing computer effectively. The discussions that follow describe some of these options and/or requirements.

Furniture and lighting. Desktop publishing can require long sessions at the keyboard and video screen. Set up your work station to help avoid the neck strain or eyestrain that can result from long work sessions. You also should find a chair in which you can sit comfortably, one that can be adjusted for the height of the seat and the support of your back.

In planning your work situation, be sure you leave room at a comfortable location for use of the mouse. Consider also whether you might be able to benefit from a copy stand that holds original documents from which you may be transcribing text.

Balance room light to minimize eye fatigue. You don't want an abnormally dark room. The idea: You should be able to read the display on your VDT screen with the same comfort as a book.

Mouse and mouse pad. The standard mouse provided with most desktop systems has a ball at the bottom. The ball operates through friction with the desktop or the pad on which it rolls. Movement of the ball translates to movement of the pointer on the screen.

One tip about use of the mouse is that it pays to get a special pad on which to roll it. The use of such a pad with a mouse is shown in **Figure 3-21.** A normal desktop will contain enough paper, clips, and lint to block up or wear out the ball. As alternatives, many devices can be interchanged with the standard mouse. One is a light-sensitive unit that eliminates the rolling ball. The mouse is moved across a pad with a number of points that engage a light beam. As the mouse is moved over this special pad, the visible points act as a grid. The screen pointer travels as the light senses these markers.

Figure 3-21. The mouse is used for cursor movement and a number of operating functions.

 DESKTOP JARGON

page makeup software Program packages that support on-line assembly of text and illustration into finished pages.

menu Display that presents or lists options for user selection.

hierarchy A top-down plan of organization. Describes method for organizing and accessing multiple levels of programs.

module A portion of a program or a unit within a set of programs.

icon A pictorial representation of programs or functions for user selection on Macintosh and similar systems.

folder A set of programs joined for coordinated storage on Macintosh system.

click Use of mouse to select text or a program function.

As an option to a mouse, you may want to consider a **track ball.** This is a device in which a ball mechanism is at the top. You roll the ball with your hand to control movement of the screen pointer.

Glare screens. If you are going to work at a desktop computer for long intervals, pay special attention to the possible effects of glare. If your system has a monochrome monitor, you may want to experiment with different colors of displayed images. Some people prefer colors such as green or yellow against a black background. Others find it easier to work in white on black or black on white.

Regardless of the type of screen, you may find it restful and efficient to install a "glare screen" in front of the picture tube. This is a light-filtering unit that eliminates reflections from the room and sharpens the images you see on the screen. **Figure 3-22** shows a special anti-glare shield being positioned on a PC screen. It may be even better to look for a monitor that has an anti-glare display. Many modern monitors have non-glare faces that do not require special filters.

Large monitors. If you are using a system with a small-size monitor, you might want to consider installing a larger display unit. Auxiliary monitors are available that display full, page-size images. It can be helpful to display full, page-size images when you are composing and editing publications. The offsetting disadvantage is that, at the present time, the large monitors cost about the same as the basic system. However, for some situations, the investment may be justifiable. A large-screen desktop system is illustrated in **Figure 3-23.**

Supplementary cards. A wide range of plug-in memory and coprocessor cards are available. Among these are units that add extra memory to the system. With larger memory capacities, more software and documents can be stored for high-speed access. This can be a big help in composing finished pages on a desktop system. To illustrate this potential, cards can be added to a one megabyte Macintosh Plus to expand memory to four megabytes.

Figure 3-22. Easily installed anti-glare radiation shields reduce CRT reflected glare.
Courtesy of ACCO International, Inc.

Figure 3-23. A large-screen display makes it possible to view a page in full size. This can be an advantage.
Courtesy of Apple Computer, Inc.

A coprocessing device that is being publicized widely is known as a "hypercard." This is a circuit card that provides a set of programming language commands. These commands can be used to manage data and compose publication pages. Among other capabilities, a hypercard establishes the ability to provide high-speed links between multiple software packages and multiple documents created by users.

MATCHING SYSTEMS AND APPLICATIONS

It is safe to summarize by saying that there are virtually no limits on ways you can spend money to enhance a desktop publishing system. Experience has led to formation of a policy worth passing on: Never buy add-on devices or software packages for their own sake. Review each offered item and decide what it can do for you. Make your purchasing decisions on the basis of the results you anticipate in comparison with the costs involved.

Consider the description of the computer equipment used to write this book. Under the author's value system, it makes sense to use a $600 machine to compose text. The idea is to avoid tying up more than $4,000 worth of hardware and software simply to capture text. The logic becomes even better when experience proves that the $600 tool is more efficient for writing.

Think results! Then find the best, most cost-effective way of getting them. This doesn't mean that the cheapest solution always is best. It does mean that decisions should be geared to the needs and best interests of the publications themselves.

 DESKTOP JARGON

track ball A cursor movement and option selection device that can substitute for a mouse.

THE MAKEUP DESK

1. Visit the computer lab in which you will work as you move along in this course. Prepare a list of all equipment available within the computer configuration you will use.

2. Prepare a list of system software items available in your computer lab.

3. Prepare a list of the application software packages you will have available and write a short description of the functions, strengths, and weaknesses of each. Interview the instructor or lab assistant to gather this information.

THE COMPOSING ROOM

1. Assume you have been assigned to prepare a newsletter for which a series of stories and several files of line art already exist. On the basis of information in this chapter, prepare a descriptive list covering steps you would follow to create camera-ready art for the finished publication.

Manuscript Preparation

Editorial Budget

❏ **Manuscript preparation** for desktop publishing systems involves the use of word processing software. In some instances, the author writes the text directly on a word processing computer. In other cases, text is captured by word processing operators.

❏ **Text capture** should be handled under programs that are compatible with the desktop publishing system to be used.

❏ **Manuscript review and revision** will be necessary for most publishing projects. With a desktop publishing system, these functions are best handled under control of word processing software.

❏ **Release of a manuscript** for typesetting should occur after the author and editor are convinced of quality. The idea is to minimize the number of corrections that will be needed to format type.

❏ **Typesetting** can be handled either through direct input to a desktop publishing system or through transfer of text from other computer systems. Desktop software provides a variety of tools that can be used to format text into professional looking type.

❏ **Proofreading** should be regarded as an opportunity to assure the quality of a publication.

❏ **Finished type** can be made up into pages through manual or electronic techniques, depending upon the nature and economics of individual projects.

MANUSCRIPT SOURCES

The manuscript, remember, is the product to be packaged through the publishing process. This packaging begins with the capturing of text under control of word processing software. To appreciate the value of word processing software, consider things the way they used to be.

A particularly dramatic example can be seen in the way news copy was handled. Assume that a reporter for a major New York newspaper covered an event in Washington. The reporter would come to the paper's office in Washington, where the story would be written on a typewriter. The copy would be edited at the bureau, then turned over to a teletypewriter operator. The text would be keyed again—from beginning to end—in the course of transmitting the story to New York.

In New York, the copy received via teletypewriter would have to be edited once more. The editing was needed because teletypewriters transmitted text in all capital letters. The editor had to mark the manuscript for capitalization, as well as read it for sense and style. The text then was keyed a third time by a Linotype operator. After that—and if time permitted—proofs from the type were read and Linotype corrections were made. All told, each story had to be keyed three times, edited twice, and proofread once—all within a matter of hours. **Figure 4-1** illustrates the volumes of text that had to be handled this way. This photo shows a portion of a "wire room" with teletypewriter receivers.

Now compare this with what happens today on a computer network with word processing capabilities: The reporter writes the story on a computer terminal. Text is transmitted to a central computer in New York in seconds. The story is added to the day's budget automatically. It then is called up from the computer file by the editor assigned to handle it. The editor makes changes and writes the headline on a computer

Figure 4-1. This is the "wire room" where a newspaper receives text via teletypewriter. Before computerized text processing systems were introduced, it was necessary to key text three times to get it in print. With computer systems, one keying does the whole job. Photo by Benedict Kruse.

screen. After editing, the story is in type in a minute or so. If the newspaper does page makeup on computers, the story goes all the way to platemaking film on computers. The story may never have to exist as **hard copy.** Hard copy is the term for any manuscript typed or printed on paper.

Word processing techniques such as these succeeded in eliminating some 80 percent of the handling of copy between creation and publication. These savings alone often are enough to pay for purchase and use of desktop publishing equipment. Eliminating duplication places extra responsibilities on the writer. Extra care is needed in preparing the manuscript because the needs for editing and proofreading are reduced.

For the desktop publisher, a first step is to find out where the manuscript is being created— and by whom. In some instances, copy will be written in the same department or group that produces a publication. In other instances, manuscript sources may be high-ranking officials of the company. Also, individuals who are completely outside the organization may be originating manuscripts. Each of these sources presents different requirements and challenges.

In-House Authorship

If the text is being developed in-house, there should be an opportunity to coordinate writing and publication. Ideally, when the writer finishes a manuscript, it should be possible to use the same diskette for typesetting input. To continue this discussion, assume it is possible to establish compatibility with typesetting needs if a manuscript is written in-house. The same diskettes used to create the manuscript can be withdrawn from files and used as typesetting input, as illustrated in **Figure 4-2.** Methods for transferring word processing files into typesetting programs are covered later in this chapter.

External Authorship

Opportunities for coordination between text creation and typesetting may be lost or lessened if writing is done externally. If you are dealing with external authors, the possibility for coordination should be explored before a project begins.

The potential benefits of author-publisher collaboration can be great. To illustrate, some book publishers have agreed to buy complete desktop computer systems for outside authors. Suppose, for example, that you are working on a magazine that receives 100 pages per month of manuscripts from outside authors. If these manuscripts have to be retyped completely, keying the text and proofreading will be expensive. For 100 manuscript pages, these costs can easily run close to $1,000 per month. For a 500-page book manuscript, costs for the single job can run more than $4,000. This is greater than the price of a desktop computer.

Coordination Tips

Some tips that can help establish a link between manuscript preparation and production are identified and discussed next. These principles apply regardless of whether the manuscript is prepared internally or externally.

Pick a word processing package. Word processors generally are included within page makeup packages. However, these usually are not as efficient as compatible software tools that can be used separately. This has been the author's experience in working with Macintosh equipment. The same is true for Ventura Publisher systems for IBM and compatible computers. Under present conditions, **it is best to use the word processing software that the author prefers.** Then, you can find a way to integrate manuscripts from any word processing system with your desktop publishing software.

Include a capability to communicate and translate. The desktop publishing field is extremely dynamic. Introduction of new, advanced products is an almost daily occurrence. Since you can't tell what the future will bring, it is best to keep as many options open as possible. This can be done with existing software/hardware communication products.

 DESKTOP JARGON

hard copy Any manuscript typed or printed on paper.

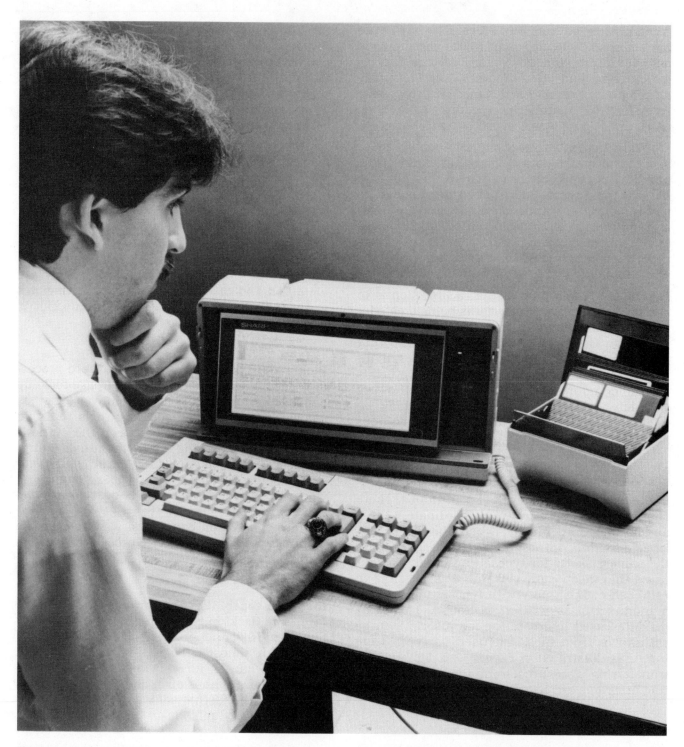

Figure 4-2. Control and efficiency are aided if text is captured on diskettes for direct transfer to desktop publishing computers. Courtesy of Sharp Electronics Corporation.

For example, this book was produced with the aid of a package called MacLink Plus. This package links IBM PC or compatible units with a Macintosh Plus system. Original manuscripts can be read from 5.25-inch diskettes in any of 10 word processing formats that run on the PC. The text is translated as it is read from the PC and recorded by the Macintosh. An entire book manuscript is carried over from the PC to the Macintosh in Microsoft Word format in a few hours. Individual chapters take perhaps 10 to 15 minutes each. An installation in which a PC

compatible computer is linked to a Macintosh for this kind of operation is shown in **Figure 4-3.**

In this specific case, the conversion capabilities preserved the value of seven in-place PC computers. This approach also minimized the amount of hardware needed for desktop publishing. The PC units were installed and paid for before the desktop publishing system was installed. In this instance, the MacLink capability was a key to making desktop publishing affordable and financially feasible.

Today, this approach would make it possible to set up writing work stations on PC clones. These units can cost as little as $600 each. In the current market, the Macintosh Plus would still appear to represent a good cost-benefit trade-off. Macintosh Plus systems with 20 megabyte hard disks can be purchased for $1,300 to $1,500. Later-model equipment is more costly. IBM Personal System/2 or Macintosh 2 or SE hardware would cost $3,000 or more per work station.

There are, of course, considerations other than money. But cost-benefit comparisons never hurt. In some shops, it might be worth the extra

Figure 4-3. Text can be transferred from an IBM PC to a Macintosh with an installation like this one. The two computers are connected by cables.
Photo by Benedict Kruse.

money to acquire systems with faster processing speeds and larger displays. These decisions are individual. That's why this book provides value comparisons, rather than specific advice.

Study the potential for document scanning. If your publishing process begins with a type-written manuscript, text scanning can be an attractive alternative. Scanning devices can read complete pages of manuscript and record the text in computer files. This job can be done with a high degree of accuracy. If you can't afford a scanner in your own shop, there are service bureaus that will scan the manuscript for you. These services deliver diskettes with the text encoded in a format you can use.

For some jobs, an attractive option is a device that permits scanning with a hand-held optical reader. Manuscript pages are placed in a special holding device. The user scans the text one line at a time with an optical "wand" that looks like a pen. This option can be particularly attractive if the manuscript is to be edited on input. The user can turn to the keyboard and modify the text as it is being captured. **Figure 4-4** illustrates this application.

If you consider scanning, be aware of some preconditions. Scanning works best if the entire manuscript is imprinted in a single typeface on pages of uniform size. If the manuscript has a mixture of typewritten, printed, and hand-written text, or if it is edited heavily, scanning

Figure 4-4. Text can be scanned directly into computers with devices like the one this operator is using.
Courtesy of Kurzweil Computer Products, Inc.

probably won't work. At best, scanning will be difficult if the manuscript is edited manually.

Acquire software that will translate between multiple word processing formats. There are, literally, scores of word processing packages on the market. People tend to adopt one package—two at the most—and resist change. This means a desktop publisher must be prepared to accept manuscripts formatted under a wide variety of programs.

One way to handle this need is to be ready to learn different programs quickly. Be aware that you must learn each program well enough to edit text for input to word processing. The other way is to acquire translation tools. One translation program, MacLink Plus, is described earlier in this section. In addition, many word processing packages come with translation utilities. For example, one popular package, WordPerfect, includes translation programs that interact with a number of other popular packages. There also are general purpose translators.

Most word processing software packages record text under some standard system, or **protocol.** For example, many microcomputers use circuits set up for coding under the **American Standard Code for Information Interchange (ASCII).** This format was devised originally for the communications industry. Therefore, almost all modems use ASCII format for transmission. Other formats include DIF, an IBM convention, and EBCDIC, a format used chiefly for large-scale computers. To make your life as a desktop publisher easier, learn to check format protocols for word processing software. Be sure you have the software tools that enable you to accept and deal with text formatted under each system.

Learn whether each word processing package is command- or menu-driven. Users can access the capabilities of a word processing package in two ways: menus or commands. A menu is a listing or set of icons that identify available software packages and information files. The menu on a microcomputer screen, like a menu in a restaurant, is a basis for making selections. A typical menu for a word processing program is shown in **Figure 4-5.**

Menus are designed to make access to programs or files easy, or user friendly. However, it

```
┌─────────────────────────────────┐
│        ┌─────────────────┐       │
│        │  Word Processor │       │
│        │    Main Menu    │       │
│        └─────────────────┘       │
│                                  │
│  1) Edit an Old Document         │
│  2) Create a New Document        │
│                                  │
│  3) Print Document Utility       │
│  4) Printer Control Utilities    │
│  5) Merge Print Utility          │
│                                  │
│  6) Document Handling Utilities  │
│  7) Other Utilities              │
│  8) Spell Check a Document       │
│  9) Return to DOS                │
│                                  │
│         DESIRED FUNCTION:        │
│  Enter the number of the function; press RETURN │
│    Hold down Shift and press F1 for HELP menu   │
└─────────────────────────────────┘
```

Figure 4-5. The main menu of a word processing program presents a choice of functions that can be selected.

does take computer processing time to generate and process menu displays. For an experienced user, it can be faster to enter a command than to wait for menu processing. **Command-driven** software responds to coded instructions entered by a user. In command-driven operations menus are not used. The user should know the programs and files in a given system. The user also should know the commands for the full set of instructions that are available. A display for a set of commands for a popular software package is shown in **Figure 4-6.**

Experienced operators or people who use a software package regularly generally are able to memorize the commands they need. Therefore, it is a good idea to select software packages that offer alternatives for entering instructions or selecting services.

Early word processing packages—those introduced during the late 1970s—were primarily command-driven. Menu-driven packages were

 DESKTOP JARGON

protocol A standard procedure, or system, for computer use.

American Standard Code for Information Interchange (ASCII) A binary coding format; standard in data communication and for many microcomputers.

command driven Reference to software that responds to coded instructions entered by a user.

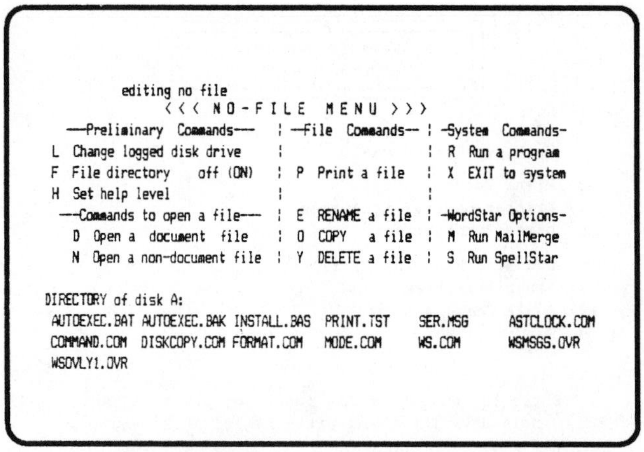

```
        editing no file
           <<< N O - F I L E   M E N U >>>
   --Preliminary Commands--  :  --File Commands--  : -System Commands-
 L  Change logged disk drive :                     :  R  Run a program
 F  File directory    off (ON) :  P  Print a file   :  X  EXIT to system
 H  Set help level           :                     :
   --Commands to open a file-- :  E  RENAME a file  : -WordStar Options-
   D  Open a document file    :  O  COPY   a file   :  M  Run MailMerge
   N  Open a non-document file :  Y  DELETE a file  :  S  Run SpellStar

 DIRECTORY of disk A:
   AUTOEXEC.BAT AUTOEXEC.BAK INSTALL.BAS  PRINT.TST  SER.MSG    ASTCLOCK.COM
   COMMAND.COM  DISKCOPY.COM FORMAT.COM   MODE.COM   WS.COM     WSMSGS.OVR
   WSOVLY1.OVR
```

Figure 4-6. This screen display shows some of the commands that can be used to drive a popular word processing software package.

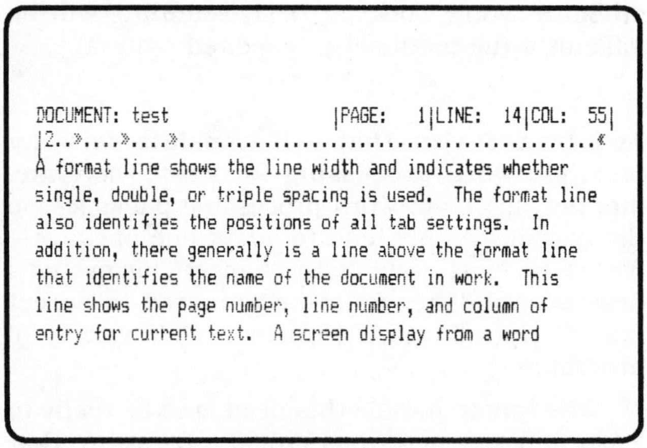

```
 DOCUMENT: test            |PAGE:  1|LINE:  14|COL:  55|
 |2..»....,»....».................................................«
 A format line shows the line width and indicates whether
 single, double, or triple spacing is used.  The format line
 also identifies the positions of all tab settings.  In
 addition, there generally is a line above the format line
 that identifies the name of the document in work.  This
 line shows the page number, line number, and column of
 entry for current text.  A screen display from a word
```

Figure 4-7. This screen display shows how a format line establishes controls for line width, tab stops, and line spacing.

developed to accommodate increasing numbers of executives and office workers who need word processing capabilities.

As numbers of users increased, there were pressures to make VDT displays look more like the outputs to be generated. Command- or code-driven software generally displays symbols on a screen to indicate tab and return entries. The correspondence between displays and printed outputs can make a difference to some users. That is, some software packages are able to show text exactly as it will appear on paper. Other packages display symbols to represent such control functions as tabs and returns. Also, many packages display text in single-spaced format even though the printout may be double spaced. These features may be decision factors for some users. So, these options are worth a brief description here.

Learn about the display capabilities of your word processing software. One option for word processing displays is to show the complete file, with all software control codes in place. This kind of display may include a *format line* at the top of the screen. This shows the line width and indicates whether single, double, or triple spacing is used. The format line also identifies the positions of all tab settings. In addition, there generally is a line above the format line that identifies the name of the document in work. This line shows the page number, line number, and column of entry for current text. A screen display from a word processing text that includes a format line is shown in **Figure 4-7.**

The alternative is an approach called "what you see is what you get," or *WYSIWYG.* With this capability, the display can replicate the content of the page of text to be printed. Thus, if the output is to be double spaced, the text on the screen will be double spaced. If boldface type is to be used, the display will be boldface, and so on. When tabs are used, the line is indented, but the tab entries are not shown. Neither are RETURN entries. Most packages have an option that permits the user to view displays that include control codes. Under these programs, key entries by the user cause the system to generate displays either in WYSIWYG or with control codes.

WYSIWYG displays can have the advantage of permitting the user to preview the appearance of a document. But there can be drawbacks as well. For example, if double spacing is used, only half as much text is visible to the user as under coded entries. Also, a special operation is necessary to transfer from single spacing to double spacing or vice versa. This step seems to take a long time if you have to reformat a large file. By comparison, to change the format for a file with displayed codes, only the number representing spacing is changed. Spacing and other controls are applied automatically on output, so there is no need to reformat stored files.

THE MANUSCRIPT DEVELOPMENT PROCESS

As described in Chater 2, developing a manuscript is the first, critical step in the overall process of publishing. In turn, manuscript development also involves a series of steps that make up a process or procedure:

- Text capture
- Review and revision
- Release to typesetting
- Format
- Proof
- Release for makeup.

Anyone involved in production of publications under desktop systems should be familiar with these basic steps. Especially important are their roles in scheduling and delivering work. **Figure 4-8** is a flow diagram that shows the sequence of the steps in the manuscript development process.

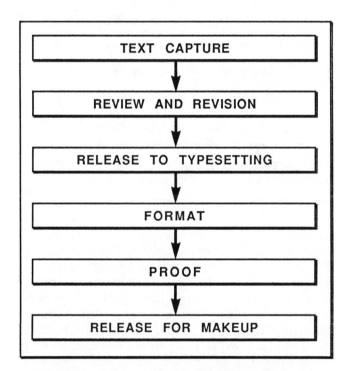

Figure 4-8. This flowchart shows the steps in manuscript preparation and the relationships of the steps to one another.

TEXT CAPTURE

As indicated earlier, this book is not going to attempt to teach anyone how to write. It is necessary to recognize, however, that a written text must be created first. Then, the text must be captured—entered and recorded on a disk file—for desktop computer processing. Toward that end, there are common requirements and techniques of text capture that can be valuable for anyone. These methods can be helpful whether you are writing an original manuscript or copying a typed document prepared by someone else.

Starting Work

The procedure you follow to begin using a word processing package will depend upon whether your computer has a hard disk or diskette drives. If you have a hard disk, the computer will load the operating system into memory automatically. All you have to do is turn on the power. At that point, you may see a menu that lists available options. As an alternative, you may find a series of icons that identify available software. Under either method, you can select the application package you want to use.

If your computer has diskette drives only, a software diskette has to be inserted before you turn on the power. Usually, needed elements of the operating system, such as the COMMAND file, can be loaded onto diskettes that contain application software. In addition, it is a good practice to add an AUTOEXEC file to the software diskette. This will cause the system to load the application program automatically. This is done after the COMMAND program has been moved to memory.

This description applies to any PC or compatible computer that uses the DOS operating system. If you have a Macintosh or other computer that is to be used for desktop publishing, you should have a hard disk. Full-scale desktop publishing capabilities can be frustrating to implement without a hard disk.

When your word processing package is loaded, you will see a menu listing the services available. Included will be options for creating a new file or selecting an existing file for further

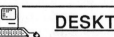 **DESKTOP JARGON**

format line Displayed line at the top of a screen used in word processing. Identifies the line width, tab positions, and line spacing.

WYSIWYG (what you see is what you get) A word processing display in the same format as the printed text that is to be developed.

work or editing. Refer to **Figure 4-5** to review a typical main menu that appears when you load a word processing package. Once a file is created or recalled, working on your word processing system is similar to using a typewriter. Some important differences are covered in the tips and procedures that follow.

Word Wrap Feature

If you haven't used word processing software before, allow time to get used to the *word wrap* feature. Word processing software eliminates the need to enter a RETURN at the end of each line. Instead, when you get to the end of a line, the computer ends the line at the last complete word that fits. The next word is moved, or wrapped, automatically to the beginning of the line below. RETURN entries are needed only at the ends of paragraphs.

When you first begin using a word processor, you may find yourself reaching for the RETURN at the end of each line. This is bound to happen if you have used an electric typewriter previously. It takes some time, perhaps an hour or two, to get used to letting the computer do this work for you. A word wrap operation is illustrated in **Figure 4-9.**

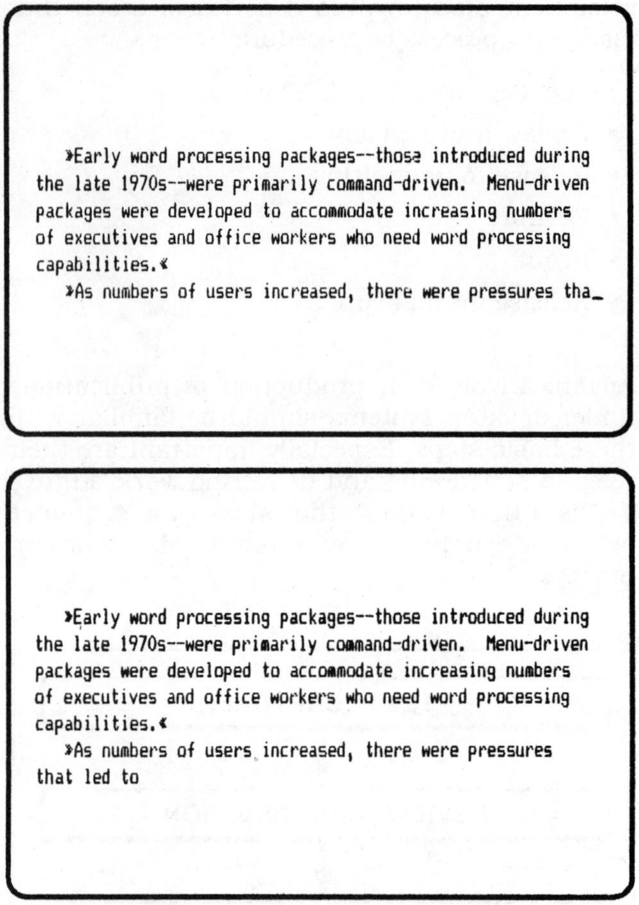

Saving Text

Entering text into a word processing computer is like writing on a chalkboard. The message is erased easily. The keystrokes you enter into most systems are recorded in the memory of the computer. The text also is displayed immediately on your video screen. If you turn off the computer or lose power, you probably will lose all the work you have done. This is because computer memory is volatile. When power goes, memory is wiped clean.

To be sure your text will be available for future use, you have to record your file on a secondary storage device. To do this, you use what is known as a *SAVE* operation. When a SAVE command is entered, everything in the active file in memory is written to secondary storage. That is, the text is recorded on either a hard disk or diskette, whichever you are using. (You can save to both kinds of disks if your system is equipped accordingly.)

Because of the importance of this protection, some word processing packages have a provision

>Early word processing packages--those introduced during the late 1970s--were primarily command-driven. Menu-driven packages were developed to accommodate increasing numbers of executives and office workers who need word processing capabilities.<
>As numbers of users increased, there were pressures tha_

>Early word processing packages--those introduced during the late 1970s--were primarily command-driven. Menu-driven packages were developed to accommodate increasing numbers of executives and office workers who need word processing capabilities.<
>As numbers of users increased, there were pressures that led to

Figure 4-9. These two screen displays demonstrate how the word wrap feature of a word processing package works.

for saving text automatically. These packages are known as *page-oriented.* That is, one page of text at a time is transferred to memory. The rest is maintained in storage. Each time you move from one page to the next, the page from memory is written to disk. The repeated writing operations take time and packages with this feature appear to be slow. But, if you are working on long documents, the protection can provide peace of mind. Under a page-oriented system, the file also is written to disk automatically when you return to the selection menu. If you don't have this feature, you have to be responsible for protecting your work by executing special SAVE operations.

One way to recognize a system that has page-protection capabilities is by the procedure for setting up a file. Some packages require that you establish a name for a file before you begin entering text. When you name a file, you record its name on your disk directory. The operating system then will be able to assign space for the file as you create text. On other systems, you are permitted to begin entering text before a file is established. Some packages simply note that you are working on an unnamed file. You then have to go through a series of steps to name and record the file. If this is the case, you have no disk backup for the file currently in work.

This is not to say that one type of design is better than another. Just be aware if your word processing package does not have automatic file saving. It is up to you to be sure your files are saved frequently. It is recommended that, either in writing or transcribing text, your work be saved at least once every 15 minutes. If it isn't, you will learn the value of this precaution the hard way. Sooner or later, a power surge (or failure) will wipe out the work you have done.

Typesetting Codes

If text is captured on a desktop publishing computer, you may have the ability to select typefaces at the time of original keyboarding. Instead of capturing and displaying all of the text in a single face, you may be able to select actual reproduction typefaces. For example, you can set some body type in italic and bold, as well as in Roman faces. Also, headings can be set in a different face from the body type.

You have to decide whether you want to deal with the details of font selection while the text is written or transcribed. As an alternative you can use a typewriter-like face to capture text, then format your type later. The choice of methods can depend on the situation. If you have a long manuscript, productivity may be a factor. If so, it usually is faster to prepare text on a PC, then convert to a desktop unit and format later. For short items and/or small jobs, it may be better to complete the whole job at once.

If text is captured on a PC, some plan must be established to identify fonts other than the body face. This will serve as a guide to formatting. One method is to generate a printout of the text and mark the printout with special coding instructions. Another method is to include codes in the original text recorded on the PC. With this method, the operator of the desktop publishing system can search for the words that require special formatting. In some instances, the computer may be able to search for and replace the identified words automatically.

In preparing the manuscript for this book, the author used a special code available in the word processing software to identify **boldface** items. This coding carried forward automatically into the word processing system. To identify italicized elements, the caret (^) symbol was used at the beginning and end of the selected text items, as shown in **Figure 4-10.** This method was used because the italic coding of the word processing program did not transfer to the typesetting software.

```
»With this word processing package, you mark characters
to be printed in ▌boldface▐ type by enclosing the word with
a special printer control character, specified by pressing
the Alt-Z key combination.«
    »Italics, on the other hand, cannot be printed with many
professional word processing packages.  To specify to a
typesetting system that a word should be ^italicized,^ the
author of this book used the caret symbol as a typesetting
code.«
```

Figure 4-10. This screen display shows the coding used to designate boldface and italic typefaces.

Proportional Spacing Decisions

Typeset fonts generally are designed for proportional spacing. This means that silhouettes for letters, numbers, and symbols have varying widths. The letters *i* and *l* have the narrowest spacing while *m* and *w* are considerably wider. Most typeset text uses proportionally spaced fonts. However, there may be special situations

 DESKTOP JARGON

word wrap Feature of word processing software that ends entry lines and starts new lines automatically.

SAVE Software command that causes the system to write a file to disk.

page oriented Type of word processing software that organizes and stores files in page segments.

that require *unispacing,* or allocation of the same width to all letters. Unispacing fonts may be used if you want an element of a publication to look like a typed letter. Unispacing also might be used for a financial report or a computer printout.

At the time text is captured, it is a good idea to identify any special type or formatting needs. Advance preparation can reduce the need to reset type later in the project.

REVIEW AND REVISION

If you want quality in a publication, it probably will be necessary to review and revise the manuscript. This should be done before the manuscript is released for typesetting and/or production. Revisions are required to meet a series of needs:

- An author may want to change wording.
- A reviewer or editor may find that a portion of a manuscript is not clear. Changes or additions may be necessary for clarity.
- Technical omissions or errors may be discovered.
- Copy or production editors may require changes for compliance with rules of grammar, style, or usage.

In any case, consider it highly unlikely that an original manuscript will be carried through to production without any change. In planning for review and revision, you can follow either of two effective methods:

- You can edit on paper copies of the manuscript and use the marked copies to update text files. If you do this, it can be easier to check and verify any questions you have with the author or reviewers.
- You can do your editing on line. You display the text on your video screen, move the cursor to the positions that require revision. Then, use special keys to control insertion and/or deletion of text elements. If you edit on-line, you do not establish a "paper trail" for validating your corrections. It can be difficult to check an original manuscript against the revision to validate the changes.

Under either approach, it still is necessary to update the text files by using your word pro-

cessing software. Be aware that making corrections is highly error prone.   All corrections should be checked carefully. After each correction is made, verify accuracy before you go on to the next item. If you have edited on hard copy before updating, you can print out a new copy for proofreading. The idea: Be sure the corrections have all been picked up and that they all are accurate.

Inserting New Text

An important advantage of electronic word processing lies in the ability to insert material within text without having to retype. Another advantage: You don't have to sacrifice legibility, as is necessary under manual methods. To illustrate, consider the insert technique available under most word processing applications that run on PC or compatible computers: You move the cursor to a point where you want to begin an insertion or deletion. To insert text, you press one key or a combination of keys to put the system into INSERT mode. The computer will move the existing text to the right ahead of your entries. Or, it will open a blank area on the screen for your entries, as shown in **Figure 4-11.** Then you key in the new text.

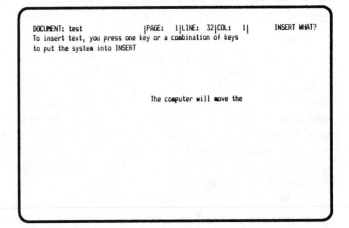

Figure 4-11. This screen display demonstrates how one word processing program opens a window area on the screen for entry of inserted text.

Deleting Text

To delete text, you move the cursor to the point at which the deletion is to begin. Then you press the DELETE key. Depending on your system and your needs, you can delete one character at a time or whole passages of text. To delete passages, you have to mark, or **delimit,** the elements to be removed. These functions are covered next under descriptions of the MOVE and COPY functions. **Figure 4-12** illustrates the delimiting and deleting functions.

```
To delete text at any time, you move the cursor to the
point at which the deletion is to begin.  Then you press
the DELETE key.  Depending on your system and your needs,
you can delete one character at a time or whole passages of
text.
```

```
To delete text, you move the cursor to the point at which
the deletion is to begin.  Then you press the DELETE key.
Depending on your system and your needs, you can delete one
character at a time or whole passages of text.
```

Figure 4-12. These screen displays show how a section of text is delimited through highlighting, then deleted.

Moving or Copying Text

Editing often requires use of "cut and paste" methods. That is, the editor moves parts of manuscripts to new locations within the text. The order of text elements is rearranged. Also, some publications may have standard text elements that are repeated in multiple sections or chapters. To handle these needs under word processing software, MOVE and COPY commands are used.

To complete text MOVE or COPY operations, it is necessary to mark the segments to be handled in the same way as described for iden-

tification of text to be deleted. That is, the text to be moved or copied is marked with special symbols or highlighted. Once the affected text is highlighted, the cursor is placed at the point in the copy where it is to be reentered. If a MOVE command is used, the text will be written at the new location and deleted from the original position. A MOVE is illustrated in **Figure 4-13.** If a COPY command is used, the text appears in both the new and old locations.

```
Text can be moved easily from one location in a document to
a new location.  A MOVE operation is a convenient feature
for relocating blocks of text without having to reenter
phrases, sentences, or paragraphs.  __
```

```
A MOVE operation is a convenient feature for relocating
blocks of text without having to reenter phrases,
sentences, or paragraphs.  _Text can be moved easily from
one location in a document to a new location.
```

Figure 4-13. These screen displays show how a block of text to be moved is highlighted, then inserted into a new position.

 DESKTOP JARGON

unispacing Display and print formats in which all characters occupy the same, uniform line widths.

delimit Entry that marks a block of text for use in move, copy, or delete functions.

Relative Efficiency of Electronic Methods

Electronic text systems were pioneered at large newspapers. At the time, it was assumed that on-line writing and editing would be slower than traditional techniques. The reasoning was that people could work faster and more efficiently if they could shuffle sheets of paper. A problem was anticipated because computer systems made only one page visible at a time. Experience has disproved this theory. During the late 1970s, it was common for a newspaper to add copy editors when on-line systems were installed.

After the staff gained experience, it turned out that on-line writing and editing actually are considerably faster. The point: If you are just starting to handle volumes of text under word processing software, give yourself time. Once you understand what is happening within the computer, your productivity will increase.

RELEASE TO TYPESETTING

To summarize the information just presented: It is best to bring a manuscript to a condition that is as complete and "clean" as possible before typesetting begins. There are several reasons for this recommendation:

- If you plan to set copy that may contain errors and to make corrections later, costs will be higher.

- If you wait until a manuscript is in type before looking for final changes, you add risk and make the job of checking more complex. **Making corrections is an error-prone job.** Proportionately, more errors are made in handling corrections than in preparing the original manuscript.

- If you are using electronic page makeup, several pages (perhaps an entire publication) can be affected by a simple change in text. If you add to or shorten text through last-minute changes, you may run into layout and design problems. Though the software has these capabilities, it is far more efficient to do electronic page makeup from "clean" type.

Once an electronic manuscript has been released, the next job is to convert the text to the needed typefaces and formats. Advertising claims indicate that this can be done directly under page makeup software. Certainly, this is possible if the finished publication involves just one or a few pages. However, for anything longer, experience has shown that it pays to handle formatting under control of separate software, as described next.

FORMAT

Typesetting for this book was handled by transferring text created on PC and compatible systems to a MacIntosh Plus under control of MacLink software. The type was formatted under the Microsoft Word program. The capabilities appear to be typical for desktop publishing systems.

The MacLink software transfers text from the MultiMate format on PC diskettes to a Word file on a Macintosh Plus. When this is done, the operator is ready to begin formatting simply by calling up the file. When the requested file is displayed, the operator uses the main menu to choose the FORMAT option. The menu appears on a bar at the top of the screen. When the mouse is clicked on this choice, the system displays a *dialog box* screen that permits entry of type-setting specifications. Under Macintosh terminology, a dialog box is one that enables the user to present instructions or information to the system. An example of a dialog box that is used to enter type formatting instructions is shown in **Figure 4-14.**

In this instance, spaces are provided for entry of typesetting specifications. Entries cover the size of type, the line width, the typeface to be used, and the *leading* required. Leading is the amount of space between typeset lines. For example, a common specification for textbooks is 11-point type on 13-point spacing. This means two points of space are added to the height of the basic type—one above and one below. The term derives from the days when typesetters used to insert slugs of metal into Linotype lines.

When a typeface is selected for application to an entire file, all of the text is set in that face. The type follows the size, width, and leading specified. Then, the operator edits the file to handle special type formatting requirements. Headings are *selected* through use of the mouse and dialog boxes are used to specify the special faces to be used. Coding searches identify the segments to be set in italic and those words are changed to the proper face.

As a shortcut, one of the Word programs still in use makes it possible to set up a split-screen

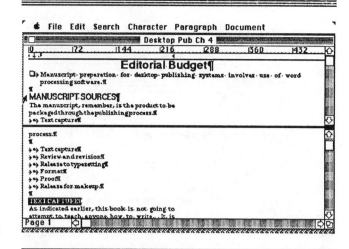

Figure 4-14. These two dialog boxes show specifications for typeface and size (top) and for line width and leading (bottom).

Figure 4-15. This display shows a technique under which the screen is split during type formatting. The upper portion of the screen contains reference entries showing how the type is to be set. In the bottom portion, type to be formatted is selected, then matched to the sample at the top.

Another method for formatting selected type is to establish a series of *style sheets* for the text. A style sheet, in effect, is a set of type specifications for a given element of text. Under the software used, a dialog box serves as a style sheet. A dialog box is created for each separate text element. When an element is encountered in text, its style sheet is referenced on a menu, as shown in **Figure 4-16**. Then, the specifications on the style sheet are applied to the selected text.

arrangement for type formatting, as shown in **Figure 4-15**. Sample lines set in proper faces are positioned at the top of the screen. The remainder of the manuscript is *scrolled* in the area below the model display. Scrolling moves text up, down, or side-to-side across the face of the screen. When a segment to be modified, such as a heading, is identified, the operator selects this copy element with the mouse. This causes the selected element to be displayed in reverse video. That is, the image becomes white on black rather than the normal black on white. Then, the mouse is moved to the top of the screen and the operator clicks on the appropriate model type. The font and format of the selected type are changed to correspond with the model element. Under this procedure, a chapter of a book like this one can be formatted in an hour or two.

 DESKTOP JARGON

dialog box A display within a desktop publishing program in which user can enter service requests or formatting and operating specifications.

leading Spacing inserted between lines of type.

select Operation in which a mouse is used to identify type or art element to be acted upon by a desktop publishing system.

scroll User function that causes displayed image to move up, down, left, or right on the screen.

style sheet A set of type specifications entered through a dialog box and used to format type.

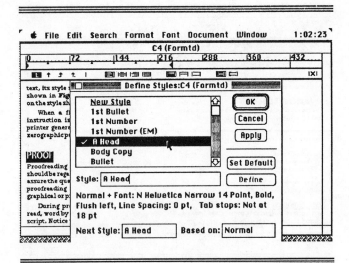

Figure 4-16. Typefaces can be specified through selections on menus like the one shown here.

When a file has been formatted, a print instruction is selected and an attached laser printer generates galley proofs on inexpensive xerographic paper.

PROOF

Proofreading is an opportunity and always should be regarded as such. The opportunity is to assure the quality of your publication. In effect, proofreading is a last chance to locate typographical or processing errors.

During proofreading, the typeset output is read, word by word, against the original manuscript. Notice this procedure, which should be a characteristic of production and quality control in all publishing operations. At each phase of preparation for any publication content, a thorough check is applied. Then, that corrected product is compared with the previous version. The idea is to validate the corrections and to be sure that the entire content is included.

To illustrate, one of the steps in proofreading should be to compare the original manuscript against the typeset version. This is done for each paragraph in the text. The idea is to be sure that the entire manuscript has been typeset. It is not at all uncommon to have lines or paragraphs dropped or positioned incorrectly through operator error or other causes. It is easy to put a series of words or an entire paragraph in an incorrect position during a COPY or MOVE operation. Computers also make mistakes. A portion of a file may be dropped in transmission from a PC to a desktop publishing computer. Or, in formatting, an error may be commited before the SAVE operation and cause a loss of text. There are other reasons as well. But the point has been made: One of the proofing steps should be to make sure the text is complete. The other should be to validate accurary.

After proofing, it is necessary to go back to the electronic files to make any needed corrections or revisions. The operator should check all corrections visually as they are made. Also, care should be taken to make sure that the disk file is updated to reflect corrections. The printout will come from the disk file; updating the display is not enough.

RELEASE FOR MAKEUP

At this point, you are ready to begin assembly of the pages that will form your publication. In some instances, you may be able to generate finished pages from your word processing software. This is done for reports, newsletters, and some other publications that consist entirely of text. The chapter that follows describes several types of publications that can consist entirely of typeset content. These can be processed completely under word processing software.

THE MAKEUP DESK

1. Using a word processing computer and supporting software (either a PC or a desktop publishing unit), prepare a manuscript of at least 200 words. Your topic: *The role of word processing in desktop publishing.*

2. As an alternative to Assignment 1, pick a section of this chapter that contains at least 400 words. Then, capture that text on a word processing system.

3. Select typefaces for the formatting of your manuscript. Assume your text will be used in a report that has a single-column format. Your text should be set 30 picas wide. Select body and headline typefaces from those available on the system you are using. Be ready to explain your choice of typefaces.

THE COMPOSING ROOM

1. Format your text according to the specifications determined in Assignment 3.

2. Print out your formatted text.

3. Proofread and correct the file for your text. Then print out a new set of proofs.

4. Deliver the completed work to your instructor.

5 Text-Only Publications

Editorial Budget

❑ **Word processing software** can be used to produce finished publications if only text content is required.

❑ **Text-only publications** can include reports, requests for proposals, proposals and bids, contracts or other legal documents, newsletters and bulletins, and manuals and books.

❑ **Professional appearance** is one of the main reasons for using desktop publishing techniques—rather than typewritten text—for business documents. In some instances, typeset text will use fewer pages and will lead to production economies.

❑ **Borders or "white space"** play important roles in publication design. Borders frame each page. Use of white space can set off type elements and improve readability.

❑ **Typeface selection** can contribute to readability. Also, contrasting typefaces can be used to avoid the gray appearance of full pages of type only.

❑ **Line width** of type columns can help to shape a publication to the needs of its readers. Narrow columns are appropriate for some newsletters. Wider columns often are best for professional publications.

❑ **Page layouts** and elements such as running heads and folio numbers for pages can create professional appearance and reader appeal.

❑ **Production methods** also should match needs of individual publications.

❑ **Budgets** should be monitored through each phase of production. Production managers are expected to stay within budgets.

TEXT-BASED DOCUMENTS

A lot of desktop publishing can be accomplished without ever going beyond the capabilities of word processing software. This is worth stressing: The job of most publications is to package and present a message contained in a manuscript. In many cases, the manuscript is the publication. Consider the list and descriptions below of publications that can be organized and presented with word processing capabilities alone:

- Reports
- Requests for proposal
- Proposals and bids
- Contracts or other legal documents
- Newsletters and bulletins
- Manuals and books.

Reports

The term *report* refers to almost any document that conveys information— other than correspondence such as letters or memos. In school, you have been required to prepare and submit reports. These assignments undoubtedly have covered a range of topics. These topics may have covered books you have read, trips you have taken, or laboratory and shop observations.

In business, owners and managers depend on reports for information they need to evaluate results and/or to reach decisions. Some reports are informal and can be made orally or dashed off in handwritten notes. However, many reports require more formality. For some reports, appearance can be an important requirement. Examples can include:

- Status reports from management to stockholders
- Reports to customers (clients) by professional firms such as accountants, consultants, or attorneys
- Reports by departments or divisions to top management of an organization.

These and other situations share a common requirement. Each report must convey information in textual form and must make a good impression. In the past, the choices were limited. Most reports were produced either on typewriters or through the comparatively expensive procedure of conventional typesetting. With desktop publishing capabilities, a typeset report is not much more difficult to produce than a typewritten document. The value in improved appearance can be vast.

Case situation. Consider a relatively typical business situation. A large corporation hires a consulting firm to study and make recommendations about one of its divisions. The division has been producing lower levels of profits than management wanted. Corporate management wants to know whether to sell the division off or to introduce changes to improve profits.

The study is to take six months and the consultant is to report to the board of directors. The final report is to be ready within a few days after the conclusion of the study period. The study itself will cost hundreds of thousands of dollars. Decisions based on the report may involve tens of millions.

Professional appearance of the report is important. So is care in protection of the confidentially of the information involved. It would be unacceptable to go to outside sources for typesetting or production. In this situation, a desktop publishing system becomes a sensible, highly affordable tool.

For such organizations, desktop publishing can do more than merely improve the appearance of documents. Desktop publishing calls for a higher degree of care and review of documents than traditional, typewriter-oriented methods. The greater care required by desktop publishing is bound to enhance the quality of each publication.

Requests for Proposal

A *request for proposal (RFP)* is a document asking potential suppliers to submit proposals

DESKTOP JARGON

report Any document that conveys information.

request for proposal (RFP) A document that asks potential suppliers to submit proposals to sell required goods or services.

offering to sell required goods or services. In many instances, a formal RFP requires a statement of technical specifications for the product or services to be purchased. If so, desktop publishing techniques represent a distinct advantage over traditional typing or word processing methods.

The reason: Desktop publishing is far superior to traditional word processors for presenting equations or scientific and mathematical notations. Typefaces available with desktop publishing systems include special sets of scientific and mathematical symbols. In addition, the graphics controls provide a better way to position equations or scientific terms for page makeup.

Appearance can play a role in RFP preparation, just as it does in reports. If an RFP involves a multimillion-dollar program, desktop publishing can make a better impression because of its professional appearance. This appearance, in turn, can impress bidders with the importance of an RFP.

Another factor—one that plays a role in many business documents: Desktop publishing actually can save money because typefaces often condense the text. This can make it possible to use fewer pages than with typewritten output. Fewer pages means that money is saved in platemaking, printing, and assembly of final documents. For an overview of the purchasing cycle that can benefit from use of desktop publishing methods, see the flowchart in **Figure 5-1**.

Figure 5-1. This diagram identifies the steps in the purchasing process and shows their sequence.

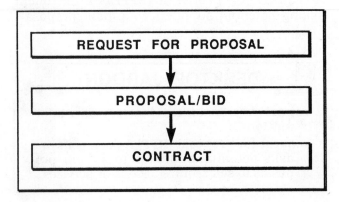

Proposals and Bids

In many instances, a *proposal* responds to an RFP by describing products or services being offered. A *bid* also represents a response to an RFP. In some instances, bids and proposals are synonymous. However, some industries prefer one term or the other. For example, bids are typical for industries in which highly detailed specifications are provided to vendors. This applies in engineering, manufacturing, or construction. Proposals, on the other hand, tend to represent the term of preference for professional organizations. Examples include accounting or consulting firms.

Regardless of terminology, a proposal or bid will do at least three things. First, it will offer specific products or services. Second, and equally important, a proposal presents information on the qualifications and capabilities of the company that submits it. Third, the proposal quotes terms, prices, and schedules for delivery of the products or services that are offered.

All this means that the proposal or bid is an instrument of competition. It represents the company that makes the offer and attempts to convince the prospective buyer in the awarding of a contract.

Many proposals and bids are prepared under tight deadlines. The combination of tight schedules and the need for quality appearance makes this type of document an ideal candidate for desktop publishing.

Contracts or Other Legal Documents

Attorneys, basically, are in the business of preparing documents for which accuracy and appearance can be vital. Some of these documents are of a one-time nature and do not lend themselves to typesetting on desktop systems. An example would be a legal brief that initiates a lawsuit. In some states, typewriter-based spacing is mandated for these documents. Certainly, there is no advantage to typesetting.

On the other hand, there are legal-type documents for which typesetting is mandated. For these, desktop publishing can be a major advantage. As one example, consider a filing with the Securities and Exchange Commission (SEC). The document requests permission to sell a new issue of common stocks or other securities to the public. Part of the documentation filed is a draft of the prospectus to be offered to potential investors.

Prospectus documents must be typeset and must conform to special formats. At one time, this work was restricted to comparatively few, specially equipped typesetters. These firms had line-casting machines that could handle widths up to 42 picas (seven inches). The standard line width for typecasting machines was 30 picas. Only a few specialized companies had tailor-made machines to handle the needs of investment prospectus documents. A typical investment prospectus is shown in **Figure 5-2.**

Before electronic typesetting, Linotype or similar machines were the only practical method for handling SEC filing documents. This was because attorneys and financial specialists require extensive changes and many drafts of a document. Retyping was out of the question. With hot metal techniques, individual slugs could be replaced to accommodate changes. **Figure 5-3** shows a close-up view of a Linotype keyboard.

Under electronic typesetting and desktop publishing methods, this kind of job is relatively easy—routine. Manuscript changes are made on-line as requests arise. Desktop publishing programs provide a capability for printing out, proofing, and checking changed pages as corrections are made. Under some software, it is possible to correct a second page while the first is printing. Remember that one of the strengths of desktop computer typesetting lies in its flexibility. Changes are accommodated readily and accuracy can be checked with comparative ease.

Other legal documents for which type-only methods are appropriate include standard contract and/or agreement forms. For these situations, typesetting can represent a psychological advantage. The reason: A contract that looks standard because it is typeset can help to overcome sales resistance.

To illustrate, think about what happens when a consumer buys a car, a major appliance, or even a home. The size of these commitments requires that the seller spell out all of the terms of sale. The buyer, in turn, must review the terms in detail and has to sign the contract before the transaction is final. If the buyer is presented with a printed contract form, the arrangements seem to be routine. There is less sales resistance

to a typeset contract than to a lengthy typewritten document.

Therefore, such documents as sales contracts, written releases, waivers, or other agreements or commitments often are set by desktop publishing systems. Order forms and other working documents also fit into this category.

Newsletters and Bulletins

This category brings the discussion into the area of periodical publishing. Producing a newsletter or information bulletin can lead to special challenges. A pressure point is that periodicals generally impose deadlines. To meet deadlines, in turn, the editor/publisher must put pressure on the writers who are providing copy.

This pressure is apparent in comparing the categories. For example, suppose you work for an in-house facility that provides desktop publishing services for other departments. An assignment might involve preparation of a proposal for the marketing department. A representative of the marketing department brings you a draft for the proposal and a word processing diskette. You transfer the text, format type, and present proofs. At this point, you have done your job. You have no other responsibilities until the marketing department representative returns with corrected proofs or other requests. There is comparatively little pressure on you.

By contrast, if a periodical is involved, you may have to put pressure on others to meet deadlines. Other special responsibilities may involve work with printers and with the people who will produce labels and handle mailings. **Figure 5-4** presents a page from a typical newsletter that could be produced through desktop publishing techniques.

 DESKTOP JARGON

proposal A document that offers to sell products or services, usually in response to a request for proposal.

bid A document that offers to sell products or services. Like a proposal, except that a bid usually stresses price quotations.

PROSPECTUS

SUMMIT CASH RESERVES FUND

Financial Institutions Series Trust

Box 9011, Princeton, New Jersey 08543-9011   **Phone No. (609) 282-2800**

The investment objectives of the Summit Cash Reserves Fund (the "Money Fund") are to seek current income, preservation of capital and liquidity available from investing in a diversified portfolio of short-term money market securities. These securities will primarily consist of U.S. Government and Government agency securities, bank certificates of deposit and bankers' acceptances, commercial paper and repurchase agreements. For purposes of its investment policies, the Money Fund defines short-term money market securities as securities having a maturity of no more than two years. Management of the Money Fund expects that substantially all the assets of the Money Fund will be invested in securities maturing in less than one year, but at times some portion may have longer maturities not exceeding two years. There can be no assurance that the objectives of the Money Fund will be realized. The Money Fund is a separate series of Financial Institutions Series Trust (the "Trust"), a no-load, diversified, open-end investment company organized as a Massachusetts business trust.

The net income of the Money Fund is declared as dividends daily and reinvested daily in additional shares at net asset value. It is anticipated that the net asset value will remain constant at $1.00 per share, although this cannot be assured. In order to maintain a constant net asset value of $1.00 per share, the Money Fund may reduce the number of shares held by its shareholders.

Shares of the Money Fund may be purchased at their net asset value without any sales charge. The minimum initial purchase is $5,000 and subsequent purchases generally must be $1,000 or more, except that lower minimums apply in the case of purchases by certain retirement plans and for accounts advised by banks and registered investment advisers. Shares may be redeemed at any time at net asset value as described herein. See "Purchase of Shares" and "Redemption of Shares".

Shares of the Money Fund are being offered by certain securities dealers which have entered into securities clearing arrangements or have other business relationships with Broadcort Capital Corp.

THESE SECURITIES HAVE NOT BEEN APPROVED OR DISAPPROVED BY THE SECURITIES AND EXCHANGE COMMISSION NOR HAS THE COMMISSION PASSED UPON THE ACCURACY OR ADEQUACY OF THIS PROSPECTUS. ANY REPRESENTATION TO THE CONTRARY IS A CRIMINAL OFFENSE.

This Prospectus is a concise statement of information about the Money Fund that is relevant to making an investment in the Money Fund. This Prospectus should be retained for future reference. A statement containing additional information about the Money Fund, dated September 30, 1987 (the "Statement of Additional Information"), has been filed with the Securities and Exchange Commission and can be obtained, without charge, by calling or by writing the Money Fund at the above telephone number or address. The Statement of Additional Information is hereby incorporated by reference into this Prospectus.

The date of this Prospectus is September 30, 1987.

Manuals and Books

Manuals and books have many features in common—from a publication production viewpoint. Both tend to be of similar size—8.5 by 11 inches or smaller. Both can be used for instruction and/or education. And both lend themselves extremely well to production through desktop publishing techniques.

Manuals. Manuals consist of sets of instructions or descriptions that cover use of products or performance on jobs.

Companies that make products usually provide instruction manuals for customers and/or

Figure 5-2. This is the first page of a Prospectus for securities investment. The type line is 37.5 picas wide.

Figure 5-3. The operator of this Linotype keyboard could set just a single line if necessary to accommodate changes.

users. Manuals of this type support products. Therefore, an attractive appearance can help to create a favorable impression upon customers. **Figure 5-5** shows a typical manual for a computer software program.

Job-performance instructions outline responsibilities and procedures to be followed by workers.

The material in this chapter applies to text-only manuals. A later chapter deals with manuals that require illustrations.

Books. Some books consist entirely of text. (Those that require illustrations are covered in a later chapter.) Examples of full-text book

Denicola & Mason Co., L.P.A.
Attorneys at Law

Report From Counsel

Insights and Developments in the Law   Summer 1988

Reviewing Your Estate Plan

Given the major changes in the federal estate and gift tax law over the years, and the changes in an individual's personal or financial situation that can occur at any time, wills and related estate planning documents should be reviewed on a regular basis. The following discussion highlights areas that you may need to consider.

Significant Tax Laws

Two federal tax laws have had a significant effect on estate planning. One is the unconditional exemption of $600,000 of a decedent's assets from estate tax: regardless of any other factor, a testator can pass $600,000 worth of his property upon his death to whomever he wishes and not concern himself with federal estate tax liability. The second, the unlimited marital deduction, allows for an unrestricted amount of property to be passed to a decedent's surviving spouse without tax liability being incurred. Will clauses based on earlier rules governing the marital deduction, although not necessarily fatal to the deduction, should be replaced by provisions reflecting the current law. Careful will drafting can utilize both these changes in the law so as to eliminate or minimize tax liability upon the first spouse's death.

A third federal tax law with important implications for estate planning is the annual gift tax exclusion of $10,000. This means that an individual in any given year can make tax-free gifts of up to $10,000 each to an unlimited number of donees. If the donor's spouse joins in the gift, the maximum amount of each tax-free gift is doubled to $20,000. A program of such gift-giving can drastically alter the com-position of the estate and requires rethinking of the testamentary estate plan.

Short-Term Trusts

The lifetime estate planning device of shifting income to one's children by transferring property to them under a short-term trust is no longer viable. Under most circumstances, as long as the grantor will get the trust property back after a term of years or at the trust beneficiary's death, there will be no shifting of income, and all income earned during the period of the trust will be taxed to the grantor. It should be noted, however, that the earlier rules continue to apply to short-term trusts established before March 2, 1986.

A Checklist for Periodic Review

Lost or Misplaced Wills: Oftentimes steps are taken to revise an old will or draft a new one, but the task is left incomplete. Meanwhile, the old will may have been destroyed or misplaced, and all that is available at the testator's death is a set of notes concerning the new instrument. While it is possible to "recreate" the old will and have it probated, this is a troublesome undertaking that can be avoided by making certain that a valid, current will exists.

Beneficiaries: Changes in the circumstances of beneficiaries named in a will (e.g., through death, marriage, or incompetence) may well require corresponding changes in the will itself.

Major Life Events: As a general rule, important events like marriage, divorce, or the birth of a child should occasion a reexamination of your will to make sure it accurately reflects where you would like your estate to go.

INSURANCE

Settlement Without Insured's Consent

In a recent case an oral surgeon alleged that his insurance company had breached an implied covenant of good faith after the company settled a medical malpractice claim against him without his consent. The Fourth Circuit Court of Appeals held, however, that the decision to settle the malpractice claim was unquestionably one of reasoned good faith on the insurer's behalf. The court acknowledged that even a provision in the policy at issue stating that the insurer could settle claims as it "deem[ed] expedient" did not give the insurer the absolute right to settle any claim within the policy limits. Nevertheless, it did find ample justification for the insurer's decision to avoid a trial in this matter.

The court observed that the likelihood of a substantial award of damages was great: the plaintiff in the underlying malpractice suit was a young man who had suffered horrible and permanent injury; the attorney for the physician, employed by the insurer, learned that the plaintiff had secured an expert witness prepared to testify that the physician had breached the applicable standard of care; and the physician during the time of the malpractice suit was charged criminally with conspiracy to murder his business partner, which, with the attendant stress and unfavorable publicity, raised serious doubt about his ability to function effectively as a witness in his own behalf. Accordingly, the court reasoned, the insurer's decision to settle the matter was made in good faith.

Denicola & Mason Co., L.P.A.
701 Fifth & Race Tower • 120 West Fifth Street • Cincinnati, OH 45202 • (513) 621-9660

Figure 5-4. This is a page from a newsletter with a simple design that can be produced entirely with word processing software.

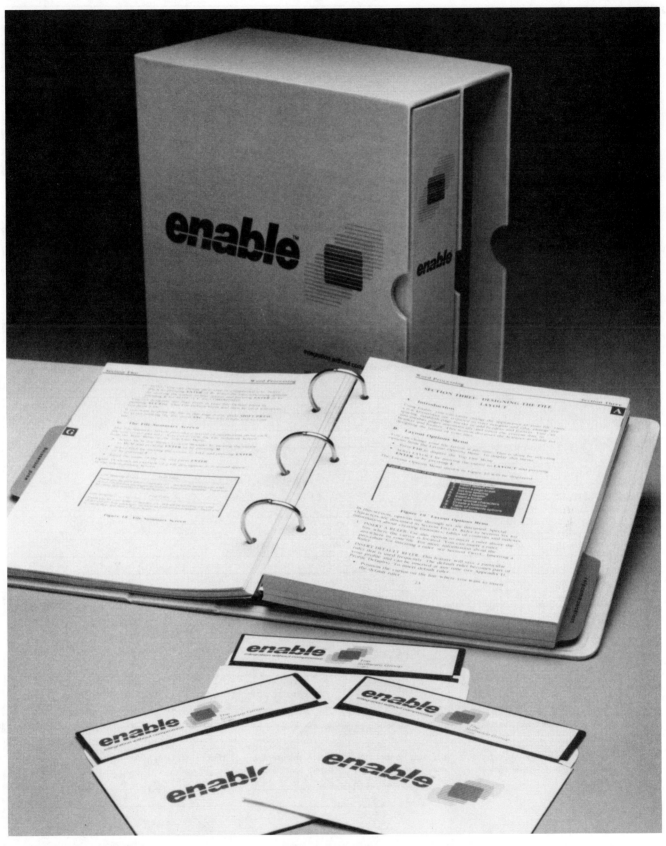

Figure 5-5. The manual in this photo is typical of those furnished with computer software programs. Courtesy of The Software Group.

JOB SPECIFICATION SHEET

Customer Name _____ Date _____

Address _____ Zip _____

Person to Contact _____ Phone _____

Author/Title _____ No. Ms. Pages _____

LAYOUT & SPACING

Trim Size _____ Chapter Start: ☐ run-in ☐ new page ☐ new right-hand page   Amt. of Drop _____

Page Layout: Top to Baseline of Running Head (or 1st line of type) _____

No. of Lines on Page (include running heads and folios _____

Gutter to Type _____ Running Head to Type _____ Folio to Type _____

Extra Paragraph Spacing _____

Internal
Spacing
(it is best to
use baseline-
to-baseline
in points)

#1 head _____ Space Above _____ Space Below _____

#2 head _____ Space Above _____ Space Below _____

#3 head _____ Space Above _____ Space Below _____

Extracts _____ Space Above _____ Space Below _____

Front Matter: i. _____ vi. _____ Page 1 _____

ii. _____ vii. _____

iii. _____ viii. _____

iv. _____ ix. _____

v. _____ x. _____

TYPE SIZE, STYLE, LEADING & MEASURE

Text   _____

Extracts   _____

Subheads   First _____ Second _____

Third _____ Fourth _____

Notes   ☐ Foot   ☐ End of Chapter   ☐ End of Book   _____

Captions   _____

Tables   _____

Bibliography ☐ End of Chapter   ☐ End of Book   _____

Index   _____

Running Heads   ☐ Outside Flush   ☐ Inside Flush   ☐ Center   _____

Folios   ☐ Flush Outside   ☐ Center   ☐ Drop   ☐ Above   _____

Proofs   (1 galley, 1 page supplied regularly) _____

Please mark other data on Ms, e.g. chapter titles, etc., front matter. If possible, enclose layout of front matter & part openings.
If a sample layout is not enclosed, we will make one and send it for OK before beginning.

Completion Date Requested _____

Signed _____

products include many novels, books of poetry, some professional books, and many educational texts.

For publications of this type, complete, camera-ready outputs can be generated from word processing software. The word processing packages have the potential to create book (or manual) pages that include *running heads.* These are the descriptive headings at the top of each page, and *folios,* or page numbers. The shop where this book was created uses word processing application software for educational publications. Included are study guides (also called workbooks) and instructor's guides.

DESIGN CHECKLIST

Design of publications is a creative process that doesn't lend itself to hard-and-fast rules or step-by-step prescriptions. Each publication can have its own personality and can be designed to appeal to readers on an individual basis. There will be no attempt in this book to lay down rules about what a publication should look like.

Creative freedom can, however, benefit greatly from suggestions and constructive examples. Many examples and guidelines are provided. In addition, some general guidelines and technical limitations are identified. A model of a form that can be used to prepare type and page layout specifications is presented in **Figure 5-6.**

Borders and 'White Space'

Borders, text positions, and allocation of blank, or "white," space can be important. Both technical and aesthetic considerations are involved. The technical requirements must be observed. The aesthetic values can be a matter of taste.

A main technical consideration is that a xerographic laser printer cannot apply imprints to a full sheet of paper. From experiments, the author has learned that it is necessary to leave margins at the edges of pages. A safe practice is to allow at least three-quarters of an inch for outside margins. The xerographic drum within a laser printer simply won't retain and output an image over a full, 8.5-inch width. There also are problems at the top and bottom margins. At

these points, the contact between drum and paper is not good enough to produce a quality image. Each printer is individual. If image area is important to you, experiment with your own printer. Develop your own guidelines for image limitations. A general set of guidelines for laser printer image area is provided in **Figure 5-7.**

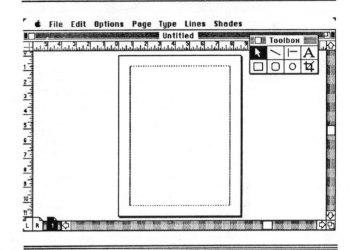

Figure 5-7. This simple illustration shows minimum borders that should be used for publications in an 8.5-by-11-inch size.

The attractiveness of the use of white space can vary in the designer's eye and with the nature of the publication. The guidelines that follow are provided within a context of type-only composition and layout. Different guidelines apply for publications that include drawings and photographs within text.

One valuable guideline is that a solid page of type projects an image of overall grayness. The effect can be dull and uninteresting. One way to break up solid body type is through insertion of headings and subheadings set in bold, contrasting type. The idea: The bold headings and different type styles present contrasting, black values that break up the grayness. An example of a newsletter that uses type for visual interest is shown in **Figure 5-8.**

Figure 5-6. A control form establishing specifications for type to be used in a publication is easy to create and can be a valuable project management tool.

DESKTOP JARGON

running head A descriptive heading at the top of a publication page.
folio A sequential page number.

ααp

Monthly Report

Vol. V, No. 8　　A Newsbulletin for Members of The Association of American Publishers　　August 1988

ISSN 0748-8173

NEWS FROM WASHINGTON

Trade Bill Will Benefit Copyright Industries

The Omnibus Trade Bill passed by the Senate on August 3 and awaiting President Reagan's signature is expected to aid in the fight against international copyright piracy, help open overseas markets for U.S. copyrighted works, and generally benefit U.S. copyright industries by strengthening the international trading system. Four years in the making, the legislation is the most sweeping revision of U.S. trade law since the end of World War II, and mandates a tougher stance by the U.S. government against the unfair trade practices of other nations.

Of specific concern to publishers are provisions strengthening Section 301 of the 1974 Trade Act to combat piracy and open foreign markets unfairly closed to U.S. intellectual property industries. The new provisions will broaden and strengthen existing trade law protection of intellectual property by requiring the U.S. Trade Representative to identify "priority" countries where the level of piracy and/or the lack of fair market access creates significant trade problems for U.S. firms. The process of negotiating improvements with these "priority" countries and of recommending remedial action to the President will be accelerated. The legislation also provides the Administration and future administrations with negotiating authority in the ongoing "Uruguay Round" of trade talks under the General Agreement on Tariffs and Trade (GATT).

AAP anti-piracy counsel Eric Smith is preparing an analysis of the specific weapons the new trade law will give publishers to combat piracy and to open overseas markets. The analysis will be available to AAP members in the next few weeks.

Education, Library Funding Measure Passes Senate

The Senate has now passed its Labor/HHS/Education appropriations measure calling for $21.8 billion to fund education programs, a $1.5 billion increase over the 1988 appropriation. The House bill, passed on June 15, provides for education funding in excess of $22 billion, $1.7 billion over the 1988 level. House

and Senate conferees are expected to resolve differences in the two bills when Congress returns from its August recess.

The House bill asks for $489 million for Chapter 2 programs; $4.6 billion for Chapter 1 programs for disadvantaged students; $142 million in federal library assistance; $577 million for higher education; $10 million for the Star Schools Program (improved instruction in selected areas); and $8.5 million for the RIF inexpensive book distribution program. Senate appropriations are generally lower for all of these programs. In addition, the House measure would allocate $25 million for Even Start, a literacy initiative strongly supported by AAP. Although this is only half of the $50 million authorized in this year's education reauthorization act, it is a vast improvement over the Senate bill which contains no appropriation for Even Start.

Cavazos Named to Replace Bennett as Education Secretary

Lauro F. Cavazos, President of Texas Tech University, has been named to replace Secretary of Education William J. Bennett who will leave his post on September 20. Bennett had announced last spring that he would leave his Cabinet post to lecture and write.

Prior to assuming the presidency of Texas Tech in 1980, Cavazos was Dean of the School of Medicine at Tufts University. He received his bachelor's and master's degrees from Texas Tech in zoology and cytology, and holds a doctorate in physiology from Iowa State University. If Cavazos' nomination is confirmed, he will become the first Hispanic-American to hold Cabinet rank.

COPYRIGHT

Sovereign Immunity Question Continues to Trouble Publishers

Publishers and other segments of the copyright community continue to be concerned over assertions that the 11th Amendment to the Constitution grants states and state agencies protection from damage suits for copyright infringement. The seriousness of that concern is underscored by several recent developments.

In *Anderson v. Radford University*, a case in which AAP participated as a friend-of-the-court, (see *Monthly Report* July/August 1987), the Court of Appeals for the Fourth Circuit has refused to reverse a lower court finding that the Commonwealth of Virginia, of which Radford is an official arm, is protected by the 11th Amendment from damage suits for copyright infringement. AAP will file an *amicus* brief in support of Anderson's petition for Supreme Court review, and if such review is granted, will file an *amicus* brief in the Supreme Court.

AAP has filed an *amicus* brief in the Supreme Court in *Commonwealth of Pennsyl-*

vania v. Union Gas Company. Although the case does not deal directly with copyright, its outcome is seen as critical to the question of whether states can be held liable for copyright infringement. The underlying issue in the *Union Gas* case is whether or not Congress has the power under Article I of the Constitution to abrogate 11th Amendment immunity. AAP's brief, filed jointly with the Association of American University Presses, argues that whenever it enacts legislation under its plenary

(continued on page 2)

IN THIS ISSUE

New Technology 2
Joint Programs at ALA 3
New Members 3
Divisions:
　General Publishing 3
　Higher Education 3
　Professional & Scholarly 4
　International 4

2005 Massachusetts Avenue, N.W., Washington, D.C. 20036 • (202) 232-3335 • 220 E. 23rd Street, New York, N.Y. 10010 • (212) 689-8920
Judith Platt, Director of Communications

The dull appearance of solid type also can be broken by allowing extra space between paragraphs. The effect can be to break the gray area with narrow lines of white. This book follows that design principle. Instructions were entered into the typesetting software to add an extra three points of space between paragraphs. This "extra" space is added each time the software senses a RETURN symbol.

The amount of blank space at the top and side borders should be an aesthetic, as well as a technical, consideration. In effect, the outside borders of a page form a frame. Within this frame, you picture the text you are presenting to the reader. The top and side borders set off the type to reduce eye strain and to make the printed page more attractive. As is true for framing a picture, the relationship between a page of text and its borders is a matter of taste. A good practice is to try several possibilities for each publication. Then, you can pick the combination of top and side borders that looks best. Also, once a choice has been made, the style should be followed throughout a publication. The selected margins should be violated only for good, specific reasons.

Typeface Selection

If your entire publication consists of text, readability of the typefaces you use is particularly critical. You can't count on illustrations to attract interest. Type is all you have.

Typefaces selected should depend on the overall size and scope of the publication and on the length of individual published items. As an illustration, consider a typical daily newspaper. Generally, the newspaper presents a number of small items set off by headlines that attract reader attention. Because there is so much news to present, the typical paper uses a condensed face for body type. The idea is to cram as much information as possible into narrow column widths. Because individual lines are short, the leading between lines can be minimal. The reader's eye movement covers short distances. It is relatively easy to pick up the beginning of the next line after the current line has been scanned.

At the same time, use of tightly packed type can present an overall gray image for relatively long stories. This is why most newspapers break up long stories by inserting subheads within the text. Almost all newspapers use condensed Roman faces for body type. Headlines and subheads generally are set in bold type and may be either Roman or Gothic. For a "classic" look, Roman headlines generally are used. Gothic faces generally are used to present a "modern" or "lively" appearance.

By contrast, publications such as business reports or professional books generally have wider line widths. For such publications, body type generally will have a wider silhouette. That is, there will be fewer characters for each inch of line width in a "book face" than in a "news face."

To illustrate, a typical hard-cover book will have type set in line widths of from 26 to 32 picas (4.3 to 5.3 inches). On lines of this width, readability requirements generally demand a larger typeface and greater leading than for narrower newspaper columns. To illustrate, a typical newspaper might use a body face of 8.5 or 9 points on either 9- or 10-point leading. By contrast, a book set 30 picas wide might use 10- or 11-point type on 12- or 13-point leading.

This means the typical report or book will have larger type and more leading. The principle is that the extra size and leading make it easier to read the text as line widths become wider. **Figure 5-9** illustrates comparative widths of the silhouettes of a number of typical body and headline typefaces.

Line Width

The choice of line width for a publication can represent an exercise in reader psychology. The idea: Individual designers have varying views of type layouts that attract readers. For example, some newsletters published in 8.5-by-11-inch formats use type in the full width of the page— 30 or 36 picas. Others organize their presentations into two columns of 18 or 19 picas each. Still others use three-column formats and a few use four-column layouts.

One theory is that busy people feel they are accomplishing more if they read quickly through the length of a column. This kind of thinking justifies narrow column widths. Other designers feel that readers don't want to jump around on the page or have information metered out in narrow columns. They seem to feel that

Figure 5-8. This newsletter shows a satisfactory balance in placement and type selection for headlines.

This is a sample of 9 point Times
Roman type set on 10 point leading. The line width is 12 picas.

This is a sample of 11 point Times Roman type set on 13 point leading.
The line width is 26 picas.

This is a sample of 9 point Century
type set on 10 point leading. The
line width is 12 picas.

This is a sample of 11 point Century type set on 13 point
leading. The line width is 26 picas.

This is a sample of 9 point Palatino
type set on 10 point leading. The
line width is 12 picas.

This is a sample of 11 point Palatino type set on 13 point
leading. The line width is 26 picas.

This is a sample of 9 point
Bookman type set on 10 point
leading. The line width is 12
picas.

This is a sample of 11 point Bookman type set on 13
point leading. The line width is 26 picas.

This is a sample of 9 point Avant
Garde type set on 10 point
leading. The line width is 12 picas.

This is a sample of 11 point Avant Garde type set on 13
point leading. The line width is 26 picas.

This is a sample of 9 point Helvetica
type set on 10 point leading. The
line width is 12 picas.

This is a sample of 11 point Helvetica type set on 13 point
leading. The line width is 26 picas.

This is a sample of 9 point Helvetica
Condensed type set on 10 point leading.
The line width is 12 picas.

This is a sample of 11 point Helvetica Condensed type set on 13 point
leading. The line width is 26 picas.

Figure 5-9. Typefaces come in a variety of silhouettes, as
demonstrated by these samples.

wider columns give the impression of seriousness and solid information content. To illustrate, **Figures 5-10** through **5-14** present samples
of newsletters that use different column widths.

The idea: Judge your own audiences and
come up with a column layout that appears best
for them.

BOOK MARKETING UPDATE

Ad-Lib Publications, 51 N. Fifth Street, P.O. Box 1102, Fairfield, IA 52556-1102

March / April 1988 — Issue #7   ISSN 0891-8813   Subscription Price: $48.00 / year

How to Get Publicity in Newspapers — More Tips

My experience, and that of most independent book publishers I've spoken with, is that it is very difficult to get reviews in newspapers — and far easier and, in many cases, more effective to get news or feature writeups.

For example, last year USA Today featured Gregory Stock's *The Book of Questions* in a week-long series on the front page of the Life Section. Within a few days of that series, Workman had to go back to press for another printing of 25,000 copies. The last time I looked, the book had sold over 540,000 copies and is still on the *Publishers Weekly* trade paperback bestseller list. Plus, it sold to Book-of-the-Month Club and negotiations are in the works for spinoffs of the book as a game and as a TV series. Any questions?

Here are just a few of the ways to work your book or author into a newsworthy story:

Sponsor a Celebration — Every year Liberty Publishing Company sponsors Muffin Mania Week during the first week in February. This year, *USA Today* published a notice about the week in their Lifeline section. As a result of their annual publicity, they have received many inquiries from individuals and libraries — and, as a result, have sold many copies of their book, *Muffin Mania*.

Set Up an Information Bureau — Reebok, manufacturers of athletic shoes, sends out many of their background information releases under the auspices of their Reebok Aerobic Information Bureau. Recently, for example, the Associated Press featured a blurb about a study done by USC researchers that showed that exercising improves problem-solving abilities, concentration, and short-term memory. What a way to sell shoes! Why not books as well?

Sponsor a Poll — Gallup did a poll for a book by speech therapist Lillian Glass (*Talk to Win* published by Perigee). The results were featured in many news stories.

Work with Local Columnists — Many newspaper columnists will feature a book by a local author or book publisher. For example, I've seen books mentioned in Herb Caen's column for the *San Francisco Chronicle* and in David Cataneo's Hot Stove sports column for the *Boston Herald*.

Here are a few other local columnists: Jim Klobuchar for the *Minneapolis Star Tribune*, John Crumpacker and Rob Morse for the *San Francisco Examiner*, and O'Malley and Gratteau's INC. column for the *Chicago Tribune*.

Work with Specialized Columnists — Besides the above general columnists, many nespapers also publish special interest columns such as the following:

- Couples, by Cheryl Lavin and Laura Kavesh, for the *San Jose Mercury News*.
- On Food, by Jeremy Iggers, for the *Minneapolis Star Tribune*.
- Tidbits, by Lee Svitak Dean, in the Taste Section of the *Minneapolis Star Tribune* (which recently featured *Uncle Gene's Bread Book for Kids* published by Happiness Press — and which even gave the press's address: P. O. Box 218, Montgomery NY 12549-0218).
- Tender Years, by Pat Gardner, in the *Minneapolis Star Tribune* (an advice column on parenting).

Volunteer to Be an Expert — Let the newspapers know that your authors are available as experts. Send them an author bio and background news release about the author's latest book. For example, every week *USA Today* features a special section, Ask Money, where they invite readers to ask questions which are, in turn, answered by leading experts around the country. If appropriate, let the Money Section editor know that your authors are available to answer such questions.

USA Today uses experts often. In a recent article describing a survey they conducted on sex, they interviewed about ten authors, including Judith Sills, Maggie Scarf, Maxine Rock, Paul Pearsall, and David Viscott.

There are many other opportunities to be an expert:

- The *Minneapolis Star Tribune* has a regular column called Fixit, which answers reader's questions about consumer problems, from insurance to real estate.
- *St. Louis Post-Dispatch* has a Help Yourself department in its Sunday paper. In this instance, readers answer each other's questions.
- *San Jose Mercury News* has an Action Line column.
- The *Boston Herald* has a Sound Off column.

Get Listed in Community News — When your authors go on tour (or even just to visit), arrange for an autograph session at local bookstores or libraries. Then make sure your local contact gets the event listed the Calendar section of their newspaper. The *Minneapolis Star Tribune*, for example, has separate calendar listings for events of interest to senior citizens and families as well as the regular arts calendar.

Figure 5-10. Many layouts and page styles are acceptable. The idea is to match the presentation of text to the tastes and needs of readers.

SUMMARY OF BASIC TAX POINTS
WHEN PLANNING CHARITABLE CONTRIBUTIONS

As indicated in the first page letter, Congress has recently imposed a number of important restrictions on the deductibility of charitable contributions. We shall cover the field broadly below and emphasize the recent changes:

I. Ceiling on Charitable Deductions.

1. An individual taxpayer may deduct cash contributions up to 50% of his or her adjusted gross income. Any excess may be carried forward for five years.

2. Individual taxpayers may deduct the fair market value of securities, real estate or other long term capital gain property. The amount of the deduction is limited to 30% of adjusted gross income, but the excess may be carried over for five years.

3. Only the cost basis of short term gain property and Section 306 stock is deductible.

4. Gifts of tangible personal property are deductible only to the extent of cost, except where related to the charitable donee's function, such as a gift of a painting to an art museum or a gift of computers to a university. The limits are 30% of adjusted gross income for related gifts and 50% for other gifts, with a five-year carryover.

5. The ceiling on charitable deductions by corporations is 10% of taxable income, with a five-year carryover. Contributions are deductible by a corporation on the accrual basis if its board of directors approves them in the taxable year and payment is made within 65 days of the succeeding year.

6. Contributions of marketable securities and other capital gain property to provide foundations are limited to 20% of an individual's adjusted gross income, unless such contributions are made to one or the other of the following two types of private foundations:

(a) If to a private "operating" corporation, 30% of adjusted gross income is the limit.

(b) If to a "pass thru" private foundation, where the assets received are distributed to public charities within 2 1/2 months after the end of the taxable year, 30% is the limit.

II. Tax Savings of Gifts of Appreciated Property.

1. We are familiar with the income tax advantage of making charitable contributions of property that has appreciated in value over its cost basis. A deduction is allowed for the entire fair market value of the property given, provided it has been held longer than 6 months. The income tax on the appreciation is thus avoided, except as discussed below. If you do not wish to change your security portfolio, you can simply use some of your cash to replace the securities given to the charity.

2. One plan that has received qualified approval of the courts involves a gift by the owner of closely held stock to his private foundation, followed by the redemption of the stock by the corporation. The stockholder receives a deduction equal to the value of the stock given, and the foundation receives cash from the corporation. The Internal Revenue Service has approved this type of plan, provided there is no legal obligation or other complusion on the foundation to sell or the corporation to buy. This type of gift is an excellent way to save income taxes, but you will need the help of very able tax counsel if you expect to avoid opposition from the Internal Revenue Service.

3. The main problem today with the contribution of appreciated property is that the appreciation is a tax preference and subject to the alternative minimum tax (AMT). This tax preference will now be treated the same as a dozen other tax preferences, such as the net loss from passive investment activities and the excess of market value of stock purchased upon the exercise of an incentive stock option over its cost. The annual exemption is $40,000 for a joint return and $30,000 for a single return. The AMT tax rate is 21%. The amount of the tax is the excess of the AMT tax over the regular income tax. For high-income taxpayers, the exemption is phased out at the rate of 25 cents for each $1.00 of minimum taxable income over $150,000.

There is no substitute for a detailed study of your anticipated income for the current year and based on your contemplated charitable deductions.

Figure 5-11. A one-column layout was used for this newsletter page. The seven-inch line width can be difficult for some readers.

ESTATE AND TAX LETTER

Let us suppose that the life insurance proceeds and available liquid assets are not sufficient to cover your estate taxes and your funeral and administration expenses. The corporation would then have the choice of (a) borrowing money from outside sources, (b) selling the company stock to outsiders, or (c) using the installment payment provisions of Section 6166 of the Code, which permits the deferral of tax for 5 years and the payment of the tax over the following 10 years. In the alternative, your estate could pay the taxes in 10 equal installments over a 10 year period.

To qualify for the installment payment method the estate must meet these tests: (a) the value of the decedent's interest must exceed 35% of his adjusted gross estate and (b) the estate's interest must include 20% or more of the voting stock of the corporation, or the corporation must have 15 or fewer stockholders.

It should be borne in mind that the 10-year installment provisions apply only to that proportion of the estate taxes that the business interest bears to the value of the adjusted gross estate. For example, if the business interest were worth $500,000 and the adjusted gross estate were $1,000,000, only one-half the estate tax could be paid in installments. If, during the 10-year period, the corporation makes capital distributions or the beneficiaries sell stock exceeding 50% of the value of the decedent's stock, then special acceleration provisions apply. The amount paid in a Section 303 redemption, however, is not considered a distribution or sale.

The foregoing discussion has been directed to the transfer of your stock and your wife's stock to your children. If, however, you create trusts with values in excess of your and your wife's $1,000,000 generation-skipping exemptions, then there will be another extremely serious tax problem upon a child's death. This situation we cover in our first page letter.

Hopefully, this discussion underscores for you the importance of sitting down with us and your tax attorney to determine the best overall plan to follow. A small investment of your time can make all the difference in whether your family will continue to own and operate the business or whether it will have to sell it.

RECENT CASES AND RULINGS

DEDUCTIONS DENIED FOR RESTITUTION PAYMENTS TO BROKER'S VICTIMS

The Tax Court has recently ruled that restitution payments to the victims of a loan broker who was convicted of conspiracy to commit grand theft were not deductible business expenses for the convicted loan broker. In **Waldman v. Commissioner**, 88 T.C. (1987), the taxpayer was the president and sole shareholder of the loan brokerage company. The company was engaged in the business of negotiating and servicing loans secured by deeds of trust. A Government investigation into the taxpayer's business resulted in his conviction of conspiracy to commit grand theft. Following his conviction, the taxpayer's prison sentence was stayed on the condition that he pay restitution to his victims, and he made the required payments.

On his tax return, the taxpayer deducted the restitution payments as a legal or professional fee. In disallowing the deduction, the Internal Revenue Service contended that the Internal Revenue Code prohibits the deduction of restitution paid pursuant to a criminal conviction. On review, the Tax Court agreed with the Internal Revenue Service. It held that the restitution paid by the taxpayer constituted a "fine or similar penalty to a government for the violation of any law" and hence was not deductible. It was irrelevant that the taxpayer's payments were made to individuals rather than to a government entity. The purpose of the restitution was to satisfy the broker's criminal liability to the United States Government, the nominal plaintiff in all federal prosecutions.

Figure 5-12. Another page from the previous newsletter combines one and two columns.

More Marketing

(continued from page 9)

order). The following seems not to generate more orders: 1) larger than the norm discount schedules; 2) a return of the old edition for a credit on the new edition. Librarians who receive this mailing will retain the copies of the flyers for their proper budgetary time and orders will be placed for the next six months from this mailing. **Deadline for all flyers to be at PMA offices is August 30, 1987.**

Cooperative Marketing to College, Jr. College, and University Libraries

On August 15, PMA will mail a packet to more than 3,000 Junior College, College and University libraries across the U.S. This is the first time PMA has entered into this program, which will be similar in concept to the cooperative library mailing program. Please send 3,100 8 1/2 x 11 unfolded flyers, designed on either one or two sides, not to exceed 70# stock weight to the following address—West Coast Mailers, 5630 Borwick Ave., South Gate, CA 90280. Mark in bold letters on the outside of the box "PMA - College Mailing Program." Submit the registration fee of $125 and the registration form to the PMA offices. **Do not place the check and registration form inside the box to West Coast Mailing.**

Books for Review

The final 1987 quarterly mailing to 2,500 daily metro newspaper reviewers across the U.S. will be mailed on October 15. If you wish to participate in the program, the following information needs to be supplied with your reservation form — a 100 -word description of your title, a 5 x 7 or smaller black and white photo of your book. If your copy exceeds 100 words, it will be edited. The most effective way to utilize this program is to make your distributors aware of those geographic area publications that have requested your title for review. Based on previous experience, approximately 80% of those books requested end up getting reviewed. By making your distributors aware of the geographic region requesting the review, they can tell their sales staff to stock that area with your title. This helps both the distributor and you in selling more books. A bingo card is included with the mailing, and all requests are forwarded from the PMA office directly to the publisher on a weekly basis. The newsletter is limited to 35 title participants, which are categorized with like titles and listed alphabetically. Please include your specific category designation when sending in your copy. Fee for participation in this program is $90 per title.

Fall Bookstore Mailing

On September 1 PMA will mail 4,500 newsletters featur-

[10] PMA Newsletter, August 1987

ing new and backlist titles to independent booksellers across the U.S. All books will be categorized by subject matter and all publishers wishing to participate in this program must agree to offer the same discount terms if orders come direct to the PMA offices. The promotional newsletter states that the independent booksellers should check with their normal distributor(s) first before placing an order with PMA. If they are unable to find your title(s) with their regular distributor, we then encourage them to order through the PMA postcard which is attached to the mailing. The following discount terms will then apply: 1 book-no discount; 2-5 books 20%; 6-10 books-30%; 11-25 books-40%; 26-74 books-45%;75 or more books-50%. Return policy is 90 days for full refund of undamaged material. If you wish to participate in this program, the fee is $100 per title. The following material must be sent with your reservation: a 50-word descriptive about your title; a 5 x 7 black & white photo or stat of your front cover; number of pages; ISBN(s); price(s). Deadline for submission of material is August 15, or whenever we reach the 35-book-limit.

PMA-Staffed Exhibits

The following shows will be staffed by PMA and/or its affiliates during the Fall. The first group of shows will be attended by booksellers from a specific geographic region. Based on previous shows, the following book categories are of special interest to this group: those specific to the region; crafts; self-help; cookbooks, tour books, history and/or ethnic (as they refer to the specific region); children's books; diet books, and all others that have a horizontal interest. Fees for display at any or all of these shows is $30 per title for 1-2 titles; $25 per title for 3 or more. If you wish to send the same title to all shows, the fee will be a flat $25 per title/per show. Please send two copies of each book, along with a 50-word description, including price and ISBN to PMA's offices by no later than September 11. The regional booksellers shows for PMA this year are: **New England Booksellers Association** in Boston, MA on September 18-20; **The Upper Midwest Booksellers Association** in Minneapolis, MN on September 18-20; **The Northern California Booksellers Association** in Oakland, CA on September 26-27. A special show for the target marketing area of **Self-Help/Pschology** books will be attended by Leigh Cohn, co-chair of the Marketing Committee. PMA members wishing to display their titles at the **American Association of Marriage and Family Therapists** on October 29-November 1 in Chicago, IL can submit two copies of each title, along with a 50-word description, including price and ISBN, to PMA offices by no later than October 16. Fee for participation in this show is$40 per title for 1-2 titles; $35 per title for 3 or more titles from the same publishing company.

Figure 5-13. A two-column layout is shown here.

ANNUAL MEETING HIGHLIGHTS
continued

(John Wiley & Sons); Treasurer—Lawrence Hughes (Hearst). The Executive Committee will be composed of these officers and Board members Bruce Harris (Crown) and Lawrence Levenson (Simon & Schuster).

Crown Publishing's Nat Wartels Wins Curtis Benjamin Award

Nat Wartels, founder and chairman of The Crown Publishing Group, was named recipient of the 13th annual Curtis Benjamin Award for Creative Publishing. Administered by AAP for its founders, the award is given each year to honor a publishing career of exceptional creativity and innovation. The award was presented on March 21 at the AAP Annual Meeting by long-time friend and colleague Richard E. Snyder, President and CEO of Simon & Schuster. Snyder praised Mr. Wartels' "integrity, wisdom and unabashed enthusiasm for the book business," noting that he has earned "not only the universal respect of his colleagues, but also our affection and love."

Beginning as a 31-year old alumnus of the Wharton School of Business, Mr. Wartels' publishing career has spanned nearly sixty years. Since he established the Outlet Book Company in 1933, Nat Wartels has remained the quintessential book man, publishing more than 15,000 titles by such authors as Ernest Hem-

ingway, Sholom Aleichem, Langston Hughes, Padraic Colum, Alex Comfort and Albert Einstein. He built that first publishing venture into a company which now employs more than 800 people and which includes Crown Publishers, Inc., Outlet Book Company, Harmony Books, Clarkson N. Potter, and Publishers Central Bureau.

Mr. Wartels recalls as his most memorable publishing project *Men at War*, an anthology of great literary accounts of battle edited by Ernest Hemingway. The book, which Nat Wartels conceived in 1939, is still in print.

In his introduction, Richard Snyder remarked that Nat Wartels' creativity "has had a profound influence not only on publishing in this country but on the reading habits of many Americans."

The Curtis Benjamin Award was established to honor the late President and Chairman of the McGraw-Hill Book Company. Even after his retirement, Curtis Benjamin remained an active and enthusiastic ambassador of American books until his death in 1983. The award is given each year to a member of the U.S. publishing industry still living who has demonstrated extraordinary creativity, embodied in an entire career or manifest in a special publishing project. A list of previous winners reads like "Who's Who in American Publishing" : Charles Scribner, William Kaufmann,

Chester Kerr, C. Stewart Brewster, Ursula Nordstrom, Arthur Rosenthal, Ian Ballantine, W. Bradford Wiley, Kenneth McCormick, Frederick G. Ruffner, Simon Michael Bessie, and Herbert S. Bailey, Jr.

The plaque presented to Mr. Wartels reads: "His tireless efforts to discover new and better ways to reach readers with books of quality has changed the nature of publishing in our time."

COPYRIGHT

House to Hold Hearings on "Artists Rights"

Rep. Robert Kastenmeier (D-WI), Chairman of the House Judiciary Subcommittee on Courts, Civil Liberties and the Administration of Justice, has announced that his subcommittee, which has jurisdiction over copyright, will hold hearings this spring on the subject of "artists rights," an issue that gained a great deal of public and media attention during the hearings on U.S. adherence to Berne. The subcommittee will look at several legislative proposals including Rep. Gephardt's bill on movie colorization (H.R. 2400) and Rep. Markey's bill on rights for visual artists which parallels Senator Kennedy's bill S. 1619 (*Monthly Report* December '87). AAP's Copyright Committee is reviewing the proposed legislation to determine what, if any, implications there are for AAP members.

Countervailing Duties on Books Dropped from Trade Bill

Senate and House conferees on the Omnibus Trade Bill have accepted the recommendation of AAP and others and have eliminated language extending the provisions of the countervailing and antidumping duties laws to books that might be regarded as "technical publications." In August of last year AAP expressed it objections to this provision, stating that it violated both the letter and the spirit of U.S. obligations under the Florence Agreement and that it might have serious repercussions on American imports and exports of publications (Monthly Report, Sept. '87). The Trade Bill is expected to be reported out of the Conference Committee in the next few weeks.

Administration Delays Decision on Ending Thailand Trade Benefits

On April 1 President Reagan announced that he would defer until December 15, 1988 a decision on whether to strip Thailand of trade

NEWS FROM THE GENERAL PUBLISHING DIVISION

GPD Business Managers Agree on Benefits of Acid-Free Paper

At its April 11 meeting, the GPD Business Managers Committee met with a panel of experts to discuss the advantages and problems inherent in the use of acid-free paper. The panel included author Barbara Goldsmith, Ellen McCrady (Alkaline Paper Advocate), John Baker (New York Public Library) and Linda Amster (New York Times). Publishers were generally in agreement on the advantages of acidfree paper and voiced a preference for using it, but cited problems of availability. In most cases, it was noted, a first printing can be done on acid-free paper, but paper manufacturers are often not able to provide the same paper for a second and subsequent editions. A number of economic causes contribute to supply limitations. Among the factors cited were the resources required to build new mills, problems arising from the difficulty of dying acid-free paper, and the relative ease of

converting smaller rather than larger machines to this production, generating limitations on the quantities available. There was general agreement that supply rather than price is the problem. Publishers expressed their willingness to use acid-free paper but noted that time constraints make it impossible to wait for an available supply. Since the paper supply is uncertain, publishers are not able to print the acid-free symbol on their books. Both groups—publishers attending the meeting and the panelists agreed that the dialogue was valuable, bringing the parties together to address the practical problems involved.

As a result of the wide interest in the use of acid-free paper, Congressman Sidney Yates (D-IL), chairman of the House Appropriations Interior Subcommittee, has convened an informal meeting on April 21 to discuss the issue. Congressman Yates is reportedly willing to consider appropriating funds to encourage the use of acid-free paper by American publishers in order to support and conserve our literary heritage.

(continued on page 4)

Figure 5-14. This newsletter page uses a three-column layout.

Technical note: In setting type on desktop publishing systems, it is best not to try to use automatic hyphenation. Also, it generally is best not to **right-justify** really narrow columns. Right-justified type has even right-hand margins. If you get down to column widths of 12 picas and narrower, it is recommended that you use **rag right** (for ragged right) margins. On narrow columns, the system is likely to use too many hyphenations. Therefore, it is better to look at the results you get on proofs and insert hyphens yourself on the basis of appearance. Rag right lines should vary in width. This avoids the appearance of columns that were intended for right justification but missed the mark. **Figure 5-15** shows a three-column layout that uses rag right lines. The newsletter in **Figure 5-16** also uses rag right lines, but in a two-column layout.

For column widths of 18 to 36 picas, most desktop publishing systems now have adequate hyphenation programs. However, it still is best to review proofs and to look for opportunities to improve the line spacing of your type. Reason: Most programs hyphenate from a dictionary. If you use words that are not in the dictionary, the system can give you badly spaced lines. In particular, your hyphenation program will not be equipped to enter hyphens in people's names.

When you use automatic hyphenation, the system inserts **soft hyphens.** A soft hyphen is placed temporarily at the end of a line to support automatic hyphenation. If you change text and eliminate the need for a soft hyphen, the system should erase it automatically.

Type Size and Leading

The idea is to leave at least one point of space above and below each line of body type. This space is necessary to avoid having the tops and bottoms of letters touch. The lines are easier to read when there is space between them. Some designers leave additional space. Also, at least a full blank line should be inserted above each subhead within text. Generally, a half-line of space below a subhead is adequate. As indicated above, some desktop publishers prefer to leave about three or four points of extra space between paragraphs.

For adult audiences, 10-point type generally is considered a basic, readable, acceptable choice for the body of text. For younger audiences, 11-point type often is used. Headings generally are two to four points larger than the body face.

Running Heads

Running heads, identified earlier, are title lines that can appear at the top or bottom of each page. In general, designers allow about a half-inch of space between the top or bottom of the body text and the running heads. The typeface selected for these lines may either blend with or represent a contrast from the body face. One option is to use the italic of the body face for running heads. Another is to use a light-face version of the type used for headings. Still another is to use an entirely different face.

The best bet: Examine a series of books or reports similar to the one on which you are working. Determine your own preferences. Then try one or two options on test pages before you make your final selection.

Folios

Folios are page numbers. They can run alongside the running heads, usually on the outside of the page. You also can use **drop folios,** numbers at the bottom of the page. Traditionally, drop folios can be placed in the center of the page or at the outside corner.

Folio positions can be varied. For example, many books use folio numbers on top, outside corners for all pages except those that open

DESKTOP JARGON

right-justify To set type with even right margins.

rag right Description of type column with unjustified right margin.

soft hyphen A hyphen placed temporarily at the end of a line to support automatic spacing and justification of text. The soft hyphen is eliminated if the text is altered.

drop folio Page number placed at the bottom of a page.

TAX & DEFERRED GIVING

*A Bi-Annual Newsletter
for the Alumni and Friends of
Occidental College
Fall 1988*

Charitable Annuity Trusts

The Charitable Remainder Annuity Trust is particularly suitable to meeting the financial needs of retired individuals desiring a fixed rate of income from their investment. Retired individuals can frequently increase spendable income by reinvesting low yield highly appreciated securities or real estate in a higher yield charitable remainder annuity trust, at the same time completely avoiding the payment of capital gain tax on the appreciation. With capital gain tax currently at 28%, and for most taxpayers, 33%, avoidance of capital gain tax is an important consideration for individuals contemplating asset reinvestment to increase spendable income.

The annuity trust shares many common features with the charitable remainder unitrust, the principal difference being the manner of calculating the payment to the income beneficiary. Whereas the unitrust provides for a payout that may vary, the annuity trust provides for a fixed payout. This amount must equal a sum certain of not less than 5% of the initial fair market value of the assets used to fund the trust. Currently, the College is writing annuity trusts with

a 7% return to donors. Another difference is that the annuity trust cannot permit additional contributions.

A charitable deduction is immediately available when the annuity trust is funded. The charitable deduction is determined by the net fair market value of the assets transferred, the annual percentage payout and the age or ages of the income beneficiaries.

Depending on the donor's financial planning objectives, a choice may be made to increase the amount of the charitable deduction by choosing a lower percentage of annual income or reducing the charitable deduction by selecting a higher annual income return.

Charitable Gift Annuity

The Charitable Gift Annuity is among the oldest, simplest and most popular methods of making a charitable gift to the College and retaining income for life from the philanthropic act. It is a combination of a gift and an investment in an annuity. In exchange for the transfer of cash, marketable securities, or, under some circumstances, real estate, Occidental College will, by legal written agreement, guarantee to pay a specific annuity amount to one or two income beneficiaries for life. The income rates are the same for males and females.

The annual income rate or percentage is based on the age or ages of the donors. At age 50, a one life annuity would pay an annual income of 6.5% of the annuity amount compared to 11.4% at age 85. A two life annuity, for individuals both age 50, would pay 6.3%, compared to 9.4% if both annuitants were 85 years of age. The annual income remains the same over the life or lives of the income beneficiaries.

A charitable deduction is received for the charitable gift element, which is the amount by which the total gift exceeds the value of the annuity re-

ceived. In addition, a portion of the annual payment to the annuity beneficiaries is received tax free.

A deferred payment gift annuity has great appeal to younger donors in the 40 to 60 year age bracket who have high current income, need to benefit now from a current tax deduction, and are interested in augmenting potential retirement income on a tax-sheltered basis. With the deferred gift annuity, the donor transfers cash, marketable securities or, under some circumstances, real estate, in exchange for an annuity where the College agrees to pay annuity payments starting at a future date, usually at the individual's retirement. The individual realizes an immediate charitable deduction for the gift portion of the gift annuity plan. When income payments begin, the annuitants receive a tax-free return of principal over their life expectancy. When appreciated securities or real estate is used to fund a regular annuity, or a deferred annuity, that portion representing the cost of the annuity is subject to capital gain tax. Fortunately, the applicable capital gain tax for a regular gift annuity may be paid ratably over the life expectancy of the annuitants. With the deferred gift annuity, the applicable capital gain tax must be paid when the annuity is established.

Important

The *Tax & Deferred Giving Newsletter* is distributed twice each year to Alumni and friends of Occidental College by the members of the Deferred Giving Class Agent Committee. The Bequest and Trust information is of a general nature and is based on existing Federal tax law and regulations. In addition, this publication provides information on tax changes or revisions being considered by the Administration and the Congress. Because of space limitations, giving methods and examples may be oversimplified, readers are urged to consult their legal counsel or tax adviser regarding the applicability of this information to their own particular circumstances. The Newsletter is prepared by the Occidental College Endowment Development Office.

Figure 5-15. This newsletter uses a rag right line.

aap
Association of American Publishers
220 East 23rd Street/New York, New York 10010/(212) 689-8920

Publishers of books, journals, looseleaf,
software, and databases in technology, science,
medicine, business, humanities, law, and the
behavioral sciences.

PSP

**PROFESSIONAL
& SCHOLARLY
PUBLISHING
D I V I S I O N
BULLETIN**

Volume 2, No. 3, Spring 1988

NEW PROGRAMS AND ACTIVITIES
Robert E. Baensch, Chairman, PSP Division

Greetings! PSP '88 gave us some major new
issues to think about and reinforced what
the Planning Committee had identified as
important new directions for the Division in
the coming months. For example, there were
two major sessions on the role of the retail
bookstores for professional and scholarly
publishers. It's obvious we need to explore
how we can build sales growth through the
retail channel. As a result, **Linda Scovill**,
Vice President of Marketing at Appleton &
Lange, will serve as Chairperson for a new
American Booksellers Association Liaison
Committee. We also need to determine how we
can relate to the Government as customer,
competitor and source for research funding.
Therefore, **William Begell**, President of
Hemisphere Publishing Company, has accepted
the Chairmanship of a new Government
Relations Committee.

We want to focus on Electronic Technology,
not only as a production tool but as a
provider of information services such as
CD-ROM. A new committee will be established
to address the complex and fast moving
developments of computer technology as it
affects and involves our (cont'd on p. 8)

PSP'88: AN INSIDER'S VIEW
James H. Cooper, Executive Vice President,
McGraw-Hill Book Company

This year's annual meeting of the PSP
Division took place at the Washington Grand
Hyatt on February 4-6. Why go to such a
meeting? I go to get what I need to do my
job better. I don't care if there are
subjects on the program I'm not interested
in as long as there is enough to keep me
busy. I went to the meeting with three
goals: First, to learn more about
publishing matters on the program of
interest to me. Second, to meet old and new
friends and exchange publishing information

and ideas with them. Third, to see the 1987
PSP Awards and examine the entries that were
up for awards. My goals were met, and my
wife and I had an extremely pleasant time
socially as well.

There were a number of speakers covering
material designed to meet a variety of
needs; I'll mention just a few that were of
particular interest to me.

In this age of acquisitions and
consolidations, the words of Robert J.
Jachino, Executive Vice President of
International Thomson Organization, Ltd.,
were timely, thought provoking, and gave the
audience an insider's view of acquisition
strategy. His talk also drew a firm
response from Kate McKay of (cont'd on p. 8)

PROFESSIONAL & SCHOLARLY PUBLISHING DIVISION
BUSINESS MEETING February 5, 1988 - Brief
Report to the Membership
Barbara Meredith, Director, PSP Division

President's Report. Ambassador Nicholas
Veliotes' report to the PSP membership will
be published in the Fall 1988 issue of PSP
Bulletin.

Chairman's Report. The Division is in
excellent health, Myer Kutz reported, and
has experienced a 10% increase in membership
in 1987, The Boston Contingent presented
a strategic plan, to revitalize the Division
emphasizing education and information. Two
of the plan's objectives have been met: the
PSP Bulletin was launched and the Annual
Conference (PSP '88) was expanded, improved
and moved to a major city location. A new
PSP statistics program will be undertaken in
1988 to improve and update the STM portion
of the AAP Industry Statistics
questionnaire. PSP Committees have run a
series of highly informative and well
attended seminars.

Library Survey. Michael Boswood reported
that the questionnaire had (cont'd on p. 7)

chapters. For chapter opening pages, drop folios are used. Occasionally, folio numbers are placed in outside margins at the center or bottom of each page. Folio placement is a relatively small detail. But this item is part of your responsibilities as a desktop publisher.

Overall Page Layout

The previous sections talk about the parts of a page for a text-only publication. Selection of these elements, of course, is made against an overall design for page layouts.

Page layout should be regarded as the packaging of your information content for the benefit of the reader. There are almost as many theories about what makes an attractive page as there are designers or layout editors. Although there are no fixed rules, there are some principles that are worth keeping in mind:

- Page layouts generally are structured from the top downward. That is, designers expect that readers will direct their attention to the top of each page first, then scan downward.

- Pages are designed to direct reader attention to the top-right or top-left corners, rarely to the middle.

- Headlines and/or subheads should be used to create a pattern, or balance, of black-on-gray effect. The idea is to help the reader's eye travel across the page and pick up information the publisher is stressing. A headline on one side offsets a headline on the opposite side. The less-important heading generally is placed lower on the page or set in smaller type. Toward the bottom of a page, a headline may be used in a center position. This can help to promote visual eye movement from top to bottom.

- If a special point of interest is needed on a type-only page, *quotation boxes* can be used. These are areas on the page that are enclosed in ruled lines (boxes). Within these boxes are quotations or abstracts from the text printed in headline-sized letters.

- In designing publications on which the reader turns pages, be aware of the total appearance of each *spread.* A spread consists of

two facing pages. Balances between headlines and other elements should carry across each spread.

Figures 5-17 through **5-20** offer, without recommendation, reproductions of several newsletter pages that are felt to be attractive for their intended audiences.

Top and Bottom Alignment

Production management also requires attention to the relationship of text placement throughout all pages of a publication. As a reader turns pages from spread to spread, there should be a consistency and/or regularity of appearance. This means the text should start and end on each page at consistent distances from the top and bottom of the paper.

The top border is more critical than the bottom. Some publishers permit a variance of one or two lines in "bottoming out" pages. This book was designed for consistency at both the top and bottom of each page. Of course, the beginnings and ends of chapters have their own, specific designs. Each publisher should understand the need for setting guidelines. After that, individual taste can prevail.

Other factors also can affect the appearance of the first and last lines of pages:

- Some publishers avoid—as much as possible—ending pages with hyphenated words. A page-ending hyphen can be particularly objectionable on a right-hand page, since it forces the reader to turn pages in mid-word.

- Most publishers prefer to avoid **widows** and **orphans.** A widow is a short line at the bottom of a paragraph or page. Short lines at the bottom of the page can have a jarring effect on the eye. An orphan is a short line at the

Figure 5-16. This two-column newsletter uses rag right line. Note the ruled line used to divide the columns.

 DESKTOP JARGON

quotation box An area enclosed by a ruled box in which a quotation from text is used in large type.
spread Two facing pages in a publication.
widow A short line at the bottom of a paragraph or page.
orphan A short line at the top of a page.

aap

Monthly Report

Vol. V, No. 7   *A Newsbulletin for Members of The Association of American Publishers*   July 1988

ISSN 0748-8173

A WORLD OF BOOKS ILLUMINATED BY IPA CONGRESS

The pervasive power of the written word was reaffirmed as some 1,000 publishers from 50 countries gathered in London June 12–17 for the 23rd Congress of the International Publishers Association. The theme of the 1988 Congress was "The World Hunger for Books."

Noting that "freedom to write, to publish and to read are among the most important human rights," the Congress issued a formal declaration calling for:

- freedom from restrictions on the publication, distribution and reading of books.
- freedom of books from taxation and tariffs;
- effective international and national copyright systems;
- constructive relationships between authors and publishers in which both can play their particular roles;
- commitment by governments to increasing library, school and university book acquisitions;
- increased international cooperation to encourage the establishment and growth of effective publishing industries in developing countries;
- optimum use of new information technologies to increase access to works of the mind.

For only the second time since the U.S. joined IPA in 1947, an American assumed the presidency of the organization. Former AAP chairman Andrew H. Neilly, Jr. (John Wiley & Sons) began a four- year term as IPA president with a speech calling for the strengthening of copyright worldwide and the forging of alliances among various groups with a common interest in intellectual property.

AAP was well represented on the speaker's rostrum throughout the week. AAP chairman Richard Morgan (Scott, Foresman) was a featured speaker on the panel addressing educational publishing. Richard Snyder (Simon & Schuster) debated the future of publishing with a distinguished group of international industry leaders; Ursula Springer (Springer Publishing Co.) and Barbara Morgan (Reader's Digest) participated in a panel on women in publishing; and George Davidson (Ballantine) took part in a program on production and distribution.

AAP President Nicholas Veliotes spoke on the ambivalent relationship between the U.S. government and American publishers, noting that a unique factor in the equation is our First Amendment and the role it plays in the battle for intellectual freedom. Carol Risher, AAP's Director of Copyright and New

Technology, outlined recent developments in the fight to end international piracy of copyrighted works, calling for a comprehensive intellectual property code within the framework of the General Agreement on Tariffs and Trade. In this respect, Ambassador Michael Samuels, U.S. Ambassador to the GATT in Geneva, argued effectively in a keynote speech that adoption of such a code within the GATT would supplement existing international agreements by adding needed enforcement mechanisms. The success of PUBNET, the college textbook industry's electronic ordering network co-sponsored by AAP and the National Association of College Stores, was discussed by Barbara Meredith, director of AAP's International and PSP divisions, who noted that the network may soon be expanded to professional and scholarly publishers as well as trade publishers.

In a statement of solidarity with those denied freedom of expression, the Congress sent a telegram to jailed South African activist Nelson Mandela, congratulating him on the occasion of his 70th birthday and expressing the "fervent hope that he will soon be able to enjoy freedom and liberty of expression so long denied to him." The Congress applauded the position of the AAP opposing boycotts of books and other intellectual and informational media to South Africa.

(continued on page 5)

BOOK SALES $11.45 BILLION IN 1987; TRADE BOOKS SHOW GREATEST GROWTH

Book sales in 1987 totalled $11,447,200,000, an increase of 9.2 percent or $963 million over 1986, according to figures released by AAP on July 1.

Trade book sales were $2.4 billion, reflecting the highest percentage of increase (15.9%). Other categories showing high percentage increases were: religious books (up 13.4% to $539 million); rack-sized mass market paperbacks (up 12.8% to $894 million); book clubs (up 11.6% to $779 million); and college textbooks (up 7.9% to $1.5 billion). University press books showed an increase of 7.2% in sales

($172 million) and professional books increased 7.1% to $1.8 billion.

1987 estimated sales in other categories were: elhi textbooks—$1.7 billion; standardized tests—$101.9 million; subscription reference—$516.2 million; mail order publications—$627.4 million; audiovisual and other media—$213 million. "Other sales" totalled $104.2 million.

Copies of the complete AAP Industry Statistics Report for 1987 will be available for purchase from the AAP New York office. For additional information: Thomas D. McKee, AAP New York.

IN THIS ISSUE

Copyright 2
Washington 2
Joint AAP/ALA Programs 3
Divisions:
    Paperback Publishing 3
    Higher Education 3
    General Publishing 4
    Professional & Scholarly 4
    School 4
    International 5
Noteworthy 5
Coming Events 6

2005 Massachusetts Avenue, N.W., Washington, D.C. 20036 • (202) 232-3335 • 220 E. 23rd Street, New York, N.Y. 10010 • (212) 689-8920

Judith Platt, Director of Communications

Figure 5-17. This and the following three newsletters were selected to show that many different layout styles can be acceptable.

The official publication of Publishers Marketing Association

PRES PROOFS
Robert E. Alberti, Ph.D., Impact Publishers - PMA President
What Is A Publisher?
Part VIII: Selling Translation Rights

One of my major goals in this column has been to explore some subjects which readers may not have thought much about, as a way of expanding your perspective on the book publishing industry. Nobody in this business does *everything* possible to exploit the potential of a book, but it helps to keep in mind the range of possibilities.

One area of book sales often overlooked — or ignored because of its apparent "mystery" — is that of rights for non-English editions. "Translation rights" — or "foreign rights" as they are often called in our ethnocentric society — are one element of a literary property which may be licensed to another publisher, granting the right to produce an edition in another language. Such licenses may be very restricted (involving only hardcover book rights, for example) or very broad (including hardcover, paperback, mass market, excerpts, audio and video, film, book clubs, and more).

Translation deals generally start in one of the following ways:

Continued on page 12

Marketing Programs Explained — Exhibits

By Leigh Cohn and Jan Nathan

We thought it would be a good idea to explain the types of exhibits PMA attends, and what publishers might realistically expect from exhibiting their titles.

Prior to going to the show, the PMA representative in charge of the exhibit familiarizes him or herself with each title being displayed. They are also sensitive to the importance of having a professional appearance and sales manner. Sometimes we ask that members assist by working in the booth. We attempt to train each person who works with us to understand that we are a cooperative effort, so they must work as hard for a book that they haven't published as they do for their own titles. An advantage of displaying with PMA instead of some other cooperative exhibits is that we are attentive to each title and actively sell! For example, we were at the New England Bookseller Association show when an attendee requested books on teenage pregnancy. Though we didn't have the books with us at that show, we were able to give this bookseller our 1987 Catalog, which contained the name and address of a publisher who specialized in that type of book, and showed other books on display that dealt with teen problems.

Continued on page 13

April 1988
Volume 6, Number 4

Newsletter

Figure 5-18. In this newsletter, type elements are used to create visual interest and to make the one-column text more readable.

Editorial Comment

Avoid Restrictive Contracts, Be Wary of Ads

(Continued from Page 1)

the year 2000. Other than Social Security, Medicare payments are the biggest item in governmental expenditures for this age category. Since cataracts are the most common disabling affliction among senior citizens, more cataract removal operations are performed than any other type of surgery for those covered by Medicare. So, when they start looking at where federal dollars go, cataract surgery and related services become an obvious area to examine.

A study by a subcommittee of the House Select Committee on Aging and the federal Health and Human Services Department charges that some operations were done unnecessarily and that some intraocular lens manufacturers gave kickbacks to surgeons for using their lenses. As in many cases, however, early publicity about broad government allegations is likely to be much louder than any media coverage of follow-up facts and responses.

The government is also trying to group together large segments of patients and potential patients through various quasi-social programs. Medicare tells these health plan providers specifically how much they will pay them to provide various health services. Then the organizations are forced to limit medical care to fit the level of federal payment. As a result, they attempt to increase patient volume by requiring members to see only doctors who are participants in their plan.

The bottom line here is obvious. These patients have given up their right to choose their own physicians. This applies to all kinds of services, ranging from treatment for the flu to cataract surgery.

Patients, regardless of age, should never give up their right to decide which doctors will treat them. The federal government, however, has been chipping away at that right for some time. It's a kind of socialized medicine, and it does not lead to improved health care.

What can you do to protect your rights and still receive high quality medical service? First, avoid enter-

AARP: You Pay The Bills

It takes more than $1 of every $10 produced in the United States to pay the yearly health care bill. The nation's total health care bill is now more than $1 billion a day, every day. At that level of spending, the bill will be $2 billion a day by 1990.

These statistics are from a booklet entitled "Cut The Cost, Keep The Care" published by the American Association of Retired Persons (AARP).

Who pays for health care? The AARP said, "You pay for health care through your taxes, your insurance premiums, your out-of-pocket health costs, and increases in the cost of everything you buy. You are paying that $1 billion a day bill."

Under a section of the booklet asking "What can you do?", the AARP advised: "If you require an operation, ask your doctor if 'same day' or 'outpatient' surgery is appropriate. This can help you avoid unnecessary hospital room charges."

Out-Patient Cataract Surgery Takes An Average 15 Minutes

Cataract removal procedures at the Valley Eye Center Out-Patient Surgery Suite usually require patients to be at the Center only about an hour and a half. The actual small-incision surgery by Thomas R. Mazzocco, M.D., takes an average 15 minutes. There is minimal out-of-pocket expense to patients.

For patients requiring a hospital, Dr. Mazzocco also performs surgeries at Valley Presbyterian Hospital next to Valley Eye Center and at Valley Hospital, which is just a few minutes away from the Center.

Surgery appointments are scheduled about two weeks earlier, at which time patients' eyes are measured and complete instruc-

tions are provided about what to expect on the day of surgery. Patients are given eye drops to put in on the morning of surgery.

An anesthesiologist is with patients before, during and after surgery. A "twilight" sedation is given to last two to three minutes while a local anesthetic is administered around the eye. Patients remain awake throughout surgery.

Afterward, patients are able to walk into Valley Eye Center's home-style recovery room, where their vital signs are monitored as they receive something to eat and drink. Within about a half hour they go home and are able to resume most normal activities.

---

ing into contracts that restrict your ability to choose your own doctor. Second, be wary if you see advertisements by organizations offering health care "free" for Social Security recipients. Quite frequently, these groups merely take the benefits the government has already promised to you, subtract their own profits—and tell you who will be your doctor!

When the government has to spend more money for health care—or anything else—all of us end up paying for it. We understand that here. Valley Eye Center is an in-

dependent eye treatment facility. For years, Valley Eye Center has worked to reduce the cost of cataract removal and lens implant surgery by utilizing its own outpatient surgery suite, as well as hospital out-patient surgery facilities, and by developing small-incision procedures that shorten recovery time, whether done in the hospital or as an out-patient procedure. You may be sure that we will continue to work toward the goals of cost containment while maintaining quality care.

BY ALBERT H. BRADSHAW, EDITOR

Figure 5-19. In this layout, a two-column box is used to attract attention.

EXPERIENCES OF AN SPC SCHOLARSHIP RECIPIENT

Three weeks before the Stanford Publishing Course began, the course director sent the participants a letter suggesting that we get plenty of sleep because the 12 days at Stanford were going to be busy. She wasn't kidding.

For 12 days the 160 course participants attended SPC events from 8 A.M. to 9 P.M. To get to classes, we rushed across campus. (Do you realize how big the Stanford campus is? Ask me.) After classes we worked on group projects and tried to find time to sleep. Now that it's all over, I find myself wanting to go back. Even with the nonstop schedule and no sleep, there wasn't enough time.

There wasn't enough time to meet all the Type-A participants from 35 states and 18 foreign countries—all of us deadline driven, inquisitive, and on the move. There wasn't enough time to question the faculty, whose credentials and experiences were dazzling. There wasn't enough time to go to the magazine classes (I was in the book division) and find out what really makes those magazine people tick. What there was time for, however, was wonderful.

There was time to meet other publishing professionals and learn from their experiences as well as to teach from my own. We shared knowledge about everything from specific design situations to four-color printing. There was enough time to learn that we publishers do know what we are doing—and in some cases those of us here in the western United States are ahead of the game. We had enough time to laugh (such horror stories I heard!) and refine some rough edges.

All of this, in 12 days, gave me an insight into myself as a publisher and into the publishing industry. I also caught glimpses of what the future may hold for text and trade publishing. And, thanks to the Stanford Publishing Course, I can say, "What a future!"

—Larry Lazopoulos

BOARD OF DIRECTORS ELECTION IN FEBRUARY

Absentee ballots for the February Board of Directors election will be mailed in January to member companies not located in the Bay Area. Ballots will include biographical sketches of the persons running for the Board.

Each member company is allotted one ballot and those members whose dues are outstanding will not be eligible to vote. Ballots must be returned prior to February 16, 1987.

NEW MEMBERS COVER MAP

Cover and components printer Philips Offset of Mamaroneck, NY, and H.M. Goushā Company, travel publishers in San José, show some of the diversity of Bookbuilders membership—and the range of skills needed in our ever-changing profession. Also welcomed as members at the September meeting were Central Graphics of San Diego; Midwest Publications, an el-high book packager and publisher from Pacific Grove (you're right, not very Midwest a place); and freelancers Judy Mason of San Francisco and Linda Caviglia of Redwood City.

people going places

Charles Goehring has left Mayfield Publishing Company of Palo Alto to pursue other publishing interests.

Kelly Hicks has been hired as executive vice president, manufacturing, for the Viking Press, Eden Prairie, Minnesota. Prior to the change he was president of the Murray Printing Company of Westford, Massachusetts.

Mark Shoemaker has been named senior vice president of the book division of York Graphic Services, York, Pennsylvania. Mark, who has been with York for 12 years, was vice president of sales before his recent promotion.

New faces in new places for Edwards Brothers, Inc. of Ann Arbor, Michigan: **Ann Lawrence** has joined the San Francisco office as an account executive. **Carole Major** has been named district sales manager for the western division, and **Sue Olson** has joined the San Francisco sales office as a sales technician.

Leland Moss has been promoted to senior production editor at the Wadsworth Publishing Company of Belmont, California. Leland also directs *Life of the Party* and directed *The AIDS Show*, which is the subject of a documentary that will be aired nationwide on PBS this fall.

Keith Nicholl, previously U.S. sales representative for SanType International of Salisbury, England, has joined Katerprint Typesetting Services of Oxford, England. Call Keith at (0865) 773408.

Michael Oates has transferred from Brooks/Cole Publishing Company of Monterey, California, to Wadsworth Publishing. A production editor, Michael was with Wiley Law Publications before joining Brooks/Cole in 1985.

In the Brooks/Cole art department, **Vernon T. Boes** has been promoted to the position of art director, **Roy R. Neuhaus** has joined as an associate designer, **Judith Macdonald** has resigned her position as senior art coordinator to devote more time to her painting, and **Suzi Shepherd** has been promoted to art coordinator.

Mary Kay Hancharick has resigned her position in the Brooks/Cole permissions department and has entered a premed program at Chico State.

Phyllis Larimore has been promoted to production editor at Brooks/Cole.

Tony Siani is calling on Northern California accounts for La Salle Paper Company of Los Angeles. His office telephone is (213) 269-1131.

—Bill Ralph

The Newsletter Committee is eager is receive information about promotions, new hires, and changes in organizations active in publishing. Please send contributions to Bill Ralph, BBW Newsletter, Wadsworth Publishing Company, Ten Davis Drive, Belmont, CA 94002.

STOCKTON TAKES ON BOSTON

A voice from Bookbuilders West recently rang out in the East.

Jim Stockton of James Stockton Associates served as one of the judges of the Boston Bookbuilders' New England Book Show on September 4. The results of the judging will be presented in Boston at the awards banquet on January 12, 1987.

SURVEY RESPONSE CONTINUES

The initial response to the Educational Survey from the last newsletter has been encouraging. Results are being compiled for the January/February issue, so there is still a little time to get yours in.

NOVEMBER/DECEMBER 5

Figure 5-20. Notice the use of boldface type in this newsletter page.

top of a page. Orphans also can mar appearance. It is considered good practice to begin and end each page with a full line of type. It is, however, not always possible to do this.

- Special care is needed when headings or subheadings fall near the bottom of the page. There should be at least two or three lines of type below the lowest heading on any given page. The idea: A heading introduces information. The purpose is defeated if a head or subhead falls at the bottom of a page.

PRODUCTION TECHNIQUES

The design and layout principles discussed above are general in nature. The presentations that follow highlight techniques for implementing the principles under control of page makeup and/or word processing software.

The need for special techniques occurs because text rarely fits perfectly into page layouts or other space allocations. To avoid widows, orphans, or a heading at the bottom of a page, you may have to add or delete space between some type elements. For example, suppose you have a heading near the bottom of a page. You need to put an extra line of type below the heading. If you are leaving two spaces above subheads, you will need to delete one space. To eliminate an orphan, you may want to add space to move an extra full line to the next page.

Manipulation of type elements for appearance and fit is a common requirement. If you are dealing with full lines, you can cause the computer to display all formatting and control symbols and codes on your screen. Then, you can add or delete lines at the appropriate places. To add or delete points within paragraphs, you might have to "select" the affected type and change the format just for the individual element. Just bear in mind that flexibility is a requirement of page makeup. Become familiar with the typesetting and formatting functions of your system. Then, figure out comfortable procedures that enable you to adjust to needs for insertion or deletion of spaces within text.

You have to learn to vary formats and placement of running heads and/or folios between left and right pages. The technical name for a left-hand page is *verso.* A right-hand page is called *recto.* (As a memory jogger, remember the letter "r." Right equals recto.) Type may be placed in staggered positions, with more space on the outside of the page than at the inside, or **gutter.**

Generally, a word processing or page makeup application package will provide dialog boxes you can use to position type columns. These tools enable you to create separate recto and verso layouts. Similarly, there will be provisions for positioning running heads and folios. The page numbers should be on the outside, with the running heads at inside positions. Understand the necessity for these layout capabilities. Then check the user manuals for the software packages you are using to be sure you know how to meet these requirements.

A special need might lie in pickup of page-numbering continuity between text files. For example, assume you are producing a book with the manuscript for each chapter stored in a separate file. You are using the chapter title as one of your running heads. This means that you will have to print your text on a chapter-by-chapter basis with changes in running heads. You also will have to keep notes on page numbers as you proceed. To do this, you will have to learn how to enter the correct starting number for each file that you print. The idea: You have to wind up with a book in which pages are numbered consecutively from chapter to chapter.

BUDGETING AND MANAGING PROJECTS

Costs and working time requirements will vary widely for different kinds of publications. However, there are common requirements and challenges for any publication. This applies even to a simple text-only job of relatively few pages. Some of the requirements and challenges you should know about are discussed below.

Scope the Job

A good idea for any publication production job is to list all of the steps or tasks to be performed. Start with your present status. Don't worry about dates or schedules at this point. You can start by breaking a job into its components. These include manuscript completion, copy editing, capturing text, typesetting, proofreading, dummying, and pasteup. Go over the step-by-step requirements several times to be sure you have covered everything you need. The reason for completeness: You will use this list as a basis for scheduling. If you forget anything, your schedule will be thrown off.

Schedule the Work

The first thing you need to know in setting a schedule is what the final delivery date MUST be. People you deal with in publication production may tend to ask for impossible deliveries. You need to establish realities. To get the real delivery date, you may have to ask challenging questions. For example, you may want to ask how the publication will be used. If it must be distributed at a scheduled meeting, you have your answer.

Once you have your completion date, work back. Start from the beginning. Figure out how long each listed task or step will take. Then allow a little time for rework or slippage. Carry this activity from start to finish. If the schedule is loose when you reach the end of the job, you can add time between steps. This will provide a margin for review and safety. If the job comes out tight, you may have to overlap some of the tasks to find enough time to complete everything. The point: Time will almost always be tight when you schedule production of a publication. By using your delivery date as a guideline, you can look for realistic results.

Set Budgets and Monitor Costs

People who ask for publication services rarely know what to expect to pay for the work. Budgeting and cost control can be important even for in-house operations. A main reason that people install desktop publishing systems internally or buy these services from outside sources is to save money. Don't fool yourself on this point. If top quality is essential and cost is not a factor, the job probably will not be done on a desktop publishing system.

Therefore, it is important that you be able to relate the time for individual tasks to the costs involved. This will help you to develop a budget for the entire project. Then, as the work is done, you should monitor actual time and cost factors against your budget and make adjustments as you go. Jobs tend to take longer than expected and to cost more than budgeted.

The best way to overcome budgetary and cost problems is to stay on top of each project and to be aware of where and why any cost overruns occur. As you gain experience, you will learn which people and what types of jobs tend to cost more than expected. Allow some budgetary cushions at the points where you know you can expect overruns.

Finally, expect and be ready to deal with revisions on any publishing job. The pattern rarely varies: People who present jobs provide "tight" schedules. They will assure you that the manuscript you see is final and will not be changed. Then, when the job is in process, you can expect a steady stream of "small" or "minor" alterations. Keep track of all changes and their consequences in terms of costs for working time and delays for schedule purposes.

Your sanity—or at least your composure—may well depend on your ability to plan, schedule, and monitor production jobs on a step-by-step basis.

With the discussion on type-only methods in this chapter, you have established a limited knowledge about publishing production. As indicated, many publications use type only. However, greater opportunities lie in capabilities for combining illustrations with type. Accordingly, the next chapter deals with techniques for creating illustrations for use in desktop publishing projects.

 DESKTOP JARGON

verso Term for a left-hand page.
recto Term for a right-hand page.
gutter The space at the inside margins of two facing pages.

THE MAKEUP DESK

1. Select one publication from among those reproduced in this chapter. Or, if you prefer, choose another text-only publication for this assignment. Evaluate the publication you select according to the topics covered under the DESIGN CHECKLIST section of this chapter. Specifically: Evaluate the use of borders and white space, the selection of column widths, the selection of typefaces, and the general layout. You can present your comments in a written report or an oral class presentation. Follow directions from your instructor.

2. Select two publications, one with a three-column format, the other with a one-column format. Compare the body and heading faces used in these publications. Comment on whether you feel the designer selected appropriate faces. If you disagree with the choice of typefaces, explain why. If possible suggest other typefaces that might be used.

THE COMPOSING ROOM

1. Select one page of any text-only publication upon which you think you can improve.
2. Capture the text from that publication.
3. Format the text into typefaces that you think will be appropriate for the publication.
4. Format a single page of the type-only publication under word processing or page makeup software.

Line Illustration Techniques 6

Editorial Budget

- ❏ **Line art** consists of illustrations that can be reproduced through use of line negatives.
- ❏ **Drafting software** provides the tools necessary to create line art on desktop computers.
- ❏ **The tool kit** that comes with a drafting software package provides a selection of lines and shapes that can be used to create line art. Shapes available include rectangles, circles, and elipses.
- ❏ **Background patterns or tones** also are available for selection from drafting software tool kits. These tones can be introduced into drawings under control of a mouse.
- ❏ **Text illustrations** should appear on the same spread as the corresponding text reference. If possible, the illustration should be after the text reference. If there is only one illustration on a spread, try to use it at the top of the right-hand page.
- ❏ **Stock art** illustrations are available on diskettes and can be used to enhance the appearance of some publications.
- ❏ **Generated line art** can be produced by computers under control of electronic spreadsheet software.
- ❏ **Existing art** sometimes can be input to a desktop publishing system through electronic scanning.

WHAT IS LINE ART?

To a publisher, the term *line art* has a specific meaning: Line art consists of illustrations that can be reproduced on line negatives. These negatives are the same as those created to reproduce type.

As a further qualification, line art consists of illustrations created entirely with lines and/or tone values that already have been separated into dot patterns. Recall the description of how photographs or paintings are reproduced by breaking the images into halftone dot patterns. Printing reproduction cannot handle *continuous tone* or *gray scale* values of photographs, paintings, or other similar images.

In many instances, line art illustrations can be positioned on the same pasteup boards or desktop system outputs as type. That method has been used for this book. This means that illustrations are captured on the same film used to reproduce the type.

By contrast, continuous-tone and gray-scale art must be photographed separately. This separate step generates halftone negatives that can be integrated with the line negatives for platemaking.

ROLE AND USES OF LINE ART IN PUBLICATIONS

As discussed in the previous chapter, it is possible to create many complete publications entirely with type. However, the appearance and communication value of most publications is improved if illustrations are included. Line art enhances publications in two distinct ways:

- An illustration can be a far more effective way to describe something or to demonstrate comparisons of values than words alone.

- A presentation that uses type exclusively can present a gray, dull appearance. Line art is an effective way of adding visual interest to a publication.

LINE ART PREPARATION SOFTWARE TOOLS

Dozens of graphics application packages with line drawing capabilities are available. All share a basic common denominator: Work begins with display of a menu or pallette. The display provides access to lines, forms, and tone patterns that may be selected with a click of the mouse.

Typically, the selectable art elements are positioned around the edge of a work area, or desktop. The work area is at the center of the screen. The accompanying, general explanations are illustrated with the MacDraw II program that runs on Macintosh computers. Reason: MacDraw was the first package in this field to achieve a high level of acceptance and market success. Most of the many packages that have followed are similar in operation.

Drawing a Line

Figure 6-1 shows a MacDraw II screen display after a user selects this application. Along the left side, the display provides drawing tools that can be reproduced, a text insertion tool, and a box for changing the percentage of the drawing.

Across the top of the screen is a set of pull-down menus. Under the menus is a display for choosing fill patterns and tones.

Figure 6-2 is a sequence showing use of this software to place a simple line in the working, or "desktop," area. In **Figure 6-2A**, the user clicks the mouse to select the line drawing tool. Then, in **Figure 6-2B**, the pointer is moved to select the desired line weight.

In **Figure 6-2C**, a starting point for the line is established by clicking on the desired position.

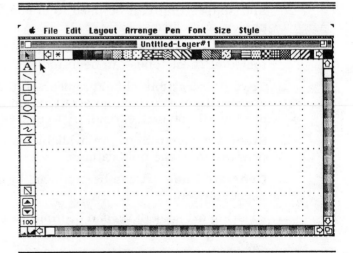

Figure 6-1. This is the main menu used to begin specification functions to be used in the MacDraw II program.

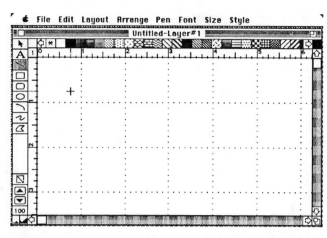

Figure 6-2A. This screen display shows the beginning of a sequence of operations for drawing a line. The user makes a selection that causes the system to display the MacDraw II toolbox.

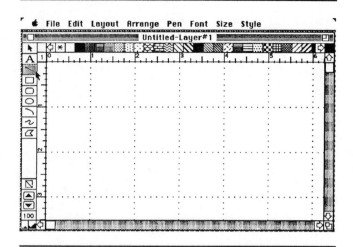

Figure 6-2C. The user clicks the mouse at the point on the desktop where the line is to begin.

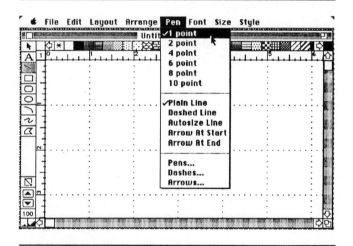

Figure 6-2B. The user uses the MacDraw II toolbox to select the weight, or thickness, of the line to be drawn.

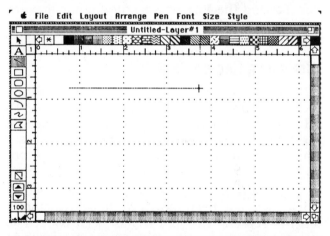

Figure 6-2D. The mouse is dragged and clicked at the end point on the line and the line is drawn in place. This line still is temporary.

To create the line, the user clicks at the starting point, then **drags** the mouse across the screen by holding down on the mouse button, or switch. A dark black or dotted tracing line is displayed along the path over which the mouse is dragged. When the terminating point of the line is reached, the mouse button is released. In **Figure 6-2D,** the line is at the terminating point.

As shown in **Figure 6-2E,** the software generates the desired line after the mouse button is released. Note that there are "handles" at the

 DESKTOP JARGON

line art Illustrations that can be reproduced on line negatives.

continuous tone Type of art presented through tonal values, rather than lines.

gray scale Series of tonal values that apply to reproduction of continuous-tone art.

drag Technique for use of mouse in which button is held down while cursor is moved across display screen.

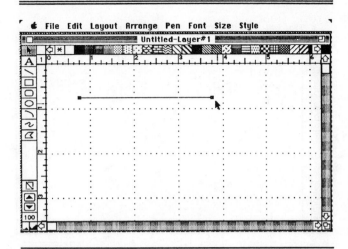

Figure 6-2E. A final click of the mouse sets the line in the display.

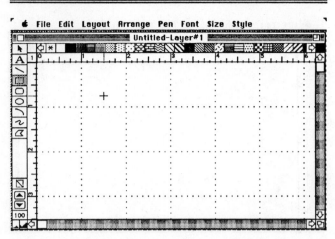

Figure 6-3A. To draw a rectangle, the user starts by selecting the shape from the toolbox. Then the user clicks at the starting point for the rectangle on the desktop.

ends of the line. These can be used as base points for altering the line or attaching other lines or forms to this element.

Creating a Rectangle

The same technique is used to control the positions and sizes of line-based shapes. To illustrate creation of a rectangle, assume the user has selected the desired shape. The user then clicked on a starting point for its positioning.

Figure 6-3A shows a screen display on which the cursor has been moved to the starting point on the screen. The mouse has been clicked to start the drawing operation. The cursor then is dragged from the starting point to a completion point. **Figure 6-3B** shows a rectangle on the screen.

Note that the operator has elected to use a background grid on the screen. This provides working guidelines, but the grid is not included on printouts of drawings. As an option, the user also can work against a background without the grid.

Special Effects

Once a form has been created, it can be duplicated or changed with simple clicks of the mouse. To illustrate, **Figure 6-4A** shows a display screen with two separate rectangles placed side by side. The second is an exact replica of the

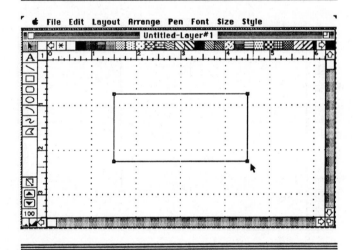

Figure 6-3B. The mouse is dragged to establish the size of the rectangle. When the mouse is clicked, the shape is displayed on the screen.

first. It was created by clicking on the image to be copied, then selecting the option to duplicate an image. Finally, the user drags the duplicate to the position where the copy is to be placed. This is a practical demonstration of the power of graphics software tools.

The original shape, the new shape, or both shapes as a set can be duplicated as many times as the user wishes. To illustrate, **Figure 6-4B** shows a first stage in duplication of the two

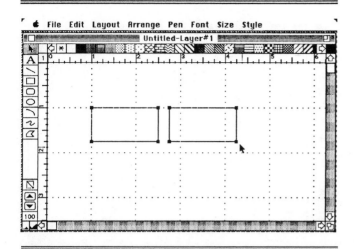

Figure 6-4A. Demonstration of duplicating and filling drawn shapes begins with two rectangles placed on a screen.

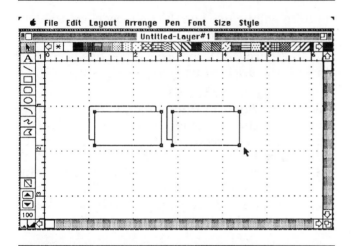

Figure 6-4B. In this display, the two rectangles have been selected for duplication.

modification, the same method can be used to create floor plans for offices or homes.

As a further demonstration, **Figure 6-4D** shows the two rectangles from the previous illustration filled with different design patterns. These were selected from the application software package's "Fill menu."

The point: Desktop graphics software provides almost infinite latitude for creative use of forms for development of illustrations and/or design patterns.

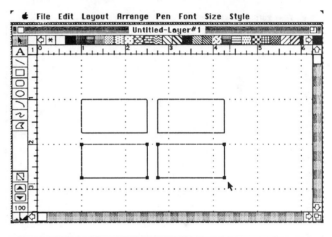

Figure 6-4C. The duplicated rectangles are moved to a new position on the screen, away from the originals.

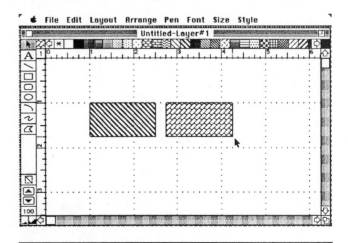

Figure 6-4D. A pattern has been selected from the toolbox and used to fill the original rectangles.

rectangles displayed in Figure 6-4A. Note that the duplicated forms have handles indicating their availability for manipulation or relocation. Images with handles have not yet been fixed in place by the software.

In **Figure 6-4C,** two new rectangles have been moved into a position beneath the original set. This is done by selecting and dragging the duplicated shapes through use of the mouse. This technique, obviously, permits considerable savings in time, effort, and money for creation of such illustrations as organization charts. With

Adding outline shadows. To demonstrate another capability available with little effort, consider **Figure 6-5A.** This shows a single box that could be part of an organization chart for a company. A sequence of operations demonstrates how simple drawings can be enhanced easily to produce a shadowed effect.

In **Figure 6-5B,** the box has been duplicated. The second box overlaps and is positioned above the first.

In **Figure 6-5C,** a design pattern is selected from the MacDraw system's Fill menu. This

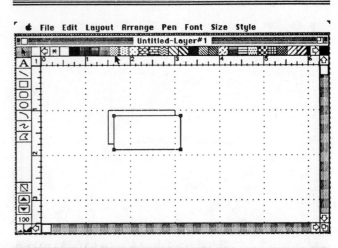

Figure 6-5C. A pattern to be used for the drop shadow is selected from the toolbox.

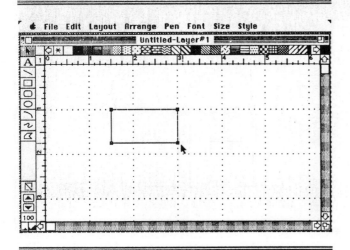

Figure 6-5A. To begin a demonstration on use of drop shadows, the user starts with a single box on the screen.

pattern will be used as the shadow effect to highlight the box as an art element.

In **Figure 6-5D,** the second box has been filled in with the selected pattern.

Next, as shown in **Figure 6-5E,** the user selects the **Send to Back** function of the Arrange menu of the graphics package. When this instruction is executed, the system places the filled box behind the clear one, as shown in **Figure 6-5F.** Notice that this illustration retains the ruled line of the original box. This line provides a solid image border for the shaded area.

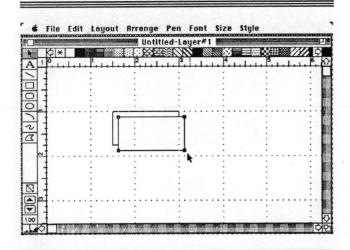

Figure 6-5B. The initial box is duplicated and offset from the first in an overlapping position.

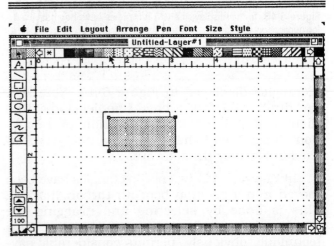

Figure 6-5D. The duplicated box is filled with the selected pattern.

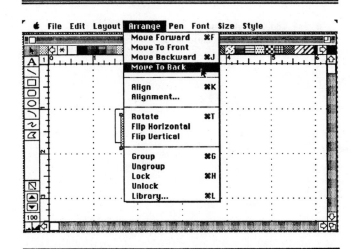

Figure 6-5E. The user selects the *Send to Back* option for the duplicated box.

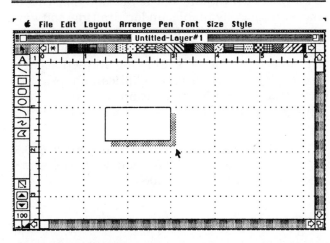

Figure 6-5G. As an option, the lines of the drop shadow box can be removed, leaving only the shading.

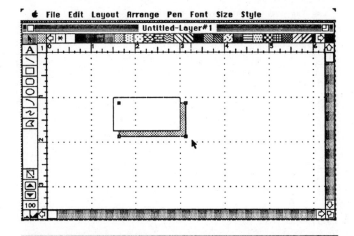

Figure 6-5F. When the *Send to Back* function is executed, the shaded box is moved behind the white one. Only a shaded, drop shadow border shows.

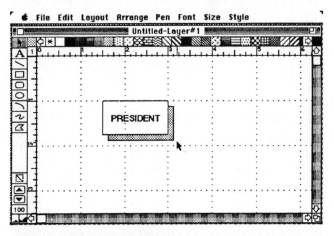

Figure 6-5H. The title PRESIDENT is entered to demonstrate mixing of art and type. This display could be the beginning of a business organization chart. An organization chart is completed in a later sequence of illustrations.

The outside line can be eliminated at the option of the user, as shown in **Figure 6-5G.** Some publishers prefer this effect. However, the unenclosed dot pattern presents a jagged-looking edge for the shaded area. This effect is objectionable to some people. These are examples of the kinds of results you can deliver with little effort through use of standard graphics software packages.

Finally, **Figure 6-5H** shows that type can be mixed with line art through the use of application software tools. In this final illustration of the sequence, the designation "PRESIDENT" has been added to the shadowed box.

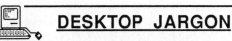

DESKTOP JARGON

Send to Back Drafting software command that moves an art element from foreground to background.

Combining shapes. For some line art, two or more shapes available under drafting software tool kits are combined. To demonstrate, the accompanying sequence of illustrations shows the development of a drawing formed from a rectangle and two oval, or eliptical, shapes. The resulting form, a vertical drum, is used in flowcharts of information systems to represent a storage device.

A starting point, illustrated in **Figure 6-6A,** is a vertical rectangle formed with the same techniques already described.

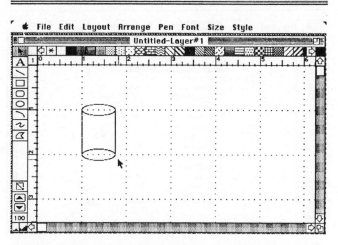

Figure 6-6B. Oval shapes, or elipses, are selected from the toolbox and placed at the top and bottom of the rectangle.

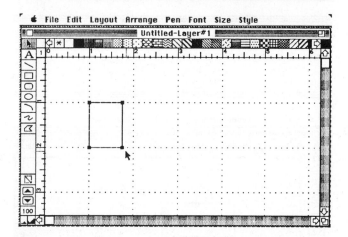

Figure 6-6A. To demonstrate the mixing of shapes to create finished art, this sequence shows development of the symbol for a storage device. The symbol is used on computer system flowcharts. The process starts with creation of a vertical rectangle, as shown on this screen.

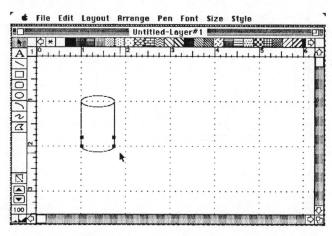

Figure 6-6C. The combined shape formed by the rectangle and ovals is filled with solid white.

To this basic shape, the user adds an oval to the top and bottom of the rectangle, as shown in **Figure 6-6B.**

Next, the unneeded lines are eliminated by filling the area they occupy with solid white, as shown in **Figure 6-6C.** This produces the finished image in **Figure 6-6D.**

When multiple images are joined in this way, it is a good idea to take a close look at the points where the lines are joined. This can be done by using the enlarged-display feature available with virtually all drafting packages. The idea of examining drawings in this way is to be sure there are solid connections at the points where lines meet. If there is any break in the pixel patterns, the software may treat the art element as two separate images. Then it will break up the image when it is copied or processed.

With an enlarged image like the one shown in **Figure 6-6E,** the user can check the images to be sure they consist of continuous lines. If there are any breaks in the lines, elements can be moved or lines can be extended as necessary. The end result should be an image that consists of continuously joined lines.

As a further assurance, the combined image can be "grouped" through use of a command that is available within programs like MacDraw. Grouping causes the system to treat the combined image as a single art element.

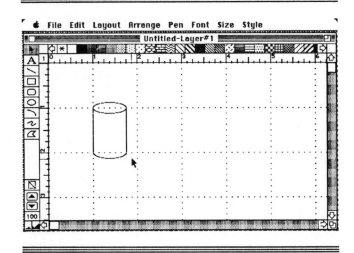

Figure 6-6D. This display shows the finished flowchart symbol.

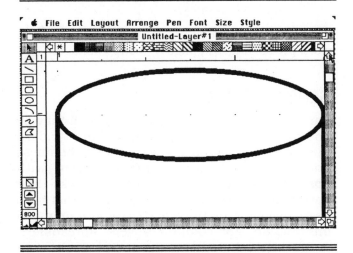

Figure 6-6E. Line drawings can be smoothed or corrected by enlarging images to display pixel patterns. Black pixels can be erased or added, as needed.

STOCK ART

The techniques just described above create the kinds of line art used frequently in publications produced on desktop computers. This book will not go into advanced drawing or painting techniques that require the skills of a trained artist. However, software tools are available with which you can incorporate professional illustrations into your publications with push-button ease. You can do this through use of ***stock art*** packages.

For a relatively small investment, you can purchase diskettes that contain drawings of a wide variety of subjects. You can examine printouts of the available illustrations in any computer store. You can insert disk files of these art elements into your own computer. Then, any of a wide variety of drawings can be selected for inclusion in your own publications. A representative sampling of art elements available in stock art packages is shown in **Figure 6-7.**

Figure 6-7. These are just a few of thousands of art elements available in stock art files.

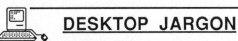 **DESKTOP JARGON**

stock art Drawings that can be purchased on disk files for import to desktop publications.

LINE ART AS A LAYOUT ELEMENT

Remember the two main reasons for using line art: to illustrate text and for visual interest.

Illustrating Text

If you are illustrating text, you have to lay out your pages to establish connections between text and illustrations. Some guidelines can help you in doing this:

- If at all possible, an illustration referenced in text should appear on the same spread of a publication as the reference.

- If at all possible, the illustration should appear *after* the text reference. However, it is acceptable to use the illustration *just before* the text reference, if the illustration and reference appear on the same page or spread.

- If there is only one illustration on a spread, try to place it on a right-hand (recto) page. This provides better visual impact as a reader turns pages.

- If there is only one illustration on a spread, try to run it at the top of a page. This also makes for better, more interesting visual impact. However, if there are two or more illustrations on facing pages, it is okay to balance appearance. One illustration can be used in a top-of-page position, the other at the bottom of its page.

To demonstrate, **Figure 6-8** shows a screen display of a publication spread on which balance is achieved through top-and-bottom positioning of illustrations.

Building Visual Interest

If you are using illustrations primarily for visual interest in your layouts, you have a lot more flexibility. The guidelines described above also apply to the positioning of illustrations used for visual interest. That is, your first choice for placement generally will be the top of a right-hand page. Also, visual balance should be sought if possible.

As a final guideline, the subject matter of your illustrations should relate to the content of the text and/or to the interests of your reader. **Figure 6-9** illustrates use of a decorative box for the first letter of a paragraph. This kind of

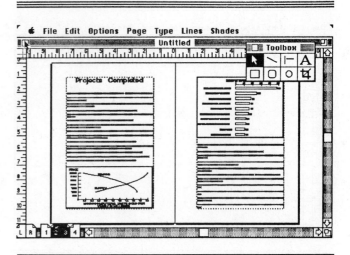

Figure 6-8. This screen shows an in-work layout for a two-page spread.

decorative treatment is available with several word processing and page makeup packages.

GENERATED LINE ART

For financial or management reports, it may be possible to derive illustrations from standard business application software. Many business and accounting reports are produced with *spreadsheet* software. Spreadsheets take their names from wide sheets of ruled paper that have been used for many years to report financial information. For computer users, spreadsheet preparation has been streamlined through software tools that produce documents that have become known as *electronic spreadsheets.*

An example of a screen display that will generate a financial report under control of spreadsheet software is shown in **Figure 6-10.** For electronic publishing purposes, a tabular report of this type can be treated as a line illustration. As described earlier, spreadsheets can be "imported" into word processing or page makeup software and used as part of a publication.

In addition, a number of spreadsheet application packages have built-in capabilities to generate line art directly from statistical information. Specifically, many spreadsheet packages can generate *pie charts, bar charts,* and *line graphs* directly from the content of spreadsheets. This means that, if you have spreadsheet

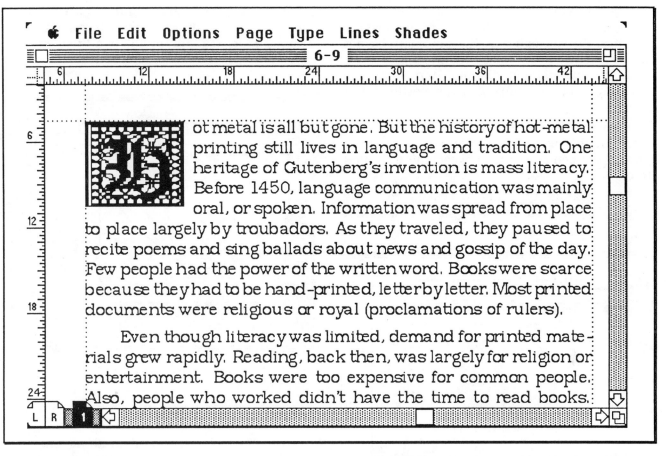

🍎 **File   Edit   Options   Page   Type   Lines   Shades**

6-9

ot metal is all but gone. But the history of hot-metal printing still lives in language and tradition. One heritage of Gutenberg's invention is mass literacy. Before 1450, language communication was mainly oral, or spoken. Information was spread from place to place largely by troubadors. As they traveled, they paused to recite poems and sing ballads about news and gossip of the day. Few people had the power of the written word. Books were scarce because they had to be hand-printed, letter by letter. Most printed documents were religious or royal (proclamations of rulers).

Even though literacy was limited, demand for printed materials grew rapidly. Reading, back then, was largely for religion or entertainment. Books were too expensive for common people. Also, people who worked didn't have the time to read books.

software available, you can enter numbers in tables that you create under spreadsheet control and generate line art automatically.

Figure 6-9. Visual interest can be promoted through use of large initial letters in boxes with design elements.

Figure 6-10. The computer screen in this photo displays a typical spreadsheet report prepared through use of an application software package.
Courtesy of Lear Siegler, Inc.

  DESKTOP JARGON

spreadsheet Columnar document, usually used for financial reporting.

electronic spreadsheet Software package for creation of spreadsheet reports on computers.

pie chart A graphic diagram that shows the relationships of parts to a whole, represented as slices of a pie.

bar chart A graphic diagram that shows the relationships of values in terms of lengths of bars or lines.

line graph A graphic diagram that shows trends by linking points on a grid with connecting lines.

Figure 6-11 presents a pie chart diagram of the type that could be generated by spreadsheet software. As you can see, the pie chart format can be used to show relationships of parts to a whole. In this instance, the pie chart illustrates percentage relationships of major portions of a budget.

Figure 6-12 arranges the same data into a bar chart. In this instance, the length of the bars reflects the comparisons between the indicated items.

Line graphs typically are used to show trends. For this reason, this type of illustration

sometimes is called a *trend line.* **Figure 6-13** is a trend line that shows comparisons for sales income, expenses, and profits of a business over a five-year period.

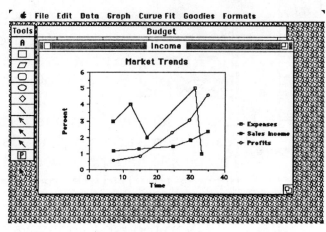

Figure 6-13. A line graph helps viewers to visualize trends in business situations.

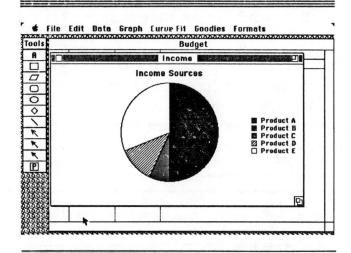

Figure 6-11. A pie chart illustrates the relationships of parts of an item to the whole.

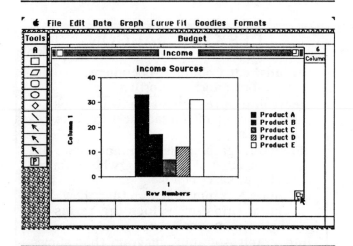

Figure 6-12. A bar chart shows comparative values for multiple items.

An important consideration about generated art: Tools such as electronic spreadsheet software make it possible to develop illustrations directly from an organization's business information files. That is, many businesses develop spreadsheets routinely. The files that produce the spreadsheets often can be imported directly into desktop publishing programs.

LINE ART EXAMPLE: ORGANIZATION CHART

To develop an organization chart, this demonstration starts with a single rectangle at the left of the screen. Then, the user selects the line weight to be used in linking boxes into the chart, as shown in **Figure 6-14A.** This box is measured to establish a width that will provide room for the widest row of entries. For this purpose, the operator causes the system to display rulers at the top and left sides of the work area. It can be handy to display rulers in this way as an aid in positioning of graphic elements.

In **Figure 6-14B,** the operator creates a short line at the top center of the box. This establishes a basic element of the chart. The short lines will connect the boxes to the rest of the chart.

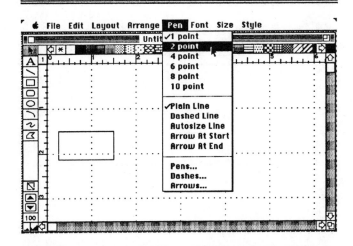

Figure 6-14A. Development of an organization chart starts with placement of a single box. Note that the artist has asked the MacDraw system to place a ruler at the top of the desktop. This will serve as a guide in positioning other boxes as the chart is developed.

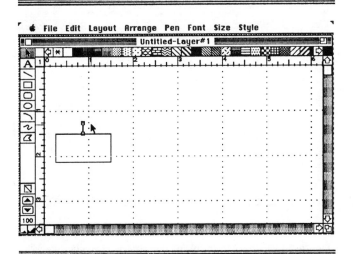

Figure 6-14B. In building a single element for duplication, the user adds a short line to the top of the initial box. This will serve to connect boxes within the final organization chart.

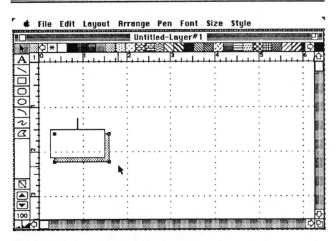

Figure 6-14C. Drop shadow is added to the single box, following methods demonstrated earlier.

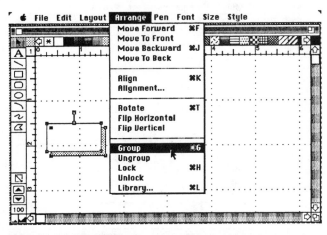

Figure 6-14D. Elements of the first box are "grouped" so they can be handled as a single art element.

Figure 6-14C shows that the artist moved through a series of steps needed to create the drop shadow in the initial box. The idea is that it is easier to finalize each element as much as possible before it is repeated.

Figure 6-14D shows the use of the Arrange menu to group the elements of the first box into a single unit. Again, the idea is to create a final element before the box is copied and repeated.

In **Figure 6-14E,** the repeating process is started. The entire group of elements is copied as a unit.

Figure 6-14F shows a full line of boxes ready for incorporation into the organization chart.

 DESKTOP JARGON

trend line Another name for line graph.

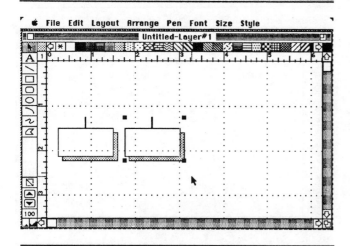

Figure 6-14E. The process of duplicating the master box has begun.

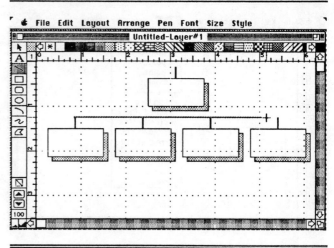

Figure 6-14G. Lines are added as necessary to connect the boxes that will form an organization chart.

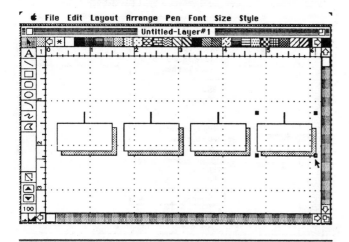

Figure 6-14F. A full line of organization chart boxes has been completed.

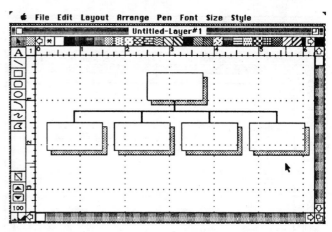

Figure 6-14H. This is a completed organization chart structure with the boxes still blank.

The process of linking the lines to connect boxes is shown in **Figure 6-14G.** Note that the cursor is about to link a connecting line to the box at the lower right.

In **Figure 6-14H,** the framework of the organization chart has been completed. All boxes are linked by lines. The line above the top box has been removed.

The final organization chart, with all of the descriptive type in place, is shown in **Figure 6-14I.** Note how the type is centered in the boxes.

LINE ART EXAMPLE: FLOWCHART

At the shop where this book was produced, there is a continuing demand to develop computer system flowcharts. Because this work represents a continuing need, the art director has prepared and maintains a library of basic shapes to develop flowcharts. This file is shown in **Figure 6-15.**

The artist works from sketches like the one illustrated in **Figure 6-16.** These are provided by authors. From this type of sketch, the artist

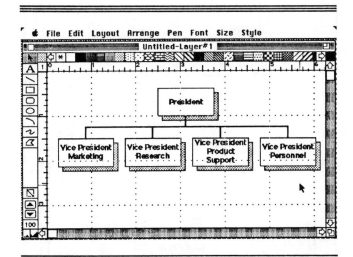

Figure 6-14l. This is the final organization chart. Type has been added to identify the positions represented by the boxes.

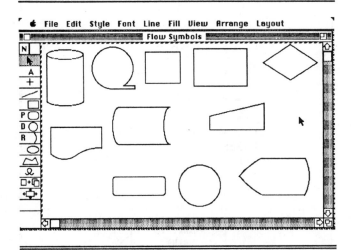

Figure 6-15. This is a set of symbols used to create computer system flowcharts. Elements of this display can be used to build new flowcharts.

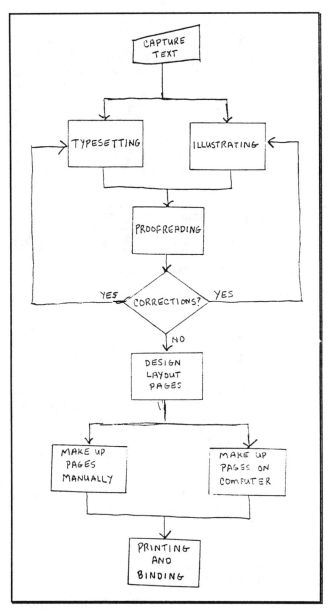

Figure 6-16. Flowcharts generally are developed from rough sketches like the one shown here.

develops a screen display like the one in **Figure 6-17.** Note that the lines in the screen display fall short of touching the succeeding shapes in the flowchart. Also, there are no arrowheads on the lines.

This design demonstrates how one user deals with limitations inherent in desktop publishing software. It is possible to create arrowheads on the desktop system and to position them at the ends of lines. However, laser printouts from these displays did not provide the degree of

quality desired. Apparent reason: The display on a desktop computer screen and the printed image generated by a laser output have different pixel patterns. Adjustments are made by applying mathematical computations to the input from the computer to generate the output from the laser printer. These calculations apparently treat the lines and arrowheads as separate art elements. At any rate, the result has been that, on printouts, the arrowheads often do not match the lines on which they are positioned.

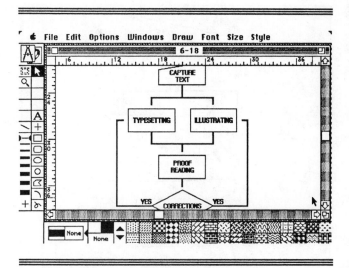

Figure 6-17. This is a screen display showing a flowchart ready for printout.

To deal with this situation, a practical solution has ben adopted: Sheets of *rubdown art* elements have been purchased. The arrowheads are positioned by rubbing them onto the laser printer output. A finished drawing is shown in **Figure 6-18.**

A sheet of arrowheads like the ones used for the flowchart is shown in **Figure 6-19.**

LINE ART EXAMPLE: ELECTRONIC DIAGRAM

Another example of how a file of drawn shapes can be used to create finished art is shown in the accompanying set of illustrations. These demonstrate development of a schematic diagram for an electrical circuit on a desktop system.

Figure 6-20A shows a display of symbols and elements that can be used to build diagrams of electrical circuits. This display comes from a commercially available software package.

In **Figure 6-20B,** component symbols and lines have been positioned to form a circuit. In this instance, note that the diagram has been enclosed in a box measuring 5 by 3 inches (30 by 18 picas). Note that rulers are positioned at the top and left as a guide for sizing of the illustration. This makes it possible to tailor the drawing to fit the layout of a publication.

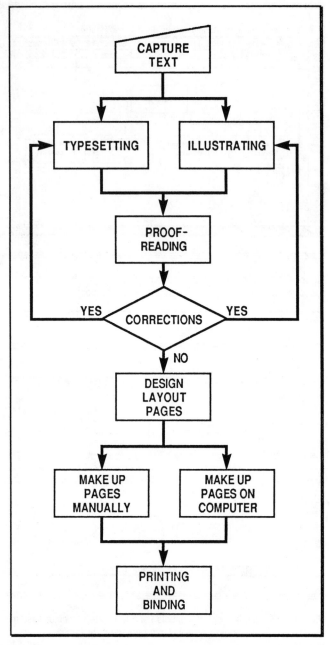

Figure 6-18. On the printout, arrowheads are added to the flowchart through use of rubdowns.

LINE ART EXAMPLE: FLOOR PLAN

The accompanying set of illustrations demonstrates another typical line drawing application: preparation of a floor plan for a residential building. The display in **Figure 6-21A** is a mixture. Some of the elements are taken from a commercial software package. Others were developed for demonstration purposes by the art director who prepared these samples.

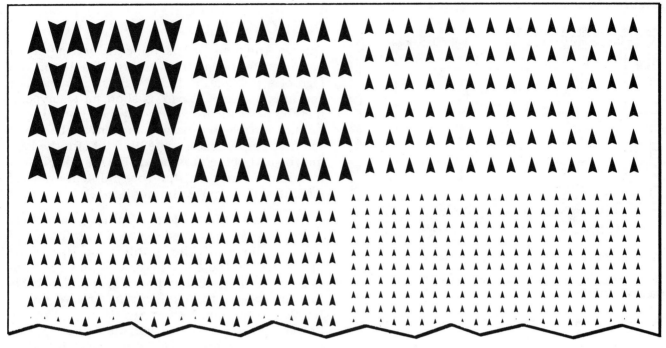

Figure 6-19. This is a sheet of rubdown art elements like those used to place arrowheads on flowcharts.

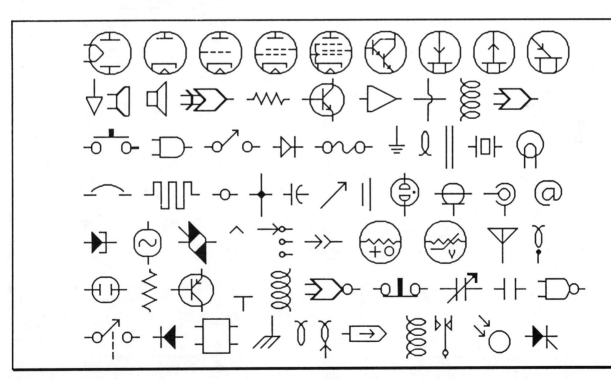

Figure 6-20A. This is a set of symbols used to develop circuit diagrams.

Figure 6-21B is a floor plan developed by selecting and positioning the art elements and linking them with lines generated by a general drafting pakage.

 DESKTOP JARGON

rubdown art Illustration elements affixed to sheet that is rubbed to transfer the image.

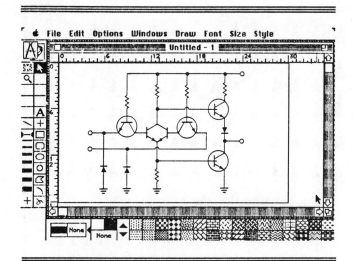

Figure 6-20B. This is a circuit diagram created with the aid of standard art elements.

Figure 6-21A. This is a set of symbols used to produce architectural drawings.

LINE ART EXAMPLE: PUBLICATION LOGO

One of the jobs to be done in setting up a periodical publication is to create a *logo.* The logo of a publication is the design element that contains its name. "Logo" is short for logotype, a metal type element used in hot-metal printing. A publication's logo generally appears at the top of the first page of each issue. In addition, the logo may be part of the *masthead.* The masthead is an information box within the publication that identifies its purpose and publisher.

For this illustration, assume you are to produce a newly formed newsletter, to be called "Flower Power." The publication is to be sponsored by the Cut Flower Growers' Association. It will be published on a bi-monthly basis for circulation to restaurants, private clubs, hotels, motels, and other regular users of cut flowers. The newsletter will use photographs and articles about successful, attractive floral displays created by customer organizations.

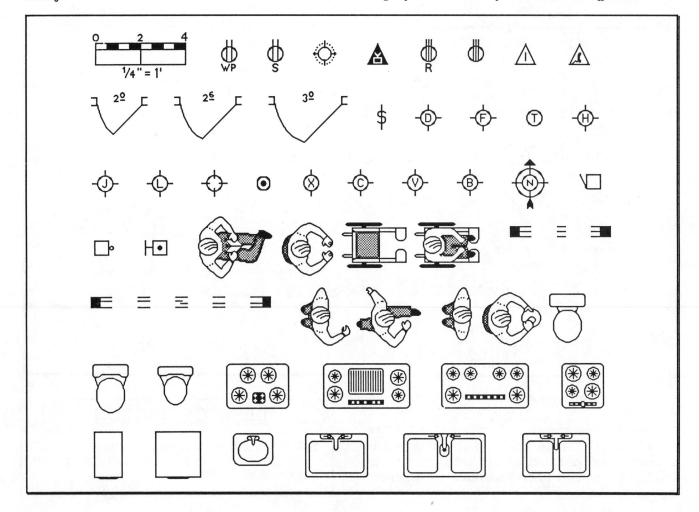

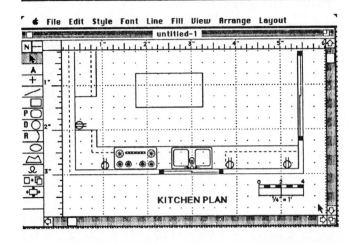

Figure 6-21B. This is a floor plan created with the aid of standard architectural symbols.

There also will be articles describing availability and potential uses of flowers that are available from grower-members of the association. Finally, each issue will carry an article about one selected grower.

It is decided that the finished logo will occupy a space of 1.5 inches high and 5 inches wide. Now, the artist must select potential elements that can be combined to create the desired image. The artist searches through stock art files to find floral art elements that can be used as parts of a logo. A selection of floral elements selected from actual stock art software packages is shown in **Figure 6-22.**

Next, the art editor keys in the title of the publication, Flower Power, and sets these words in a number of available faces. The examples in **Figure 6-23** show type samples from fonts available routinely to users of Microsoft Word software.

Figure 6-22. These floral elements taken from a stock art file will be used to create a logo for FLOWER POWER, a newsletter.

 DESKTOP JARGON

logo Design element that contains the name of a publication.

masthead The information box within a publication that identifies its purpose and publisher.

Figure 6-23. In developing the logo, the user prepares a series of type samples.

Flower Power
Flower Power
Flower Power
Flower Power
Flower Power

Finally, a series of alternative logos is assembled under a page making application package. These alternatives will be shown to people in management as a basis for selecting the final logo for the newsletter. **Figure 6-24** presents a series of alternatives. It is typical practice to provide alternate designs. The final design is selected from among them or as a combination of elements from different designs.

Figure 6-24. Stock art and type are used to prepare a logo for the newsletter, FLOWER POWER.

SCANNER INPUT

Another alternative is available for the creation of line art for use in desktop publishing systems. Art that exists on paper can be scanned electronically and included as files for use in publications. A wide range of scanning devices is available for this purpose. Some are low-cost units that can be attached to matrix printers. Others are high-resolution devices that can cost as much as your desktop computer itself.

Although this chapter will not go into a detailed review of scanning equipment, you should

know about this option. In general, a scanner operates in much the same way as the facsimile machines now being offered as attachments to telephone systems. A document is placed in an automatic feed device and drawn into the unit gradually. As this happens, a light-emitting electronic device moves back and forth across the face of the document to sense light-dark values.

Within a desktop publishing system, the scanner records its signals on a disk instead of transmitting them over a telephone line. The recorded information file then can be recalled and the images can be used within publications. Also, a scanned image can be modified as necessary under control of drafting or painting software. **Figures 6-25** and **6-26** show photos of some available scanning devices.

POSITIONING PHOTOGRAPHS

Though photographs have to be reproduced separately as halftones and stripped into plate-

making film, you provide for their use through line art. For each photo to be used, you provide a *key line* shape to show where it will be placed. Key lines are rectangles or other shapes positioned on pasteup boards or pages generated by desktop publishing software to indicate photo positions.

A widely used convention that identifies a photo position is to place angle marks in the corners of the box, as in **Figure 6-27.** Each box of this type should be labeled with an identification, which can be a number or description.

DESKTOP JARGON

key line A box that indicates where an illustration is to be placed in a publication.

Figure 6-25. Scanners like the one shown here can be used to enter text and line art from images on paper.
Courtesy of DEST Corporation.

This identifier will enable the stripper to match each photo to its appropriate position.

Another method is to fill the photo shapes with solid black. When this is done, the photo areas appear as clear spaces on the film negatives for platemaking. Halftone negatives are stripped into these clear areas.

Figure 6-26. This scanner features page makeup and text recognition capabilities with IBM-PC, Apple II, and Macintosh compatible microcomputers.
Courtesy of Microtek Lab.

USING ILLUSTRATIONS

The demonstrations in this chapter are performed on Apple Macintosh equipment. These samples are general in nature. Other computers are available for line art preparation and other desktop publishing functions, as shown in **Figure 6-28.**

Preparation of illustrations represents a special skill within the spectrum of desktop publishing operations. To be useful, of course, illustrations must be incorporated into layouts along with text. The seven chapters that follow deal with the design and production of a number of different types of illustrated publications.

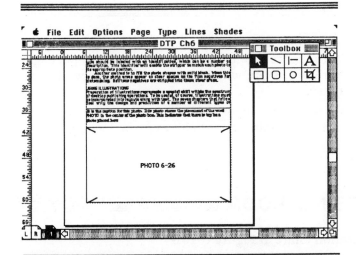

Figure 6-27. This screen display shows the placement of key lines to indicate positions for photos.

Figure 6-28. The operator at the IBM microcomputer in this photo is making a selection from a Graphics sub-menu.
Courtesy of Index Technology Corporation.

THE MAKEUP DESK

1. Through a visit to a software store or by reading personal computer magazines, get the names of at least two drafting packages, other than MacDraw. Compare the features of each of these packages with those of MacDraw. From the information you have, state which package you believe is best for a desktop publishing program. Explain your reason.

2. Review stock art packages shown in a software store or advertised in a desktop publishing magazine. Assume you have been asked to start an employee newsletter in a local hospital. Describe uses you might have for stock art.

THE COMPOSING ROOM

1. Using a drafting package, reproduce the organization chart in Figure 6-14I.

2. Using stock art and a drafting program, design a logo for a publication entitled STUDENT NEWSLETTER for your school.

Manuals and Illustrated Reports 7

Editorial Budget

❑ **A manual** presents instructions for use of a product or performance of a job.

❑ **A report** communicates information. Generally, a report is a one-time publication.

❑ **Many manuals and reports** lend themselves well to production through desktop publishing systems.

❑ **Manuals and illustrated reports** use the same text selection and formatting principles covered earlier. The new dimension is the placement and visual use of illustration elements.

❑ **Line art elements** can be prepared with drafting software and positioned within text.

❑ **Photos** must be reproduced separately from line copy. Key-line boxes are used to indicate positions of photos.

❑ **Copy fitting** or **cast-off** of text is a starting point for production of many publications. The idea is to determine whether copy fits in the available number of pages or how long a publication must be.

❑ **Illustrations** should be selected and positioned to lead the reader's eye into the text portion of the publication.

❑ **A layout grid** is a series of lines that assists in placement of copy and illustrations.

❑ **Layout drawings** or **dummies** can be prepared as guides to final placement of copy and illustrations.

❑ **Page making software** can be used to create complete publications. One package, PageMaker 3.0, is demonstrated.

TYPES OF REPORTS

A *report* is a document designed to communicate information— usually on a special, or one-time, basis. The reports covered in this chapter are of the same general type as those described in Chapter 5. Inclusion of illustrations is the major difference. Therefore, all of the principles that apply to text-based reports also apply to those described in this chapter. Typical applications for the methods described here will include:

- User guides or *manuals* describe care and use of products or procedures for job performance. These publications contain textual instructions on product operation. Illustrations become part of the instructions.
- *Financial* or *status reports* are prepared by companies for stockholders, bankers, or government agencies. They usually are illustrated by photos of key people or products. Also, statistical tables and graphs are used to report on company status.
- *Project reports* are prepared by scientists, engineers, or consultants. These reports describe the status of experiments or product development projects.
- "Reports to customers" are prepared by many companies, particularly those that serve other businesses. These reports describe product applications, particularly for new products or services.

CHARACTERISTICS AND FORMATS

As publications go, the designs and formats for the documents covered here are relatively simple. Most will be designed for reproduction on simple offset presses, usually in 8.5-by-11-inch format. Some may be printed on xerographic duplicators. Photos may be used in some reports; but line art will predominate. Typically, budgets will be low. This will provide strong motivation to use in-house desktop publishing systems if they are available.

As a desktop publisher, you would be justified in classifying most of this work as "quick and dirty." That is, designs and layouts can be rudimentary. Generally, emphasis will be placed on low cost and quick turnaround.

These job characteristics mean that you should look for production shortcuts. Work usually will be initiated within the same organization that employs the desktop publishers. So, it should be possible to coordinate production with manuscript preparation. Your goal should be to receive manuscript on disks that can provide input into your desktop publishing system.

Some Special Situations

Some manuals and illustrated reports definitely should not be quick and dirty. For example, *annual reports* on company condition are among the most attractive and "slick" publications produced. These publications generally are supported by large budgets. Many annual reports are printed in full color. However, desktop publishing systems still may play a role. Desktop computers can format type for annual reports. Final typesetting then could be done on phototypesetting systems. Diskettes from desktop computers could serve as inputs.

Also, many companies issue quarterly reports to their stockholders and other financial readers. These reports are less formal and definitely could be produced on desktop publishing systems.

Another special situation may be the preparation of user guides or manuals. These publications may be designed for consumers. If so, companies may treat them as advertising pieces. Slick design and production may be required. However, many product and job manuals fall well within the quality standards of desktop publishing systems.

TYPES OF ILLUSTRATIONS

All of the line-art techniques covered in the previous chapter can be used for manuals and illustrated reports. In addition, these publications provide many opportunities to use photos.

Special Line Art Possibilities

Even if no illustrations are provided by the author, you may be able to create your own visual elements. These elements are different from the line-art illustrations that are covered in Chapter 5 in that they are text based. Use of these elements, described next, can add visual interest and make your publication look more professional.

Copy boxes. These are quotations from text that are reproduced in large type. These quotes usually are boxed to establish points of visual interest. Generally, a copy box will appear on a page that consists predominantly of body type. The quotation from the text serves two purposes. First, it provides a visual focal point to break up the grayness of body type. Second, it gives the reader something to look for. Most readers will look for the quoted passage as they read the text.

To illustrate, **Figure 7-1** shows a copy box based on the content of the preceding paragraph.

Special treatment for equations. Technical publications frequently contain equations or statements in scientific or mathematical notation. Including this kind of material within text can cause problems: Frequently, equations or scientific notations require multiple lines. This is because they include fractions, superscripts, or subscripts. Fractions, of course, require placement of type above and below horizontal lines. Superscripts are small type characters placed slightly above regular characters. Subscripts are positioned slightly below regular characters.

All of these elements invade lines above or below the technical text items. This means that the spacing pattern of text must be altered. You can minimize typesetting problems and also enhance the appearance of a publication through special treatment for this kind of content.

Place equations or special notations on separate lines. Center this content in the middle of your page. Then, for extra emphasis, place this material in boxes or on a tint block (shaded area). Most readers will want to devote special attention to mathematical or scientific content anyway. Visual emphasis, as demonstrated in **Figure 7-2,** can help the reader and make the publication more interesting.

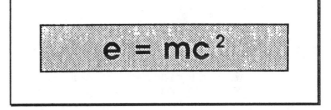

$$e = mc^2$$

Figure 7-2. Mathematical or scientific expressions can be boxed for emphasis.

Abstracts. Reports that present financial or experimental data can be long and complex. These reports take time to read. Readers who are in a hurry may not have time to cover the entire document. To help with reader understanding, it

Figure 7-1. This is an example of a copy box.

A copy box... consists of... a quotation from the text. It provides a ...point.

  DESKTOP JARGON

report A document designed to communicate information—usually on a one-time basis.

manual Publication that describes care and use of products or provides instructions for job performance.

financial report Statement on condition or status of a company.

status report A document that describes the condition of a company.

project report Document that describes the status of experiments or product development effort.

annual report A document issued at year-end to describe financial condition and operating achievements of a company.

can be a good idea to include an **abstract.** An abstract is a short statement that summarizes the content of a document. If a report contains an abstract, the main points are delivered to all readers. An abstract also provides a way for a person to decide if the full document should be read. Further, an abstract can help direct a reader's attention to key parts of a report.

As an illustration, financial statements tend to become highly detailed. It can be profitable to present, as visual elements, brief abstracts that convey key points. One method is to create a table that shows only income, expense, and profit figures for two or more years. A table of this type can focus reader attention and highlight key information. An example of this treatment is shown in **Figure 7-3.**

Roles for Photos

Photos can be used for the same basic reasons as line illustrations. That is, they can add visual interest to a publication and also convey information.

Photos for visual interest in manuals or reports can include pictures of key people or products. For example, in a manual, visual interest can be generated with photos of the product being described. In a report to employees of a company, it is common to use portraits of executives who are quoted.

As information sources, photos often are presented in a series. In this capacity, photos can be instructional. Instruction manuals for product assembly, for instance, may be illustrated with a series of photos showing a worker performing the job, step by step.

In most situations, photos relate to the text of a publication. However, photos also can tell stories on their own, with little or no text. The art of telling stories with pictures is called **photojournalism.**

Photojournalism. The previous chapter notes that it is not possible to teach the fine points of drawing in a book on production. The same is true for photographic skills. As a publisher, however, you should be aware of the value and potential uses of photos.

Photos that tell stories are proven ways to attract reader interest. Examples appear regularly in newspapers, magazines, and on TV screens. The ideal story-telling picture needs little or no text— perhaps only a short caption. In many situations, a picture may reduce the amount of text needed to tell a story. Another

Figure 7-3. Summary statistical or financial tables can be used as illustrations.

OPERATING RESULTS
(000 DROPPED)

	LAST YEAR	THIS YEAR
SALES INCOME	$1,200	$1,456
OTHER INCOME	150	150
TOTAL INCOME	1,350	1,606
OPERATING COSTS	650	765
PRODUCT COSTS	575	615
TOTAL EXPENSE	1,225	1,380
GROSS PROFIT	$ 125	$ 226

Figure 7-4. Photos can help to express mood or feeling. Photo by Liane Enkelis.

function of a photo can be to attract reader attention to the story it accompanies.

Story-telling photos are individual and should be selected to serve specific purposes. Though there are no firm rules about story-telling photos, there are some general categories that can serve as guidelines:

- Some individual photos tell their own stories, without requiring supporting text. Often, a photographer "grabs" a shot when an unexpected opportunity occurs. The resulting photo can be strong enough to stand on its own. Examples include unusual weather scenes, accidents, or outstanding sports plays. There also is a broad category of people pictures classified as "human interest." The general idea: If a picture has audience appeal on its own, an astute editor will find a place to use it effectively. To illustrate, **Figure 7-4** is a photo that shows concern for appearance, which is part of a person's self-esteem.

- A series of pictures often does an excellent job of conveying a theme, or mood, story. Often, these stories consist of one overall, *establishing photo* and a series of close-up, individual pictures that detail what is happening. Think of picture stories you may have seen about a state or county fair, or of other events. Typically, one large picture

 DESKTOP JARGON

abstract A short summary of the content of a document.

photojournalism Technique for telling a story with photos.

establishing photo In a picture story, the photo that sets the scene.

will present an overall view of the area. (A favorite at a fair is a picture taken from the highest point on a Ferris wheel.) Then, there will be separate shots that might include individual rides, judging of animals, food displays, and even children eating cotton candy. The idea may be used frequently. But it generally works.

- Another idea for a picture story is the step-by-step sequence. These are used for sports events, demonstrations, or instruction. An example of an instructional sequence of photos is shown in **Figure 7-5.** These photos show the steps in changing a carburetor air filter in an elementary book on automotive maintenance.

- A special kind of photo sequence is the "day in the life" story. An individual or group is tracked through a series of activities that occur during a single day. A number of books have conveyed the lives of entire countries, states, or cities. Many other publications have used this type of story. Among them are reports to stockholders or employees and major consumer magazines.

The point: Use of photos can help enhance both the products you produce and your own professional skills.

DESIGN PRINCIPLES

In general, the type specifications and layout principles for illustrated manuals and reports are similar to those for the type-only publications. Type-only publications are covered in Chapter 5. Additional design techniques are covered in later chapters. These include publications with multicolumn formats. At this point, discussions still are limited to single-column publications.

When you include illustrations in manuals and reports, you open new potential: You can place your illustrations within the body of your text. This opens the way for use of *runaround type.*

In typesetting terminology, runaround describes type that varies in column width to accommodate, or run around, illustrations. A typical example, might be the use of a photograph of the company's president in a report to customers or employees. The photograph may be

Figure 7-5. This is a series of photos that instructs readers on how to change a carburetor air filter.

in a corner of the first page of a report. The type alongside the photo will be narrower than full column size. Then, below the photo, the type will spread out to full width. An example of a display screen that uses runaround type for a report-type page is shown in **Figure 7-6.**

Two approaches can be used to establish the varying column width needed for runaround type. One is manual. You simply select a section of type and tell the computer to set it in the desired, narrow width. Then, when you have enough depth in the narrow size, you select the regular column width and continue.

A more convenient method is to let the computer adjust the type for you. Under the PageMaker 3.0 package, for example, you can place your type on a page first. Then you can position your illustration. The type will adjust automatically around the position you block for the illustration. This technique is demonstrated later in this chapter.

LAYOUT AND PRODUCTION

The positions of photographs—and some line illustrations—can require special attention. The idea, remember, is to blend illustrations into text to create visual interest. A good place to start, therefore, is to find out how much space you will need to fit in the copy and illustrations you have.

Copy Fitting

One good starting point for laying out any publication is to determine the space needed to hold the copy you want to use. People in the business generally call this step *copy fitting* or *cast-off.* Either term implies that you will estimate the space required for your copy and illustrations. Then, you will figure out how many pages these elements will occupy. If the space requirement is too great, you may have to cut some text or eliminate some illustrations. If you don't have restrictions on page length, this is the point where you should set targets.

The procedure is simple: After your text has been formatted, determine the total length of all your copy, in *column-inches.* A column-inch is a depth of one inch on a single column of text. If appropriate, separate the copy according to categories based on importance. This definitely should be done if you are producing a newsletter,

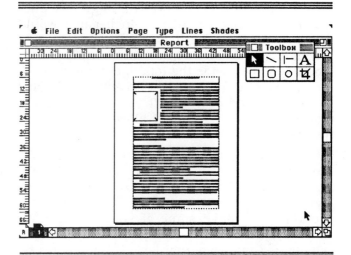

Figure 7-6. Runaround type changes column widths to accommodate illustrations.

magazine, or newspaper. Often, these publications receive more copy than they can use. One method is to classify your copy elements as MUST, IF POSSIBLE, and FILLER. This sets up a system of priorities. The priorities can have two values. First, classifications help to determine which copy gets used. Second, priorities determine where copy is placed within the publication. The copy with the highest priority should get the best placement.

Once you have your copy measurements, you do the same for illustrations. Allow space according to the column depth and number of columns to be occupied by each picture. Of course, your figures must be adjusted to reflect the layout of your publication, in columns or parts of columns. For example, even within a single-column layout, a picture can occupy less than a full column of width. If so, adjust your estimates to reflect the corresponding amount of type, in column-inches.

DESKTOP JARGON

runaround type Type that varies column width to accomodate illustrations.

copy fitting or **cast-off** Procedure for estimating space requirements for text and illustrations.

column-inch A depth of one inch on a single column of text.

To illustrate: A report running in a one-column format on 8.5-by-11-inch paper would have a column length of about nine inches. Therefore, to determine how many pages of text you have, you divide the total inches by nine. In doing this, allow for space that will be occupied by logos, headings, etc. If you have a three-column format, you might allow for 27 inches per page.

Once you have your actual measurements, you can adjust your layout accordingly. For example, your cast-off may show you have more type and illustrations than space. If so, one option is to make some of your illustrations smaller. Another possibility would be to eliminate some copy that isn't absolutely necessary. Conversely, if your measurements are just a little short, you might make some illustrations larger. Another possibility would be to increase leading or type size.

You do all this by taking stock of your product and the package into which it is to be fit. Then, you adjust as necessary.

Positioning Illustrations

Illustrations are an opportunity. They represent reader appeal. Your challenge is to place your illustrations to make your publication attractive to its readers.

One obvious example of how pictures can be placed to advantage can be demonstrated with portrait photos. Usually, a portrait shows the subject looking to the left or right.

A good rule for use of portrait photos is to have the subject look into the page. That is, if the subject is facing right, the picture should be at the left of the page or column if at all possible. Conversely, a left-looking picture should be at the right. If the subject is looking straight ahead, the picture can go anywhere. However, "head-on" photos often are of less interest visually. Most people look better from a partial side view than in a "full-face" picture.

On other types of illustrations, either photos or line art, evaluate placement by examining content. For example, in a photo of an assembly line, the reader's eye would travel from the point at which work is being done back to the starting point. In a photo of a highway or railroad, your eye would travel in the direction of normal movement. With line art, the reader's eye would move to match the information being presented.

As an example, suppose you were using a bar graph that showed rapid growth when the information was read from left to right. It would be natural to place the illustration in the center or to the left of a page.

Sketching Layouts

For some publications, advance planning of design and layout may be unnecessary. Assume you are doing a text-only report that will be printed on a small offset press. You don't have to worry about where illustrations will fall on your pages. Nor are you worried about the number of pages in your publication. You simply quit when you run out of text.

Your design decisions center around relatively simple choices. These include type selection, type size, leading, and column width. Then, you simply paginate the text through use of a word processing or pagemaking application package. When all the text is positioned, your job is done. The software can be instructed to create running heads and folios. If you are not restricted to a set number of pages, there should be no problems.

That's desktop publishing at its simplest. Things become more complex if you are aiming for a set number of pages and/or are including illustrations that correspond with references in the text. To combine elements and to preview the overall appearance and scope of a publication, you probably will want to plan a layout.

Start by developing a *grid,* or plan for positioning elements on individual publication pages. The grid is a line drawing that shows column positions and locations for running heads and folios. There also may be guide rules that divide the column into vertical halves and horizontal thirds. **Figure 7-7** shows a simple layout grid that contains these elements.

A layout grid like the one shown can be created and used in a number of ways. The classic method is to rule the grid on a sheet of paper, then create duplicates on a copying machine. These layout sheets, can be used to mark positions of text and illustrations in pencil. As an alternative, these may be used as dummy sheets and proofs can be pasted in place to establish layouts. For a one-time job, the pencil-and-paper method may be most convenient.

Another method is to create a master through use of pagemaking software, then print

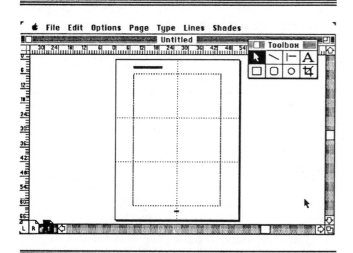

Figure 7-7. Layout forms with grids can guide the design and layout of a publication.

out copies on a laser printer. A third method is to display the layout grid on your video screen and do your design plans on-line.

Whatever the method, the idea is to have a form for planning the placement of type, headings, art, and other elements. Generally, it will prove efficient to generate paper copies of your layout grid. Use layout sheets to draw rough designs that can be used to position elements in screen displays of desktop systems. This will be unnecessary for very simple publications, such as reports that include text and few illustrations. However, if you are working on newsletters, magazines, or newspapers, use of rough layouts as working plans can be a big help.

Figure 7-8 shows a rough layout for a single page of a newsletter. Note that the layout uses the

logo for which a design was created in the previous chapter. The logo position is indicated on the layout sheet. The remainder of the elements are indicated with rough lines. This layout uses procedures standard at many newspapers. That is, the key word of a headline is lettered into place and the name, or *slug* for the story is indicated. A slug line in publishing is similar to the file name assigned to publication elements under desktop systems. A slug was the name for a line of machine-cast metal type. Use of slugs or file names in a desktop system makes it easy to find and place all the elements of a publication.

Dummying

A step beyond rough, penciled layouts is the dummy. To dummy a publication, all of the type is printed in galley form. Then, on either layout sheets like those illustrated above or a blank sheet, the type elements are pasted in place. Generally, illustrations are indicated by drawing boxes where they fit.

Rather than printing layout forms, some artists prefer to work on *light tables.* A light table is a back-lighted glass or plastic work surface. The light enables the artist to see through a pasteup board for the positioning of type and art elements. For this kind of operation, the artist prepares a *template* that consists of layout lines ruled on a sheet of clear acetate. The template then is positioned on the surface of the light table. When the lights are on, the template can be seen through the sheets of paper or board used for dummying. The show-through lines are used to guide placement of type and ruling of boxes for illustration positions.

In many shops that handle volume jobs, dummying and pasteup are facilitated through

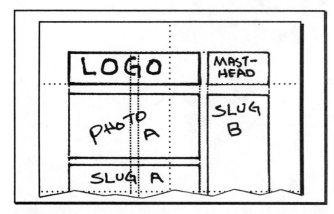

Figure 7-8. Preliminary designs for publication pages can be created by positioning and identifying elements on a form like this.

DESKTOP JARGON

grid Set of lines that guides the positioning of text and illustrations in a layout.

slug Working name for a publication element. Derived from slug of linecast type.

light table A work station with a back-lighted glass surface; used for pasteup.

template A guide used to position type on dummies and pasteup boards.

use of a *pin-register* system. Metal tabs with round pegs facing upward are positioned on the face of the light table with masking tape. The template, which is punched with holes that match the pins, is placed over the register pins, as shown in **Figure 7-9.** The paper or boards to be used for dummying or pasteup are punched with matching holes. In this way, dummy sheets can be slipped quickly over the pins to set them up in working position. A partially completed dummy is shown in the photo in **Figure 7-10.**

Pasted-up dummies are valuable, sometimes necessary, as review and communication tools. Dummies are valuable if publication design must be approved by someone who is not directly involved in production. In these instances, the decision maker, or "client," can review the dummy in detail. Any required changes are easier to make at this stage than after production mechanicals have been prepared. Even with

desktop techniques, rework on finished publications can be time consuming and frustrating. It usually is better to handle reviews and to make changes on rough layouts or dummies.

USING PAGE MAKEUP SOFTWARE

The content of this book is organized, in part, to help a beginner avoid a major misconception about desktop publishing: The only way to do desktop publishing is through use of page makeup software. This is the reason Chapter 5 demonstrates creation and completion of entire projects entirely with word processing software.

For the same reason, traditional dummying and pasteup techniques are covered in earlier descriptions. There are some jobs, such as full-sized newspapers, for which traditional pasteup remains the best production method. This is because newspaper-size pages are too large for desktop publishing makeup techniques. However, as described in Chapter 12, large newspaper pages can be made up on large computer systems.

Figure 7-9. A template drawn on clear acetate provides a dummying and pasteup guide.
Photo by Benedict Kruse.

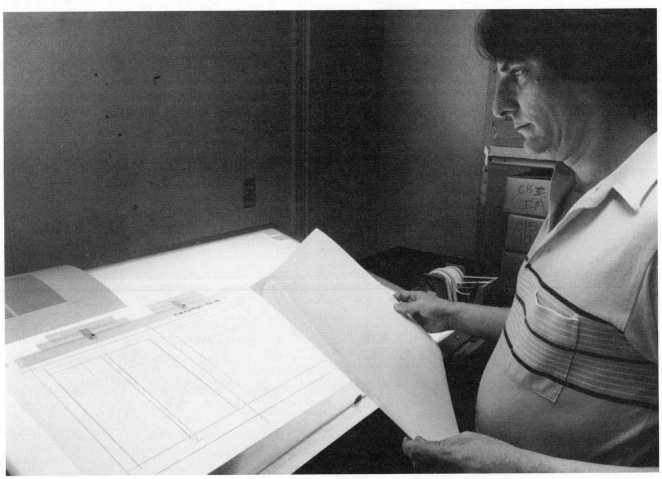

Figure 7-10. Dummy or pasteup boards are positioned over templates as a guide for placing type and illustrations. Photo by Benedict Kruse.

When traditional pasteup is used, desktop publishing still is a valuable tool. Substantial savings can result from the preparation of type and line art on desktop computers.

The idea behind the content organization of this book is to establish a practical perspective: Desktop publishing provides general-purpose tools that can be applied to virtually any publishing situation. The user has a great deal of latitude and flexibility. At the same time, it is worthwhile to recognize that page makeup software is largely responsible for the current desktop publishing boom. Anyone going into desktop publishing should be familiar with and should be able to make use of page makeup software.

Having established this perspective, this is a good place to introduce an illustrated, step-by-step discussion of how page makeup software works. The presentation that follows covers the layout and electronic formatting of a simple, single-column, illustrated report. It is based on use of an extremely popular pagemaking application program, PageMaker 3.0 from Aldus Corporation, headquartered in Seattle, Washington. The reasons for selecting this particular package and version are worth noting.

About PageMaker

At this writing, PageMaker stands out as both a pioneer in and a dominator of the microcomputer page makeup market. PageMaker was the first successful application package to adopt and

 DESKTOP JARGON

pin-register A technique for positioning publication elements accurately through use of metal pins that locate pasteup boards on work surfaces.

implement the PostScript graphics formatting language for a microcomputer-based publishing program. PostScript is a software package that controls the formatting and printing of type fonts and graphics images. PostScript applies a bit-mapping technique for the processing and output of computer graphics.

PageMaker 1.0, released in 1985, was tested in the shop where this book was developed. It was found to be less than satisfactory for full-scale use. To qualify this, the same shop was equipped fully for traditional dummying and pasteup operations before desktop publishing computers were introduced. Software bugs and limitations of PageMaker 1.0 quickly became apparent.

Among these was a major type formatting bug: When a format called for comparatively wide spacing between lines (four or five picas), the program mixed up the specifications. Lines of type were set to the height of the interline spaces. Another problem, not a bug, was a limitation of the size of publication that could be handled by PageMaker 1.0. Sixteen pages was the maximum size for any individual document. The original software was extremely limited in its capabilities to flow long segments of copy from page to page. It also was difficult to make adjustments after copy had been positioned. Given these limitations, it actually was faster to handle dummying and pasteup manually.

Accordingly, a decision was made. It was more efficient to output type under control of MicroSoft Word and continue to handle dummying and pasteup manually. However, use of drafting software was an immediate success. As indicated earlier, savings on line illustrations alone were enough to pay for the cost of desktop publishing equipment.

PageMaker 2.0, released in 1987, made a big difference. The type formatting bugs were eliminated. Capacity was expanded to 128 pages per document. Also, provision had been made to chain multiple documents—up to a limit of 9,999 pages. Copy can be flowed through from page to page under user control. That is, when you finish working on one two-page spread, you turn to the next. The text that left off on the previous page is flowed into the available space on the new spread. In short, PageMaker 2.0 came close to electronic replication of the artist's drawing board.

In 1988, PageMaker 3.0 was released. This package introduced some advanced capabilities that are especially useful in many production shops. Some advances incorporated in 3.0:

- Text flow is automatic from beginning to end. That is, when the beginning of a text file is positioned, the remainder of the file flows into place automatically. The type is positioned, column by column and page by page, until all text is used. If adjustments are made for style or to eliminate widows, the text flow is adjusted through the entire document. The same is true if illustrations are inserted into text. This capability has been of major value in production of multi-page publications.

- PageMaker 3.0 supports style sheets in the same manner as MicroSoft Word. That is, the user can specify type for body copy and heads. Then, the user can refer to those specifications and cause the program to format the text accordingly. This is an advance in type formatting capability. But, PageMaker is still more limited than Word as a formatting tool. Therefore, the value of this feature is limited for an application such as this textbook.

- Hyphenation and justification can be handled automatically as the text is flowed into place. PageMaker uses an extensive dictionary to look up correct hyphenations as text is positioned. The system works well as long as the words used in the manuscript are listed in the dictionary. The system will not hyphenate terms not in the dictionary. This can make for awkward spacing if a long, unlisted word comes at the end of a line. The line above can have large gaps between words. The same is true for proper names. Therefore, to get a quality publication, you still have to review your type and handle some hyphenation manually.

- Text wrap around illustrations is automatic. In PageMaker 2.0, the user has to fill run-around areas with manually entered instructions.

- Version 3.0 has a color separation capability.

Offsetting these features is a demand for much more memory and storage than required for 2.0. Also, because 3.0 is color-separated and must process four sets of graphic data instead of one, it runs noticeably slower. However, the automatic flowing of copy seems to make up for the loss of processing speed.

Using PageMaker

When PageMaker 3.0 is used to produce a multipage publication, such as a manual or book, a separate file is created for each element. In this sense, each illustration is an element. Each chapter of text is a separate element. Other text elements also are placed in separate files. For example, illustration captions would be one file. In this book, the *Desktop Jargon* definitions also were placed in a separate file.

It has worked best to format text in MicroSoft Word 3.0 (or later version) and to import copy into PageMaker. There are no problems because PageMaker 3.0 recognizes and uses the Word style sheets. When PageMaker is to be used, the Word files are not set up in column width. Rather, PageMaker handles column formatting as the copy is flowed into place.

It works best to flow in all text first. Then, line illustrations can be positioned and spaces for photos can be blocked over the positioned copy. Captions also can be inserted below or above the illustrations. PageMaker adjusts the body type to accommodate the inserted elements.

PageMaker demonstration. The above information and insights provide background. Next comes a practical demonstration. The following presentation provides a "walkthrough" of steps involved in calling the PageMaker 3.0 program from storage and formatting simple, illustrated pages. More complex work is demonstrated, as appropriate, in later chapters.

Bear in mind that the descriptions that follow assume that PageMaker and necessary supporting software have already been loaded onto hard disk. The demonstration illustrations were created on a Macintosh Plus.

First, the PageMaker icon is clicked on the Finder menu, as shown in **Figure 7-11.** Then, the system generates the display shown in **Figure 7-12.** The displayed box includes the Aldus logo and a copyright notice. Operationally, the significance of this screen is the main menu across the top line.

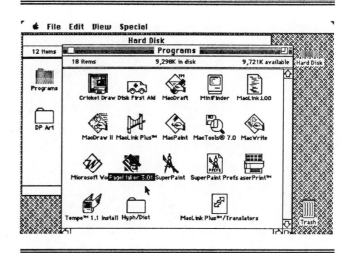

Figure 7-11. The PageMaker program is selected from the Finder menu.

Figure 7-12. The title screen and main menu for PageMaker are presented together.

In **Figure 7-13,** the operator calls the File menu and positions the cursor to highlight the option for creating a new file. If the user wanted to work with an existing file, the Open option would be selected from the same menu. For the purposes of this walkthrough, it is best to demonstrate opening of a new file.

Selection of the New file option causes the system to generate the dialog box shown in **Figure 7-14.** Note that the user has idicated that the document will be letter size—8.5 by 11 inches. Page dimensions can be stated in inches

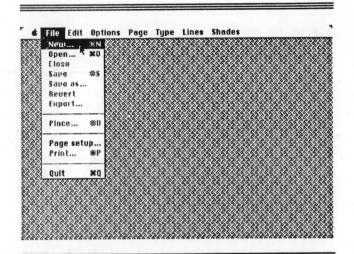

Figure 7-13. The File pulldown menu is used to indicate that a new file is to be created.

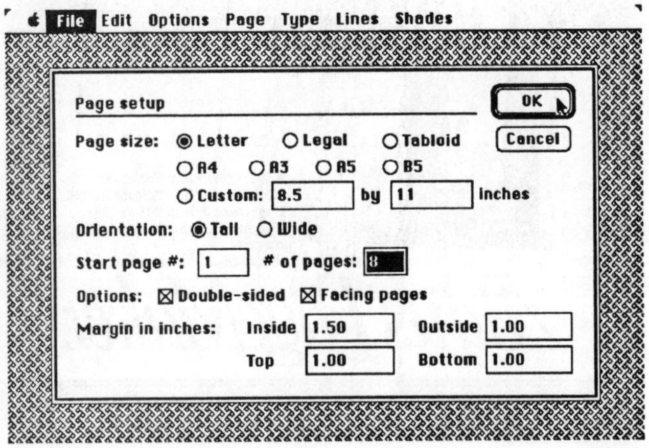

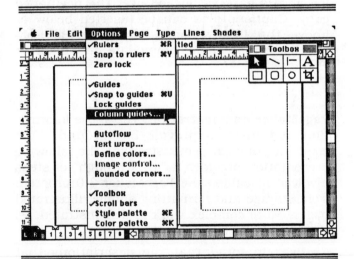

Figure 7-14. Entries in the Page Setup dialog box establish layouts for the document.

with decimal values for parts of inches, as is done here. Other measurement options include millimeters, picas, or ciceros (an alternate, type-based measurement).

Another entry indicates that the format will be vertical (Tall). The document to be created will be eight pages long. If no length is indicated, the software will flow text automatically to its maximum limit of 128 pages. An entry is made to indicate the page number will start at 1.

The user also specifies the document will have double-sided and facing pages, or will use

two-page spreads. These options, together, control use of margins so the copy is in matching positions on the front and back of each page. This option makes it possible to specify inside, outside, top, and bottom margins. The software will position text according to these instructions.

The operator clicks on the OK position in the dialog box. The system then creates, internally, an electronic page layout template according to the Page Setup specifications.

Next, the operator uses the Options item on the main menu to display the pull-down menu in **Figure 7-15.** Note that the specified layout is presented in the background. On the pull-down menu, the operator has told the system to display rulers at the top and left side of the desktop. These rulers can be useful in placement of copy and illustrations. The system also has been told to display column guides and to place entered elements at the guides automatically. The reason for selecting this option is apparent in the next illustration. The user also has told the system to display the PageMaker toolbox and to provide scroll bars.

Figure 7-15. The Options menu is used to select the ability to set column guide specifications.

When the user clicks on the Column Guides option, the system generates the display in **Figure 7-16.** The reason for selecting this option now is apparent: The *default* setting of Page-Maker 3.0 is for a two-column format. A default is a standard setting that is applied by software.

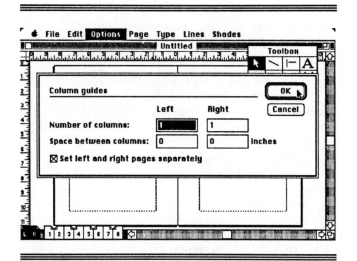

Figure 7-16. The entries in this dialog box override the default settings to create single-column pages.

The default setting is used automatically if the operator fails to override with another entry. So, within the margins entered in the Page Setup box, PageMaker automatically goes to a two-column format. The entries in this screen display change the default settings. The user has asked for a one-column format on both left and right pages. Also, the system has been asked to set up left and right pages for separate measurements.

When the dialog box is okayed, the format displayed on the screen is changed as shown in **Figure 7-17.** Note that the bottom of this screen

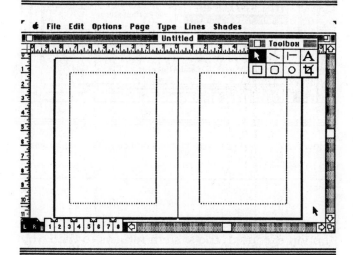

Figure 7-17. The screen now displays the master layout for the document.

indicates that provision has been made for eight pages in a left-right alternating format.

In **Figure 7-18,** the operator has created a working grid as a guide for positioning text and illustrations. The uses and values of grids in laying out pages are covered earlier. To create this dotted-line grid, which will not reproduce on printouts, the operator clicks on the desired positions. The rulers at the top and left are used as guides. The operator clicks on a position on a ruler and drags the mouse across the page layout form. When the mouse is released, the lines are straightened and positioned automatically.

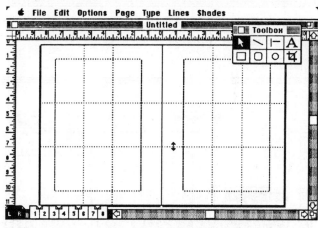

Figure 7-18. A design grid is established to help position the copy for the title page, or cover sheet, of the report.

Next, the operator clicks on the position for page 1, at the bottom of the screen. This causes the system to display a single page, since page 1 is recto and there is no corresponding verso. The layout for the first page of the document is shown in **Figure 7-19.**

To begin actual makeup, the operator selects the File menu and highlights the Place option, as shown in **Figure 7-20.** This tells the system

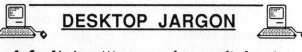

DESKTOP JARGON

default A setting or value applied automatically by a system if an operator does not enter other specifications.

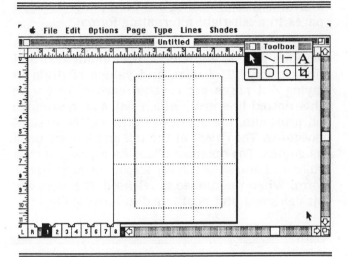

Figure 7-19. When page 1 is selected for page makeup, only a single-page layout is displayed.

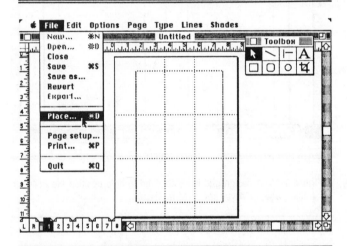

Figure 7-20. To begin flowing copy into the document, the Place option is selected.

that the operator wants to select a stored file document for placement in the page.

Author's note: This is a good point to pause to take note of the knowledge and skills you will need to use page makeup software. There are seven options on the main menu. Each of these has multiple options and sometimes dozens of file names as well. All of these options represent knowledge you will need and actions you will have to take to put a layout together.

This review is intended to provide a valuable guideline. But, to become a qualified user, you

still have to allow time to study, master, and practice use of basic commands. In addition to the page makeup package, you also must master line art and type formatting software.

The process is akin to learning to drive a car. You can read a book to learn about the different controls and what they do. But it takes a few thousand miles on the road to develop competence. Similarly, page makeup software becomes easier to use as you gain experience.

Now, return to the page makeup walk-through. Execution of the Place command causes the system to display the dialog box shown in **Figure 7-21.** This dialog box includes a list-type menu in which the names of available text and graphics files are shown. The operator scrolls through the list to highlight the text file to be used for the first page of the report. This procedure assumes that a file has been created and stored previously. In this instance, all files are stored in MicroSoft Word 3.0. In the illustration, the selected file is entitled Title Page. The operator then clicks on the Place option.

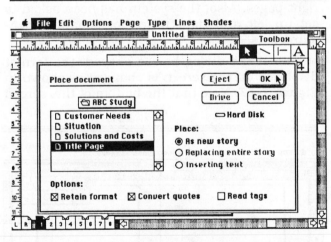

Figure 7-21. To carry out the placement of copy, the user selects the file to be imported.

With the file name identified and the Place option executed, the system returns to the layout for the first page. A special copy placement cursor is positioned in the upper-left corner of the copy area, as shown in **Figure 7-22.** The operator simply drags this special cursor along the layout area to where copy is to be placed. The copy will flow into position automatically.

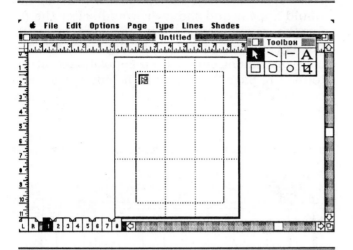

Figure 7-22. The copy-positioning cursor is placed in the upper-left corner of the page to import text.

When the cursor movement is completed, the text file is placed in the formatted copy area, as shown in **Figure 7-23.** The system also introduces "handles" at the top and bottom of the copy block. The configuration of these lines also leads users to call them "window shades." The blank handle at the top of the page indicates that

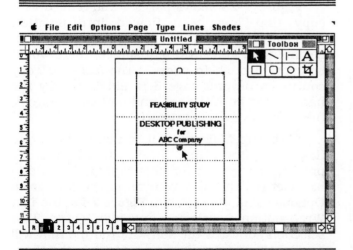

Figure 7-23. Copy appears on the title page. The handle at the top of the page is blank, indicating the start of a file. The # in the bottom handle indicates the end of the file.

this is the beginning of the copy block. The # symbol in the bottom handle indicates the end of a copy block. If the text file had more copy, a + symbol would appear in the handle at the bottom of the page. As indicated, this report will be on a feasibility study for introduction of desktop publishing for an interested company.

In **Figure 7-24,** the operator has elected to put the program into a mode that will permit movement of copy under simple scrolling commands. The crossed arrows at the top of the image area indicate that the text can be moved. This symbol appears when the user clicks on the upper-left option in the Toolbox at the top-right of the screen. In this operating mode, the operator can select and drag the copy block to any desired position on the page. Note how the grid pattern aids the user in centering text on the page, both horizontally and vertically.

The copy movement operation represents just one use of the PageMaker Toolbox. Other Toolbox items can be used to add lines, boxes, circles, or rectangles to a layout. Tools also are available for on-line editing functions. The user can edit text or change the sizes of illustrations through Toolbox controls.

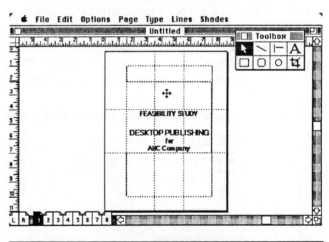

Figure 7-24. The symbol above the copy indicates that the Move Copy option has been selected from the Toolbox.

Figure 7-25 shows the first page of the report as it approaches its final state. The move mode has been discontinued and the handles are in place. The handles can be removed by clicking the mouse at any point outside the copy area. In the illustration, the mouse is in position to eliminate the handles.

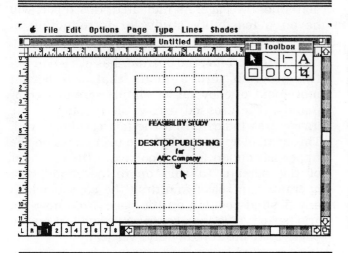

Figure 7-25. The copy for the report cover, or title page, is centered with the aid of the grid.

In **Figure 7-26,** the operator has moved on to the spread for pages 2 and 3 of the report. This move is triggered by clicking the mouse on the positions for pages 2 and 3 at the bottom of the screen. Note that these page numbers are high-lighted.

After the page layouts are positioned, the user selects the Options menu and highlights the Autoflow function. This tells the system to flow

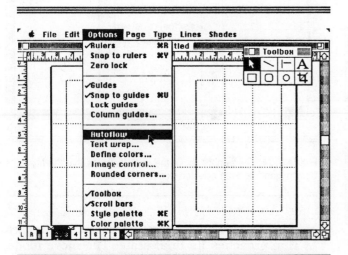

Figure 7-26. The layout for pages 2 and 3 is positioned and the Autoflow option is selected.

in the complete copy file that is to be called. For your information, the full text for this document contains about five-and-a-half pages.

As a next step, the operator would initiate a Place operation. The Select document dialog box would appear and the user would select the file for the report text. Then, the system would display the layout shown in **Figure 7-27.** The copy-placement cursor then is positioned at the top-left of page 2. Note that the copy-placement cursor takes on a different symbol when the Autoflow option is to be used.

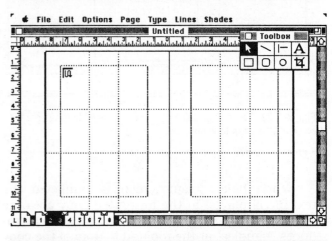

Figure 7-27. The Autoflow cursor is positioned on the top of page 2.

Figure 7-28 shows pages 2 and 3 filled with copy that has been flowed into position automatically. The file flows continuously from beginning to end. In this instance, there would be copy through to page 7. The fact that copy continues beyond page 3 is illustrated by the handles. At both the top and bottom of page 3, the handles have plus signs (+).

With PageMaker 3.0 it is more efficient to flow copy first, then insert illustrations. To prepare the system for illustrations that are to be inserted, the user returns to the pull-down Options menu. As shown in **Figure 7-29,** the Text Wrap option is selected and highlighted. This selection activates the software routine that will control the wrapping of text around the illus-trations.

Figure 7-30 shows a dialog box used to select the specifications for Text Wrap operations.

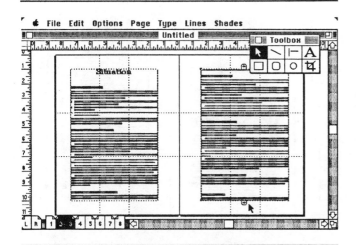

Figure 7-28. Copy is flowed into position on the document. The plus signs in the handles for page 3 indicate that the copy extends to more pages.

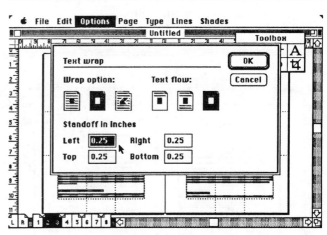

Figure 7-30. This dialog box is used to specify the Wrap and Text Flow options for runaround text.

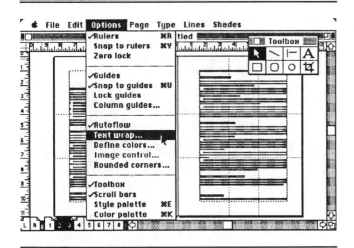

Figure 7-29. In preparation for the placement of illustrations, the Text Wrap option is selected.

Note that there are diagrams to be highlighted for selection of the method of text wrap and text flow. At the left is the Wrap Option. The user can instruct the system to place text over the position occuped by an illustration. As a second option, the one selected in this illustration, the text will flow around a rectangular illustration. As a third option, the system can be instructed to wrap text around an irregularly shaped art element.

There are separate options for text flow. In one option, the text can be terminated just above

the illustration. A second option stops the text above the illustration, then continues below the inserted image. The third option has been selected for this application. It instructs the system to flow copy around the illustration.

Note that the operator also is asked for a specification called **Standoff.** Standoff is the distance between the outside edge of an art element and the closest copy element. In this instance, the specification is for a quarter-inch of standoff on all sides of each illustration.

After Text Wrap specifications are entered, the operator is ready to insert illustrations. To do this, the Place option is selected again. Then, the files for each of the art elements are selected in turn. Each element is flowed into its desired page position through use of the copy-placement cursor. The illustration sizing tool can be used to finalize the position of each illustration. As this is done, the copy flows around the newly placed art element. The result is shown in **Figure 7-31.** Note that the standoff area is marked on the screen by a series of four diamonds connected by dotted lines. If captions are to be included, they

DESKTOP JARGON

standoff The distance between the outside edge of an art element and the closest copy element.

could be entered through the computer's keyboard or imported from a file.

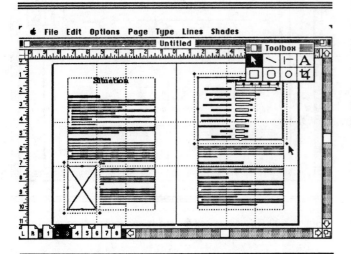

Figure 7-31. The two illustrations for this spread are positioned through use of the Place option and a Toolbox option to control sizing. Note the marked area for standoff.

Even after all elements have been positioned on a page, PageMaker supports almost any changes or revisions a user might want to make. For example, in **Figure 7-32** the illustration on page 2 has been moved from the lower-left to the center of the page. As long as the system remains in Text Wrap mode, PageMaker will adjust to any layout alterations a user makes.

Other PageMaker options. The illustrations presented in this walkthrough have been in the "Fit the Window" mode of the PageMaker program. This means simply that entire pages or spreads are displayed within the desktop area provided. PageMaker also has a number of other options: The user can view the working image in 50, 75, 100, or 200 percent of full size. In these larger sizes, only a portion of a page image is displayed at any time. The user has to scroll the image to see the desired areas.

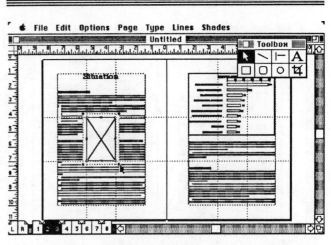

Figure 7-32. This display demonstrates the ease and flexibility available for modifying layouts under control of PageMaker software.

Other options include the ability to insert or delete elements or to insert or delete entire pages.

PageMaker 3.0 also has the ability to highlight portions of layouts for color reproduction. It even is possible to select the colors in which the selected elements are to be printed.

PAGE MAKEUP TOOLS ARE FLEXIBLE

The walkthrough you have completed is for a relatively simple publication. However, even this example is enough to highlight the reason for the way this book is organized: Desktop publishing tools are flexible. The possibilities for their use are infinite. The tools can produce almost any products the publisher can imagine. Now you know the basics of how page makeup software can be used. You are ready to move along to applications for other kinds of publications. The next chapter reviews use of these tools for presentation graphics and for color outputs from desktop publishing systems.

THE MAKEUP DESK

1. Draw a layout form like the one illustrated in this chapter. Set up your layout form for a single-column format. The column width should be 30 picas and should be centered on the page. Allow for one-inch margins at the top and bottom.

2. Select a report publication or a one-column newsletter that is reproduced in this chapter or a previous chapter. Prepare a layout for the publication you select. If you don't find anything you like in this book, you can use any one-column publication of your choice.

3. If you wish, rework the layout you selected. You may want to add illustrations or other visual interest items. Be as creative as you wish.

THE COMPOSING ROOM

1. Input text from a publication of your choice.
2. Format the text in any typefaces you feel are appropriate.
3. Prepare an electronic page layout for the design you have created.

Presentation Graphics and Principles of Color Reproduction

Editorial Budget

❏ **Presentation graphics** are **visual aids** used in meetings and instructional sessions.

❏ **Overhead transparencies and slides** are the main presentation graphics prepared on desktop publishing systems.

❏ **Desktop publishing** advantages in preparation of presentation graphics include speed, convenience, and cost.

❏ **Use of color** can enhance the effectiveness of presentation graphics. Work on presentation graphics provides a good opportunity to gain experience with color graphics.

❏ **Color methods** that can be applied include special slide cameras, color plotters, color cartridges in laser printers, and hand coloring with transparent markers.

❏ **The primary colors** are the main components of visible light. These are red, green, and blue. Color slides are photographed in these "additive primaries."

❏ **Subtractive primaries** are used for printing reproduction. These are formed by filtering the additive primaries. The subtractive primaries are magenta, cyan, and yellow. In addition, printing reproduction uses black to form images.

CHALLENGE AND OPPORTUNITY

Presentation graphics sometimes are called *visual aids.* These are the illustrations used to support personal, or "standup," speeches or explanations made to groups of people. Typical forms for presentation graphics include:

- *Posters* are large, printed signs that convey a message. Posters often are hung in work or conference areas.
- *Flip charts* are large pads. Information presenters can write information on flip chart sheets. Also, flip charts can be prepared in advance and pages can be turned to support presentations.
- *Slides,* generally 35 mm photographic color transparencies, can project images onto screens.
- *Overhead transparencies* are acetate sheets that are laid on the viewing table of a device that projects images onto screens.
- Electronically generated displays are created on computers for audience viewing. The images can be projected or shown on large-screen video monitors.
- Videotape presentations are used in some situations.

The most popular types of presentation graphics are slides and overhead transparencies. Electronic displays have been growing in popularity, particularly for large companies. However, the techniques used for slides and overhead transparencies can be used for the preparation of computer-generated displays as well. This chapter deals chiefly with overhead transparencies. Slides also are covered. This emphasis reflects the fact that transparencies and slides lend themselves especially well to preparation under desktop publishing techniques.

Videotape production techniques are beyond the scope of this book, which concentrates on print media.

Special requirements and opportunities are connected with preparation of presentation graphics on desktop publishing computers. One of these is to limit the content of any given presentation. Be aware that the average audience can understand only small amounts of information at a time. In part, this is because transparencies or slides usually are shown only for short periods. **Figure 8-1** shows a presentation situation.

Another challenge lies in the fact that most users of presentation graphics prefer color transparencies or slides. As a desktop publisher, this field could be your major exposure and opportunity to use color. There will be limited opportunities to work with color in the production of publications. The great majority of publications developed on desktop publishing systems are printed in black and white. If a second color is to be used on a publication, it generally is incorporated after mechanicals are finished. The color can be set up during the platemaking and/or printing stages—from black-and-white mechanicals.

SOME BASICS ON AUDIO-VISUAL PRESENTATIONS

The first requirement in preparing presentation graphics is to understand your user (customer) and audience. In most cases, the presenter who uses your visuals will be either a manager or an instructor. The major types of presentations that use desktop publishing outputs are:

- Management briefings
- Information and instruction sessions.

Management Briefings

Meetings or staff *briefings* are major channels of management communication. A briefing is a

---

 DESKTOP JARGON

presentation graphics Pictorial materials used in meetings and instructional sessions.

visual aids Pictorial materials used to support oral presentations.

poster Large sign that conveys a message; may be printed and illustrated.

flip chart Large pad used for information written during a presentation or prepared in advance.

slide Image on transparent color film, usually 35mm, prepared for projection.

overhead transparency Acetate sheet for use on overhead projector.

briefing A meeting at which people receive information needed for their jobs.

Figure 8-1. Presentation graphics are used to convey information and focus audience interest at meetings or training sessions. Courtesy of Octel Communications Corporation.

meeting at which people receive information needed on their jobs. Management briefings usually are held to present information on executive decisions to others in an organization. The members of the audience need the information to perform their jobs. Words alone generally cannot convey the information to be presented. Ideas and information can be summarized and emphasized with visual aids.

A special contribution of graphic presentations is that they can save time in getting ideas across. Visuals that can save time also can save money. Top-level meetings are expensive. They require the time and attention of the highest-paid people in a company. Sessions of this type can cost thousands of dollars per hour. The time of the people involved is worth that much.

Information and Instruction Sessions

In today's business environment, technical people spend as much as a quarter of their working time in training sessions. This training is needed to keep people current on the latest technologies and methods. Technical information changes so quickly that any person who does not receive continuing training would fall behind—very quickly. **Figure 8-2** shows a typical training session.

The term "half-life" is used to describe the outdating of knowledge among engineers, technicians, and managers. Half-life is the time it takes for half of a person's professional knowledge to become out-of-date, or obsolete. Half-life time spans for engineers, scientists, and technicians now run three to five years. This explains why a person is expected to spend a quarter of his or her working time on learning. This effort is necessary just to keep up with change.

To meet this challenge, many organizations operate extensive training facilities. The training sessions, in turn, are major users of presentation graphics. Overhead transparencies of the type that are produced easily on desktop publishing systems are in great demand. Transparencies provide a convenient and practical way for an instructor to interact with a group of learners. An instructor can face a class while a transparency projector is in use. He or she can point to specific items or can write on a transparency master. Pointing or writing can be done right on the lighted display surface of a projector. Thus, the instructor can point to or add

Figure 8-2. Information and technical workers, as well as managers, spend much of their time learning about new developments. Courtesy of Fujitsu Office Automation.

information while the image is displayed. The instructor has all the convenience of a blackboard without having to turn his or her back to the learners.

Desktop publishing systems can generate professional-looking transparencies in minimum amounts of time. Transparency masters can be produced simply by feeding acetate sheets through a laser printer. Only a few simple application program commands are needed, as discussed below.

If a classroom is equipped with a video projector or display, the production of transparency masters can be eliminated. The art work is generated on a desktop computer. The instructor calls up display images through entries in the computer keyboard. Then the mouse can be used to identify or modify elements of the display.

ROLE OF DESKTOP PUBLISHING

Some special values from use of desktop publishing systems for presentation graphics include:

* Desktop publishing generally can reduce costs for the preparation of transparencies, slides, or electronic displays. In the past, preparation of professional-looking materials has involved typesetting services and manual production. Even if the work is done manually by an in-house department, desktop publishing costs are less.
* Service is faster. Desktop publishing systems can output some presentation visuals in minutes.
* If electronic display capabilities are available, a presenter has the flexibility of being able to project visuals directly from stored files. **Figure 8-3** shows equipment that can project computer-generated images.

COLOR AND COMPUTERS

It may be possible to get by with black-and-white outputs for overhead transparencies. However, even those who accept monochrome products may want to add at least some color. Certainly, anyone interested in 35-mm slides or electronic imaging will want color.

Color Boards and Monitors

To produce color outputs, your desktop computer will need additional hardware components. At the very least, this will involve installation of a color coprocessor and a full-color monitor. A board like the one in **Figure 8-4** is installed within the computer itself. It will have to match the monitor you select.

Many categories of video displays and projection devices are available. These devices carry a wide range of prices. The technology is moving so quickly that it would be meaningless to cite specific products. New devices are introduced frequently. The principle, however, is simple: The higher the image resolution you want, the more the monitor will cost. Also, the higher the resolution, the better your outputs will be. If you plan to make 35-mm slides, you will need at least a medium level of image quality.

Slide Attachments

One way to produce slides from desktop computers is to mount a camera on a tripod and focus it on the display screen. Darken the room before each shot and use a range of exposures to be sure you will get one that is useful. Photos should be taken at shutter speeds of one-fifteenth of a second or slower. Reason: This allows time for the video image generator to run

Figure 8-3. Presentation graphics can be projected directly by devices that are connected to computers.
Courtesy of Electrohome Limited.

Figure 8-4. To process graphics and color images, desktop computers require special circuit cards.
Courtesy of Imaging Technology Incorporated.

through two or more display cycles. A TV image is generated in an electronic scan pattern that takes one-thirtieth of a second. If you shoot at speeds faster than one-fifteenth of a second, you lose part of your picture.

As an alternative, you can use a special attachment that has its own color output controls and film recorder. The device seals out light, so there is no need to darken the room. One commercially available unit of this type is illustrated in **Figure 8-5.**

Plotters

If your system has a color plotter, you can generate finished transparencies simply by having outputs drawn on acetate sheets. If you plan to do a lot of transparencies, you may want to think about acquiring a color plotter. An example of a plotter that can be driven by a microcomputer is shown in **Figure 8-6.** At this writing, a number of acceptable units are available within a price range of $1,700 to $2,200. The outputs from plotters are usable directly as overhead transparencies.

Color Cartridges in Laser Printers

You can work with a black-and-white system and generate color outputs. However, you have to be willing to invest extra time and just a little money. You would separate the images of a transparency master into elements to be reproduced in different colors.

For example, suppose you are generating a graph with a series of bars. You could reproduce the bars in two or three different colors. Simply save the image for each color on a different document file. As an alternative, you can use an application package with color-separation capabilities. One such package, as described earlier, is PageMaker 3.0. Working with a monochrome system, you can identify elements to be reproduced in different colors. The system generates color-separated outputs automatically.

To generate color transparencies from black-and-white outputs, you need to change the cartridge in your laser printer. These cartridges can be purchased with toner in a variety of colors. You have to change cartridges to record outputs in different colors. If you need multiple colors on a single transparency, you can make multiple impressions on the same sheet of acetate.

If your transparency master is to have only one color, load the cartridge you want before producing your outputs.

Note: The toner used in laser printers produces solid, highly opaque images. Light can't pass through an opaque imprint. Therefore, to generate transparency masters that will project in color, you should screen back your

type or illustrations. Screened areas on your transparencies will project colored images.

Output Format

If overhead transparencies are your outputs, you almost certainly will want a horizontal image. That is, you will want an image that is wider than it is long. For most document outputs, you will want a vertical image as your output. This means the width of the image will be smaller than the length. Most publication pages use a vertical format.

One reason for wanting a horizontal, rather than a vertical, image is that most projection screens are horizontal. It takes a special command to cause a computer to generate horizontal output. Generally, you have to select a mode that is called "landscape," "turn page," or "wide" to get

Figure 8-5. Devices like the one shown can be attached to computers to create color images on photographic slides. Courtesy of Eastman Kodak Company.

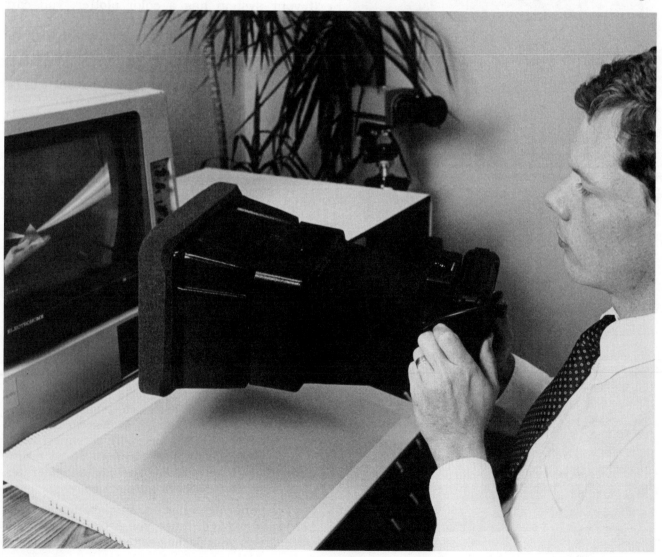

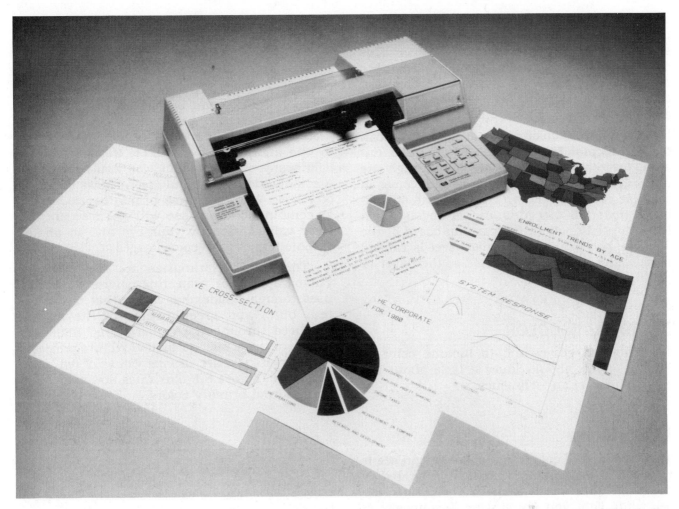

Figure 8-6. Plotters can be used to create color transparencies. Courtesy of Hewlett-Packard Company.

horizontal outputs. A space in one of the dialog boxes for printer output usually can be used to designate the printing mode you want. This option is demonstrated in the dialog box reproduced in **Figure 8-7.**

Hand Coloring

Another option is to generate monochrome transparency masters and color them manually. You simply buy a series of marking pens with transparent inks and add colors. The same result can be achieved with color acetate film. This material comes in sheets. The color film is peeled off the backing sheet and is positioned on the transparency master.

Use of an Office Copier

A longstanding tool for the production of overhead transparencies is the office copier. Most copiers will generate satisfactory transparencies if you simply reproduce your images

Figure 8-7. A PageMaker dialog box like the one shown can be used to indicate whether the output format is to be vertical or horizontal.

on acetate. This leaves the option of generating paper copies from your desktop publishing system and reproducing them on a copier. This option may seem attractive if you are assigned to prepare a number of sets of transparencies. You can use the desktop publishing system to prepare a quality master which is duplicated on a copier.

If you have a color copier available, you can make full-color transparencies from color images. Your originals can be created through use of **rubdown type** or **transfer type** that comes in multiple colors. Rubdown type consists of wax-based materials placed on carrier sheets. Each letter is positioned on the pasteup board at the desired spot. When the carrier sheet is rubbed briskly, the letter is transferred to the paper or pasteup board.

DESIGNING IN COLOR

To design in color—and to include color in graphics—you should know a little about the color reproduction techniques.

Primary Colors

The full range of colors that your eye can see is included in the normal, white light generated by the sun. This is known as **visible light.** When you see white light you are viewing a composite of the colors red, green, and blue. (This is why some color monitors for computers are designated RGB.)

Red, green, and blue also are called **additive primary** colors. The term "primary" means basic. All colors can be formed through combinations of red, green, and blue. The term "additive" describes the ability to add the colors to one another. For example, if you combine light beams of red and blue, you would see violet. A combination of red and green shows the color of yellow. When all three primaries are viewed in combination, you see white. These are the color values used by your eye and in photographic film to form color images.

The additive primaries are the basis for photographing or projecting colors. Color film used to create slides has layers that record the red, blue, and green values of the images captured through the camera lens. Similarly, when you see a slide or motion picture projected on a screen, you are viewing values of red, blue, and green. **Figure 8-8** illustrates how images are formed from primary colors.

Figure 8-8. Additive primaries get their name from the fact that they can be combined, or added to one another, to produce white light. This drawing shows beams of red, green, and blue light converging to form white.

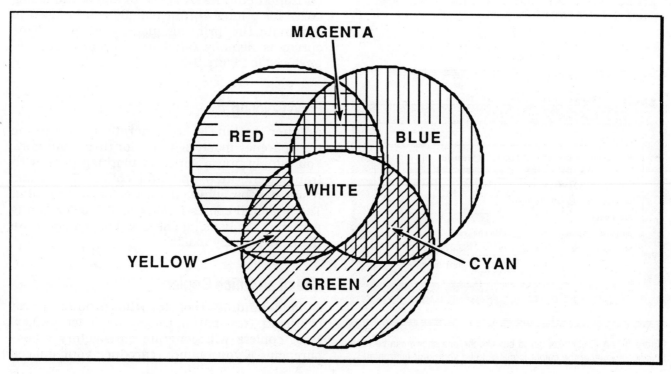

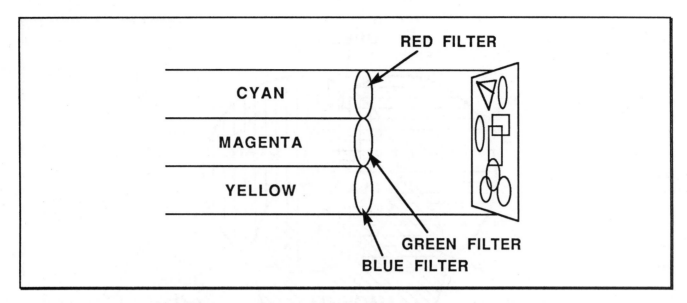

RED FILTER

CYAN

MAGENTA

YELLOW

GREEN FILTER
BLUE FILTER

To produce printed images, a different set of color values is used. The colors used in printing are called **subtractive primaries** or **reflective primaries.** "Subtractive" means that the additive primary colors are removed from a light source. When the color values of red, green, and blue are removed, the subtractive primaries remain. The "reflective" reference indicates that you see a reflected image when you look at color printing.

The subtractive primaries are magenta, cyan, and yellow. These colors result when white light is passed through red, green, and blue **filters.** A filter is a device that permits only selected portions of a beam of light to pass.

For example, when you pass white light through a red filter, the red is permitted to pass through. But the blue and green are blocked. The combination of blue and green comprise the subtractive primary cyan.

Similarly, using a green filter blocks passage of red and blue, a combination that forms magenta.

A blue filter blocks passage of red and green, which combine to form yellow.

Thus, using the colors red, blue, and green to filter white light creates the complementary, or subtractive, primaries: magenta, cyan, and yellow. **Figure 8-9** illustrates the filtering process.

Subtractive primaries have the reverse effect. Remember that the subtractive primaries are used to form images on paper or other materials. When cyan and yellow inks are printed together, the effect is green. When cyan

Figure 8-9. This diagram illustrates that use of red, green, and blue filters retains the color values of magenta, cyan, and yellow.

and magenta are combined, you get a blue image. And when magenta and yellow are combined, you see red. **Figure 8-10** demonstrates these effects.

What does all this mean to your activities as a desktop publisher?

The points you have to remember: When you are creating projected images, you are dealing with red, green, and blue as your primaries. When you are producing a printed end product, your primaries are magenta, cyan, and yellow.

 DESKTOP JARGON

rubdown type or **transfer type** Type elements supplied on waxed sheets. Characters are applied to pasteup sheets by positioning and rubbing them to complete transfer.

visible light White light viewed by the human eye.

additive primaries Basic components of white light: red, green, and blue.

subtractive primaries or **reflective primaries** The basic colors that result when white light is passed through red, green, and blue filters. The subtractive primaries are magenta, cyan, and yellow.

filter A device that permits only selected portions of a beam of light to pass.

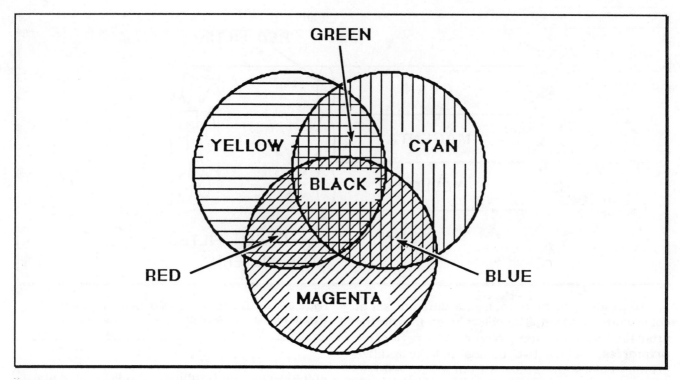

Figure 8-10. This diagram demonstrates how reflective primaries are combined in printing to produce visual effects of the additive primaries, red, green, and blue.

Color printing has an extra dimension as well. Four inks are used: magenta, cyan, yellow, and black. The subtractive primaries, by themselves, cannot form a really pure black. Therefore, a black plate is added to the printing process to provide shadow values and, usually, to present type.

Balance and Control

Reproducing photographs in color presents few problems (aside from the comparatively great expense involved). The original color image can be a transparency (such as a slide or other film size). The image to be reproduced also can be reflective art (such as a drawing or photographic color print). The original image is photographed (or scanned electronically) through a series of transparent filters. This operation produces a separate sheet of black-and-white film for each of the printing colors: magenta, cyan, yellow, and black. In addition to separating colors, the camera or scanner establishes half-tone dot patterns during the same operation.

Color values of the finished image can be represented on photographic proofs made from the separated film. Adjustments can be made on the basis of the color values in these images. That is, the values of magenta, cyan, and yellow can be adjusted by using filters that control image density. Densities of the primary colors are graded, usually in degrees of 5 percent. For example, an editor viewing a proof of a portrait might find that the skin tones are too pale. The editor could instruct the technician to "add red." In more correct technical terms, the instruction could be "plus 10 percent magenta."

When color is used, you also must be aware of the aesthetic (taste) values that can be involved. Taste, of course, is a matter of personal judgment. Color values and contrasts depend on what a given editor likes and also on the purpose of a given piece of printing. Some products are judged to require bright colors that contrast with one another. For example, many products introduced around Christmas time use combinations of bright green and red. A different effect usually is sought on products for babies, which generally use pastel colors.

For publications, be aware of the expectations of your readers and the readability of your products. For instance, images in yellow ink are pale looking and not readable on their own. Yellow is generally used within a design where it is surrounded by other colors. Reds, or mixtures of red and yellow are felt to deliver a "warm" image. By contrast, greens and blues are felt to create a "cool" image.

Be aware also of how colors will blend when they are printed one over the other. As one example, a common error of design judgment involves the printing of information in light black type on dark blue backgrounds. This color treatment appears in many publications, particularly instructional books. When this is done, the type becomes extremely difficult to read.

Color can add appeal and effectiveness to a publication. But it does take judgment and experience to use color well. A good starting point is to be conscious of the different ways color is used in publications that you read. Ask yourself how different color values and combinations might look in publications on which you work.

Type in Color

In some instances, type elements will be run in color for impact and emphasis. For example, the headings of many books are run in color. This helps call them to the attention of a reader. Color type also helps to break up the gray image of large amounts of body type. To reproduce type in color, use a few experience-based guidelines:

- It is best to use solid, dark colors for type. Light or pastel shades can be hard to read.

- Try to avoid using two-color or three-color combinations for large amounts of type, such as headings in a book or report. You can run into trouble with printing registration of delicate portions of letters.

INTEGRATING GRAPHICS INTO A PRESENTATION

Use of graphics in an oral presentation recognizes that people learn (or absorb information) in different ways. Through hearing, people retain only about a third of the information presented. If visual impact is added, the retention level moves up to the range of 50 percent.

Further improvements occur if learners do something themselves. For example, when you take notes at a lecture, you contribute to your ability to remember what you hear. Similarly, when learners or listeners take some action themselves, their memory spans increase. The goal of presentation graphics is to improve the transfer of information between presenter and audience.

Determining the number of graphics to use. When a visual is presented, a listener's attention is focused. Learning is enhanced. Then, after the visual has been noted, the listener's attention drifts again. The point: Use of visuals increases the effectiveness of a presentation. Thus, each presentation should have enough visuals so that audience attention is refocused frequently.

In general, it is a good idea to keep the information content of any single visual to a minimum. In planning a presentation, allow enough display time for each visual for the audience to absorb the information fully. Then, as the presenter moves to new information, new visuals should be shown. There are no firm rules. But it is a good idea to change visuals each 60 to 90 seconds.

Be especially careful about visuals that consist of type only. Provide some graphic images on as many slides or transparencies as possible. If color is available, use color backgrounds that set off type in contrasting hues. If you are working in black-and-white, consider using colored acetate sheets to reduce glare and increase interest. If you are creating transparencies with black type, try several different background colors. Project your transparencies and examine the results to identify the best background color.

Remember also that, if you are generating outputs on laser printers, you may be able to enhance your results with color cartridges. You also may be able to enhance the appearance of your transparencies by using outline or screen type. You do not have to limit yourself to solid, bold typefaces.

In this chapter, you have reviewed the challenges of presentation graphics. In doing so, you have covered some of the principles for coordinating use of graphics and type. This can be an important capability for users of desktop publishing systems. Virtually all of the publication areas covered in the chapters that follow require the blending of pictures and text. Thus, you can put the principles covered in this chapter to work as you move to the next chapter. The chapter that follows deals with brochures, catalogs, and other market-support publications.

THE MAKEUP DESK

1. Assume you are to present a lecture to your class on one of the following topics: presentation graphics, text-only reports, or illustrated reports. Your lecture is to last 15 minutes. Prepare a brief outline of the information you would present. Within the outline, identify the visuals you would use.

2. Prepare hand-drawn layouts for at least two visuals you would use with the presentation described in response to Assignment 1.

THE COMPOSING ROOM

1. Use a desktop publishing system to produce, on paper, a proof of two of your presentation graphics designs.

Marketing Support Publications

Editorial Budget

❏ **Market-support publications** are used to promote sales of products or services. Types of publications covered include brochures, catalogs, product information sheets, price lists, and capabilities/facilities descriptions.

❏ **Design emphasis** in publications such as catalogs is on placement of illustrations. This is because pictures convey most of the information the reader needs. Text supplements illustrations.

❏ **Grid patterns** can provide major design and layout tools in the development of catalogs and other market-support publications. Grids are used to break pages into modules that contain illustrations and/or text.

❏ **Page makeup** on a computer can follow grid-based layouts. Files of illustrations or copy are identified according to grid location. Grids can be used to indicate the page number and column in which a copy block or illustration appears.

❏ **Color separation** can be handled with overlays to indicate location of color elements. Another method is to use a tissue that covers the pasteup board. The tissue is marked to identify and locate color elements. Still another method is to separate color elements on a computer through use of a program such as PageMaker 3.0.

THE IMPACT OF DESKTOP PUBLISHING

Most companies exist by selling products and/or services. Therefore, sales activities are as important to survival of a company as breathing is for a person. Thomas Watson, Jr., when he was president of IBM, used to say: "Nothing happens around here until someone sells something."

To sell their products and/or services, companies must provide information to prospective buyers. Special **market-support publications** are produced for this purpose. Total costs for these product-information publications represent a multibillion-dollar annual investment.

This discussion refers to publications created especially to support marketing of products or services. A large segment of these informational publications can be classified as **sales literature.** A substantial amount of sales literature consists of colorful, "slick" material produced by advertising agencies or professional art services. These are top-quality materials that promote expensive products or services.

Beyond these top-of-the-line publications is a variety of simpler, less glossy publications. The capabilities of desktop publishing systems are proving ideal. The advent of desktop publishing has expanded—greatly—the ability of in-house departments to create sales literature of acceptable quality.

Where quality proves adequate, desktop publishing can deliver major cost savings. In addition, and often just as important, desktop publishing can save time. A company rushing a product to market can create press-ready literature in hours with a desktop system. Then, printed copies can be generated in minutes more if an internal printing facility is available. By contrast, external services usually take days, often weeks.

For the desktop publisher, the area of market support presents some special challenges and opportunities. One challenge lies in quality. Sales literature represents the quality, appearance, and capabilities of the products or services described. Therefore, the publications must be at a matching level of quality.

Required quality often must be delivered under less-than-ideal working conditions. Demands can include ultra-tight deadlines and, frequently, last-minute changes. Demands from marketing personnel can, at times, seem impossible and can lead to tensions and frustrations.

Yet, friction at any point in the publishing process is useless, counterproductive. The best way to deal with tension is to follow established procedures. Do so calmly. Be organized in your own mind about what you are supposed to do.

Follow process! Remember that the steps listed in Chapter 2 provide a process that applies to production of publications of every type. These steps, again, include:

- Writing a manuscript
- Copy editing
- Production editing
- Typesetting
- Illustrating
- Proofreading
- Designing and laying out pages
- Making up pages
- Printing and binding
- Marketing and distribution

The process approach assumes, of course, that a product is defined before you go to work on it. Before a manuscript is written, the topic and information content must be identified. If a long manuscript is involved, there will be a detailed outline. The process approach makes publication production manageable. Once the manuscript is in work, you have a series of steps that carry you through to job completion.

Regardless of the size or type of job, the first step, always, is to define the work to be done. Once the publisher and the customer agree on a job definition, the work can be scheduled realistically. If deadlines really are impossible, compromises can be worked out. Also, any special costs, sacrifices, or adjustments that must be made can be understood by all parties.

For example, to meet a deadline for a new, urgent project, delivery dates for other publications may have to slip. As a typical example, a last-minute price change may be needed on a product description sheet. To do this job, staff time may have to be taken away from another job. The consequences of such decisions should be understood and approved by all involved parties.

The point: Pressures are normal in product marketing. It is inevitable that these pressures will spill over into the preparation of market-support literature. Your best strategy for coping with pressures is to understand and organize your work to avoid frustration. You also have to establish a process that makes realistic scheduling and control possible.

TYPES OF MARKET-SUPPORT PUBLICATIONS

The purpose of market-support publications is to promote the sale of products and/or services. Therefore, the form and design of publications will vary widely with the nature and type of product or service. However, as with other areas of publishing, some common denominators and typical categories can be established. These include:

- Brochures
- Catalogs
- Product information sheets
- Price lists
- Capabilities and facilities descriptions.

Brochures

A **brochure** generally is a multipage (four or more) publication. Brochures present in-depth information on individual products, product lines, services, or companies. Brochures usually are the highest in quality and most costly among market-support publications. Also, brochures are most likely to be produced by outside agencies or art services. Many brochures, such as those that describe lines of automobiles or housing tracts, are printed in full color on slick paper. **Figure 9-1** illustrates the quality of these publications.

Catalogs

A **catalog** is a publication that illustrates and describes a number of products or services. Catalogs can range in size from two to hundreds of pages. Design and production quality also can vary widely. At the low end, you might produce a black-and-white publication printed on low-cost paper. At the high end, catalogs are slick products that are sold to consumers.

For some companies, catalogs are the only or main selling tool. That is, catalogs are the places where customers see products and decide whether to buy. This is true for "mail-order" or

Figure 9-1. Brochures are quality publications that feature products, product lines, or services.
Courtesy of Griffin Printing & Lithographic Co., Inc.

"direct-mail" organizations. These companies distribute large numbers of catalogs to prospective customers who order by mail or telephone. In other instances, catalogs supplement marketing efforts. For example, a furniture store may have a limited number of items, sizes, or colors on display. Catalogs supplement the floor samples. They are shown to interested customers, who can place orders for the exact items they want.

DESKTOP JARGON

market-support publications Publications that promote products or services.

sales literature Publications that support the sale of products or services; another term for market-support publications.

brochure A multipage (four or more) publication that presents information on products, product lines, services, or companies.

catalog A publication that illustrates and describes a number of products or services.

For the desktop publisher, catalogs can represent complex, detailed jobs. Typically, there will be large numbers of photos or line illustrations and many small blocks of copy. Laying out a catalog and getting all of the elements in their proper places can be a major challenge. Large catalogs can involve many uncertainties and changes due to last-minute problems or decisions.

To illustrate, a product offered through a catalog may be discontinued after you have included it in a layout. Prices may change. Market demands may change. As a result of any of these developments, catalog designs and layouts may have to be adjusted.

Each product position in a catalog is like display space in a store. Products are shown to be sold. The desktop publisher who works on catalogs must learn to deal with changeable market conditions. **Figure 9-2** reproduces pages from a catalog.

Figure 9-2. Catalogs use illustrations prominently; copy supports the pictures.
Courtesy of ECZEL Corporation.

Product Information Sheets

A *product information sheet* often represents a compromise, or sometimes a stopgap, that substitutes for a full-scale catalog or brochure. As the name implies, a product information sheet is a single piece of paper. It describes an individual product, a single family of products, or a service.

Generally, a product information sheet will not be as "slick" as a brochure or retail catalog. Suppose a new product has been introduced since the last printing of a catalog or brochure. A product information sheet can be prepared and distributed quickly. These can be used until new catalogs and/or brochures are ready.

In some industries, product description sheets are market-support mainstays. Examples include items such as scientific, medical, technical, computing, or electronic equipment. That is, product information sheets may take the place of catalogs. **Figure 9-3** shows an example.

Product information sheets often have to be prepared under tight production schedules.

Figure 9-3. Product information sheets feature a single product or product line.
Courtesy of the Columbus Show Case Company.

Speed is required because the product sheet may be needed for use at a specific event. For instance, many companies introduce their new products at conventions or trade shows. Most of a company's customers may attend these shows. Product information must be ready by show time or a major sales opportunity is lost. This kind of schedule presents priorities. To meet deadlines, desktop publishing personnel may have to put in overtime. Whatever happens, the deadline cannot be missed.

Price Lists

Although they are publications on their own, *price lists* often supplement brochures, catalogs, or product information sheets. A price list typically is made up of a series of columns. The information in one of the columns identifies products by name and/or number. Other columns may show size, number of units in a package, color, weight, price, and discounts.

Many organizations do not include prices, which are subject to frequent change, in brochures, catalogs, or even product sheets. Instead, they use price lists, which normally are dated to permit flexibility in issuing changes.

Price lists are least demanding in quality of layout and appearance among all market-support publications. However, they are highly critical in terms of required accuracy. Errors in pricing are embarrassing and may be costly. If there is a pricing error, a company is required to ship products at a low, unprofitable price. **Figure 9-4** presents a sample price list.

Capabilities and Facilities Descriptions

Companies that sell services or made-to-order products face a special marketing job. Customers are, in effect, buying the ability of a supplier to make and deliver needed products and services. Therefore, these companies are selling the capacities of their facilities and the capabilities of their people.

One way to handle this type of selling is to get prospective customers to visit the facilities where the needed work would be done. However, it usually is impossible to arrange personal visits for everyone. Instead, many companies publish descriptions of their capabilities and/or facilities.

Capabilities statements generally describe the kinds of work a company can do. The markets served also are identified. In addition, there usually will be descriptions of available factories, laboratories, test equipment, and warehouse areas. In some instances, companies include resumes of the qualifications and experience of key personnel.

Capabilities and facilities descriptions tend to be more technical in their content than product brochures. Brochures tend to be "hard sell" documents. In effect, a capabilities statement says: "This is who we are and what we do. Can we be of help?" Capabilities descriptions may take the form of brochures. They certainly can include multiple pages and, in many cases, are printed in color. In other instances, capabilities statements may consist of loose sheets delivered in binders or folders. The idea of loose sheets is that information items can be selected to match the needs of the prospective customer. Design and production quality can range from low, informal levels to slick publications produced under liberal budgets.

DESIGN PRINCIPLES

The most important factor in the appearance of market-support publications is that they represent the company and its products or services. Therefore, the appearance of these publications should match the company's image. That is, the publications should equal the quality of the logo, product labels, stationery, and annual report.

As one illustration, many companies design product information sheets and capabilities

---

Figure 9-4. Price lists provide the information needed to order products.

 DESKTOP JARGON

product information sheet A document, usually a single page, that describes an individual product, a single family of products, or a service.

price list A document that gives pricing, packing, shipping, and other information needed to order identified products.

Photo Composition

A photo composite is the combination of several images from separate originals onto a single piece of film or paper. The new images are photomechanically composed from the separate pieces of film or artwork.

A photo composite is generally more economical than multiple color separations. High quality is assured since the elements are color balanced and density matched to each other.

The prices apply only if original transparencies/negatives and mechanicals are supplied. (ColorHouse provides a mechanical preparation service.) Contrast masking will be done if required by the original.

On Black	Transparency		Cibachrome Prints				Ektacolor Prints			
	8x10	11x14	11x14	16x20	20x24	24x30	11x14	16x20	20x24	24x30
Straight edges (images dropped into squares, rectangles, etc.)	60.00	72.00	60.00	75.00	85.00	96.00	85.00	105.00	120.00	136.00
Soft edges (irregular shapes, overlapping or butting images)	150.00	180.00	150.00	180.00	210.00	245.00	150.00	180.00	210.00	245.00
Letters, lines (Standard)	35.00	42.00	35.00	42.00	50.00	56.00	50.00	60.00	70.00	80.00
(PMS)	65.00	78.00	65.00	78.00	90.00	105.00	90.00	108.00	125.00	145.00
Background color (Standard)							50.00	60.00	70.00	80.00
(PMS)							90.00	108.00	125.00	145.00
On White or Color										
Straight edges (images dropped into squares, rectangles, etc.)	85.00	102.00	85.00	105.00	120.00	136.00	60.00	75.00	85.00	96.00
Soft edges (irregular shapes, overlapping or butting images)	150.00	180.00	150.00	180.00	210.00	245.00	150.00	180.00	210.00	245.00
Letters, lines (Standard)	50.00	60.00	50.00	60.00	70.00	80.00	35.00	42.00	50.00	56.00
(PMS)	90.00	108.00	90.00	108.00	125.00	145.00	65.00	78.00	90.00	105.00
Background color (Standard)	50.00	60.00	50.00	60.00	70.00	80.00				
(PMS)	90.00	108.00	90.00	108.00	125.00	145.00				

On Grey Tone	Black & White Prints			
	11x14	16x20	20x24	24x30
Straight edges (images dropped into squares, rectangles, etc.)	64.00	79.00	90.00	102.00
Soft edges (irregular shapes, overlapping or butting images)	112.00	135.00	157.00	184.00
Letters, lines	45.00	54.00	63.00	72.00
Grey tones	55.00	66.00	77.00	88.00
On White or Color				
Straight edges (images dropped into squares, rectangles, etc.)	45.00	56.00	64.00	72.00
Soft edges (irregular shapes, overlapping or butting images)	112.00	135.00	157.00	184.00
Letters, lines	31.00	37.00	45.00	50.00
Grey tones	38.00	46.00	55.00	62.00

In-plant service time: 5 days

Note: One edge per composite will be punched with registration holes.

descriptions to match the formats of their proposals and bids. In this way, the market-support materials can be included within proposals or bids.

Another design factor: A company wants its market-support materials to be competitive. This doesn't mean that all marketing publications have to be slick or expensive. Rather, the publications must match the company's position in its markets. If a company seeks an image of quality and leadership, it should produce superior sales literature. Conversely, a company with a low-price, "bargain" image can afford to have publications that are less elaborate.

Design also should be influenced by the kind of information and the number of pictures and text elements to be included. As one example, a catalog may have many, perhaps hundreds, of brief product descriptions. These may be designed for use in narrow columns. Copy elements of this kind can be set effectively in a condensed Gothic face, such as Univers Condensed or Helvetica Narrow. If column widths are extremely narrow (less than 10 picas), it often is best to set type ragged right. This avoids the risk of a "spacey" appearance in right-justified format. Right-justification on narrow columns also leads to extensive use of hyphenation. This usually is avoided in sales literature. Also, if time is a factor, it is quicker to set in "rag right" than to take time to adjust spacing and hyphenation.

A catalog may contain blocks of descriptive text in addition to brief product identifiers and pricing copy. If so, it can be effective to contrast Gothic, rag right pricing information with right-justified, Roman body copy for the longer text elements.

For catalogs, the rules for typeface selection and text formatting are different from most other publications. This is largely because the role of text elements is different. Text blocks in catalogs support photos or drawings that depict the products offered. The information that readers use is chiefly in the pictures. Therefore, type elements can be smaller and more compact. Also, readability is less critical because text blocks are short and pictures are the main design elements.

DESIGN TECHNIQUES

Chapter 7 introduces use of a design grid for the positioning of copy on the cover of a report.

In preparing catalogs, the grid is a major design tool. Grids also are used for publications covered in the chapters that follow this one. So, this is a good point for an additional review of grid design techniques. The grid technique works well for desktop publishing applications because:

1. It is simple and easy to apply.
2. It is easy to use with the major desktop publishing application packages.

The Grid Approach

The basic idea of a design grid is to allocate space on a publication page. Each page is divided into a series of modules that provide a framework for design and layout. Generally, a single grid layout can be applied to all pages in a given publication. However, it is possible to use variations on a grid for special sections of a publication.

To illustrate, many full-size (wide sheet) newspapers use a six-column grid format on front pages and eight-column layouts on inside news pages. Also, some business-section pages, particularly those that carry stock market listings, often have columns set to a special, wide measure. Another variation occurs with classified advertisements. Classified advertising pages use a grid with a narrower column format than other pages.

A catalog is a good example of a publication that often is designed to fit a basic grid. A typical grid, illustrated in **Figure 9-5,** divides an 8.5-by-11-inch page into three columns. Margins of six picas are allowed on all sides, except that folio numbers can appear above or below the grid area—on outside corners. Each column measures 13 picas, with 1.5-pica spaces allowed between columns. This makes for a copy area that is 42 picas wide. The six-pica margins fill out the total sheet width of 54 picas (8.5 inches). Column length for the copy area of this grid is 54 picas. The six-pica top and bottom margins fill out the page length of 11 inches (66 picas). Dotted lines are used to indicate headline areas at the top of the page. These areas are used for headlines that announce page content. Also, the mid-point and center point of the page are marked.

A basic three-column grid then can be used as a layout pattern for the placement of illustrations and type. Layouts can be prepared flexibly and rapidly if deadlines are tight. One approach is to use the three columns as

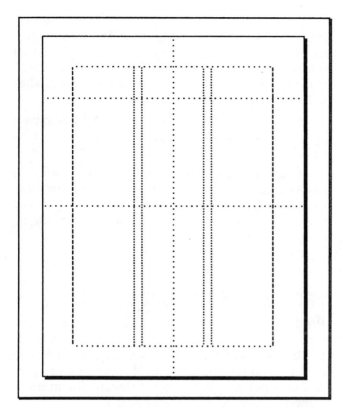

Figure 9-5. This three-column grid is a typical layout tool for a catalog.

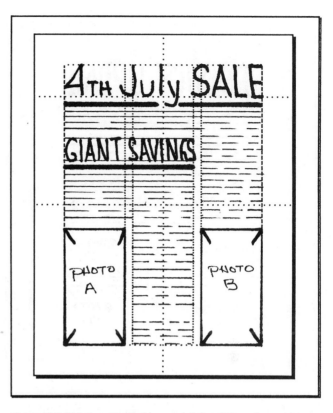

Figure 9-6. This is a penciled layout developed through use of a three-column grid.

boundaries for placement of illustrations and type, possibly with headlines that carry across multiple columns. This method, which also is popular for many newsletters, is illustrated in **Figure 9-6.**

For presentation of important products, or for design variations, it is possible to allocate space that crosses over the grid areas. For example, **Figure 9-7** shows a page layout that uses two-column spaces for large illustrations. When a grid approach is used, this can be done without violating the design balance of a page.

It also is possible to subdivide, or invade, the modular areas established by a grid. For example, illustrations can be allocated widths of 20 picas and a two-pica space can be used between them to fill out the text width for the page. A treatment of this type is illustrated in **Figure 9-8.**

Another kind of treatment varies both the size of illustrations and the column width of the type. In some instances, runaround type can surround an illustration. This technique is described in Chapter 7. A catalog layout that uses runaround type is shown in **Figure 9-9.**

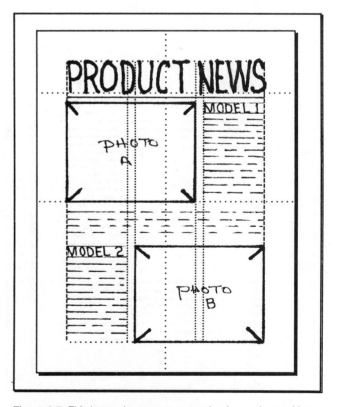

Figure 9-7. This layout demonstrates use of a three-column grid to place art elements that are two columns wide.

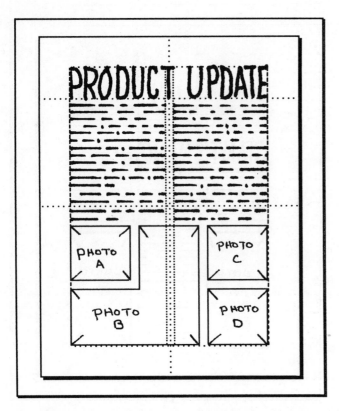

Figure 9-8. This layout demonstrates how grid lines can be violated to provide a framework for odd-sized art elements.

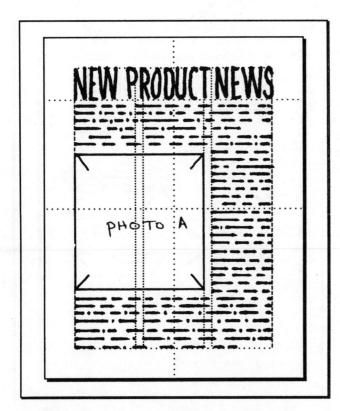

Figure 9-9. This layout shows placement of art elements within a grid to allow for runaround type.

Grids themselves can be varied almost infinitely. To illustrate, **Figure 9-10** shows a grid in which a page has been divided into four equal quarters, or **quadrants.** This is a convenient arrangement for newsletters or magazines that will use a two-column format.

As a final illustration, **Figure 9-11** shows a six-column format for a grid that could be used to lay out front pages of a full-sized newspaper.

Other design considerations center around the use of color printing in marketing publications. Design considerations connected with the use of color are dealt with below, in discussions on production.

PRODUCTION CONSIDERATIONS

Production knowledge and skills are cumulative. All points made in previous chapters apply to the publications described in this and succeeding chapters. Two production techniques not covered previously are relevant for market-support publications. These are:

- Some types of market publications lend themselves ideally to development under page makeup software.
- Marketing publications frequently use color. Therefore, this is an ideal time to discuss preparation of mechanicals intended for color reproduction.

Page Makeup Software

Most market-support publications lend themselves well to use of page makeup software. In most instances, page makeup software will work better than word processing or drafting packages. To demonstrate, the discussion that follows covers advantages of page makeup software for a typical catalog.

To use page makeup software for a catalog, it it best to begin by establishing a grid. Development of a suitable, three-column grid is demonstrated above in the discussion of design. Once your grid is established, it is best to position all of your illustrations before you place the copy. In this way, the illustrations set boundaries for placement of copy. Also, by having pictures in place first, you have a chance to evaluate how the illustrations and text tie together visually.

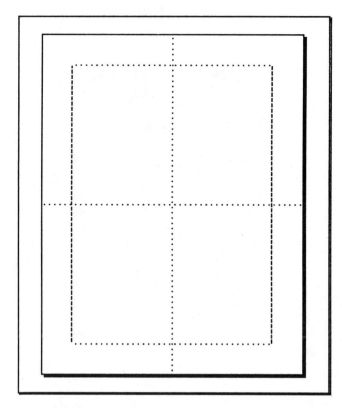

Figure 9-10. This grid uses a quadrant approach. The page is set up in four equal quarters.

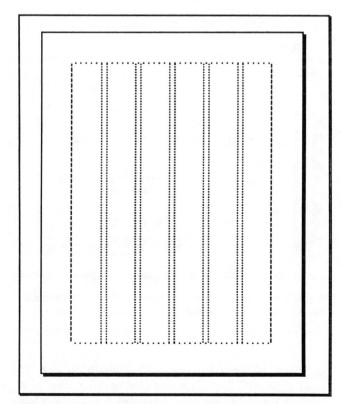

Figure 9-11. This grid could be used to lay out newspaper pages.

A good practice is to create a separate document name and storage area for each line illustration and copy block. This enables you to call up and place copy elements individually. This approach generally is easier than having large text or illustration files from which you have to extract individual elements as you make up pages.

On a Macintosh system, graphic elements should be stored as PICT files. This option is available under most draw and paint software. To illustrate, **Figure 9-12** shows a dialog box for a MacDraw application package. The user is offered options for saving either in the MacDraw or the PICT formats. If you are still working on an illustration and may modify it in the future, it is best to keep this in MacDraw. However, if the art has been finalized and is ready for inclusion in a publication, the PICT format gives you more flexibility. In addition, the PICT format condenses the file space needed (as compared with MacDraw). When you include a PICT file in a layout being created under Page-Maker software, you can resize the drawing

Figure 9-12. This dialog box is set up to store an illustration in PICT format.

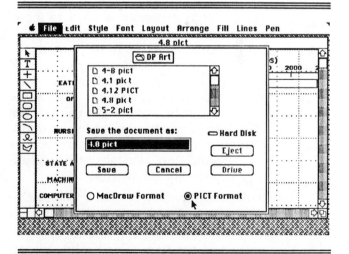

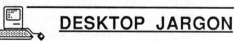

DESKTOP JARGON

quadrant One-fouth of an equally divided item. In layout, a grid that divides a page into quarters with mid-point vertical and horizontal lines.

easily. The PICT illustration can be expanded or contracted in any direction.

You may have many art and copy elements. Assembling them can be confusing and difficult if they are bunched together with multiple elements in each file. It is a good idea to key the file names of art or copy elements to their positions in your publication. One method is to identify each file with a page number and grid-location letter. For example, in a three-column layout, the columns can be identifed with the letters A, B, and C. Thus, a copy element labeled 3C would go in the right-hand column of page three.

Figure 9-13 shows a layout form on which illustrations and text elements have been labeled. This layout serves as a guide to assembly of a catalog page through use of page makeup software. **Figure 9-14** shows a PageMaker list-type menu that identifies a number of files to be used within a publication.

Preparing for Color Printing

Special copy preparation and pasteup techniques are required for color. The most common color designs are for two- and four-color reproduction.

Two-color design generally is used to focus attention on text to add visual interest. For example, a common practice is to print headings, key words, or other text elements in a color, rather than in black. Used in this way, color helps to focus reader attention. Also, some elements of copy can be enclosed in color boxes or screen tint blocks can be used as background. These techniques also help to emhasize text or illustrations. In addition, portions of line illustrations may be reproduced in color.

Four-color reproduction makes it possible to reproduce photographs, drawings, or paintings in full color.

For either two- or four-color books, special preparation of mechanicals is needed. In printing, each color of ink is applied from a different plate. This means that separate platemaking film and printing plates must be prepared for each color on every color page.

Pasteup mechanicals for color pages must be prepared and/or marked to guide the stripper. The stripper must be able to identify the exact color requirements for each image and text

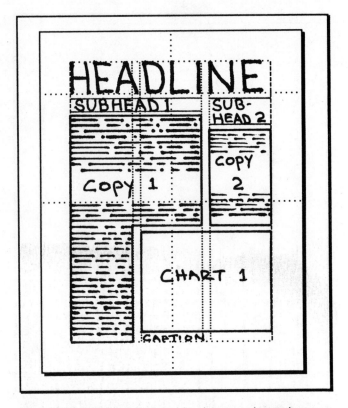

Figure 9-13. This layout is marked for placement of art and copy elements. The system uses file names that correspond with layout positions.

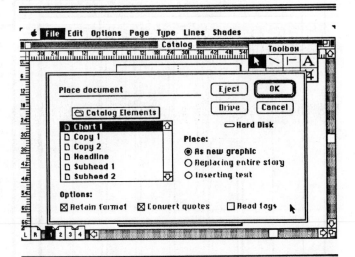

Figure 9-14. This is a PageMaker document file that indicates use of file names that correspond with layout positions.

element. Except for color photographs, the text and line art for all colors generally are positioned on a single set of pasteup boards. Color photographs are *separated* in a different opera-

tion to create platemaking film in each of the colors to be reproduced. **Figure 9-15** is a photo of a color separation scanning machine that creates separated film from color photos.

Color elements in type and line art are identified in three general ways:

- Overlays
- Color-marked tissues
- Computer separation.

Overlays. One requirement occurs when a portion of a drawing is to be run in a second color. Another use of color occurs if a black-and-white photo is to be overprinted in a second color. For example, in using an old, or historic photo, a light-brown tint might be used to give the effect of aging. Either of these color treatments can be handled with an *overlay.* As overlay is, as its name indicates, an art element that is laid over

the basic mechanical. When color ink is to be applied over black, the color area is indicated on an overlay.

 DESKTOP JARGON

separate For color reproduction, the preparation of separate lithographic film and plates for each color to be printed.

overlay An art element that is laid over the basic mechanical, usually to indicate the position of a color element.

An overlay is prepared with either of two materials: *amberlith* or *rubylith.* Both are acetate sheets with a thin, removable layer of amber-colored or deep red film that can be peeled off the carrier sheet. The artist fastens a section of amberlith or rubylith over the pasteup board. This is done by taping one edge of the acetate to a part of the board outside the image area. Then, with a sharp, pointed knife, an outline of the image area to be printed in color is traced on the face of the overlay material. The unneeded colored film is pulled away. This leaves a pattern of color film covering the area to be printed in color. The camera operator then uses the overlay as a basis for creating separate film for the black and color plates. **Figure 9-16** shows how an overlay is cut.

Figure 9-16. Overlays are cut on amberlith or rubylith film with sharp knives. Then, the excess color material is removed. Photo by Benedict Kruse.

Color-marked tissues. When elements of type or line art are to be run in color, a different identification technique is used. A sheet of tissue, or onion-skin paper, is attached to the pasteup board. The translucent tissue covers the entire image area of the board. The type and line art can be read through the tissue. Any instructions written on the tissue can be related readily to the underlying mechanical. Marking pens are used to identify the elements of the type or drawings that are to be run in color, as shown in **Figure 9-17.** These tissues serve as guidelines for the strippers who assemble the platemaking film.

Computer separation. PageMaker 3.0 gives a user a chance to separate colors for type and art elements electronically. Two methods are available. Under one, color can be specified on a style sheet. Remember that, in both Word 3.0 and PageMaker 3.0, typefaces and sizes are specified in dialog boxes. To illustrate, suppose an artist has specified a style for "A Head." This will be a heading used throughout a publication. Using

Figure 9-17. One way to identify color elements is to place a tissue over a pasteup board and mark the elements that are to run in color. Photo by Benedict Kruse.

the Type option on the main menu, the artist selects the Define Styles option. This choice displays a dialog box with a menu that lists all of the style sheets that have been established under Word or PageMaker.

On the Define Styles dialog box, the user selects the A Head style sheet for editing. This selection is shown in the background dialog box in **Figure 9-18.** Then, the user selects an option that indicates the A Head style sheet is to be edited. When this option is selected, an Edit Styles dialog box is presented. This also is shown in **Figure 9-18.** The Edit Style dialog box provides an option that enables the user to specify that color is to be used. With this entry, the system presents another dialog box, like the one in **Figure 9-19.** This provides options that enable the user to identify colors. Also, the

percentage of saturation for each color can be indicated.

As another option, the user can select one block of type or art element to be run in color. Then the Options menu is called and the Define Colors option is selected. On the dialog box that is presented, the user selects the color to be used. If the user simply wants to use solid printing in a standard color, this operation completes the color selection process. However, if the user wants to use a percentage of color or to specify a special color value, the Edit Color option is selected. This causes the system to display an Edit Color dialog box. This provides choices for available colors and densities. The set of

 DESKTOP JARGON

amberlith or **rubylith** Acetate sheets with removable layers of colored film; used for overlays to indicate positions of color elements.

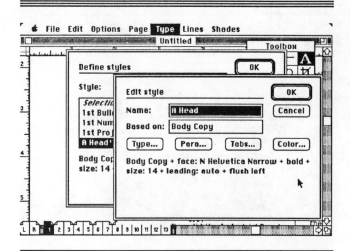

Figure 9-18. The Define Styles dialog box is used to access the Edit Styles box. The user then indicates that the A Head elements are to run in color.

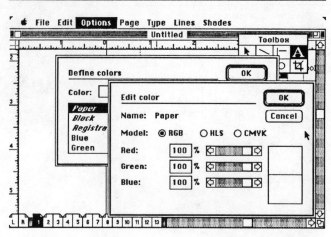

Figure 9-20. To specify color for a single, selected element, the user works with the Define Color and Edit Color dialog boxes.

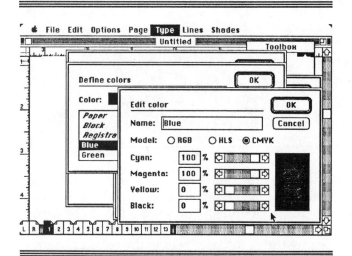

Figure 9-19. The Define Color and Edit Color dialog boxes are used to enter specifications for separated color elements.

Options boxes used for this selection method are shown in **Figure 9-20.**

Under PageMaker, a separate output page is generated for each specified color. Each of the color pages contains *registration marks* and a code identifying the color. A registration mark is a symbol used to match the impressions of multiple colors. Registration marks are used to produce film and plates for printing.

Although the content of this chapter focuses specifically on market-support publications, many of the concepts and techniques apply equally to the preparation of newsletters. Newsletters represent an important and growing area of publishing activity for desktop techniques. Creation of newsletters on desktop computers is covered in the chapter that follows.

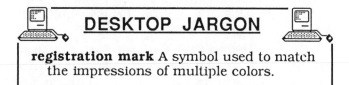

DESKTOP JARGON

registration mark A symbol used to match the impressions of multiple colors.

THE MAKEUP DESK

1. Find a catalog of your own or use one of the catalogs reproduced in this chapter as a model. Based on the catalog's layout, draw a design grid that represents a typical page layout.

2. Develop a plan for preparation of a facilities brochure about your school. There should be one page or spread about the school itself. Then, each major department should be covered on a separate page. For your design, indicate a reasonable amount of copy for each page. Also identify the subjects and positions of the illustrations you want to use.

THE COMPOSING ROOM

1. Capture the text from any single page of any catalog you have available. Develop a grid for the catalog. Indicate photo positions with key lines. Place the copy blocks you capture in positions that support the illustrations. The idea of this assignment is to change typefaces and layouts for the catalog.

10 *Newsletters*

Editorial Budget

❏ **A newsletter** is a periodical that is issued on regular schedules to an established group of readers.

❏ **Classifications for newsletters** are established by the types of readers served. Groupings include profit making, nonprofit, and sponsored newsletters.

❏ **Newletter formats** can use one-, two-, or three-column layouts.

❏ **Design elements** for newsletters include a logo that presents its name. Another element is the masthead, which identifies the publisher, mailing address, telephone number, and gives subscription information.

❏ **A mailing indicia** is necessary for newsletters that are delivered by mail. This area includes a postal permit number, the name and address of the publisher, and a space for a mailing label.

❏ **Special production concerns** include responsibilities for meeting deadlines for text capture and page makeup.

❏ **Careful copy checking** is recommended because a newsletter requires handling of many different copy elements. Copy checking is a quality control measure that assures completeness and correct sequence for text.

❏ **Binding and distribution** operations affect the ability of a publisher to deliver newsletters on schedule. Therefore, the production manager should work closely with the people who handle these operations.

THE NEWSLETTER MEDIUM

A *newsletter* is an information medium that generally is intended to serve an audience that shares special, common interests. The interests that attract and hold audiences can vary widely. Readers can share job or career interests. They can share hobbies or even political beliefs.

To establish appeal for its readers, each newsletter should be unique. Differences among newsletters can lie in their information content, design, layout, and methods of distribution. However, some general characteristics apply to the majority of newsletters:

- Newsletters are periodicals. Each newsletter generally is issued at specific, regular intervals (such as monthly, bi-monthly, or quarterly).

- Each newsletter is distributed to a regular, established group of readers. Publication management responsibilities thus include distribution and distribution-list maintenance. These responsibilities are added to the basic jobs of design and production.

- The most typical *trim size* for newsletters is 8.5 by 11 inches. Trim size gives the dimensions of a page. Different trim sizes are possible. But larger or smaller trim sizes often serve to classify publications as newspapers or magazines.

- The *folio count,* or number of pages, generally is small. In general, newsletters contain between two and 16 pages.

- A newsletter typically is laid out to be read from beginning to end, in sequence. Information content begins on the first page. This is a difference from magazines that often use art on their covers. On newsletter pages, the important stories generally begin at the left of the page. Additional copy is sequenced from the left of the page to the right. This is a difference from newspapers, in which the most important story runs at the top right of the front page.

- Newsletters need not use photos or line illustrations. They can consist of copy only. By contrast, photos or other illustrations generally are considered necessary for newspapers and magazines (covered in chapters that follow).

These features add up to an important conclusion: Newsletters are designed for serious reading by audiences who need or want the information they contain. Newsletters are prepared under regular schedules. Their emphasis is on information content. **Figure 10-1** shows several newsletters.

TYPES OF NEWSLETTERS

The discussion above establishes that newsletters are audience-oriented. Therefore, the type of audience served tends to shape the publication. Audiences also tend to affect the methods that should be used for development and production. Audiences vary widely; however, there are some broad categories of newsletters:

- Profit making
- Nonprofit
- Sponsored.

Profit-Making Newsletters

A profit-making newsletter is a business venture. That is, the publication is intended to generate a profit. To have a profit, in turn, income must be greater than operating expenses. The needed income can stem from two sources:

- Sale of subscriptions
- Advertising revenues.

Both of these income sources represent topics that have not been covered previously in this book. The explantions that follow focus on the effects of these revenue sources on publication management.

DESKTOP JARGON

newsletter A periodical that delivers information to a specialized audience.

trim size Measurements for the size of a publication page.

folio count The number of pages included in a publication.

Subscription sales. In the periodical field, the term *paid subscription* has some special meanings. A subscription is a fee paid by a reader in exchange for receipt of a periodical. Paid subscriptions set their publications apart from *free circulation* periodicals that are given away.

Publications that do not charge for subscriptions are sometimes classified as having a *controlled circulation.* This means copies are given away. But information is gathered that helps to identify the reading audience. This

Figure 10-1. Desktop publishing can be an effective method for developing and producing newsletters.
Courtesy of Apple Computer, Inc.

information is presented to advertisers to help attract their business. Often copies are given away only to specific, qualified readers.

Most newspapers and magazines do not realize enough income from subscriptions to support them. Many sell subscriptions largely because it gives them an image of "quality" readership.

Profit-making newsletters are different from newspapers and magazines in this respect. Many newsletters rely on subscription revenues as their main or only income. When a profit-making newsletter relies on subscription income, charges often are high. Profit-making newsletters often have subscription charges that range from $35 to $200 per year, sometimes more. Most of these publications serve audiences that require the information to perform their jobs. Examples can include technical information newsletters for engineers or computer scientists. There also may be legal newsletters for attorneys and market-information newsletters for sales executives.

When a newsletter relies on subscription sales, editors and publishers face a special challenge: The content of the newsletter must be timely and important enough to justify continued payment of subscription fees.

Advertising sales. Income from the sale of advertising space can be a main source of support for any publication. This certainly is true for most newspapers or magazines. Television and radio broadcasting are supported by income from commercials.

Some newsletters sell space for advertising messages. Sales are based on the factors of circulation numbers and quality. In general, the greater the circulation of a publication, the more its space will be worth to advertisers. Quality of audience also can be a factor. In some situations, comparatively few readers may make up the majority of a market for an advertiser. If so, a newsletter that reaches these people becomes a valuable communication medium. Advertising space may be worth premium rates.

From a production and publication standpoint, advertising commitments translate to a need to allocate space for the paid messages. Generally, advertising space is sold in modules that start with a full page. Other modules generally include half-page, quarter-page, and sometimes one-sixth page sizes. In some instances, advertisers buy specific positions in a publication, such as the back cover, page two, etc.

For a makeup editor, advertising placement can be something like a jigsaw puzzle. Generally, advertisements are positioned before editorial copy is placed in the remaining space. The point: If you work on a newsletter that accepts advertising, recognize that the ads are paying your salary. Treat them with respect; give the advertisers the value they are paying for.

At the same time, remember that it is the readers who give any publication its value. Don't make the mistake of shortchanging readers because short-term advertising revenues are available. If your readers become dissatisfied, there will be nothing to sell to future advertisers. **Figure 10-2** reproduces a newsletter page that contains both advertising and news copy.

Nonprofit Newsletters

A nonprofit newsletter faces some of the same requirements as profit-making publications. The term *nonprofit* means what it says: The publication does not produce a profit for its owners. However, every publication has production expenses. There must be a source of income to pay for production and to cover salaries. The major difference is that a nonprofit publication does not seek to have any money left for profits.

Readers of nonprofit newsletters often share membership in an organization or group. For example, many churches and other religious organizations publish newsletters for their members and/or supporters. Political parties

 DESKTOP JARGON

paid subscription A confirmed order from a reader who pays to receive a publication.

free circulation Description of a periodical that is given away.

controlled circulation Description of a publication that does not charge for subscriptions but does check on the interests of its readers.

nonprofit A type of organization that serves a special function and does not develop income that exceeds expenses.

(SERVICE cont'd)

with zest and inspected firsthand the resources and talents of book manufacturers nationwide, and perhaps even worldwide. In relation to the client the publication service should also act in a spirit of service and responsibility that welcomes the challenge of handling all details and resolving all problems as soon as they arise.

Having found such a service, the publisher should then ascertain that it is at least well-equipped for cost-effective editing and typesetting. Start by scoping the service's computer configurations and proficiencies. Today's services layout publications at a fraction of the cost and time in previous years due almost totally to advanced computer technology. It is well-known among typesetters that typing time accounts for as much as 53% of typesetting costs. Therefore the publisher will only save considerably if typing during editing and typesetting can be avoided — that is, if the service in question can make use of a word processing file prepared on the publisher's own personal computer.

The service should be equally comfortable accepting the file via diskette or modem. Alternatively, the service should be able to scan your manuscript pages with an OCR (optical character recognition) scanner.

Once the service has your file, it should be adept at file conversion — the ability to take the file and translate it cleanly into the software format in which the book will be set, such as Pagemaker or Ventura Publisher. To confirm the service's capabilities in this area, look for both an IBM PC and an Apple MacIntosh wedded via communications and file translation software or a local area network. Remember that less formal means of file format conversion, relying on the 8-bit American Standard Code for Information Interchange (ASCII), may require more "clean-up" and operator time.

The existence and efficient operation of appropriate computer technology is more critical than ever to savings in time and money, quick turnaround, accurate transcription, and document control (your ability to make last-minute and, if necessary, global changes, quickly and inexpensively).

The next thing to look for is that the publication service shows a willingness and ability to creatively cut print costs

(Cont'd from page 6)

BBW/South Invites Job Listings

As a service to its members and the local publishing community, Bookbuilders West/South has initiated a Job Bank to list openings for positions in publishing companies or their suppliers.

All relevant job listings are welcome. You need not be a member to post positions or to receive the current listings. If you have a need for an experienced publishing professional, and would like to reach a highly-targeted market, simply send a job description, salary range, and relevant company information to:

Joe Hollander
4046 Stoneybrook Drive
Sherman Oaks, CA 91403

Requests for current listings can be mailed to the same address.

If you are not a member of Bookbuilders West/South and would like more information on this fine publisher's association, contact Helen Hawekotte at Unisource, 213-725-3700.

4

and elected officials often issue newsletters for supporters and/or voters. Professional organizations publish newsletters as a service to members, often in partial exchange for dues paid by the members.

Nonprofit newsletters generally have lists of readers and must have mailing or distribution procedures. Some nonprofit newsletters may have paid subscriptions. Others may be sponsored by organizations or may operate with voluntary contributions. In any case, there must be a source of income to cover operating costs. Therefore, publishers of nonprofit newsletters also have financial responsibilities.

The common denominator factor for appeal to an audience of members is service. People belong to organizations or vote for candidates because of shared beliefs or commitments. A newsletter that serves an audience of members or supporters should concentrate on the common interests of its readers. The interests that attract members to an organization must guide the editorial policies of its newsletter. Headlines and story content should stress this focus.

Sponsored Newsletters

A sponsored newsletter also may be classified as a *house organ.* This term implies that a sponsor, the "house," is the publisher. In some ways, a sponsored newsletter is similar to a nonprofit newsletter issued to members of an organization. The difference is that readers do not have to pay, contribute, or join an organization, except possibly as employees.

Sponsored newsletters fall into two broad categories: internal and external.

Internal. Internal newsletters generally go to employees or others associated closely with an organization. For employees, the newsletter provides a medium for sharing information about the company and about fellow workers. Other internal newsletters may go to dealers or distributors who handle the company's products. The purpose of dealer/distributor newsletters is to provide product and marketing information.

For both employee and dealer newsletters, an important element of editorial content generally is recognition of outstanding performance. Employees who turn in exceptional performances or dealers who achieve high levels of sales and/or service can be praised. A good feeling of achievement can come with recognition for work that is done well. Internal publications also provide vehicles for management information. The newsletter may be a source of information on a company's operations, policies, and plans.

External. External newsletters generally are aimed at customers. Their purpose is to provide information about products and/or benefits to prospective buyers. In this sense, an external newsletter or house organ can be regarded as an advertising medium. In fact, many external newsletters are funded through the advertising budgets of the companies that issue them.

Because they are designed to appeal to prospective customers, external newsletters often are "slick" publications. Comparatively large budgets may be available for such items as color printing, photographic layouts, and line illustrations.

DESIGN AND LAYOUT CONSIDERATIONS

Many elements associated with the design and layout of newsletters are the same as those covered earlier for other types of publications. To illustrate, the selection of typefaces for body copy and headlines is similar for all publications. The same is true for the preparation of line art or the positioning of photos in a layout.

Therefore, as is true throughout this book, only new concerns or techniques are covered in the next discussions. A special consideration is that the *letter size* format is used most widely. A

Figure 10-2. Many newsletters sell advertising space.

 DESKTOP JARGON

house organ A publication that promotes the internal or market interests of the organization that acts as publisher.

letter size A page format that measures 8.5 by 11 inches.

letter-size page measures 8.5 by 11 inches. The discussions that follow apply to letter-size publications.

Column Formats

The most typical layout patterns for newsletters use one-, two-, or three-column formats.

Single-column layouts. Single-column layouts resemble the formats for reports, covered in earlier chapters.

The major difference is that some one-column newsletters choose this format to achieve a "newsy" look. This is done, in some cases, by setting type in typewriter-like fonts and rag right (unjustified) lines. This approach tries to give the effect that the news items are late, or "hot."

A single-column format is easiest to produce. This kind of layout also encourages readers to scan through the entire publication, from beginning to end. A page from a single-column newsletter is reproduced in **Figure 10-3.**

Two-column layouts. A two-column format divides the page into equal columns. Usually, each column is 19 or 20 picas wide. The columns typically are separated by a two-pica center strip. An advantage is that two-column formats create a natural left-right balance on each page. Two-column formats also encourage readers to scan through the entire content of a publication in sequence.

The two-column approach also provides for flexibility in presenting fairly large photos or illustrations. Generally, a one-column photo or drawing presented in a three-inch-wide column will be large enough for clarity.

If a publisher sells advertising, the two-column format divides the page neatly into half-page and quarter-page modules. A newsletter with a two-column format is shown in **Figure 10-4.**

Three-column layouts. Three-column layouts apply techniques similar to those used for magazines and newspapers. That is, narrow columns are used to position stories that are relatively short. Stories are topped with bold headlines. The chapters that follow on magazines and newspapers contain more information on multicolumn layouts. Within this chapter, the idea is to indicate that three-column (and sometimes four-column) layouts are an available option.

Regardless of where they are positioned within a publication, narrow columns can lead to typesetting problems. On narrow columns, hyphenation and justification are more difficult than for wider columns.

If automatic hyphenation is used, the system is apt to run into either of two difficulties—or both. First, there may be too many hyphens—so many that the copy becomes difficult to read.

The second potential problem is that there will be large gaps between letters and words. If you feel justified margins are essential, be prepared for considerable manual review and adjustment for the placement of hyphens. Many editors and designers avoid these problems by opting for rag right margins on narrow columns.

This treatment has become commonplace for both newsletters and magazines, though newspapers have continued to justify all columns. If you opt to use four-column layouts, consider that rag right columns are a necessity. Examples of three-column newsletters are shown in **Figures 10-5, 10-6,** and **10-7.**

Often, newsletter editors use a mix of layouts. Three-column formats are used for news content while wider columns are set up for longer articles. For example, a newsletter might use a three-column layout on a front page that is devoted to news stories. Three-column formats also may be used on selected inside pages. The same publication may use two-column formats on inside pages for technical papers or long articles.

The principle: Select and mix information content to serve the best interests of readers. Then, select or mix formats so that the content is presented most attractively.

Figure 10-3. This illustration shows a newsletter page with a one-column format. The wide line can be difficult to read.

THE BEST WAY TO USE THE $1,000,000 GENERATION-SKIPPING TAX EXEMPTIONS

As stated in the first page letter, Congress in the Tax Reform Act of 1986 assessed a flat rate of 55% on all generation-skipping transfers, but gave each grantor a $1,000,000 exemption. This exemption means that if you create a trust of $1,000,000 or less which pays income to your child for his lifetime, with the remainder passing to his children on his death, you can avoid the generation-skipping tax that would otherwise be assessed at the time of your child's death.

Your spouse is also given a $1,000,000 exemption from the generation-skipping transfer tax, hereinafter referred to as the GSTT. While it may be relatively simple for you to elect to allocate all or part of **your** exemption, it may be very difficult to do so for your wife's exemption. We shall try to point out the problems and outline the most effective way or ways to use her $1,000,000 GSTT exemption. In our illustration, we shall discuss only the case of a married couple with their own children.

There are variations depending on the value of the trust assets and the number, ages and wealth of the children. We shall assume that the combined assets of both spouses total $4,000,000 and that neither spouse has used up the $600,000 estate tax credit shelter.

I. The husband creates a $600,000 credit shelter trust. As you will observe later on, the part of the wife's marital trust that does not qualify for the GSTT exemption could be added to this trust and thus avoid two sets of trustee's fees.

II. The rest of the estate is divided into two marital trusts. The first marital trust would be a QTIP trust in which the decedent elects, or authorizes his executor to elect, to use the $1,000,000 generation-skipping exemption for transfers from the trust. The first trust is hereinafter referred to as the "exempt trust." The second marital trust would be a QTIP trust which would hold the residue of the decedent's estate. The second trust is hereinafter referred to as the "non-exempt trust." The provisions of the marital trusts also would permit the decedent to direct or authorize his executor to allocate to the **exempt trust** assets that are likely to appreciate in value over the years. A good example would be the common stock of a closely held business. (Any preferred stock could be allocated to the residuary non-exempt trust.)

A. **During your wife's lifetime,** the trust provisions of the **exempt trust** would be substantially as follows:

1. The trustee pays all the income to her for her lifetime.

2. The trustee would distribute corpus to her for her support, comfort, medical care and best interests, but only if there are insufficient liquid assets in the non-exempt trust. The objective is to retain as many assets as feasible in the exempt trust.

B. **Upon your wife's death,** the exempt trust estate would be divided into separate trust estates for your children or the issue of deceased children. The income and corpus of each trust estate would be distributed, in the corporate trustee's sole discretion, to the child's lawful issue from time to time living, until the expiration of the period prescribed by the Rule against Perpetuities in your state of domicile. The Tax Reform Act of 1986, in granting the $1,000,000 exemption, provided that the GSTT shall not apply to any future generation-skipping transfers. This provision means that in Illinois and the many other states that follow the common law Rule against Perpetuities, the generation-skipping tax will not apply to the exempt trust during a period ending 21 years after the death of all of your descendants and all the descendants of any other designated persons who were **living at the time of your death.** The exempt period could last 90 years! It is not necessary that the designated lives be related to you.

III. The remaining assets in the decedent's estate, after creating the $600,000 credit shelter trust and the $1,000,000 exempt marital deduction trust, are placed into the so-called "non-exempt" trust.

A. **During your wife's lifetime,** the trust provisions of the **non-exempt trust** would be substantially as follows:

1. The trustee pays all the income to her for lifetime.

2. Liberal distributions of corpus would be made to her.

3. She would have the right to draw down each year the greater of $5,000 or 5% of the value of the trust estate.

B. **Upon your wife's death,** part of the non-exempt trust estate would be added to your credit shelter trust, and part of it would be added to the exempt trust. Assuming she allocates $600,000 to your credit shelter trust and $800,000 to your exempt trust, the breakdown of the final trust estate figures would be as follows:

More Moselle

continued from page 1
Verne called because he can't find a publisher to take his wife's novel. "Worked on it 15 hours a day for weeks. Couldn't stop writing. Now it's done. It's really good," Verne insists. "Real mainstream stuff. Reads like Ayn Rand, only better."

How many times have you heard a similar story? Author writes a book without the slightest idea of who's going to publish it — and then is disappointed when no one will.

Many PMA members got started that way. We self-publish because no publisher will take the chance. And sometimes it's better that way — for us, not the publishers and agents who turned us down. My company, Craftsman, self-published our first book because no publisher would. We've sold about two million books since then.

Here's Another Example
Conari Press of Berkeley, California was started in 1979 by wife Mary Jane Ryan and husband Will Glennon. Will's a lawyer. Mary Jane knows the magazine business. Conari's total product between 1979

and 1985 was three editions of the same restaurant guide. The company was never much more than a hobby. By 1986 it was in mothballs.

Will Glennon and Mary Jane Ryan

That changed in the spring of last year. Mary Jane's a good friend of Santa Barbara therapist Daphne Rose Kingma. Daphne was writing a book on ending relationships. Mary Jane was the editor and assumed a major publisher would snap it up. In 1985 Daphne

Figure 10-4. This newsletter page is set up with a two-column format.

Griffin's
Signature
A NEWSLETTER FOR THE PUBLISHING INDUSTRY

Taxation Without Interpretation

or Writers' Write-offs

by
Eva Rosenberg
E.A., M.B.A.

If you are confused and bewildered about the mysterious changes in our tax laws, you are in good company. Isaac Asimov, who freely admits to being as intelligent as his accountant, claims that "...my understanding of what is in all those papers I sign has steadily decreased...I don't know what's going on." He complains that "If I spent enough time on taxes to gain an understanding of the subject, my writing output and my income would drop considerably, and frankly, I can't afford it."

For a man with who prefers to leave such matters to his accountant, in the June 1988 issue of Isaac Asimov's Science Fiction Magazine (IASFM) he certainly presented a very astute discussion of an aspect of the new tax laws affecting writers — capitalizing writing and research expenses.

Throughout our lives as writers, we have been able to justify all our expenses on researching our orphan books and articles by telling ourselves, "At least we can write it all off of our taxes." So much of our work is done on speculation, hoping we'll find a publisher or an editor to buy it, or *at least* print it, so we can get EXPOSURE, so someone else will see it and realize that we are gifted, brilliant and the hope of civilization and actually PAY us for our work.

Even then, it takes at least five years before a writer can actually live on the proceeds of creativity alone...and only if that writer is also gifted at marketing the outlines, books, articles, scripts or whatever. Otherwise, it could take decades to become an overnight success.

So what did the Tax Reform Act of 1986 (TRA 86) do to us?

The Internal Revenue Service interpreted the law, effective on our 1987 tax returns, to require us to expense all the costs of our creative efforts only by using the following formula:

A) This year's income
B) The total income you expect to receive, ever, for this work.

This applied to things like books, articles, films. plays, sound recordings, videotapes, photographs, music, dance, graphics and other works of art (except jewelry).

Think about this. Some books gather dust in publishers' offices and library shelves for decades before someone discovers how wonderful and entertaining they are and suddenly they become classics. Who ever thought, when it was written, especially after the initial

(Cont'd page 2)

INSIDE THIS ISSUE

| CHOOSING A PUBLICATION SERVICE | PROFITABLE PRICING & DISCOUNTS | PUBLISHERS' CHRONICLE OF EVENTS | SPOTLIGHT: NEW RIDERS' HARBERT RICE |

VOLUME 3, NO. 5   JULY/AUGUST 1988

Figure 10-5. This newsletter page uses a three-column layout.

Goodwill Tidings

VOL. 47, NO. 8/9   **AUG/SEP. 1988**

Goodwill's Del Taco Training Facility; not the same place, not the same thing

Opening a taco stand in Los Angeles is usually not a major media event. It becomes that, however, when the restaurant is actually a training program for disabled workers.

KABC news interviews Mary Concha.

The grand opening of Goodwill's Del Taco drew the attention of government officials, media and the general public. Representatives from all levels of the State Department of Rehabilitation, including Dr. P. Cecie Fontanoza, head of the Department, were on hand to congratulate the first class of trainees and sample the fare. The trainees graciously interrupted their duties to respond to the questions of reporters from network affiliates KABC and KCBS, the Los Angeles Times and the wire services. The following Monday, trainees appeared on the local talk show, "Mid-Morning L.A."

The reason for all the excitement? When Goodwill Industries of Southern California opened its Del Taco, it became the first vocational rehabilitation agency in the country to own and operate a franchise open to the public where disabled workers are trained for jobs in the fast food industry.

Del Taco trainees are accepted after demonstrating their aptitude in our cafeteria. At the Del Taco they hone their skills in an actual fast food restaurant.

"We joined with Del Taco because of its varied menu of both Mexican and American food items. The program will provide 50 trained workers per year who are able to work in a variety of fast food outlets," said GISC President Nicholas Panza.

Each 10 weeks, eight people enter the program. Working with a Job Coach they learn several job stations, receiving a raise for each they master. After learning at least four stations, Goodwill's placement staff begins the process of finding them other jobs.

The Del Taco is next to our "Arcade" store, 235 S. Broadway, in downtown L.A.

Cheri Cook dispenses soft drink order.

Ventura job testing center holds open house

On August 11, Ventura held an open house to promote our vocational testing program. Working with local agencies it matches the right person with the right job.

At the open house special tools used to match people and jobs were on display. These tools test strength, physical limits, skills and talents. To rate actual job performance a person will often work at the plant for a few days.

Using the "wobble board" to test dexterity.

Data from the tests goes into a computer. In turn, the computer lists 150 jobs the person is suited for.

"Once we have the list, we can get a person in to the right field," said Carol Morrow, vocational tester and counselor. "A person has more options when he knows what he can do. He can return to work, find another career or explore new jobs they never thought about before."

As a result of the open house, local rehabilitation agencies now know how Goodwill can find the right jobs for their clients.

Figure 10-6. Notice how photos are placed within the columns of this three-column newsletter layout.

GROWTH STOCK REVIEW

50 Broad St., New York, N.Y. 10004
(212) 558-6422 • 1-(800) 537-4494

Vol. 6 No. 8 September 1988

Breakthrough in heart monitoring technology could save your life

The San Diego Union

COMICS

Doctors Are Optimistic Cummings' Career Is Not Jeop

The numbers overwhelm the imagination. The country's number one killer —heart disease —affects 63,400,000 Americans, claims 550,000 lives annually and runs up a phenomenal $75 billion in medical bills each year.

Heart disease could be affecting you at this very moment. Fortunately, Hovik Medical Corporation (VSE symbol "HVK") has a revolutionary heart monitoring technology that could save your life.

The Hovik heart monitor saved Milwaukee Bucks basketball player Terry Cummings' life. Cummings, Rookie of the Year basketball player when he played for the San Diego Clippers, was

monitored during a game with Hovik equipment. Real time monitoring showed Cummings had a life threatening heartbeat in the 280-310 per minute range. Using this information, Cummings was treated with medication and now plays basketball better than ever.

The incident saved Cummings' life while giving the Hovik monitoring system high credibility in the medical field.

The Clippers chief physician, Dr. H. C. Palmer states: "Were it not for the Hovik monitor we, the medical staff of the San Diego Clippers, would not have been able to correctly diagnose Terry Cummings' potentially fatal dysrhythmia. Terry Cummings had received several types of ECG (electrocardiogram) tests, but they did not reveal any abnormalities. The Hovik telemetry device documented a serious ventricular arrhythmia in both the real time and recorded mode. The Hovik monitor is a definite breakthrough in ambulatory monitoring."

Figure 10-7. Note the treatment of the headline and illustrations in this layout which uses three columns rag right.

Logo and Masthead

As with most periodicals, the typical newsletter presents a logo on the front page. Identifying information also should be related to the logo. This information should include:

- Date of publication can be run as a specific day, month, or quarter.
- *Volume* refers to the number of years a publication has existed. During the first year, issues are marked Volume 1, during the second year, Volume 2, and so on.
- *Number* identifies the number of times a publication has been issued during the current year. A quarterly newsletter would go up to Number 4, a monthly to Number 12.

The *masthead* identifies the publication, the publisher, subscription information, the mailing address, and telephone number. A reproduction of the logo often is included in the masthead. Sometimes, the masthead contains a statement that describes the publication's target audience. The masthead can appear anywhere in the publication, though it generally does not run on the front page. For layout purposes, a masthead can be boxed and treated as an illustration. **Figure 10-8** shows a logo and masthead for a newsletter.

Mailing Indicia

Many newsletters are distributed through *bulk mailings.* Bulk mailing is a special postal service for volume customers. An organization that uses bulk mailings must get a special permit from the U.S. Postal Service. Then, a bulk mailing notice must be printed in specific positions.

In effect, the bulk mailing imprint replaces the use of stamps. The mailing organization gives the Postal Service an advance deposit to cover postage. Items that are bulk-mailed must be sorted in advance according to ZIP code number. This reduces the cost of handling the items and helps to earn a special, low rate for the mailer.

Similar services and savings are available to charitable and other nonprofit organizations. The mailing organization must have a permit from the Postal Service and must pre-sort items according to ZIP code number.

A final alternative involves the use of postage meters for mailings. The newsletters are processed through machines that imprint postage values.

To distribute newsletters under any of these plans, the publication must contain an *indicia.* This is an area of the newsletter, generally on the back page, that is set up specifically for mailing purposes. Any person who edits or produces a newsletter that is to be mailed should learn the requirements for its postal indicia.

The most typical position for an indicia is the bottom one-third of the back page or back cover. The bulk mailing notice must be printed in the upper right of this area. This imprint position corresponds with the position of a stamp on a letter. The name and address of the sender also must appear in the indicia area. Another requirement is a clear area for the name and address of the recipient. Address-imprinting techniques are described below. A typical indicia is shown in **Figure 10-9.**

The point: If you become involved in newsletter production, find out how your publication will be distributed. If it is to be mailed, plan for a mailing indicia. Then, for safety, take a proof or design of the indicia to the Post Office that will process the mailing. It is safest to have the postmaster approve the design and placement of the indicia in advance. The author has a standard, precautionary practice which is a good

---

Figure 10-8. This illustration shows the logo and masthead for a newsletter. Note the use of a two-column photo.

 DESKTOP JARGON

volume Value that identifies the number of years a publication has been issued.

number Identifier for the number of times a publication has been issued during the current year, or volume.

masthead The design element in a periodical that identifies the publication and its publisher.

bulk mailing A special postal service for volume customers.

indicia The area of a publication set aside for mailing information.

THE VALLEY EYE

SURGICAL-MEDICAL GROUP   **MAZZOCCO EYE INSTITUTE**   **SPRING 1988**

Technique Refined In One-Year Project

Improved Cataract Surgery Method Developed

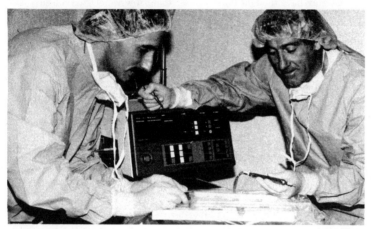

Thomas R. Mazzocco, M.D., right, and George M. Rajacich, M.D., evaluate CooperVision's latest ultrasonic cataract surgery unit. Valley Eye Center's physicians review new surgical instruments and other products for several companies.

A new cataract microsurgery procedure that appears to promote more rapid healing, faster return of improved vision and allows further protection of other segments of the eye is being used by surgeons at Valley Eye Center.

Thomas R. Mazzocco, M.D., and George M. Rajacich, M.D., have been performing the technique with patients in the Center's Out-Patient Surgery Center for about six months. They said post-operative results on most patients indicate that healing time and the period required to attain much better visual acuity have been reduced.

Dr. Rajacich worked for the past year to refine the advanced method, conducting the project within the Mazzocco Eye Institute's research program.

"Generally speaking, this surgery is advantageous to patients because it permits them to see better

(Continued on Page 2)

Our Objective

The Valley Eye Center's VALLEY EYE newsletter is published quarterly. Its objective is to provide public education about vision protection and improvement, and about rapidly-advancing technology in eye care. Each issue of THE VALLEY EYE will present information about Valley Eye Center, advances in vision care, and descriptions of common eye ailments. QUESTIONS ABOUT EYE PROBLEMS AND TREATMENT SHOULD BE DIRECTED TO YOUR PERSONAL EYE DOCTOR. Also, a staff member at Valley Eye Center will always be available to assist you. Comments are welcome to: Editor, VALLEY EYE, Valley Eye Center, 15225 Vanowen St., Van Nuys, CA 91405.

Available To Former Cataract Patients

Lens Implants Can Replace Thick Glasses, Contacts

A gentleman complained recently that it is hard for him to read for very long through his Coke-bottle-thick "cataract glasses," and his wife is finding it increasingly difficult to deal with her contact lenses.

Wearing heavy thick-lens glasses and sometimes awkward contact lenses can be a hassle, especially for senior citizens. Until the mid-1970s, however, these were the only "replacement lenses" available for cataract surgery patients.

In the majority of cataract procedures today, surgeons implant permanent intraocular lenses (IOLs), the major advancement in cataract surgery in recent years. Also, many patients whose cataracts were

removed before the lightweight IOLs were developed are now electing to undergo a secondary out-patient procedure for implantation of the permanent lenses. Most of the cost for the operation is covered by Medicare.

At Valley Eye Center, surgeons Thomas R. Mazzocco, M.D., and George M. Rajacich, M.D., have performed several hundred procedures in which patients had IOLs implanted after having cataracts removed years ago. In nearly all cases, vision is improved and patients have a more easy-going lifestyle.

The IOLs usually eliminate the need for thick "cataract glasses,"

(Continued on Page 2)

Man...Have You Guys Got It Made!

One of our customers who remembers the days 15 years ago when we started this company made that comment to me the other day. He remembers the "good old days" when he could call me on Sunday afternoon and know I'd be at work...when the work days were from 10 to 16 hours long and if it wasn't Christmas day, all the days were work days.

Well those days are over now but his comment caused me to spend the next morning, from about 4:30 to 6:00 am, wondering if he knew something I didn't. The conclusion I arrived at merely identified something that I've really known all along but never stopped to recognize.

That conclusion is that there is no business entity...or individual for that matter...that "has it made." There is no business so successful and secure that there isn't the chance of a big surprise just around the corner. Success is a thing of the past, not the future, because you can never be sure what's coming. About all you can predict is that things will change

and there will be surprises. Your own individual efforts can help make those changes positive ones but if you relax in those efforts, you can stumble.

The Super Bowl Champion rarely repeats, the American League has had 7 different champions in 7 years, Ford is now making more money than GM, Texas banks are going under, IBM is getting beaten by companies only 1/1000 their size. At one time, all these organizations may have thought they "had it made"...but they were wrong. The past isn't necessarily prologue.

I think my point is that no business can afford to relax and enjoy their "success" because that very moment there are competitors out there looking for ways to beat you. You can never stop running. If you look back, someone's going to pass you.

Fortunately, the struggle to get an organization moving forward and performing a bit better all the time is fun and that's probably the major reward in starting or running a business. There can be great per-

sonal satisfaction in witnessing results of your company's efforts.

The challenge of competing and contributing each day and seeing others around you do the same is likely the best reward you're going to have because there is no judgment day when someone says, "Congratulations! You won and you're going to live happily forever after."

Success has to be an hour by hour, day by day achievement for tomorrow is not guaranteed.

A few months ago our treasurer came into my office and told me we'd had our first $1,000,000.00 sales month and it came with a profit percentage in double digits. For a brief moment I was tempted to celebrate but then I reminded myself that that achievement was already past history. Today's challenge is this month, not last month, and I have no idea how this month will turn out. Fortunately I enjoy the effort and challenge of making the next hour, day and month as successful as is possible and to that extent maybe I've got it made.

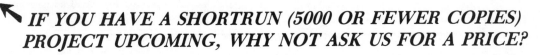

IF YOU HAVE A SHORTRUN (5000 OR FEWER COPIES) PROJECT UPCOMING, WHY NOT ASK US FOR A PRICE?

ADDRESS CORRECTION REQUESTED

> BULK RATE
> U.S. POSTAGE
> P A I D
> Permit No. 87
> Ann Arbor, Mi

Printer's Ink
Thomson - Shore, Inc.

7300 W. Joy Rd., P.O. Box 305

DEXTER, MI   48130-0305

(313) 426-3939

idea to follow: Get the Post Office official to sign and date a copy of a proof or layout to verify the approval.

PRODUCTION CONCERNS

In addition to the guidelines and suggestions about publication production provided in earlier chapters, the following areas are of special concern in connection with newsletters:

- Text capture and page makeup
- Copy checking
- Binding
- Distribution
- Scheduling.

Text Capture and Page Makeup

For newsletters and other publications covered in the remainder of this book, copy fitting and layout may require special attention. The methods that should be used can be somewhat different than for publications covered earlier.

Differences lie in the greater flexibility that can be available. Consider: In the production of reports, proposals, or bids, copy fitting is not critical. The number of pages in a document doesn't matter much because the number of copies to be produced is small. In catalogs and other market-support literature, content is controlled pretty much by marketing personnel.

In producing newsletters, however, the editor has considerably more flexibility and control. The number of pages usually is established in advance. Typically, the copy received will be more than enough to fill available space. This leaves the editor deciding what is to be left out. It can be hard to allocate space for stories. One potential problem: Your most important copy may be received at the last minute, just prior to publication.

In these situations, it generally is a good idea to establish priorities for copy as stories are received. The classification system mentioned earlier rates stories as MUST, IF POSSIBLE, and FILLER. This is one workable technique.

If you use this system, it is a good practice to capture and format the text for all MUST and IF POSSIBLE stories as they are received. Keep count of the column inches required for these stories as they are set. Compare your totals with available space. Your running totals can serve as a guide to indicate whether additional stories will be needed or whether you should set some filler items.

Setting type as copy is received can be a big advantage. The earlier your stories are in type, the more time you will have to apply quality control measures—proofreading and correction. If deadlines are tight, it may seem tempting to shortcut or short change the proofreading step.

Try to avoid this! Keep in mind that your readers are your final judges. If they see mistakes, they will not know or be interested in learning that you took shortcuts to save time. They will be aware only of the fact that their publication arrived with errors.

If you are using a three-column, news-oriented format, it may be impossible to write your headlines until you establish the position for a story. Headline writing may have to be integrated with page makeup. If you are setting up type under a word processing program before going to page making, you can write headlines on-line. Check your headlines and make sure they fit your column spaces before you go to page making. Remember that it works best to set up a separate file for each piece of copy and/or illustration.

As you lay out pages, be aware, first, that you have to adjust the copy to fit available space. Next, be aware of the "tricks of the trade" that are available to help you fit copy onto your pages:

- You can adjust the size of the illustrations you use.
- You can add or remove leading between paragraphs.
- You can reset headlines in smaller sizes or fewer lines.
- As a last resort, you may be able to cut sentences or paragraphs out of the copy itself.

Remember: There is no such thing as a headline that can't be written to fit any designated space. Also, there is no such thing as impossible. There are difficulties. But they only add challenges and interest to the job.

Figure 10-9. The indicia appears on the back page of this newsletter. Note the use of the logo.

Copy Checking

If your publication uses multiple stories from different contributors, you should plan for special quality-control measures. The idea: You want to be sure of the completeness of stories. Also, you want to be sure that copy elements are run in the proper sequence. These quality steps should be part of a **copy checking** operation.

In newsletters, stories often are handled individually, sometimes by different people. They are assembled from files by an operator who may not have seen any of the copy before. Therefore, copy checking makes sure that the stories you run have all of the copy received, in the right sequence.

The first copy checking operation should be included in the proofreading step. Compare the original manuscript and the galley proofs. Do this paragraph by paragraph. The idea is to make sure that all the copy got into type. If text was keyed from manuscript, it is possible for an operator to have dropped one or more lines during input. Entire paragraphs and pages also can be dropped. It can pay real dividends to take a few moments to be sure all of the text was captured. Then proofread thoroughly. As you do, glance back and forth between the galleys and the manuscript to be sure of accuracy.

After galleys have been corrected, recheck the type to be sure that corrections have been made accurately. Remember that, proportionately, more errors are made in the correction process than anywhere else in publishing.

When pages are made up and proofed, check the pages against the galleys. You do this to make sure all copy has been picked up—in proper sequence. Simply place the corrected galleys alongside the finished pages and scan back and forth, line by line. Check any differences. Page-making software sometimes rearranges type. Be sure any differences on the pages present copy that is complete and correct.

Binding

The binding operation includes all the steps necessary to fold large sheets, trim finished items to size, and join pages if necessary.

Folding is done on special machines that handle large sheets of paper and fold them into signatures or complete publications. If printing is done from a continuous roll of paper, or web,

folding and formation of signatures may be done on the press.

The point: In most cases, publications are printed on paper that is large enough to hold multiple pages. As part of the stripping process, it is necessary to **imposition** the pages. Impositioning is the placement of pages and illustrations for platemaking and printing. Elements must be positioned so that pages come out in proper sequence on printed signatures.

There must be a way to join pages of a publication at the fold or spine. For large-circulation publications printed on web equipment, it may be possible to glue the pages of a signature at the spine. If the pages are not joined on the press, some method of stitching often is necessary. Stitching is the process for joining signatures to hold pages together. This can be done through glueing, sewing, or stapling. For newsletters, magazines, and similar publications, the most widely used method is to drive staples into the **saddle.** The saddle is the back end, or spine, where the pages are folded. This is known as saddle stitching. **Figure 10-10** shows a commercial binding operation. **Figure 10-11** is a drawing that illustrates saddle stitching.

In many instances, a newsletter will require trimming after it has been folded and stitched. Trimming simply cuts the paper to provide even edges on the three sides of the publication, other than the saddle. As described above, presses with glueing attachments usually have trimmers as well. However, if folding and stitching are done separately, trimming is necessary.

One reason for trimming is that the sheet on which printing is done generally is larger than the trim size of the signature being printed.

Another, more important, reason is that the folding process leads to uneven edges, even if the sheets are all the same size. This is because the thickness of the saddle offsets the edges of the paper. Suppose, for example, that eight sheets are folded to create a 16-page newsletter. The outside pages will be shorter than the inside pages by the thickness of the seven sheets between the inside and outside. Trimming evens the edges and improves the appearance of a publication.

The binding operation for some newsletters involves a **three-fold** process, as diagrammed in **Figure 10-12.** The publication, in effect, has six pages folded from one printed sheet. One of the

Figure 10-10. This is a saddle-stitching machine in a commercial printing plant. The binding process assembles and joins the signatures of a publication.
Courtesy of Griffin Printing & Lithographic Co., Inc.

pages is folded inward. Then, the front page is folded over to cover the inside pages. The six-page format can represent an effective compromise. It provides more useful space than a four-page layout. And it avoids the cost of binding and extra paper needed for eight pages.

Figure 10-11 This drawing illustrates the process of saddle stitching a publication with staples.

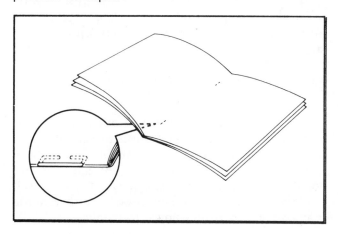

 DESKTOP JARGON

copy checking A procedure to make sure units of text are complete and in proper sequence.

folding The operation that folds press sheets into signatures.

imposition The placement of pages within signatures for printing.

saddle The point on a signature where the pages are folded.

three-fold A six-page publication folded so that the pages overlap.

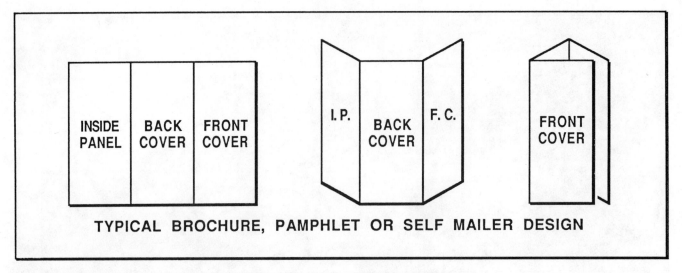

INSIDE PANEL | BACK COVER | FRONT COVER

I.P. | BACK COVER | F.C.

FRONT COVER

TYPICAL BROCHURE, PAMPHLET OR SELF MAILER DESIGN

Figure 10-12 This diagram illustrates the three-fold design that delivers a six-page newsletter.

Distribution

A publication is of no value until it is in the hands of its readers. Therefore, even if labeling and mailing your newsletter is someone else's job, distribution remains one of your concerns. The most common method for mailing or internal distribution of newsletters is to maintain a mailing list on a computer. Labels are printed at publication time and are affixed to the indicia area for distribution or mailing.

No matter who is responsible for label preparation, the person with overall production responsibility should make sure the newsletters are distributed. The task can be as simple as calling the responsible person to verify that mailing labels have been run. You also need to verify that the people who will handle the mailing are ready.

If distribution is handled in the same department as desktop publishing, you may be involved directly. At the very least, you may receive letters or notices from people who want to receive your newsletter. Or you may get change-of-address notices from readers who have moved. It is a good practice to checkpoint operations periodically to make sure that distribution lists are being updated and maintained on a current basis. Your success depends on reader service. Your concerns should extend to every operation that can help assure reader satisfaction.

Scheduling

The principles of scheduling are covered earlier. This is a good place to deal with the points at which schedules most typically break down.

One thing to watch for: People always seem ready to sacrifice quality for speed. Proofreading and copy checking should not be regarded as luxuries. They should be considered as necessities. If mistakes get into a publication, your readers won't want to hear your excuses. They will want you to know that they are dissatisfied.

To deliver publications that are both good and on time, you need to plan in advance. Start with the areas of a project that are under your control, typesetting, layout, and page production. Determine how long these jobs *should* take. Then, add about 20 percent more time to allow for things that are sure to go wrong. Use this as your basis for scheduling. Advise writers and other contributors of the date by which you need copy to carry out production.

As your input deadlines draw near, remind your contributors of their commitments. If your contributions slip, make them aware that the publication may be late and that they are responsible. Regardless of the circumstances that develop, follow process and do your best. Avoid panic. That benefits nobody.

Note that newsletters present additional challenges, as compared with publications reviewed in previous chapters. That's part of the design of this book. You build knowledge and skills as you go. The same applies to the next chapter which deals with the desktop methods for producing magazines and professional journals.

THE MAKEUP DESK

1. Assume you are appointed to develop a newsletter for one department in your school, such as the Computer Science department, the English department, or another department. Your job is to let majors and other interested students know about the activities and plans in that department. You also will invite special articles from outside sources or faculty members. The newsletter will contain eight pages. Develop a design on paper that calls for a one-column front page and two-column formats for inside pages. The back page will have a column from the department head at the top and an indicia below. Be sure to allocate room for logo and masthead.

2. Find a newsletter in your school library or bring one from home. Analyze the layout and design of one newsletter. Develop a layout that you would consider to be better than the one you select.

THE COMPOSING ROOM

1. For the newsletter you use to complete Assignment 2 above, capture enough text to prepare at least two pages of finished mechanics from your layout. You can leave key line boxes to indicate illustrations.

11 Magazines and Journals

Editorial Budget

❑ **Magazines and journals** are periodicals that deliver information and/or entertainment to readers. Magazines generally are larger and have a more "slick" appearance than journals.

❑ **Types of magazines and journals** include news and weekly magazines, feature-oriented magazines, business magazines, professional magazines or journals, and sponsored magazines.

❑ **Formats and sizes** of magazines vary. The most widely used size is 7 by 10 inches. There also are pocket-size and large-size magazines.

❑ **Magazine covers** rarely contain editorial content. Most covers promote or list the features inside the magazine. Some magazines carry advertising on their front covers.

❑ **The content ratio** for editorial copy and advertising varies. Usually, between 50 and 70 percent of a magazine consists of advertising. To qualify for special postal rates, a magazine must have a paid circulation and at least 30 percent editorial content.

❑ **Use of color** often is extensive. If a magazine sells color advertising, it becomes economical to use editorial color in the same signature as a color ad.

❑ **In laying out a magazine** it usually is best to position all of the ads first. Then, editorial copy and illustrations can be positioned around the spaces blocked for ads.

❑ **Desktop computers** are used chiefly for typesetting. Problems in attempting page makeup with desktop computers include reproduction quality of ads and handling of copy jumps.

THE MEDIA

Magazines and *journals* are periodicals. In general, these periodicals are issued weekly, semi-monthly, monthly, bi-monthly, or quarterly. Some annual publications also can be classified as magazines or journals.

TYPES OF PUBLICATIONS

One method of classifying magazines and journals is the same as for newsletters— according to type of circulation. There are paid, controlled circulation, and sponsored magazines.

Another dimension of classification lies in the types of markets served. These breakdowns are identified and described in the discussions that follow.

News and Weekly Magazines

One characteristic of news and weekly magazines is that they are issued weekly. Magazines published this frequently generally present news or other timely information.

To meet weekly deadlines, it generally is necessary to establish standard designs and layouts into which the current text can be fit. Standardization of layout grid elements eases and speeds production. Also, readers tend to scan quickly through news or other weekly magazines. A modular design is familiar to readers and makes content easier for them to review.

Feature-Oriented Magazines

The common denominator of these magazines is that they tend to use relatively long articles or fictional stories. Designs are elaborate, particularly for the opening spreads of articles or stories. These publications tend to be issued either monthly or less frequently. Examples include so-called women's and men's magazines, literary magazines, travel magazines, and airline-passenger magazines. Most magazines of this type are profit-oriented and rely on advertising revenues as their main source of income. Magazines of this type, along with news magazines, are distributed primarily by mail to subscribers. In addition, many copies are sold on newsstands and in supermarkets.

Business Magazines

This category is most numerous among the for-profit publications. There are more than 4,000 magazines published for specialized business audiences. In general, there is a magazine for each segment of every industry or trade. For example, in publishing there are separate magazines covering newspapers, magazines, and books. In retailing, there are hundreds of magazines covering every type of specialty product.

Circulation volumes of magazines in this category tend to be small as compared with large consumer publications. Large news or other consumer magazines, for example, usually have circulations that run into the millions. By contrast, circulation volumes for business magazines can run between 5,000 and 40,000.

Because of the relatively low circulation figures, advertising rates also are a fraction of those charged by large consumer publications. This means that a typical business magazine operates with a smaller budget and staff than a consumer publication. This smaller staff, however, must perform all of the publishing and production functions of any periodical. Designs are less lavish than for most consumer publications. However, publishers do strive for "clean," attractive layouts that appeal to serious readers.

Professional Magazines and Journals

Publications in this category tend to present long articles that contain many technical terms that relate to specialized fields. There is little color. Design tends to be plain. Total emphasis is on content. Articles report on developments or advanced research in the field being covered.

To stress the total concentration upon content, many publications in this field use a system under which they *referee* submitted

 DESKTOP JARGON

magazines or **journals** Periodicals issued on a regular schedule, but less frequently than daily, that present news or human-interest editorial content.

referee A person who judges the quality of articles submitted for publication in a scientific or professional journal.

articles. A board of reviewers is appointed by a publisher or technical organization. These people review and express opinions on the merits of submitted articles. Only articles that are reviewed favorably by a majority of referees are accepted and published.

Sponsored Magazines

This category corresponds with the sponsored newsletters described in the previous chapter. Magazines of this type sometimes are called "house organs" because they concentrate on the products and/or services of sponsoring organizations. Distribution of such magazines generally is to employees, customers, or members of a sponsoring organization. Content also may include news items about the sponsor's products or activities, or activities of interest to employees. There are more magazines in this category than in any other. More than 10,000 company magazines are issued regularly. These magazines probably represent the greatest potential for use of desktop publishing methods.

MEDIA CHARACTERISTICS

Tens of thousands of publications are classified as magazines and journals. Each publication, of course, strives for individuality. However, most magazines can be described in terms of a few key characteristics, described below.

Formats

The formats of magazines and journals can vary widely. At the small end, magazines can be classified as pocket size. These publications have trim sizes in the range of 5 by 7 inches. The most widely used size is at or close to 7 by 10 inches. Some magazines measure 8.5 by 11 inches or slightly larger. **Figure 11-1** shows magazines with different, popular size formats.

Figure 11-1. Magazines use formats of different sizes. Photo by Benedict Kruse.

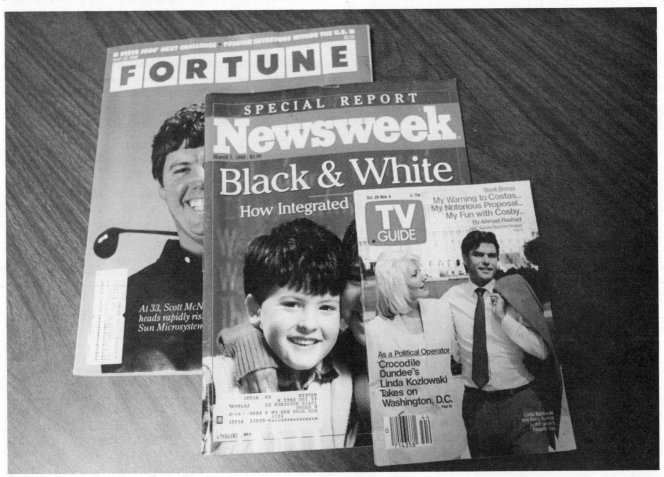

Cover Options

Regardless of size, a common characteristic of magazines and journals is that they rarely include text on the cover. Some journals have tables of contents on their front covers. Many magazines have promotional copy on the front cover that calls attention to stories carried on inside pages.

Many magazines have photos or drawings on their covers that highlight the theme of the most important or attention-getting article in each issue.

Some magazines, particularly business publications, carry advertisements on their front covers. As indicated, however, the common denominator is that there is a distinctive cover that does not carry actual articles or news stories.

The Advertising-Circulation Connection

The majority of magazines and journals accept advertising. Successful publications often gear the total size of each issue to the amount of advertising sold. In general, a successful magazine or journal will attempt to sell between 50 and 70 percent of its space to advertising. The limit at 70 percent for advertising qualifies a publication for special postage rates. With a paid circulation and editorial content of at least 30 percent, a magazine can qualify for second class mail rates. These are highly favorable.

Magazines that have controlled circulations have to pay higher postage rates and may receive lower priorities for delivery. Controlled circulation magazines are not subject to the limit of 70 percent in advertising space. However, most controlled circulation publications follow the same guidelines because they often compete with paid circulation magazines.

Layout

In general, the design and layout of a magazine says a lot about the kind of audience it tries to attract.

For example, most news magazines are issued weekly and are laid out for three-column formats. Some special pages have four columns. Most news magazines are organized into sections: international news, national news, business, sports, movies, theater, lifestyle, and so on. Within these sections, copy reads continuously. Copy starts at the top-left of the page on which a story is introduced and continues to completion. Except for situations in which ads occupy blocks of pages, there are no *jumps* in news magazines. A jump occurs when a story that is interrupted on one page is continued on a later page. If a story simply continues from one page to the next one, this is not a jump. A "jump line" tells a reader where a story is to be continued.

By contrast, most of the popular monthly consumer magazines tend to jump stories to locations farther back from the starting pages. The beginning of each story occupies a prominent position, usually a two-page spread. Sometimes a story will run four or six pages, then jump to the back of the publication. As discussed below, there can be difficulties connected with layout positions for jumps. The jumped copy often competes for space with text for special features or departments. These are smaller copy segments that are used regularly in a magazine.

Journals and some business magazines tend to use layouts that are conservative. Many journals stick with two-column layouts. Many business magazines adopt news-type, multi-column formats. Often, however, they do not have the financial budgets to support slick illustrations and designs. Most business magazines are limited to black-and-white photos as their main source of illustrations. Most journals make limited use of line art. Both business magazines and journals count on special audience interest in content to sustain readership.

Color

Many magazines make extensive use of color. The popularity of color stems, in part, from the structure of advertising rates and the effectiveness of color in selling products. Four-color magazine ads cost much more than one-color ads. However, many advertisers are committed to full color because they feel their messages gain better reader impact.

 DESKTOP JARGON

jump Continuation to a later page of a story that is interrupted on one page.

Generally, a magazine charges enough for a four-color ad to cover use of color on an entire press signature. In effect, a color ad pays the press charges for putting color onto 16 or 32 pages. The magazine does have to pay its own separation and stripping charges. However, given the extra reader appeal, use of color on editorial pages often proves to be a bargain.

Mass-circulation consumer magazines that use large-scale computers for composition and layout often have *run of publication (ROP)* color capabilities. Large-scale computer systems have word processing and typesetting systems similar to but far more advanced than those described in Chapter 9. In addition, these systems often have sophisticated capabilities for halftone scanning and for on-line page makeup.

A case example: A large, national news magazine installed computerized typesetting, page-making, and halftone scanning capabilities. The system is able to scan color transparencies or prints. Files for separated, halftone images are stored on magnetic disk files. This gives the magazine integrated control over its color processing. Separations no longer have to be handled separately. So, production delays for separations are eliminated or reduced greatly. Color photos can be positioned in layouts with on-line operator controls.

This capability enabled the magazine to change the deadline for submission of color advertisements from Tuesday afternoon of each week to Friday afternoon. The increase in revenue that resulted was enough to offset most of the costs of the computer system.

Once large magazines gained this kind of capability, the entire industry was affected. Smaller magazines, even if they can't afford multimillion-dollar computer systems, are devising ways to include editorial color. Through desktop publishing software such as PageMaker 3.0, small magazines are able to generate separations. The methods for doing this are described in Chapter 9. It is relatively simple for a magazine editor to separate headlines or line-art color to create color mechanicals. Therefore, color can be a factor in production of almost any magazine.

Photography

Almost all magazines make regular, sometimes heavy, use of photographs. Therefore, a desktop publisher who deals with magazines should know the basics of photo layout, cropping, and sizing. Selection of photos to dovetail with text and to fit into page designs also is important.

DESIGN AND LAYOUT EMPHASIS

A number of special points about the design and layout of magazines are worth noting. Bear in mind, of course, that most of the information in previous chapters also applies to production in magazines. Additional points of emphasis are covered below.

Placing Advertisements

Advertising space is paid for. It must run— often in special positions. Yet, an editor must not lose sight of the fact that advertisers buy space because of the magazine's readers. The news or feature articles get the readers. The advertising produces revenue.

When it comes to design and layout, advertising placement is the logical place to start. It is a good practice to start with a dummy. Even if page makeup is to be done on a computer, a rough layout on dummy sheets provides a valuable working guide. With paper sheets used for a rough dummy, you can keep your eye on spreads. You also can position ads to leave room for a mix of editorial and advertising content throughout the publication. **Figure 11-2** shows a layout that provides space for both ads and editorial copy.

Place all of the special-position ads first, since they must run in the spots for which they were accepted. Then, determine the mix of advertising to editorial content for the issue you are dummying. As ads are placed, bear in mind that you will need both opening spreads and jump positions for your major stories.

Identify a Role for Your Computer

The number of pages of advertising is the major factor in determining the overall page count for each issue. Also, when the ads are placed, you know exactly which areas are to be filled with text. This is a good place to determine how your desktop publishing computer can be used most effectively.

In the magazine field, desktop publishing techniques have some definite limitations.

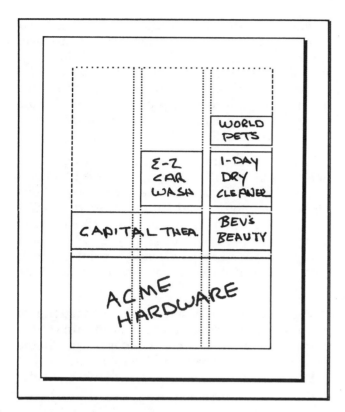

Figure 11-2. Magazine layout usually starts with placement of ads.

Quite frankly, it is next to impossible to produce an entire first-class magazine with desktop publishing tools as they exist today. One problem relates to the handling of advertising. Most quality ads, both in the consumer and business fields, are produced by advertising agencies. Agencies provide reproduction proofs or platemaking film for their ads.

With a large-scale computer system and a sophisticated scanner, original art or proofs can be scanned and incorporated in electronic files. Electronic makeup techniques can be used with these expensive tools. However, scanning systems for large computers cost far more than complete desktop publishing systems. In desktop publishing, quality scanners usually are too expensive to be justified. So, it is not likely that you will find scanners capable of reproducing quality art elements. Therefore, the most likely method for generating mechanicals is through pasteup. Reproduction proofs for ads can be pasted in place.

If you want to use page makeup methods for a magazine, you could block advertising positions with key-line boxes. Then you could position all

of the copy. The ads could be pasted on printouts for text pages. Even if you do this, however, it will be difficult to control jumps through desktop techniques. There would be a lot of page shuffling in comparatively large page makeup files. This procedure could become relatively slow and inefficient.

There are no firm statistics on how magazines use desktop techniques. However, it is obvious that one attractive alternative is to use desktop computers chiefly for typesetting. At least some pasteup probably will be required.

High-Resolution Output

Magazine production jobs can be prime candidates for use of high-resolution outputs from systems such as the Linotronic 100 or Linotronic 300. Increasing numbers of service centers are opening that will accept Macintosh or PC disks for production of commercial quality proofs or film. The Linotronic 300, for example, can generate outputs at 1,250 dots per inch or 2,500 DPI. Type fonts are set more precisely and spacing is far more professional than can be achieved on 300 DPI laser printers. A photo of a Linotronic machine is shown in **Figure 11-3**.

At the time work was begun on this text, prices for Linotronic outputs were running from $6 to $10 per 8.5-by-11-inch page. Just before this chapter was started, samples were received of high-quality work priced at a little more than $6 for an 11-by-17-inch page. This is twice the size of the 8.5-by-11-inch page.

In a period of about three months, the price at which quality outputs were available was cut in half. Further, the newly located source delivered samples of high-density, sharp, platemaking-quality film. By going directly to film through this process, a publisher can enhance output quality greatly and also reduce production costs. The film costs from this Linotronic source are comparable to those for lithographic film produced on cameras.

 DESKTOP JARGON

run of publication (ROP) Description of the ability to place specific types of content or color on any page of a publication.

Services of this type represent a potentially great breakthrough— an improvement of the type that can be expected routinely in this field.

Photo Selection and Placement

Photos are vital elements of most magazines. As a general rule, photos support and enrich the visual value of articles. At the very least, most magazines routinely try to run photos of persons described or quoted in articles. These photos can be taken at the time of interviews or events described in the articles.

Good sources for photos are the many photo libraries or agencies that can, between them, fill almost any photo need. These services can provide photos of current news events. They also can deliver photos or drawings of historic events. For example, suppose you need drawings of Shakespeare and his theater. They can be obtained from any of three or four picture research organizations. Similarly, if you want photos of an uprising in a distant country, you can call any of a dozen photo agencies.

An earlier chapter discusses selection of photos to fit layouts. One point stressed is that a photo's subject or the viewer's normal eye movement should lead into— rather than off— the page. Another factor, not covered earlier, is that experienced editors rarely run complete photos as they are received. To build interest, only relevant portions of photos should be reproduced.

The process for selecting the portions of pictures to be used and eliminating unwanted portions of photos is called *cropping.* Photos generally are cropped by placing small lines in the margins of prints or on the mounts of color

---

Figure 11-3. This machine can accept input from desktop publishing computer disks and generate commercial-quality reproduction proofs or film for printing plates.
Courtesy of Linotype Company.

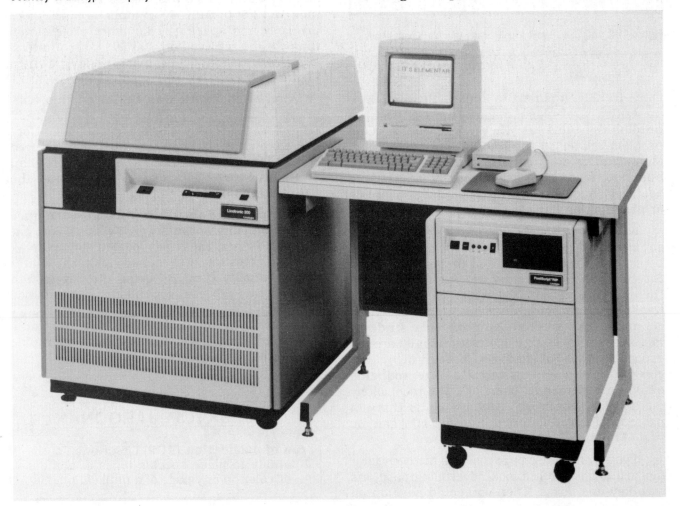

slides. The areas inside the horizontal and vertical lines identify the portion of the photo to be used. **Figure 11-4** illustrates the cropping process.

For inclusion in a publication, photos also have to be *sized.* Sizing involves preparation of instructions for the camera operator, scanner operator, and/or stripper. These people have to know the size at which the photo or other illustration will appear in the publication. Sizing is done by specifying a percentage of the original size at which the halftone or separation is to be shot. Every photo to be reproduced should be sized. One technique is to attach a tag that contains sizing instructions for the photo, as shown in **Figure 11-5.** A tag like the one used for the photos in this book is shown in **Figure 11-6.** The size percentage can be larger or smaller than the original photo. The key is that

Figure 11-4. Crop marks can be placed on the borders of photos. The crop marks identify the portion of the image that is to be published.
Photo by Benedict Kruse.

the halftone must fit the space designated for the illustration in the mechanical for the publication.

 DESKTOP JARGON

cropping Marking illustrations to indicate the areas to be used in a publication.

size To indicate the size at which an illustration is to be used in a publication.

Figure 11-5. One way to release photos for production is to attach tags that identify the picture, its location in the publication, and reproduction percentage.
Photo by Benedict Kruse.

Figure 11-6. This tag is attached to photos and contains instructions for the size of the halftone. It also identifies where the photo is to be placed in the publication.

Page # _209_

Reduce/Enlarge to _120_ %

Final Cropped Size

_42_ pi X _34.5_ pi

Description _11-4_

DESKTOP PUB.

A special tool can be used to help size photos. This is a slide rule, also called a *proportional wheel,* illustrated in **Figure 11-7.** This is a two-part device. A small circular unit rotates inside a larger one. The user matches the original size of a photo with the desired reproduction size. A window in the proportional wheel indicates the percentage of original size at which the photo should be shot.

Another device that can be used for sizing photos is a moving mask, shown in **Figure 11-8.** This device is placed over the cropped area of a photo. The mask can then be expanded or contracted to show the finished size.

PRODUCTION CONCERNS

Magazine production requires the ability to keep track of many details and to do so under pressure.

Checklists. The magazine editor's working routine generally is loaded with checklists to be monitored. There are lists of ads that must be included. Lists should be created to keep track of all stories that jump. For all jumps, there must be continuation lines at the original page. There also must be heads and pickup lines (continued from page . . .) at the beginnings of the jumped copy. There may be dozens of photos to place and captions to write. Dropping any of these details can delay production and also can detract from the quality of the publication.

An editor or production specialist has to know his or her magazine and to devise the necessary checklists or other controls.

Press checks. Monitoring or checking press runs can be a special concern for large publications. One concern is signature-to-signature balance in the image density of type and illustrations. Each time a signature is printed, there is a chance for variation in color or image values.

You probably have noticed publications in which the imprint is lighter or darker at different points. These variations often result from careless press work. There are adjustments on presses that can control image quality. Generally, it pays to make the effort needed to be there when a publication is being printed.

In doing a press check, be especially careful with the first signature that is printed. Be sure it

Figure 11-7. This is a proportional wheel used to determine the percentages of enlargement or reduction for illustrations. Photo by Benedict Kruse.

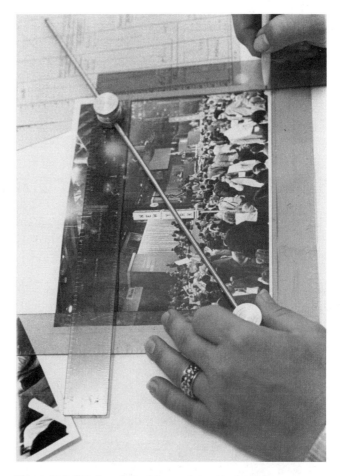

Figure 11-8. This is a photo sizing mask used to determine enlargement or reduction sizes for illustrations. Photo by Benedict Kruse.

represents the quality you want in your publication. Then, for each succeeding signature, compare a new press sheet with the imprint on your first, model signature. Printing impressions on succeeding signatures should match closely.

Magazine publishing presents challenges that are added to and different from those for newsletters and other media. Differences lie largely in both complexity of the process and the urgency of the deadlines to be met. Still further pressures for urgency exist in the newspaper field, covered in the chapter that follows.

 DESKTOP JARGON

proportional wheel A rotary slide rule used to determine the percentage of enlargement or reduction needed to reproduce an illustration at the size that is specified in a layout.

THE MAKEUP DESK

1. Bring in a feature magazine or a news magazine that you admire. Find one two-page spread in the magazine that you think could be improved, given the copy and illustrations available. Prepare a new layout for the material in that two-page spread.

2. Examine one news magazine thoroughly. Develop a grid that represents the layout for pages of this magazine.

THE COMPOSING ROOM

1. Capture the text from the two-page spread that you redesigned in completing Assignment 1 above. Prepare page makeup outputs for your layout on a desktop computer.

Newspapers 12

Editorial Budget

❑ **Newspapers are periodicals** that are given this classification partly by their production techniques. A newspaper is printed on newsprint stock, usually on rotary offset presses. Most newspapers are classified as dailies or weeklies.

❑ **Computerized production** is used throughout the newspaper industry. Large daily newspapers pioneered the use of on-line copy processing and typesetting with large computers. Many small daily and weekly papers now use desktop publishing techniques.

❑ **Many copy sources** supply newspapers. Included are wire services, news bureaus, correspondents, and copy written in the city room. Copy can be fed from computer networks or over telephone lines. Many correspondents now use laptop computers.

❑ **Copy editing** is done at computer terminals or desktop computers. When copy is released, typesetting is done by computers. At large papers, type can be set at rates of thousands of lines per minute. Desktop computers generate text at rates of hundreds of lines per minute.

❑ **Newspaper makeup** generally uses a column layout or modular approach. Most papers still handle composition through pasteup. Systems have been devised that make it possible to paste up more than 100 pages in a few hours.

❑ **Circulation paperwork** is handled on computers at many newspapers.

213

THE MEDIUM

Newspapers are actually a broad category of publications that serve a number of different markets. Classification of a publication as a newspaper is based on several key characteristics, identified and discussed below.

Paper Stock

The great majority of newspapers are printed on a paper stock known as **newsprint.** This is a coarse, uncoated paper made from wood pulp. Newsprint is among the most inexpensive printing papers. Because the surface is coarse, ink spreads through the pores of the paper when it is applied. Therefore, printing quality tends to be low, as compared with publications printed on stock of higher quality.

To illustrate differences in printing quality, magazines and books tend to use 150-line screens for half-tone reproduction. Most newspapers use 65- or 85-line screens. Some newspapers do use a better paper stock. But these tend to be special-market, low-circulation publications.

Printing Production

Virtually all newspapers are printed on web presses. For many years, low-circulation papers were run on sheet-fed presses. It used to require relatively long print runs to overcome the costs of setting up a web press. It can be time consuming to thread a continuous roll of paper through the units of a large web press. Recent design innovations, however, have made it feasible to run as few as 2,000 copies on web equipment. **Figure 12-1** shows a web press of the type used for newspapers.

Figure 12-1. Most newspaper are printed on rotary offset web presses.
Photo by Benedict Kruse.

Figure 12-2. This illustration compares the sizes of tabloid and standard newspapers.
Photo by Benedict Kruse.

Page Size

Newsprint comes in fixed roll widths and web presses have standard plate sizes. Therefore, most newspapers fit into one of two format sizes, *tabloid* or *standard.* A tabloid newspaper measures approximately 11.5 by 15.5 inches and uses a five-column layout grid. A standard-size newspaper measures approximately 15 by 22.5 inches. Most standard-format papers use six-column layouts, though some use eight columns for special sections, such as classified advertising and some news pages. **Figure 12-2** shows a standard newspaper and a tabloid together.

Publication Schedule

Most newspapers are published either daily or weekly. Accordingly, there are separate categories for *dailies* and *weeklies.* Some 1,700 dailies and more than 4,000 weeklies are published in the United States. Frequency of publication affects copy and production deadlines. There are wide differences in production practices and copy-handling routines between dailies and weeklies. Some of the requirements and differences are covered later in this chapter.

 DESKTOP JARGON

newsprint The paper on which newspapers are printed; a coarse, uncoated paper made from wood pulp.

tabloid A size and category of newspapers. Trim size usually is 11.5 by 15.5 inches.

standard A size and category of newspapers. Trim size usually is 15 by 22.5 inches.

daily A newspaper issued every day.

weekly A newspaper issued once a week.

In addition, most high schools and virtually all colleges have newspapers published by students. Some colleges publish daily newspapers. Most have weeklies. Desktop publishing techniques are being adopted widely for college newspapers.

Circulation

As with other periodicals, some newspapers have paid circulations. Others are distributed free, some under controlled-circulation procedures. Some newspapers are sponsored.

The size of a newspaper's circulation is an important factor in its operation and management. The larger the circulation, the more complex distribution management becomes. Newspapers with large circulations use computers to handle paperwork and control of distribution.

Use of Computers

Most mass-circulation newspapers use large-scale computers that have high-speed typesetting and on-line page makeup capabilities, even for large pages. These techniques are of interest

mainly because they have been the forerunners of the desktop publishing techniques covered in this book.

To dramatize the differences, consider that large-scale computer systems can set type at speeds of thousands of lines per minute. A full page of classified ads typically can be set in about two minutes. By comparison, consider typesetting output on a laser printer linked to a desktop computer. The desktop system generates about eight 8.5-by-11-inch pages per minute. Typical per-minute production rates can range to 10,000 lines for a large system, 400 to 800 lines for a microcomputer.

These figures are not intended to belittle the capabilities of desktop publishing systems. Rather, it can be valuable to understand the capabilities of the tools you may encounter if you go into publishing production. A desktop publishing system represents a valuable, powerful tool that can be purchased for under $10,000

Figure 12-3. At large daily newspapers, reporters and editors work at computer terminals.
Courtesy of Gannett Co., Inc.

Figure 12-4. This high-speed photo composition computer can set type for a complete standard-sized newspaper in 64 seconds. Photo by Benedict Kruse.

for some equipment configurations. There are bound to be major differences in capacities between desktop computers and systems that cost $1 million and up, like those illustrated in **Figures 12-3** and **12-4.**

Desktop publishing systems are used in conjunction with standard pasteup methods at many weeklies and small dailies. In these instances, desktop computers have replaced earlier electronic typesetting methods. These earlier methods have included computerized typesetters and impact-printing methods. Impact-printing typesetters, such as the IBM Magnetic Tape/Selectric Typewriter, had enjoyed wide use among weeklies and small dailies. These systems and some predecessors replaced Linotype and other typecasting machines during the 1960s. During this period, most small newspapers led the way into use of web offset printing.

At this writing, desktop computers are mainstays for typesetting at small newspapers. Many desktop computers also are used for advertising and administrative functions, including the capture and setting of classified ads. Another widely used application is the development of the *circulation blotter.* This is a computer-produced list that controls press runs and distribution of papers.

 ## DESKTOP JARGON

circulation blotter A listing of the number of papers needed for distribution.

PUBLISHING FUNCTIONS

This text does not include instruction on writing. However, it is important for anyone involved in newspaper production to be aware of the processes for newsgathering and copy handling. Also, the methods used for accepting and publishing classified advertising are unique to the newspaper field. Some of the key characteristics of unique newspaper operations are reviewed below.

Copy Sources and Handling

Newspapers have sources and methods for copy preparation and handling that are unique to the newspaper publishing industry.

Wire services. One special source is *wire service* copy. A wire service is a news agency that delivers copy via telecommunications channels. The term "wire" is a holdover from the days of Morse telegraphy. A single strand of wire could carry signals in dots and dashs.

There are two major general news agencies, or wire services, in the United States. These are the Associated Press (AP) and United Press International (UPI). In addition, financial news is distributed to many publishers on the Dow Jones (DJ) wire. Specialized city news services operate in some metropolitan areas. Also, some large newspapers or newspaper chains have their own news services, also known as *syndicates.* A number of wire services based in foreign countries also serve newspapers in the United States. A wire room is shown in **Figure 12-5.**

Bureaus and correspondents. Thousands of newspapers need a way of receiving and recording copy supplied by wire services. Also, if newspapers operate *bureaus* at which coverage is handled by staff *correspondents,* there also will be wire transmissions from these sources. A

Figure 12-5. Photos, as well as text, are distributed by news wire services.
Photo by Benedict Kruse.

Figure 12-6. Laptop computers are used for copy preparation by many news correspondents.
Courtesy of Hewlett-Packard Company.

bureau is a news-gathering facility that represents a paper or wire service. A correspondent is a reporter who works at a location away from the main office of a newspaper. A number of correspondents work on their own. They travel or work from home at points distant from the publishing office. Sports reporters work at ballparks or stadiums. Political correspondents may work at a city hall. Others may cover a legislature, while still others are stationed in foreign countries.

Increasingly, reporters who work in bureaus or at outlying locations are capturing original copy on *laptop* computers. These are portable units that run on batteries. An entire computer may weigh 10 pounds or less. Despite their small size, many laptop units have full microcomputer capabilities. These units are playing important roles in the generating of copy at the points where news is happening. The compact size of a laptop computer is illustrated in **Figure 12-6.**

Many laptop units have built-in modems that make it possible to transmit text to the home office over telephone lines. Modem is an

 DESKTOP JARGON

wire service A news agency that delivers copy via telecommunications channels.

syndicate An organization that provides news and feature materials to subscribing papers. The syndicate sells specific items and is different from a wire service that provides general news coverage.

bureau An outlying office that provides news coverage for a paper or wire service.

correspondent A reporter who covers an area distant from the home office of a news organization.

laptop computer A portable, battery operated computer.

abbreviation of the words "modulate-demodulate." These are the signal conversion functions necessary to transmit information from computer to computer over telephone lines. Thus, a correspondent can write a story during an actual news event. Then, the correspondent can walk to the nearest phone booth and deliver ready-to-use copy to the newspaper's computers. This is possible because the modems on laptop computers can be coupled directly to a telephone handset. Transmission can be at rates of between six and 12 pages per minute.

The city room. Also captured on the same central computer are stories that originate in the news room in the paper's central office. This usually is called the **city room.** Included are stories written by the reporters who gather the news personally and copy generated by **rewrite** desks. Many newspapers have home-office staff specialists who take information from reporters or other sources over the telephone. These rewrite specialists write copy on the basis of the information provided.

Information storage. At the publishing office, the computer system has to have a way to record all copy from external sources. All stories must be logged into an editorial budget maintained electronically on a computer system. This generally is done by storing text on disk files that can be accessed by editors and typesetting computers.

An editorial budget can be prepared manually. Also, copy access and editing operations can be handled by transporting disks from point to point manually. However, a more efficient method is to set up a **local area network (LAN).** This is a method for connecting a series of computing devices. A LAN can include desktop computers, printers, storage devices for on-line communication, and even large computers. Local area networks are relatively inexpensive and their cost generally can be justified even by small dailies and weeklies. A typical local area network will include a high-capacity **file server.** This is a central disk device with storage capacities into the range of 100 to 300 megabytes. At large papers, central file systems have capacities measured in **gigabytes,** or billions of bytes of data.

Within any hardware-software configuration, a basic necessity is information access.

Editors must be able to access a budget stored on a computer. Through use of the budget, the editor has to be able to access, edit, and re-record any story. The editor also must be able to control release of copy for typesetting. If on-line makeup is used, the makeup desk must have access to files of typeset copy and illustrations.

At large newspapers, story files may run into hundreds of thousands of words each day. Even at small papers, copy volumes can run into tens of thousands of words to be evaluated and processed for publication.

Copy editing. At the individual terminal, the challenges are similar for all copy editors. This is true regardless of whether the editor works at a **standalone** computer or a network terminal. A standalone computer is a complete system that is not linked with other computers.

The basic procedure is the same: The editor is given assignments. The identified stories are called up one at a time. The copy can come either from a central storage location or a diskette. The stories are edited on-line and, when they are ready, are released for typesetting. Also, necessary codes and control symbols to identify type fonts, sizes, and widths should be incorporated in each story manuscript by the editor. A separate computer operator can follow these instructions to format the copy for typesetting printout and pasteup. **Figure 12-7** shows a copy desk at a daily newspaper where copy editors work at network terminals.

Each story, at every stage of its processing, must be identified by a unique slug line. The slug line, as described in an earlier chapter, is an identifying label. Writers, copy editors, makeup editors, and composing room people identify copy by the same slug lines. Makeup and composing room functions are described in greater depth in sections that follow.

Advertising Copy

Most **display advertising,** or space ads for products and/or services, is provided in ready-to-print form by advertising agencies. Receipt of reproduction-ready ads is covered in the discussion of magazines in Chapter 11. When newspaper ads are pre-set, the reproduction proofs or film are integrated into the production process routinely. That is, the reproduction proofs can be scanned and used in electronic makeup or can

Figure 12-7. This is a newspaper copy desk set up for on-line editing.
Photo by Benedict Kruse.

be positioned on pasteup boards. **Figure 12-8** shows ads being readied for makup.

Classified advertising. Special copy-generating capabilities are required for the handling of classified advertisements. Classified ads get their name from the way they are organized in a paper. The ads are grouped into a series of classifications. Examples include apartments for rent, cars for sale, jobs available, jobs wanted, and so on.

Many classified ads are placed by volume advertisers, such as employment agencies, real estate agencies, and car dealers. These are received in written form and can be captured through keyboarding under word processing methods. In addition, many classified ads are received via telephone. These must be taken verbally and transcribed while the advertiser is still on the line. These ads are known as *telephone and transient (T and T).* To process T and T ads, the newspaper must prepare copy and also must bill the advertisers individually.

All classified ads then must be assembled in files according to category. Under desktop publishing methods, type is set in continuous columns and is pasted up on boards for film

 DESKTOP JARGON

city room The newsroom of a newspaper.

rewrite The writing of news copy from notes received over the telephone.

local area network (LAN) A group of connected computing devices located on a single floor or in a single building.

file server A central storage device that serves multiple users on a computer network.

gigabyte One billion bytes.

standalone computer A computer that is self-sufficient, with its own processing, storage, input, and output capabilities.

display advertising Advertisements that appear on a paper's news pages.

telephone and transient (T and T) Describes a classified ad received over the telephone from advertisers who are not regular customers.

Figure 12-8. Ads for a day's issue of a newspaper are sorted and stacked for makeup. Ad space controls the size of each day's paper. Photo by Benedict Kruse.

making. A special requirement lies in integrating new classified ads for each issue with those to be rerun from earlier issues.

Classified advertising personnel must keep track of the number of insertions for each ad. When an ad is to be cancelled, it is crossed out on a copy of the paper that serves as a **kill sheet.** This kill sheet then is used to update the word processing files that contain the classified ad copy. Desktop computer operators delete ads that have been killed from the computer files. They insert new ads in the proper categories for each edition. This is a complex job that has to be done accurately and quickly.

Desktop publishing techniques have made it possible to streamline classified ad typesetting at small newspapers. Traditionally, new ads were set as they were received. Pasteup personnel

then had to kill old ads and insert new ones manually—on the pasteup boards. It is much more efficient to handle kills and insertions on computer files and to generate clean type for every edition. Checking and revising are done on the computer. Pasteup people are relieved of the task of making kills and fitting new ads into their proper categories.

THE MAKEUP FUNCTION

The term **makeup** has a special meaning in newspaper production. In the newspaper field, the term "design" refers to standards for body type, heads, column widths, and so on. The makeup function uses these standard elements to lay out newspapers under tight schedules.

Headline schedules. To illustrate the kind of standardization that occurs, most newspapers have a **headline schedule.** This is a series of samples and specifications for perhaps 20 to 50 different kinds of headlines. Each headline in

---

HEADLINE SCHEDULE

1. 6-col. Banner. 60 pt. Count: 44

Council Anticipates Fight About Abandoned Dogs

2. 4-col. Cross Line. 48 pt. Count: 48

Council Members Set for Dog Fight

3. 3-col. Cross Line. 48 pt. Count: 21

Dog Fight Developing

A. 3-col. Block. 48 pt. Count: 21

City Council Expecting Battle Over Wild Dogs

B. 2-col. Block. 30 pt. Count: 28

**Battle Brewing on Proposed
$108,000 Boost in City Budget**

C. 1-col. Block. 24 pt. Count: 17

**'Dog Fight' Looms
For City Council**

10. 2-col. Drop Line. 24 pt. Count: 31

**Animal Control Department Seeks
Funds to Deal With Wild Dogs**

11. 1-col. Drop Line. 18 pt. Count: 19

**Battle Building Over
Planned City Budget**

20. 2-col. Kicker Line. 18 pt. Count: 25-30

Citizen Complaints Trigger Action

21. 1-col. Kicker Line. 14 pt. Count: 18-21

$108,000 Budget Item

Figure 12-9. This is a sample portion of a headline schedule.

---

the schedule is coded with a letter, number, or combination of letters and numbers. As an example, an "A" head might be 12 picas wide, 24 points high, and have a character count of 18. A makeup editor would note on a layout sheet that a story, identified by its slug line, was to have an "A" head. A portion of a headline schedule is shown in **Figure 12-9.**

Front page layouts. Design, then, is incorporated in the column width, typeface, and headline schedule specifications that guide the makeup desk. Thus, there is no design function in the same way as there is for other print media. Makeup editors put a newspaper together by selecting from an established set of design elements.

Makeup patterns for newspapers fall into a few broad categories: tabloids and standard-size papers.

Tabloids generally use short copy elements and attract attention with large photos and headlines. An example is shown in **Figure 12-10.**

Standard papers tend to follow one of two layout patterns. Some papers use balanced layouts based on placement of elements in column grids. Stories are positioned in vertical columns. Headlines are chosen to create a visual balance across the page. Photos usually are placed in central positions so that the headlines will balance on either side. A newspaper with a column-oriented layout is illustrated in **Figure 12-11.** Prominent newspapers that use this kind of layout include large dailies such as *The New York Times*, the *Los Angeles Times*, and the *Chicago Tribune.*

DESKTOP JARGON

kill sheet A page of classified ads marked to indicate those to be dropped.

makeup Function that places stories in newspaper layouts.

headline schedule Set of standard headlines designated for use in a newspaper's makeup.

FOUNDED IN 1801 BY ALEXANDER HAMILTON

NEW YORK POST

METRO EDITION

WEDNESDAY, OCTOBER 26, 1988 / Partly sunny, low 50s today; clear, upper 30s. tonight / Details, Page 2   35¢ in New York City 50¢ elsewhere

HITMEN SEIZED IN PLOT TO KILL KOCH

TARGETED: *Mayor Koch and Robert Stutman, top federal drug enforcement officer in New York, who cops believe were stalked by hired killers.*

Cops think coke king sent assassins after mayor, top narc

STORY
PAGE 5

ROBIN FISCHER: *A real survivor.*

WONDER WOMAN WHO SURVIVED 9 HOURS OF HELL

Page 5

Figure 12-10. Front pages of tabloid newspapers use bold headlines.

"All the News That's Fit to Print"

The New York Times

New York: Today, clouds and sun, windy, a sprinkle. High 48-53. Tonight, mostly clear. Low 31-40. Tomorrow, sun and high clouds. High 47-51. Yesterday: High 63, low 53. Details, page C24.

VOL.CXXXVIII . . . . No. 47,669 NEW YORK, TUESDAY, OCTOBER 25, 1988 — 50 cents beyond 75 miles from New York City, except on Long Island. — 35 CENTS

The New York Times/Jose R. Lopez

White House Welcome for U.S. Olympians

President Reagan was surrounded by members of the U.S. Olympic team as the national anthem was played at ceremony in the athletes' honor. "If you didn't come wearing a medal, you still were every bit a hero," the President told the 250 members of the team who attended.

TAIWAN AND KOREA ARE SAID TO IMPEDE U.S. TRADE EFFORT

CURRENCY FIXING FOUND

Treasury, in Economic Report, Asks End of Manipulation and Hails Dollar Level

By PETER T. KILBORN
Special to The New York Times

WASHINGTON, Oct. 24 — The Treasury today charged Taiwan and South Korea with fixing their currencies to spur sales of their goods to the United States, thereby impeding a reduction of the big American trade deficit.

Escalating charges that it has been leveling for two years, the Treasury said it would begin six months of bilateral talks with each of the two countries to try to persuade them to cease the manipulation, which makes their currencies cheaper relative to the dollar and therefore makes their goods more attractive.

The Treasury declined to say how it would retaliate if the talks fail. It said any action would depend on the views of Congress.

Perspective on the Dollar

In a new and comprehensive report to Congress on international economic policy, the Treasury also sought to rebuff those economists and international authorities who maintain that the dollar should fall still further from its peak of February 1985. The decline in the dollar was intended to help narrow the trade deficit, which reached a record $170 billion last year.

A senior Treasury official, at a briefing for reporters, said that "we still have exchange rates conducive to further adjustment" of the deficit.

The report — 47 pages of analyses, tables and charts — was the first on international economic policy to be issued as required under the trade law that the President signed in August.

Requirements of the Law

Under a provision sought by Representative John J. LaFalce, Democrat of Buffalo, the Treasury was ordered to look for cases of currency manipulation by American competitors in world trade and to embark on bilateral negotiations to halt any such practices.

Unlike most other Treasury reports, today's did not carry the name of the

Continued on Page D27, Column 1

A History of Big Deals

Henry R. Kravis

George R. Roberts

Transactions completed by Kohlberg Kravis, in billions of dollars.

Date	Target	Business	Price
April '86	Beatrice Companies*	Food, consumer products and services	$6.40
Nov. '86	Safeway Stores	Supermarkets worldwide	4.56
March '87	Owens-Illinois	Packaging products, health care, financial services	3.80
Jan. '88	Jim Walter	Construction industry products and services	2.43
Dec. '85	Storer Communications*	Seven television stations	2.41
June '88	Duracell	Batteries	1.80

*Has been sold or gone public since buyout. Source: Company reports

BUYOUT SPECIALIST BIDS $20.3 BILLION FOR RJR NABISCO

KOHLBERG, KRAVIS OFFER

Record Proposal Tops One of $17 Billion by Managers — New Move Is Seen

By JAMES STERNGOLD

Kohlberg, Kravis, Roberts & Company, a Wall Street investment house that has become one of the country's largest industrial holding companies, yesterday announced a $20.3 billion offer for RJR Nabisco, the nation's 19th-largest industrial company.

The staggering bid followed a $17 billion proposal made last Thursday by RJR Nabisco's top executives in partnership with Shearson Lehman Hutton, a large Wall Street securities firm. Kohlberg, Kravis said it would begin its bid of $90 a share later this week if RJR Nabisco's board approved.

The bids, which are both larger than any previous offers for a company, have opened a new frontier in the world of extraordinarily high finance. No company seems too large now for the technique used by both bidders known as a leveraged buyout.

Companies Usually Sold Off

Buyout firms such as Kohlberg, Kravis borrow heavily to purchase ownership of companies from public shareholders. So far the approach has largely been successful because it focuses all of a company's attention on the job of wringing as much profit from its assets as possible. Usually the companies are sold after a few years of ownership.

It was no surprise to find Kohlberg, Kravis present in the RJR Nabisco bidding when a new stretch of rich financial landscape was opened up. The tiny but powerful firm has been at the vanguard of Wall Street' hottest acquisition trend since it was founded on May 1, 1976. In the process, the five-man partnership has built up an enormous industrial holding company that brings in nearly as much revenues as General Electric.

Kohlberg, Kravis possesses some of the largest holdings in the supermarket, container and packaging, construction, battery and furniture retailing businesses. The buyout of RJR Nabisco, if successful, would bring the annual revenues of its holdings to more than $50 billion.

No RJR Nabisco Comment

F. Ross Johnson, RJR Nabisco's chief executive and leader of the previous buyout proposal with Shearson Lehman, would not comment yesterday.

Peter A. Cohen, Shearson Lehman's chairman, said he was slightly surprised at the Kohlberg, Kravis announcement. But, he added, "We set out to work with Ross to create value for the shareholders. We're well on the way to doing just that."

Mr. Cohen would not comment directly on Shearson Lehman's next move. "We'll collect our thoughts," he said. But most of Wall Street is expect-

Continued on Page D6, Column 1

Political Memo

Bush Is Striking Political Gold By Minimizing Silver Spoon

By E. J. DIONNE Jr.
Special to The New York Times

WASHINGTON, Oct. 23 — As a rule, Americans do not like the idea of elites and look upon this society as a place where all people are created equal.

That, in the view of many politicians, academics and voters, is one major reason the electorate does not seem to like the choice between Vice President Bush and Gov. Michael S. Dukakis very much.

They have in Mr. Bush a representative of an old family elite. They see Mr. Dukakis, the Governor of Massachusetts, representing an educated elite symbolized by the name Harvard.

What is striking about the 1988 campaign so far is that Mr. Bush has been far more successful than Mr. Dukakis in painting himself as the anti-elitist candidate, the one who is really in touch with what the Vice President calls the mainstream of American life.

Mr. Bush has managed to de-emphasize his elite background by stressing issues and values that he believes he shares with most Americans: that criminals should be punished severely, taxes should be kept low and schoolchildren should be required to pledge their allegiance to the nation's flag.

Democrats have charged that Mr. Bush's emphasis on the crime issue was veering into racism. What is clear is that Mr. Bush's attacks on Mr. Dukakis have been politically profitable.

By setting Mr. Dukakis up as a candidate who is distant from the concerns of the average American in his "liberal" views, said Geoff Garin, a Democratic poll taker, Mr. Bush "has simply given voters so many other things to think about Michael Dukakis that Bush's elitism receded into the background."

The Democrats fought hard at their national convention to portray Mr. Bush as the representative of a kind of aristocracy. "He is a man who was born on third base and thinks he hit a triple," said Jim Hightower, a Texas

Continued on Page A26, Column 1

31st St. Building Collapse Stops Subways and Trains and Hurts 10

By JAMES BARRON

Service on New York subway and commuter trains was thrown into chaos for hours yesterday because of concern that underground vibrations would endanger people who might be trapped in the rubble of a building that collapsed in midtown Manhattan.

More than 500,000 commuters were delayed as the evening rush turned into disorder just as it began. The subways and commuter trains began rolling again an hour after service had been suspended, but at top speeds of 10 miles an hour.

Officials at the scene of the collapse, two blocks from the Empire State Building, worried that if the trains went any faster, the rumblings would touch off another collapse that would demolish the sole wall that did not tumble with the rest of the building. Fire officials were also concerned that gas mains might have been ruptured, raising the fear of explosions from high-voltage rails in the tunnels.

'The Worst Situation'

The cause of the collapse, at 24 West 31st Street, was not immediately determined. But Buildings Commissioner Charles J. Smith said construction work had been going on there without a permit.

The police said one person might have been killed. Ten others, some of whom apparently worked in the building, were injured. Four others were missing in the debris, and officials held out little hope for two of them.

"This is the worst situation from the rescue point of view that I've seen," Mr. Smith said.

The six-story commercial building collapsed in a roar of concrete, bricks and shattering glass shortly after 3 P.M., hurling file cabinets, chairs, desks and debris down on the narrow parking lots that surround the cream-colored structure.

"I watched the top floors crumble," said Jeff Burgos, who works across the street. "As they fell, men were actually coming out of the side of the walls, climbing down the debris. It looked like they didn't have a choice."

Ralph Mohabbab, who works in a jewelry store behind the collapsed building, said he heard "these three big bangs."

"We thought somebody shot someone," he said. "We saw this lady walk out with dust all over her clothes. Her clothes were ripped, and she was bleeding."

An attendant at the parking lot next door, Gus Benjumea, said he watched workers pull out bricks and replace them, one by one, before the collapse. He said workers had dug a 30-foot trench along the side of the building. Some rescue workers speculated that

Continued on Page B4, Column 1

Swedish Farm Animals Get a Bill of Rights

By STEVE LOHR
Special to The New York Times

STOCKHOLM, Oct. 20 — The Swedish welfare state, long renowned for its generosity and scope, is extending its reach into a new frontier: the barnyard.

In the last few months, Sweden has begun putting in place a rights program for farm animals that may be the most stringent in the world. Under an animal-welfare law enacted in July, cattle, pigs and chickens are being freed from the restrictions of intensive, or factory-farming methods, in which animals are kept in crowded conditions and antibiotics and hormones are often administered.

'Best for the Animals'

Besides the inherent concerns about humane treatment of animals and food quality in this Scandinavian society, the legislation reflects the extraordinary political clout in Sweden of an 81-year-old writer, Astrid Lindgren. One of the world's most widely read authors of children's books, perhaps best-known as the creator of the character "Pippi Longstocking," Mrs. Lindgren demonstrated the power of the pen in Swedish affairs by writing a series of satirical allegories in leading newspapers, underscoring the plight of farm animals and fueling the animal-welfare campaign.

Associated Press

Astrid Lindgren, the author of children's books, was responsible for making the treatment of farm animals a lively political issue.

Swedish cattle have been given grazing rights under the new law. Pigs can no longer be tethered and must be granted separate bedding and feeding places. Both cows and pigs, the law states, must have "access to straw and litter." Chickens must be let out of their cramped cages. No drugs or hormones can be used on farm animals, except to treat disease.

Most of the requirements will be phased in over the next few years, but implementation of the provision making all chickens free rangers will be stretched over several years to lift some of the economic burden from farmers and to give

Continued on Page A8, Column 1

Bush Blames 'Desperation' of Foe For Charge of Racism in Campaign

By MAUREEN DOWD
Special to The New York Times

WILLISTON, Vt., Oct. 24 — Vice President Bush denied today that his campaign has any racist overtones, calling the charge by the Dukakis campaign and leading Democrats "some desperation kind of move."

"There isn't any racism," he said, speaking to reporters on Air Force Two on his way to Connecticut, Maine and Vermont for a final New England swing in Michael S. Dukakis's political back yard. "It's absolutely ridiculous."

Speaking to the Chamber of Commerce in Waterbury, Conn., Mr. Bush also denied that he had distorted or lied about Mr. Dukakis's record on crime and military issues, labeling the Democrat's charge to the contrary as "desperation."

Raising the volume of his attacks to fortissimo, Mr. Bush said his opponent was upset not because his record was being distorted but because Mr. Dukakis "is weak on crime and defense and that's the inescapable truth."

The Vice President went on to accuse his rival of lying, racism and sexism, and charged that the nation "could face an economic disaster if the liberals take over the White House."

Mr. Bush's remarks today intensified a new round of name-calling in a Presidential campaign already regarded as one of the most negative in modern history. By the final rally of the day, in Williston, even the placards in the crowd were taking on a nastier edge. "America doesn't want to become Massachusetts," read one, with a hammer-and-sickle symbol replacing the "C." A Dukakis supporter dressed in a Ku Klux Klan costume held up a Bush-Quayle sign and another held a placard that read, "Bush: Ready on Day One to be a Racist President."

The Democratic Vice-Presidential nominee, Senator Lloyd Bentsen, said Sunday in response to a reporter's question that there seemed to be a racial element in the Republican campaign's emphasis on the issue of prison furloughs in the Presidential campaign. On the same day the Rev. Jesse

Continued on Page A28, Column 1

INSIDE

Superconductivity Goals

Predictions for the usage of superconducting materials are more modest now as experts say they expect the first uses to be in microelectronics. Page D1.

Hostage Dealings Denied

The Administration denied any connection with an Italian arms dealer who is under investigation for possible schemes to release American hostages in Lebanon. Page A3.

How Arteries Get Clogged

A new theory explains how cholesterol in the blood produces the clogged arteries that cause heart attacks. The findings may yield new treatments. Science Times, page C1.

Yankees Trade Clark

The Yankees sent Jack Clark to the Padres for two pitchers and an outfielder. An arbitrator declared 14 players, including two senior Yankees, free agents. Page B11.

Baltic Lands: A Thorn in the Bear's Paw

By PHILIP TAUBMAN
Special to The New York Times

News Analysis

MOSCOW, Oct. 24 — A sense of euphoria has swept through the Soviet Baltic republics of Estonia, Latvia and Lithuania in recent weeks as the Communist authorities have seemed not only to give in to but to collaborate in the independent movements that have sprung up in those once-independent states.

To many in those seemingly downtrodden republics, the hope has grown that the same Communist Party that once pressed to Russify the region might now grant some autonomy from Moscow and, ultimately, perhaps even independence from the Soviet Union.

But there also is a sense that the harmony of the moment between the party and the independence groups may be a veneer, and that a clash will inevitably come in which hopes for more independence will be crushingly disappointed.

Most puzzling is why the Politburo in Moscow has seemed so willing to go along with the movement, which can only weaken the Kremlin's control in the Baltic republics. The republics were forcibly integrated into the Soviet Union as a result of World War II.

The question is important because the Soviet Union is made up of many ethnic groups that have been forcibly put under Moscow's control. In the past, rumblings of independence were crushed because the Government felt that if one nationalist group was given its way, others would agitate for change.

Even in the days of the Czars, Russian forces had to deal with local revolts in the Caucasuses and in Central Asia. Now, 71 years after the Bolsheviks took power, there is trouble for Moscow not only in the Baltics but in the three Caucasus republics, Georgia,

Continued on Page A11, Column 1

News Summary, Page A2

Arts	C16-23	Obituaries	B6-7
Bridge	C21	Op-Ed	A31
Business Day	D1-31	Politics	A26-28
Chess	C21	Science Times	C1-15
Crossword	C20	Sports	B10-14
Editorials	A30	TV/Radio	C22-23
Fashion	B9	Washington Talk	B8
Letters	A30	Weather	C24
Media	D31	Word and Image	C22

Classified Index .... B15 Auto Exchange B14

Figure 12-11. This is an example of a standard-size newspaper with a column-oriented layout.

VIA SATELLITE   THE NATION'S NEWSPAPER   50 CENTS

USA TODAY

NO. 1 IN THE USA...5.3 MILLION READERS EVERY DAY

Computer alarms set since 'infection'

By Mark Lewyn and Kathy Rebello
USA TODAY

Companies and universities are taking stock of their defenses in light of the worst computer virus outbreak in history.

"Every company will be looking to secure their computers in the next few weeks, if they haven't already," says David Wilson, a security consul-

tant for Ernst & Whinney.

The "virus" — a rogue program planted by a high-tech vandal — showed up last Wednesday, duplicating itself rapidly and using vast quantities of computer space. It apparently didn't destroy any information, but it clogged an

estimated 6,000 computers at universities and military labs.

Suspected of creating the virus: Robert T. Morris Jr., a 23-year-old graduate student and son of a top computer-security expert who works for the National Security Agency.

Most large companies say

they have adequate security measures against virus attacks, but many plan to remind employees of security procedures and re-evaluate their systems.

"Those who think themselves invincible set themselves up as targets for those who might want to prove them wrong," says Cole Emerson, a vice-president at First Interstate Bancorp.

The real threat, experts say,

is not from outsiders, but from disgruntled employees. Or from employees who fail to follow security guidelines, such as using unapproved software that might be contaminated with a virus, says Gary Steuck, director of computer services at Lands' End Inc.

"I know of a couple people who might do that," he says, "And I'm going to talk to them next week."

Race's last day: Round-the-clock

USA TODAY/CNN POLL
Bush holds his lead

Bush, Dukakis interviews, 4A; Voting hours, 8A; Diaries, 11A

Undecided/Others 6%

Complete poll results, 6A

Dukakis 42%

Bush 52%

How election would look

If undecided voters split the same way as similar voters who have made up their minds, the outcome would be:

Bush 55%
Dukakis 44%
Others 1%

Source: Based on 2,506 interviews with registered voters who say they are certain to vote. Interviews were taken by telephone Nov. 3-6. Gordon S. Black Corporation, Rochester, N.Y., conducted the poll.

By Sam Ward, USA TODAY

By Richard Benedetto
USA TODAY

The final day in the race for the White House climaxes with non-stop campaigning today.

A never-say-die Michael Dukakis — sleeping only in the seat of his chartered jet — plows ahead to Cleveland, St. Louis, L.A., San Francisco and Des Moines, Iowa — insisting he'll pull an upset that'll send pollsters running for cover.

The newest polls — including one by USA TODAY/CNN — show George Bush leading with a margin of five to 12 percentage points.

Meanwhile, a confident-but-cautious George Bush campaigns in Michigan and Ohio before flying to Houston, where he'll vote Tuesday.

Voters get their last chance to compare the two tonight: Bush and Dukakis each bought 30 minutes of network air time:

► At 8 p.m. EST/PST, Dukakis answers questions from voters. He ends his campaign at a 3:30 a.m. rally Tuesday in Des Moines, then moves to Boston.

► Bush, at 8:30 p.m. EST/PST, makes a final appeal for a victory.

The USA TODAY/CNN Poll predicts Bush is on the brink of a win. The Poll of 2,506 certain voters, taken Thursday-Sunday, shows Bush still ahead 52 percent to 42 percent nationally, despite gains in state races.

"There is no Poll today that shows Dukakis winning," says Nelson Polsby, of the University of California at Berkeley. "And the last 25 Polls have showed Bush winning. So it looks like Bush is going to win."

Other Polls out Sunday:

► A Gallup Poll puts Bush ahead by 13 points.

► ABC/Washington Post Poll says the lead is 10 points, 54 percent to 44 percent.

► CBS/New York Times Poll: It's Bush by nine points.

► Polls by Louis Harris Assoc., NBC/Wall Street Journal give Bush a five-point lead. Poll The two continued their war of words in weekend interviews with USA TODAY: Dukakis said he doesn't respect Bush because of negative campaigning; Bush questioned Dukakis' credentials.

► Getting out the vote, 10A

'Even freer' Sakharov visits USA

By Elisa Tinsley
USA TODAY

BOSTON — Nobel Laureate Andrei Sakharov — in his first trip outside the Soviet Union in 30 years — has brought his human rights fight to the USA.

"Two years ago I became a free man when I returned to work in Moscow," he said Sunday at Logan Airport. "Today I became even freer because I have been given the right to travel around the world."

But he noted his "duty to remember others who remain in prison," including a Soviet mathematician jailed for protesting Sakharov's internal exile from 1980 to 1986.

While here, Sakharov will:

► Check into Boston's Massachusetts General Hospital for a medical evaluation. He has heart disease and may need a pacemaker. His wife, Yelena Bonner, had heart bypass surgery there in 1986.

► Attend next week's meeting of the International Foundation for the Survival and Development of Humanity.

► Visit with President Reagan in Washington.

Sakharov was freed from exile as part of Soviet leader Mikhail Gorbachev's call for openness in Soviet society.

His friends, while applauding Sakharov's new ability to travel, remain wary of calls for Soviet democracy.

"Any overestimation of the good will of the Soviet Union is simply ridiculous," says Valeri Soifer, visiting professor at Ohio State University.

Elina Kiritchenko, a visiting Soviet economist, says, "This is obviously a good thing. It means we are opening up."

Sakharov will spend two weeks here. He's expected to visit New York City and Washington; other stops are possible.

► Sakharov's family, 2A

Inside USA TODAY — 4 SECTIONS

News
Editorial/Opinion	10-11A	Basketball	9C
Nation at large	3A	Boxing	1C, 2C
State-by-state	8A	Football	1C, 2C, 4-10C, 12C
Washington/World	4A	Hockey	9C
Weather	12A	State-by-state	10C

Money
Ask Money	3B	**Life**	
Dan Dorfman	2B	Classified	6-7D
Business Travel	7B	Crossword	6D
Your Money Plan	4B	Horoscope	7D
		Television	3D

© COPYRIGHT 1988 USA TODAY, a division of Gannett Co., Inc.

USA SNAPSHOTS
A look at statistics that shape the nation

Highest welfare payments
The average national monthly payment to families receiving Aid to Families with Dependent Children in 1987 was $360. States making the highest payments last year:

Monthly payment per family

Alaska	$571
California	$553
Wisconsin	$493
New York	$492
Massachusetts	$490

Source: House Ways and Means Committee
By Julie Stacey, USA TODAY

Family starts bedside vigil for Hirohito

Special for USA TODAY

TOKYO — Japanese royal family members gathered at Emperor Hirohito's bedside today as the ailing monarch's condition worsened.

The emperor, 87, believed to have abdominal cancer, received four blood transfusions Sunday and vomited blood.

He's now had 56 transfusions in 49 days; doctors are having trouble finding healthy veins.

Prince Aya, 22, was recalled from London's Oxford University Sunday after Hirohito suffered his largest single-day blood loss. Over the weekend:

► Doctors gave Hirohito antibiotics to fight infection.

► Hirohito's blood pressure was 122 over 62. A healthy reading is 120/80. The 5-foot-3 emperor weighs 95 pounds — but relatives say he's sharp.

Crown Prince Akihito, 54, has taken on the emperor's largely ceremonial duties.

Japanese TV gave no special coverage to the latest setback; critics had charged his illness was getting too much attention. Before World War II, the emperor was considered a god.

COVER STORY

Undecided 'are the ball game'

For Dukakis, 'they're his only hope of winning.' For Bush, 'only' way to lose

By Leslie Phillips
USA TODAY

Lillie Knoles is in a jam. Never in her 67 years has she had so much trouble making up her mind about whom to vote for president.

She can't abide by George Bush, much less his "little running mate." And she has no earthly idea what Michael Dukakis would do once in office.

"It's always been an easy choice," says the Aurora, Mo., widow. "This is the first time I don't know which way to go. I wish my husband was here. He'd clarify things."

Lillie Knoles — difficult as her predicament may be — has plenty of company. In these volatile final days, up to 20 percent of voters are still sitting on the fence or say they're uneasy with their decisions.

A USA TODAY/CNN Poll shows five key electoral states with large blocs of undecided voters: California, 7 percent; Illinois, 13 percent; Michigan, 11 percent; Ohio, 12 percent; Pennsylvania, 12 percent. Nationwide, 6 percent remain undecided after again being asked their preference.

These are the voters Bush and Dukakis will speak to in the final days of their two-year quest for the White House.

"They're the ball game right now," says Democratic poll-

Please see COVER STORY next page ►

Boomers: Toys are still us

By Michelle Healy
USA TODAY

Baby boomers aren't playing when it comes to buying kids' toys. They still like oldies but goodies — in up-to-date forms.

In December's Redbook, Joanne Oppenheim, author of Buy Me! Buy Me! The Bank Street Guide to Choosing Toys for Children (Pantheon, $11.95), lists updated oldies that are big hits:

► Motorized Mighty Tonka Tow Truck, Motorizing Power Kit. (Tonka).

► Doctor Barbie. The original party girl is now an M.D. (Mattel).

► Play-Doh Flingles. Use plastic molds, a lump of molding compound,

your finger and you've got finger puppets. (Kenner).

► Gigantik Snakes & Ladders. Oversized replica of Chutes and Ladders; played on 38-inch mat with large pieces. (The Games Gang, Ltd).

► Hot Wheels Color Racers Auto Paint Factory. Cars change colors when dipped in water. (Mattel).

► Playskool Express train set. Battery-operated train set. (Playskool).

► Etch A Sketch Animator 2000. Electronic version of Etch A Sketch uses a stylus to sketch; results appear on attached computer screen. (Ohio Art).

► The classic 1958 Hula Hoop by Wham-O. Some things never change.

The other pattern used by standard papers is called **block** or **modular.** In this approach, stories are assigned multicolumn areas on a page. Often, the stories are short and are complete on the same page. Descriptive headlines cover the entire width of the layout module. Sometimes the modules are enclosed in rules. Photos may be run within the same layout block as the copy. The most popular example of block layout methods is *USA Today*, as shown in **Figure 12-12.** Other papers in the Gannett chain, which issues *USA Today*, also tend to use block layout.

The difference between the column-oriented and block layout approaches is most evident on the front page. A column-oriented paper positions stories according to relative importance, as judged by the editors of the paper. The most important story is at the top of the right-hand column. Less-important stories are aligned, in sequence, with starting positions at the top of the page, then at the bottom of the page.

The size of the headline also represents a judgment about the importance of a story. The larger the headline, the more important a story is judged to be. Almost all stories in a column-oriented front-page layout will jump to the inside of the paper. The jumping of stories is seen as a way of getting readers into the inside of the paper. If possible, stories jumped from page one are completed in positions close to stories on related topics run on inside pages.

Modular layout still places the most important story in the upper right of the front page. However, judgment for the selection of other page one stories is based on other values. Modular-layout papers give high priorities to **human interest** stories. These are stories that appeal to readers on the basis of emotions, rather than because of the importance of the news. An attempt is made to have each front page story end within its copy module. The excption is the **lead,** or most important, story which is in the top-right position. The lead story often jumps to an inside page.

The budget meeting. Regardless of the layout approach followed, the major decisions about placement of stories are made at **budget meetings.** These sessions take place at the beginning of the production cycle for each issue. Budget meetings generally are attended by the managing editor and editors responsible for news areas or departments. Attendees, for example, might include the international news editor, national news editor, metropolitan news editor, and editors of the business, sports, and lifestyle departments.

The editors "pitch" the stories they feel are most important and a consensus is developed. However, the managing editor retains the deciding vote. The stories that are pitched are assigned orders of importance and positions on page one. Jumps for these stories generally fall into the pages assigned to the news and feature departments. Individual editors assign priorities within their own areas. Decisions by these editors are passed along to the makeup editor. The makeup desk then handles actual placement within the guidelines set down by editors.

On smaller papers, budget meetings may be less formal. However, the same evaluations have to be made and the same kinds of decisions have to be reached.

PRODUCTION CONCERNS AND TECHNIQUES

As indicated above, most papers that use desktop publishing will be too small to afford full-page typesetting and/or on-line pagemaking systems. The reasons are largely financial. Laser or typesetting output devices that can handle full-size newspaper pages are too expensive. The printers alone cost far more than the desktop

---

Figure 12-12. This is an example of a standard-size newspaper that uses a modular layout approach.

 DESKTOP JARGON

block or **modular layout** A newspaper makeup approach that assigns modules, or areas, to individual news stories.

human interest story A story that is based on an emotional appeal rather than the importance of the event.

lead story The main, or most important, story on the front page of a newspaper.

budget meeting An editorial meeting that assigns priorities to stories to be used in a newspaper.

publishing systems themselves. Also, full-page makeup for large newspapers requires processing and memory capacities greater than those available with typical microcomputers. To put this in perspective, a newspaper can install 12 or 15 desktop computers for approximately the same cost as a single typesetter such as the Linotronic 300.

Computer Work Stations

Many weekly and small daily newspapers do, in fact, have multiple desktop computers in use. For the most part, these are treated as typesetters. Individual editors handle assigned stories. Reporters have access to work stations for writing stories or handling rewrite assignments.

If the desktop computers are networked, copy can be stored on a central file server after each operation and recalled as necessary. Otherwise, copy is accumulated on diskettes and exchanged between writers and editors. The key, again, is to devise a scheduling and monitoring system. The system should log stories in when they are received. It also is important to keep track of each piece of copy through the writing, editing, makeup, typesetting, and pasteup processes.

This system can be handled manually, perhaps with a status display board. The job also can be done on a personal computer with the aid of spreadsheet software or a specialized scheduling program. Both of these are available commercially and inexpensively.

Pasteup Technique

Most newspapers have pasteup facilities that enable workers to view boards for the entire paper at the same time. Pasteup artists at other types of publications or in commercial studios tend to have one or a few work stations. Boards are mounted on pasteup tables one at a time and processed in stacks, or batches. In a newspaper pasteup area, however, it is common to have a series of flat surfaces set at an angle of perhaps 45 degrees. The effect is something like a long set of shelves placed in rows and along walls. A complete set of boards for an entire issue is set up on these shelves. Thus, all pages are visible and accessible— at all times. A typical newspaper composing room is shown in **Figure 12-13.**

Figure 12-13. Newspaper composing rooms are set up to permit work on all pages at the same time.
Photo by Benedict Kruse.

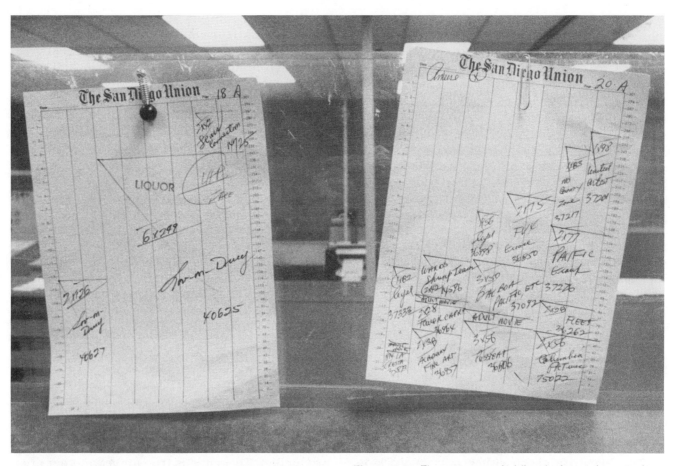

Figure 12-14. The pasteup people follow the layout sheets to place ads on boards before pasting up editorial copy.
Photo by Benedict Kruse.

Pasteup generally is done on boards that are preprinted in a light blue ink that does not reproduce on lithographic film. The printed grid identifies the standard column format for the publication and marks off column depths in half-inch units. There are no light tables and no T-squares or other art tools generally used to align copy on pasteup boards. Instead, copy is aligned visually. Quality is not of commercial caliber required for publications that seek a more polished image. But this approach makes it possible for a lot of people to take part in pasteup at the same time. Newspapers can put together 100 or more pages in a matter of hours.

Typically, the ads are placed on the boards before editorial pasteup begins. **Figure 12-14** shows layout sheets with ads marked. Then, as typesetting begins, stories are routed to the people who will paste up the pages on which they are to appear. The basis for identification and placement is the slug line at the top of the story. On some papers, the slug line also contains the number of the page on which the story will appear. In other situations, a supervisor works from a master budget listing of slug lines and positions for all scheduled stories.

Special Typography to Match Makeup

Each issue of a newspaper requires some special typography. For example, separate type must be set to cover the date and issue identification related to the first-page logo. Running heads and folio numbers must be set for all pages. Jump lines and jump heads must be set for all stories that run on more than one page. As soon as layout sheets are completed, these special type elements should be set. They should be available and waiting for pasteup—before the final rush to deadlines begins.

Circulation Documentation

In a newspaper shop that uses desktop computers, production personnel may become involved in keeping circulation records. These days, most newspapers deliver only a small fraction of their circulation through the mail. Production of labels for these copies can be handled by updating a computer-maintained subscriber mailing list. The computer can generate mailing labels for each issue—in ZIP code order. It is relatively simple to deliver these copies to the Post Office.

At most papers, the majority of copies will be delivered under a wholesaling system. On small papers of the type that will use desktop computers, carriers function as wholesalers or dealers. Copies are delivered in bulk for each route. The carrier receives delivery tickets for copies. These are, in effect, bills. At the end of each month or other billing period, the carrier must pay for the number of copies received. The carrier's price is less than the subscription fee which the carrier collects from the subscribers. This leaves a profit for the carrier. From the publisher's point of view, circulation wholesaling eliminates the need to collect from individual subscribers.

At larger newspapers, a central circulation office keeps distribution records and issues bills. A network of dealers provides destribution services. Under this system, the dealers employ carriers at fixed wages for each route. The dealer is paid by the paper and the paper collects from subscribers.

The key to making either system work is knowing how many papers are required for each route or dealer, every issue. The computer used for this application must produce documents to control press runs and shipping quantities for dealers or routes. One computer output is known as the circulation blotter. This is a listing of dealers and routes, along with the quantities to be delivered to each. The total of these requirements, developed by the computer, becomes the basis for the press run for each edition. Of course, the press run includes an allowance for office copies, advertiser copies, and reference copies of each issue.

At some papers, a separate sheet is output for each bundle of papers to be wrapped by circulation personnel. One sheet is attached to the top of each bundle of papers as it is tied and loaded onto a delivery truck. These bundle sheets provide an individual control for each distribution point. The bundle sheets also are references used if dealers or carriers want to adjust quantities for succeeding issues.

This has been a brief view of a major, multi-billion-dollar industry. There is much more to the newspaper business than has been covered in this chapter. The significance of this review is to acquaint you with new opportunities available for people with rounded training in publication production. The same is true for yet another area of publishing, the book industry, which is covered in the chapter that follows.

THE MAKEUP DESK

1. Prepare a layout for a standard newspaper that uses column layout patterns. Base your layout on stories selected from any newspapers available to you.

2. Prepare a layout for a standard newspaper that uses a modular, or block, layout approach. Pick your stories from any newspapers available to you.

THE COMPOSING ROOM

1. Set type and do a pasteup for the front page of a newspaper. You can use the logo and other top-of-page elements from any newspaper available to you. Capture copy from any newspaper. Print out, proofread, correct, and paste up your copy on a board or sheet of paper.

Books $\boldsymbol{13}$

Editorial Budget

❏ **The book business** is a major industry with annual sales of about $4 billion.

❏ **Book publishing operations** fall into two broad categories, text and trade/professional.

❏ **Book production** requirements reflect the fact that books consist primarily of text and contain large numbers of pages.

❏ **Publication development** has some special requirements in the book field. One area in which books are different from other publications lies in author relationships. Most books are written by outside authors. This means that the book publisher does not control the longest, most critical phase of product development.

❏ **Production scheduling** can be difficult because production planning often does not begin until after a manuscript is written. After that, tight schedules are needed to conform to seasonal marketing requirements.

❏ **Production efficiency** can be improved greatly if desktop techniques are used. As a manuscript is being written on a PC, typesetting codes can be included. This helps make for a comparatively short production cycle.

❏ **Typesetting operations** on desktop publishing systems rely on operator judgment. It is not practical to automate typesetting to the same degree as can be done with large computers.

❏ **Page makeup** can be handled on-line or through pasteup, depending on the complexity of design for individual books.

THE BOOK BUSINESS

Americans buy some $4 billion worth of books annually. This represents a lot of reading, especially since many books go through multiple readings. For example, an elementary or high school text will be used an average of eight to 12 semesters. Usually, a different student uses the book during each semester. College texts also may undergo multiple readings. Books read for personal improvement or entertainment tend to be swapped among family members and friends.

The importance of books for a modern society has been stressed through the attention focused on a major failure: Some 27 million Americans have been classified as illiterate. They do not read well enough to function as independent citizens. The plight of these people helps to underscore the importance of reading as a universal skill. The ability to read opens vast job and entertainment opportunities. Reading is a part of learning and succeeding. Reading skills are promoted through school experiences and through use of libraries like the one shown in **Figure 13-1.**

For this text, the book industry is important because it makes heavy use of word processing and desktop publishing computers. Services of people with desktop publishing skills are in demand at hundreds of companies. The book publishing field is dominated by a few large companies with book sales that run into hundreds of millions of dollars annually. However, the largest number of publishers are small companies that produce anywhere from a few to as many as 20 to 50 books annually.

Book Industry Segments

The book industry tends to divide itself into two major segments:

- Education
- Trade and professional books.

Figure 13-1. Libraries stock millions of books and are important centers for information and reading enjoyment. Photo by Liane Enkelis.

Educational publishing. The designation "educational publisher" generally identifies a company that provides learning materials for schools and colleges. Educational publishers are classified according to the level of materials they produce. Elementary and high school (elhi) publishers produce materials for use from pre-school through secondary levels. Textbooks certainly are familiar in classroom scenes like the one in **Figure 13-2.**

College publishers cover the post-secondary market. Within the college field, publishers tend to specialize, or to set up specialized departments. Community colleges tend to be regarded as a separate publishing market from four-year or graduate schools. Four-year colleges, of course, are a major market in themselves.

Also private post-secondary vocational or trade schools often have special textbook needs. Books used in these schools often are different from those offered to community colleges and four-year schools. Because they offer educational experiences for post-secondary (beyond high school) students, these schools generally are served by college divisions of publishing companies.

Figure 13-2. Schools and colleges are major users of books.

All told, educational publishers sell approximately $2 billion worth of books a year, about half the total for all book sales.

Trade and professional books. The term *trade,* within the book publishing industry, implies that books are produced for consumers. More specifically, trade books are distributed chiefly through bookstores.

There is a distinction between trade and *mass market books,* which are sold in supermarkets, drug stores, airport newsstands, and other busy locations.

 DESKTOP JARGON

trade In the book business, the portion of the industry that prepares books for the general public.

mass market books Books sold in supermarkets and high-volume outlets other than book stores.

Professional books are those sold directly to attorneys, doctors, businesspeople, and others who purchase books to help them do their jobs. Most of these sales are through mail offerings and specialized book clubs.

Some book stores carry professional books. In addition, professional book publishers produce study and training materials for job training. Many of these books are used in career training programs for employees of large companies. Private business organizations are reputed to spend $60 billion a year or more in teaching and training their employees. This represents a large and growing market for both professional and educational book publishers. A number of specialized organizations also prepare texts and other learning aids. Some of these companies conduct training sessions on a contract basis.

A specialized subdivision of professional publishing is known as *reference books.* As their name implies, reference books are designed to be used to look up information— not to be read from front to back. Examples of reference books include dictionaries and encyclopedias. Many thousands of special reference volumes are sold for use in specialized fields.

Trade book marketing is characterized by individual sales to readers or small orders to bookstores. This is different from educational sales, which usually involve volume purchases by school districts or college book stores. Sales to book stores involve a special risk: Industry practices permit book stores to return unsold books to publishers for credit. In effect, sales can be canceled long after books have been delivered and paid for.

THE NATURE OF BOOK PRODUCTION

Products of the book publishing industry are diverse. In particular, there are major differences between books prepared for educational and trade markets. From a desktop publishing point of view, however, there are a number of common denominators. These are the factors that relate to production applications— and to job potentials in book production.

Common Production Requirements

The main feature common to most books is that they consist primarily of text. Further, the text for any individual publisher tends to be set in a minimum number of fonts that fit into uniform layouts. In some instances, particularly for novels or nonfiction trade books, a publication consists entirely of text. There often are no subheads. Thus, the only variation from body type tends to be chapter titles and running heads. Therefore, design and layout, except for book covers, tend to be simple and easy to devise.

Educational books do have more design elements than most trade books. For example, there may be an element at the beginning of each chapter that states learning objectives. Each chapter also may have a number of elements of *end matter.* These items can include content summaries, quizzes, and project or research assignments. Together, these elements of a textbook are known as *pedagogical* material. Pedagogy is teaching. Pedagogical materials in books are designed to help students to review and remember what they have learned. Even considering these elements as exceptions, design and layout of books is relatively simple. This, of course, is in comparison with the challenges encountered on magazines or newspapers.

Book production lends itself particularly well to desktop publishing techniques. Therefore, book publishing represents a major area of potential employment for people trained in desktop publishing. Another reason why employment potential is good lies in the way book publishing companies tend to be organized. Most book publishers are set up as a series of specialized departments. This is different from the newspaper business, or even some magazines. Periodicals are produced by editors who usually are able to handle makeup and production as well as copy preparation. In book publishing, production is a specialty that is attracting increasing numbers of people.

MANUSCRIPT DEVELOPMENT

A special characteristic of book publishing is the comparative lack of control over definition and development of new products. Independent authors create the manuscripts for most books. These manuscripts are the basic products. Publishers can modify products through editing. But a publisher rarely is in full control.

Control becomes even harder as authors become successful. In bringing out a book, a publisher helps the author to build a reputation.

Once an author is known, it becomes easier to take the next book to another publisher.

A *developmental editor* must mix language skills with diplomacy. Developmental editors are the people who work with authors to coordinate the preparation of manuscripts. The developmental editor is responsible both for criticizing manuscripts and for maintaining amiable relationships with authors. The two aspects of this responsibility can leave the editor in an uncomfortable, sometimes conflict-ridden, position.

PRODUCTION SCHEDULING: A SPECIAL CHALLENGE

Since publishers do not have full control over the pace at which manuscripts are developed, scheduling can be a problem. Long periods of time can elapse between commitment to publish a book and actual printing and binding. Developmental cycles of three to five years are not unusual. Even so-called "expedited" procedures may require 18 to 24 months for development and publication of a book.

Herein is a major difference between production of books and other publications. On a magazine or newspaper, close coordination is possible from the time manuscript preparation begins until final printing. This is true even for catalogs and other in-house publications. Book publishing is different. Production tends to be something like a pipeline or assembly line. An individual publisher may have up to 50 or more publications under development. Each book works its way through the system, step by step, at its own, individual pace.

For production people, this situation means that scheduling tends to be unpredictable and difficult. Generally, book publishers wait until a manuscript is written, reviewed, and released for publication before production processes even start. This means that such steps as copy and production editing don't begin until a complete manuscript is in hand.

At that point, a manuscript that may be 500 or more pages long becomes a single work assignment. This, too, represents a major difference between book publishing and other media. A news story or magazine article rarely is more than 10 to 15 pages long. In book production, it may take months just to handle copy editing and author revision.

Production people can streamline the process significantly by helping to encourage authors to work on word processing computers. If a manuscript is received on diskette as well as in hard-copy form, the production cycle can be reduced dramatically, often by months.

Even though developmental cycles tend to be long, production schedules tend to be frantic. In part, this is because book marketing, for most publishers, is highly seasonal. Educational books must come out early in the year to earn fall adoptions, or commitments to use specific books. Trade publishers generally have fall and spring lists to coincide with consumer purchasing trends. Literally, a book that is a few weeks late can lose a whole year of revenues (sales).

Faced with tensions like this, production people tend to avoid committing themselves to schedules until a manuscript is released. Then, when a commitment is made, most publishers begin to promote a book while it is still in production. This makes for extreme pressures to deliver books on schedule.

MARKETING CHALLENGES

Bringing a book to market can be extremely expensive. Different challenges exist for text and trade markets.

Textbook Marketing

Textbooks have to be "sampled." Free "review" copies are given to educators. Sometimes, as

DESKTOP JARGON

professional books Books sold directly to attorneys, doctors, businesspeople, and others who purchase books to help them do their jobs.

reference books Books designed for looking up information rather than for continuous reading.

end matter Elements of a textbook that appear at the end of a chapter or at the back of the book.

pedagogical materials Textbook elements designed to help students to review and remember what they have learned.

developmental editor A person who works with an author to monitor and assist in development of a manuscript.

many as 5,000 to 10,000 review copies of a single title are given away. Unwanted review copies often are sold to secondary dealers, who market directly to bookstores, bypassing the publisher. Thus, sample copies reduce sales because they are sold as "used" at about half the regular prices. Publishers lose millions of sales dollars each year due to this practice.

When a book is adopted for use by a state education system or school district, the publisher takes on a major commitment. The publisher generally is required to continue to supply copies of the book at the same price for at least five years. In some states, the commitment must be backed through placement of an inventory of books in a "depository." A book depository is a specialized warehouse and distribution center.

One textbook depository, in Dallas, gained notoriety as the base from which President Kennedy was assassinated. The Texas School Book Depository, contrary to a commonly held belief, was a private business venture. This business failed and went into bankruptcy in 1988.

The point: It costs money to keep inventory tied up waiting for the possibility of orders that might not come.

Trade Book Marketing

Trade books require major promotions. Individual books can have promotional budgets of $50,000 or more. The promotional commitment, in turn, makes for major expenditures for printing and inventory. Individual titles can have press runs of one million or more. Then, the books are subject to returns.

Profit potential. Despite the expense, book publishing can be profitable. Typically, the list (retail) price of a book is six to nine times the cost of paper, printing, and binding (manufacturing costs). Therefore, many books can be profitable with sales of as few as 2,500 or 3,000 copies. A text or professional book that sells 25,000 copies or more is considered to be extremely profitable. Some trade books have sales that run into millions of copies.

Given this situation, publishers conduct extensive market research while a book is under development. Commitments for promotion and press runs are based on results of this research. The money committed to production enhancements, such as color, illustrations, photographs,

and so on, depends directly on the results of market research.

BOOK DEVELOPMENT

Book development follows the general publication-development process described in Chapter 2. Some special requirements stem from the nature of the business. These are identified and described below.

Manuscript Submission

Every book is a complete product that must be developed from scratch. Thus, a large publisher may have to create, develop, and invest money in production of hundreds of new products per year. Compare this with such consumer-product fields as automobiles or appliances. For a multibillion-dollar manufacturing company, one or two dozen new products a year can represent a heavy design and development workload.

Book development does have something in common with other products: Each new book starts with an idea. The idea can originate with an editor who seeks an author. Or, an author can seek a publisher, sometimes through a literary agent. The idea is formalized in an outline or a prospectus. If a prospectus is prepared, it includes an outline and preliminary table of contents. Also included may be information on the targeted market, any competition, and the special features of the proposed book. Significantly, the term "prospectus" typically describes a document that offers stock or other securities to investors. In much the same way, a book prospectus seeks a publisher to invest in its development and marketing.

The outline or prospectus is reviewed by specialists who are familiar with the targeted market. Each editor generally knows a number of prospective reviewers who can be called upon according to their experience and expertise.

Initial negotiations between an author and a publisher depend upon the state the manuscript is in before a contract is negotiated. As one example, negotiations may be based on just an outline and prospectus from the author. If this is the case, and if the project has appeal, the publisher generally will ask for one or more manuscript chapters as samples. However, established authors may be offered a contract on the basis of an outline or prospectus alone.

The negotiations, based on whatever initial submissions are received, culminate in an *author contract.* Though the term "contract" is used, the arrangement is far less binding than legal agreements in many other businesses. Most publishers include clauses that permit cancellation if they are not satisfied with the final manuscript. Also, most contracts can be cancelled if sales of the book are not satisfactory. Thus, although called a contract, the agreement with the author is more like an expression of mutual hope and good intentions.

Identification of authors and contracting for books generally is the responsibility of a person with the title *acquisition editor.* Once a book is under contract, the project generally is passed along to a developmental editor.

Developmental Editing

Manuscript development can be an uncertain business. At the time a contract is signed, a manuscript probably does not exist. Therefore, a contract itself does not guarantee publication. By one estimate, some 70 percent of contracted manuscripts are never brought to publication. That is, most book development projects fall by the wayside. Either the author loses interest or the publisher finds that the prospective book lacks the appeal to justify publication.

The developmental editor monitors a project from the time a contract is signed until a complete manuscript is accepted for publication. The developmental editor's responsibilities include continuing contact with the author to get the book written and to establish schedules. The developmental editor also is responsible for followup. The developmental editor receives segments of a manuscript from the author. Usually, progress is checked by asking qualified, outside people to review the manuscript as it is written. These reviews are discussed with the author. Reviews may be the basis for requesting manuscript revision by the author. Because there is so much to do, manuscript development usually is the longest single job in the book development process.

Copy Editing

The responsibilities of copy editors are reviewed earlier. These responsibilities are pretty much the same for books as for other types of publications. The unique thing about copy editing

for books lies in the relationship with external authors. At magazines or newspapers, copy usually is released as soon as the editor is through with it. For a book manuscript, the author generally is consulted. If an author and copy editor disagree about any proposed changes, negotiation follows. Thus, a book copy editor generally requires more tact and more time to complete the job than is needed in other fields.

Production Editing

The main responsibility of a production editor is to prepare manuscripts for typesetting. As indicated earlier, the work can be simplified and time requirements shortened if desktop publishing or computer typesetting techniques are used. In some instances, as was the case with this book, the production editing function can be combined with copy editing. The combined step is performed after reviews are received. The same person makes the changes necessary to respond to reviewer suggestions and to code the text for typesetting.

Design and Layout

Many design and layout requirements conform to industry standards or respond to book content. For example, many trade books use formats and sizes that conform to the measurements and shapes of display racks in bookstores. Virtually all books are designed to fit the most convenient paper sheet or roll sizes for the printing method to be used.

Editors try to select a trim size that is best for each individual book. For example, an 8.5-by-11-inch format was selected for this book. This size, which is considered a large format, provides an opportunity to present extensive illustrations. These illustrations are needed to

 DESKTOP JARGON

author contract An agreement between an author and publisher to develop, publish, and market a defined work.

acquisition editor A person who contacts prospective authors, defines products, and carries negotiations through to a contract.

demonstrate use of desktop publishing software. The two-column format was selected to achieve two purposes.

First, the two-column format accommodates more copy on each page than a single-column format with wide margins. With more copy on each page, the number of pages in the book can be minimized, as can its selling price.

Second, a large number of illustrations was planned. They would have taken too much space if a wider column format was used.

A further advantage for the two-column format is that a narrow column is easier to read. The human eye can scan narrower columns more efficiently that wider ones. Therefore, it was felt that it would be easier for readers to absorb information in the two-column format than if one wider column were used.

Typesetting and Mechanicals

Desktop publishing techniques can help to shorten the book development cycle. In part, this is because multiple functions can be combined. Also, waiting times between operations can be eliminated. This book can illustrate the benefits. As indicated earlier, the manuscript for this book was prepared on IBM PC and compatible systems. The author was experienced in the field before the project started. Because of this experience, the time required to gather information for the text was short. Writing time also was minimized. This is because the author can generate 15 or more pages of manuscript in a full day of writing.

As a checkpoint, the person responsible for the book's art and production reviewed the manuscript as each chapter was written. As part of the review, a few sample illustrations were prepared when the manuscript was under development. Given this situation, the manuscript was developed in about 40 working days spread over a three-month time frame.

Manuscript review was carried out incrementally. That is, chapters were submitted and reviewed as they were completed. Then, as reviews were received, the computer files were updated to include recommended changes acceptable to the publisher and author. By the time the manuscript was written, the staff had prepared sample layouts for the interior pages of the book. Thus, it was possible to begin formatting type for early chapters while later chapters

were being finalized. Result: The entire development cycle ran about seven months. This time span covered everything from writing through delivery of mechanicals.

Special typesetting codes. Under the typesetting techniques used for this book, coding requirements for the electronic manuscript were minimal. With the software used, one problem involved coding to control copy indentation. Notice that this book makes extensive use of indented text blocks to stress information content. To illustrate:

- Indenting makes for reading emphasis.
- Indenting stresses key content points.

The word processor used on the PC treats indentation as a key-controlled function. The author depresses the F4 key to indent all copy input until the next RETURN is entered.

The F4 key is not sensed under ASCII transmission between computers. However, the TAB code is carried across between computers. This means that the indent codes are not needed for typesetting. However, the indents are important in conveying the style of the manuscript to the publisher and reviewers. Therefore, the author needed a way to show indents in the manuscript. A separate arrangement was needed to be sure that the indented elements were picked up in typesetting.

To deal with this situation, a formatting technique was established under which indented copy is preceded by both a TAB and an F4 entry. The F4 entry indents the text on the manuscript for the benefit of reviewers. The person who handles typesetting uses a copy of the manuscript as a guide. The manuscript indicates where text is to be indented. The TAB settings that come across from the PC disk identify the points where indents are needed.

Another example lies in the coding for key words within text. The word processing software has codes that cause the Macintosh to set type in boldface and italic fonts. There has been no problem in coding type for either boldface or italic. However, the publisher of this book wanted key words to appear in ***boldface italic.*** Tests showed that the dual coding for bold face and italic were not picked up in translation from the PC to the Macintosh. So, special coding was established. Words to run in ***boldface italic*** are preceded and followed by the carat symbol (^). The Macintosh operator searches for these symbols, selects the identified words, and causes them to be set in boldface italic. **Figure 13-3** is a screen display that demonstrates use of codes for both boldface and bold-italic copy.

Another special technique involves identification of points at which illustrations are to be entered in text. In this book, note that all illustrations are assigned figure numbers. The text references to figure numbers are in boldface, as illustrated in Figure 13-3. In addition, as shown in the same illustration, the author placed descriptions of the illustrations within the manuscript. These notations were marked by strings of three asterisks (***). This coding enabled the typesetter to find and delete the descriptions. The notations in the manuscript served as guides for placement of illustrations in layouts.

The coding technique used requires judgment by the desktop publishing operator who formats text transmitted from the PC. Experience has convinced the author that it is best to rely on judgment of a skilled, trained operator. By comparison, it is too difficult and costly to attempt to automate the entire typesetting process on a desktop computer.

By contrast, when type is transmitted over communication lines for setting on a computerized typesetter, more extensive coding often is done. To illustrate, there are separate codes for regular italic and boldface italic because the large-scale typesetter makes the conversions automatically. With the smaller capacity of a desktop system, it is acceptable to have the operator do this formatting manually.

Page makeup. Makeup for this book was done through pasteup techniques. This decision followed a detailed experiment. A complete chapter was made up through use of PageMaker 3.01. **Figure 13-4** shows a dialog box used to create a style sheet for the body copy of this book.

Initially, the intent was to process the Macintosh disks through a Linotronic system. The plan was to go directly to platemaking film. The laser printer outputs would be used as final proofs that could be modified before filmmaking.

Experience showed that pasteup would cost less and be more efficient. Because the artist on this project was experienced in pasteup, this method took far less time. Pasteup production rates were about twice as fast as those for electronic makeup.

In part, this was because there are so many elements in this book. For electronic makeup, separate files had to be handled to position chapter headings, body copy, each illustration, and every caption. In particular, it took a lot of time to position and arrange the **Desktop Jargon** elements on recto pages. If a key term appeared where the copy box was inserted, the text and the terms had to be shuffled. The operations went smoothly. But they took a lot longer than comparable pasteup functions.

Figure 13-3. Boldface and bold italic coding are demonstrated on this screen display.

```
   »With this word processing package, you mark characters
to be printed in |boldface| type by enclosing the word with
a special printer control character, specified by pressing
the Alt-Z key combination.«
   »Italics, on the other hand, cannot be printed with many
professional word processing packages.  To specify to a
typesetting system that a word should be ^italicized,^ the
author of this book used the caret symbol as a typesetting
code.«
```

Figure 13-4. The style sheet for the body type of this book was created with this dialog box.

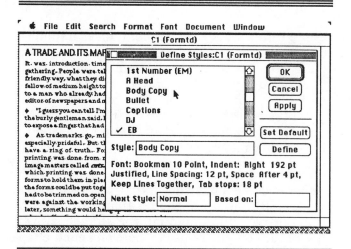

Also, the publisher found that it would cost less to shoot platemaking film on a camera than to generate Linotronic outputs.

The copy you are reading was generated under control of Microsoft Word 3.01. Reproduction proofs were backed with a makeup wax and placed on pasteup boards. Line art was pasted in place on the boards. Key lines were used to indicate photo positions. The pasteup was done in two-page spreads.

As each spread was completed, its balance and composition were checked. In a book of this type, balance is established chiefly by positioning illustrations for cross-page balance. In a two-column format, there is a choice between illustration placements. One method is to attempt to group illustrations side by side. The other is to let them run in top and bottom positions.

Positioning of headlines also affects the appearance of a book. There are four columns across each two-page spread viewed by the reader. It is considered bad makeup practice to *tombstone* headings. Tombstoning occurs when multiple headings are positioned alongside of and across from each other within a two-page spread. The name comes from the appearance: The heads are said to resemble the placement of headstones in a cemetery. It is visually more interesting to vary the positions of heads. This helps guide the reader's eye to multiple positions within each spread.

As a general practice, laser printouts are prepared for small groups of pages as they are made up. *Spooling* software permits the system to operate the printer while a user is working on other pages.

Some notes from experience: It takes a number of pages, sometimes 100, for a new toner cartridge to "break in" and begin delivering top quality outputs. It has proved best to use new cartridges for rough proofs until top quality output is realized. Then, the cartridge is removed and saved for final, quality printouts, made on top-quality paper.

Experience also has shown that it is best to use working files that are shorter than 128 pages. A full 128-page file would tax the storage capacities of the computers used. Therefore, **each chapter of this book was handled as a separate file.**

The manuscript files were saved initially on a hard disk. However, each file was copied to a diskette at the end of every day. No matter what you do on a computer, **it pays to back up your files—frequently.**

There are books for which page makeup software is efficient and practical. For example, to set type for a novel, the text could be allowed to flow into a PageMaker format automatically. Sections of up to 128 pages could be put together with minimal effort from the operator. Also, if a book had a limited number of illustrations, electronic page makeup would be efficient. For example, suppose a history text had a one-column layout and used one illustration every four to six pages. Electronic makeup would be more efficient than pasteup. The decision factor is tied to the complexity of a book's makeup.

Indexing

Most books—novels and other works of fiction are the notable exceptions—require an index. For some documents, there are software tools that permit computerized generation of an index. As a requirement for computerized indexing, however, codes must be inserted in text to identify the terms and references to be included. Although automatic indexing can be a powerful tool, the author elected not to do the index.

The decision was based on the conditions that applied for this particular book. The author has extensive writing, editing, and management responsibilities. His time was felt to be too critical to be used on an index. Instead, a professional indexer was assigned to do the job. Terms and references to be indexed were keyed into a supermicrocomputer with special software. The index was generated automatically and transmitted to a microcomputer at the shop where

 DESKTOP JARGON

tombstone A layout flaw in which headings are lined up in rows so they are said to resemble tombstones in a cemetery.

spooling software Programs that permit a computer to operate a printer while a user is working on other materials.

this book was developed. The text of the index then was carried across to the typesetting computer for formatting.

This chapter concludes your review of desktop publishing techniques for specific media. The chapter that follows moves into a new topic area that could play an important role in your future. The next chapter deals with procedures and guidelines that can be helpful in setting up a desktop publishing facility. Also covered are the major trends in desktop publishing that could affect your future.

THE MAKEUP DESK

1. Secure copies of a paperback novel and a textbook. Compare the following elements of makeup for the two books:

   A. Top and bottom margins

   B. Inside and outside margins

   C. Running heads and folios

   D. Type size and column width.

   What do these comparative features tell you about objectives for designing textbooks as compared with trade books?

2. Find a textbook that uses a one-column format. Count the number of characters per line in the one-column book. Then count the number of lines per page. Do the same for one line of this book. Then count the number of lines per page and multiply by two to get the full line count. Multiply the number of characters by the number of lines for each book. Which book gets more information on a page? From a design standpoint, evaluate the trade-offs between one-column and two-column design.

THE COMPOSING ROOM

1. Measure the page dimension for this book. Also measure the column widths, the margins, and column lengths. From this information, prepare a page makeup format for this book. Use any page makeup software available to you. Allow for up to 30 pages for each page makeup file.

14 Setting up a Production Facility

Editorial Budget

❏ **Desktop publishing requirements** should be analyzed in a series of steps that follow proven systems analysis methods.

❏ **Definition of results** expected from a desktop publishing system is the first step.

❏ **The systems analysis process** proceeds with identification of sources and inputs. Additional steps include Define Processing Requirements, Determine Needs for Storage and File Handling, Specify Equipment and Software Requirements, and Provide for Human Factors.

❏ **Storage and memory** requirements are among the keys to equipping a desktop publishing facility. Large storage capacities are needed because of software demands and large text and image files. Memory size affects the processing capacity of the entire system.

❏ **Ergonomic considerations** are important because people must be comfortable and safe to be productive. Attention must be paid to measures that will reduce effects of eyestrain, tension, and fatigue.

❏ **Trends in desktop publishing** include increased hardware capabilities, more sophisticated software, coordination between desktop and large systems, and advances in printing technology.

JOINING THE CLUB

Desktop publishing has become the thing to do. Since the 1950s, the idea of keeping up with competitors and neighbors has been a factor in decisions to purchase computers. Many computers have been installed for little reason more than the fact that everybody seemed to be doing it. It started with big computers. Then it spread to minicomputers and microcomputers. Along the way, many executives and managers installed terminals and personal computers. In some instances, the chief reason seemed to be that they didn't want to be the only ones on their floor or in their company without one. At this writing, the same kind of logic is afflicting the desktop publishing field. So, the reasons for this chapter:

- The information that follows should help in reaching decisions that evaluate desktop publishing systems on their merits. With a little knowledge and a realistic perspective, it is hoped, practical choices of hardware and software can be made.

- You may find yourself involved with a desktop publishing installation purchased by someone who joined the stampede. If so, the information presented here may help you to turn the situation around. The idea: An understanding of the factors involved may help you to develop useful results from questionable decisions.

Desktop publishing hardware and software are valuable tools when they are used effectively. The chapters up to this point are aimed at building your background. You have covered publishing operations generally. You also have learned about a number of specific techniques for applying desktop publishing tools.

Now, there is a good chance that you have developed enough interest to consider working in the desktop publishing field. If so, this chapter is aimed at helping you gain some background that can have future value on the job market.

ANALYSIS, NOT PARALYSIS

No matter where you go to work, a first step is to take stock of your situation. You need to know what is expected of you and what tools you have to work with. These needs are clear. A harder job can be to figure out where to begin. Many people just dive in at any point. Pretty soon, they find themselves going in circles. Analysis and development of systems should be an organized effort that is carried out systematically.

Many people were running in disorganized circles during the 1950s and 1960s—the days when computers were new and mysterious. In many cases, results were tragic. For example, one early airline reservation system was reported to have overrun its budget by more than $40 million. Other ambitious efforts resulted in cost overruns reported at $10 to $100 million.

Early failures got people thinking about how to manage projects for development of computer systems. The result has been the emergence of a professional specialty known as **systems analysis.** Systems analysis techniques recognize that every computer-related system is individual. However, study of problems to be solved and development of solutions to those problems can benefit from a standard approach.

Systems analysts start the study of any system development problem by defining the results or outputs needed. This identifies the destination or purpose for a project or for a computer installation. From there, study of problems and devising of solutions follows an orderly pattern.

The following are typical steps for application of systems analysis methods. This approach is especially appropriate for someone who is assigned to set up or organize a desktop publishing facility.

- Define desired results.
- Identify sources or inputs.
- Define processing requirements.
- Determine needs for storage and file handling.
- Specify equipment and software requirements.
- Provide for human factors.

 DESKTOP JARGON

systems analysis A discipline that specializes in designing procedures and determining hardware and software needs for computer operations.

Notice that the process places initial and strong emphasis on understanding and defining the results to be delivered. As illustrated in **Figure 14-1,** specification of equipment and layout of the facility are the last steps in the process.

This outline represents a general-purpose methodology that can work for any information system or computer installation. However, the review that follows is focused specifically on desktop publishing. Even if you become involved in an existing facility, the same approach applies. By starting with an understanding of the results you want, you can tell whether your equipment and software will do the job.

DEFINE DESIRED RESULTS

As a starting point, describe the publication you will produce and the number of pages it will contain. This will help even if you are assigned to work with an existing facility. It never hurts to know what is expected of you. In defining results, be specific. You need more than just an

Figure 14-1. This flowchart traces the steps in a systems analysis process aimed at evaluating existing desktop publishing facilities or determining needs of new facilities.

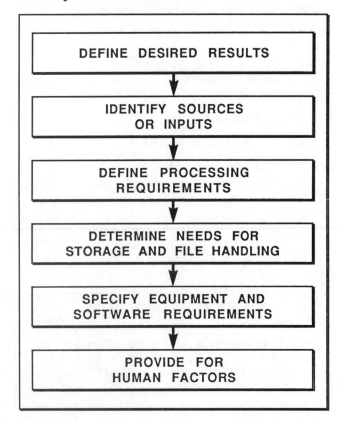

approximate page count, although that's a good starting point. You also need to project the number and type (in terms of complexity) of illustrations you will generate.

Once your outputs are identified, you also will need a description of the work flow. Are there ups and downs in work volume? Are deadlines tight and are they critical? For that matter, you have to know whether you can predict work volumes at all. If you can't, be sure that some assumptions are made about how much work the facility is to do. Put these assumptions in writing to serve as a basis for your planning. Establish what can reasonably be expected of you. Give yourself a basis for measuring your achievements.

IDENTIFY SOURCES OR INPUTS

The inputs from which desktop publishing outputs will be generated include manuscripts and illustrations.

For your text inputs, you need to know who your authors or contributors are or will be. Then, with their help, you need to predict the number of pages of manuscript that will be taken into the system. You also need to indicate whether manuscript will come to you on disk or in typewritten, handwritten, or dictated form. If you are to receive typewritten manuscripts, evaluate the alternatives of keyboarding and scanning for input. If scanning is to be considered, you need assurances of the quality of the manuscripts. If the manuscript is to be edited by hand, you have no choice but to keyboard your input.

Inputs for illustrations can be critical because of the time that can be spent in creating and reworking illustrations. If you will start with "clean," legible drawings or sketches, transposing the drawings into computer files can be easy. If the inputs will be so rough they will be hard to read, double your estimated time for creation of drawings. You will need the extra time to rework the drawings due to errors that result because the originals are hard to read.

An ideal situation would be to arrange to receive manuscripts and original drawings on disk. To illustrate, **Figure 14-2** is a screen display for the files on one of the PC diskettes for this book. Each of three diskettes contained more than 250,000 characters of text. Individual chapters were transferred to a Macintosh Plus system in minutes. If this manuscript had been

```
A>dir

    Volume in drive A has no label
    Directory of  A:\

C1        DOC      54272    1-01-80   3:39a
C4        DOC      53760    1-01-80   4:37a
C5        DOC      48128    1-01-80   8:30a
C2        DOC      50176    1-01-80   2:04a
C3        DOC      74240    1-01-80   3:25a
          5 File(s)        80896 bytes free

A>
```

Figure 14-2. This screen display shows the files for the chapters of the manuscript for this book that are on one diskette.

received in typewritten form, input would have been a major job. The work of capturing, proofreading, and correcting the input would have taken 12 to 15 working days.

The point: Great savings are possible if the people who generate manuscripts and art use personal computers. The computers used to prepare illustrations will, of course, need graphics capabilities. If this is the case, you need to find out what software is being used. Then you will have to arrange for compatibility between the source systems and yours.

DEFINE PROCESSING REQUIREMENTS

Once you have defined results (outputs) and sources (inputs), you need to determine the processing necessary to convert inputs to outputs. You have to define the operations to be performed and the volumes to be handled.

For example, suppose the workload for a given month will involve 500 pages of input received on disk. You know what the remaining jobs will involve. The text will have to be transferred to the desktop publishing system. Type will have to be formatted and proofread. Corrections will need to be made. Then, the text will have to be imported to pagemaking software. The last steps will be producing and printing completed pages. One way to document and review this analysis is by drawing a simple flow diagram like the one in **Figure 14-3.**

Similar processing descriptions can be worked out for illustrations. At this point, you

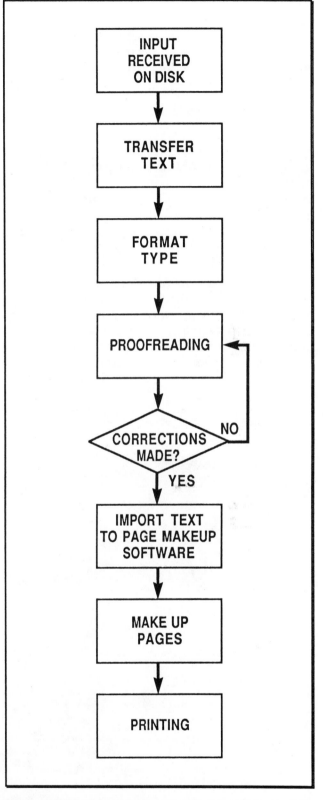

Figure 14-3. To determine equipment needs, it is necessary to define the operations to be performed and the volumes of work to be done. This flowchart identifies some of the steps needed to transform text and art inputs to outputs of finished documents. The analysis should determine the volume of each type of work to be performed.

need to identify volumes of work and tasks to be performed. Later in the systems analysis process, you will determine what equipment and how many people you need to do the defined work. Right now, the job is definition.

DETERMINE NEEDS FOR STORAGE AND FILE HANDLING

This step is particularly important to the efficiency of the desktop publishing facility you may be planning or running. Remember that desktop publishing files are large. Storage capacity is a major concern. Also, memory capacities of computers are important. The size of memory helps to determine the processing speed of your computer.

The information you develop at this time comes from the workload estimates you projected during the previous two steps. If you are processing 500 pages of manuscript, for example, the word processing source files will occupy about one megabyte of storage space.

Then, when this text is transferred to typesetting format, you probably will need two to three megabytes of additional storage space.

The page makeup files that you create probably will need six to seven megabytes of storage space.

When illustration files are added, you need additional megabytes of storage space. The idea, at this point, is to figure out how much disk storage you want for your working files.

You also need to figure out how much disk storage you will need for your software. In the desktop publishing business, storage space for system software adds up quickly. Fortunately, the technologies of disk storage have improved while prices of disks have declined. **Figure 14-4**

Figure 14-4. Hard disk files that provide extensive, inexpensive storage are necessary for desktop publishing systems. Shown here is a hard disk unit that gives the user the storage and speed benefits of a fixed hard disk, plus the removability and flexibility of a floppy disk. Courtesy of Tecmar, Inc.

illustrates the simplicity of modern disk storage devices. Tens of megabytes of capacity can be added to any desktop publishing system for only a few hundred dollars.

Regardless of what you do about hard disks, you need to think separately about memory requirements. You use memory to support actual processing. Memory also is involved in all file transfers. For example, you use memory when you back up your working files from hard disk to diskette. Thus, memory access holds the key to your productivity. It is, literally, hundreds of times faster to access files from memory than from disk storage. The more memory you have, the less time you will have to spend waiting for access to needed files. Your conclusions about your storage and memory requirements will be critical in deciding the configuration (and cost) of your desktop publishing equipment.

SPECIFY EQUIPMENT AND SOFTWARE REQUIREMENTS

In the equipment area, the personal computer and desktop publishing fields have been unique in terms of longevity of hardware and software. The Apple II computer, introduced in 1977, is still in widespread use. The IBM PC, introduced in 1981, is still the most widely used microcomputer. WordStar was the first successful word processing application package. Introduced in the late 1970s, it still enjoys widespread use. MS DOS, the operating system introduced in 1981 to support the IBM PC, is still the most widely used system software for microcomputers.

As computer development trends go, this is unusual. The computer field at large has seen a major new advance in equipment every four to seven years. With each technological breakthrough has come a related obsolescence of existing equipment. Users of large computer systems have felt obliged to go through a technological rebirth with each new generation of hardware.

The microcomputer field has been something of an exception, partly because of the nature of its users. Many microcomputers are used by scientists or businesspeople who seem to be searching continuously for greater capacities. These people flock to advanced systems as they are introduced. However, there remains a silent majority for whom advanced technology is not critical. For these people, the generation of equipment introduced in 1981 was more than they needed then. For many, it probably remains more than they ever will need. These people are content to keep using the same equipment for the same, essential jobs. These users might occasionally be interested in experimenting with new, advanced software. But there is no broad restlessness to change for the sake of technical innovation alone.

The resistance to change for its own sake is supported by economic developments. When the IBM PC was introduced in 1981, a typical system that included two disk drives and 256K (kilobytes, or 256,000) bytes of memory cost about $3,500—without a printer. Top quality printers cost an additional $1,500 or more in 1981. Today, an IBM PC with 640K of memory can be purchased for less than $1,000. Clones, or imitation systems that have come to dominate the low-price market, are available in the range of $500 to $600. Printers that represent improvements over anything available in 1981 can be purchased for $200 to $500. The low prices represent a major inducement for users to stay with their PC or clone systems.

Desktop Publishing Equipment: A Technology in Transition

This background has some special significance for buyers and/or users of desktop publishing systems. Desktop publishing equipment recently has undergone a major generation change. Both IBM and Apple have announced lines of large microcomputers that promise major breakthroughs for desktop publishing capabilities. In addition, Xerox Corporation has announced a major desktop publishing software package. This software, known as Ventura, runs on some large IBM PC systems and also on IBM's Personal System 2 (PS/2).

At the same time, more than a million Macintosh systems remain in active use. These provide the potential for low-cost entry into desktop publishing. With either the new IBM or Apple systems, a single computer equipped for desktop publishing will carry price tags in the range of $3,000 to $3,500. These prices can be expected to come down eventually. However, it also can be expected that enhanced models of these systems will add to prices. By comparison, a Macintosh Plus with one megabyte of memory and a 20-megabyte hard disk can be purchased for $1,500, possibly a little less. Similarly, laser printers that support desktop publishing now run from a low of about $1,700 to almost $15,000.

Both the established products and the new products have desktop publishing capabilities. The differences lie in individual features, as discussed below. The point: There are many trade-offs to consider when you configure a desktop publishing system.

Hardware/Software Decision Criteria

To proceed, use the information you have been gathering throughout the systems analysis process:

- You should know, by now, the types of publications you will be producing.

- You should have a good idea of your workload, in terms of number of pages and complexity of content.

- You should know what kinds of deadlines you will face.

- You should know the levels of quality you will have to deliver.

- You should have an idea of current costs for the production of the publications that you will be handling. The idea, now, is to project costs for handling the same work through desktop publishing capabilities. In most organizations, the operational savings you realize will be expected to pay for the equipment and software you want to acquire. Therefore, the benefits you project probably will have an impact on your hardware/software purchasing budget.

- Determine the attitude of the decision makers who will allocate the money for your desktop publishing system. In some companies, management tends to want the latest and best in computer systems. In other organizations, managers like to get into any phase of computing with a minimum investment. They want to realize the greatest benefit for the lowest feasible costs.

In developing plans for a desktop publishing system, be sure you know what expectations you face. First, you need a thorough understanding of the results you are expected to deliver. With this understanding, you are ready to translate targeted results into specifications for hardware and software.

The Computer

One way to select equipment is to start with the most basic, lowest-cost options available. Then go to larger units or added features one at a time. As you do, you can consider what the more expensive options make available and evaluate whether the investments are worthwhile.

Another good rule is to shop at least three sources and listen to all the recommendations you hear. Even if you are starting without much personal knowledge, the sales pitches will give you a good understanding of options and values.

Following the principle of starting low and working up, consider the minimal computer that will do the job. This would have one megabyte of memory and a small, 9-inch (diagonal measurement) display screen. It would come with a mouse that has a ball-type control. That ball rolls on a desktop or special pad to control movement of the cursor.

One upgrade to consider is to add memory. At this writing, an additional three megabytes of memory can be installed for less than $500. This will increase processing speed—noticeably. The value of this investment relates directly to the amount of work you will be doing and the complexity of the jobs. For example, consider a workload that requires you to mix multiple illustration and text files. The larger memory will make it possible for you to bring all or most of your active files into working memory. This, in turn, makes it possible to access and position the files in a fraction of the time required for repeated disk references. Memory can be added easily through insertion of circuit boards like the one shown in **Figure 14-5.**

A reason to buy a more expensive computer may be the availability of 19-inch (diagonal) monitors. These larger screens make it possible to view an 8.5-by-11-inch page at full size, compared with 50 percent of full size on 9-inch monitors. With a smaller screen, full-size viewing is available for only of a portion of a page at a time. A desktop publishing system with a large monitor is shown in **Figure 14-6.**

You also can buy full-page screens for the Macintosh Plus. As a rule of thumb, the larger screen will cost a little more than the original purchase price for the computer. But the price will be less than purchase of a Macintosh 2 or similar system. Thus, it could pay to upgrade a Macintosh Plus with added memory and a large

Figure 14-5. The size of a computer's memory affects its desktop publishing capabilities. This photo shows a plug-in memory board for a microcomputer.
Courtesy of Datatron, Inc.

screen. This could be preferable to discarding an existing system and buying a new, larger model. The value of a large display screen— or of a new, high-priced computer— depends on how it will contribute to your products and productivity. Only you can decide what it is worth to be able to view a full page on your monitor.

Another decision about the selection of your computer lies in whether you want a color monitor. The applications you project should guide you in this decision. The potential for color monitors is covered in Chapter 8, which deals with presentation graphics.

Other options lie in the choice of keyboards and mouse units. Keyboards are available with varying touch adjustments and with optional keys that support different functions. A good policy is to look at the keyboard that comes with any given system. Then ask about and evaluate options.

The same is true of the mouse. Some mouse units are shaped differently from those provided by manufacturers. Some operate electronically rather than requiring that a ball be rolled along a pad and rotated by friction. It also is possible to replace a mouse with a track ball. This is a unit on which the cursor is moved by rotating a ball at the top of a stationary device. Two track-ball devices are illustrated in **Figure 14-7.** When you are in a dealer showroom, take the time to look at all your input options. In this area, comfort and efficiency come at small prices and can represent good investments.

A microcomputer is a collection of parts that are assembled to meet the needs of a user. Scores of options are available. The best combination depends upon the judgment of the prospective user.

Disk Storage

A hard disk is a practical necessity for any desktop publishing system. The hard disk is where you will keep your software and working files. This is a good place to invest in all the capacity you can afford. You can be sure that, at

Figure 14-6. A large-screen monitor makes it possible for a user to view a full page of a publication as one image. Cost-benefit trade-offs of large monitors should be studied.
Courtesy of Apple Computer, Inc.

some time, your desktop publishing software and application files will exhaust your capacity and require extensive housekeeping. Consider that current versions of page makeup software are delivered on four disks. If you put everything you get on your hard disk, you use 2.8 megabytes. A project the size of this book will require some 10 megabytes of storage. You also will need space for graphics and word processing software packages. All this is over and above the operating system.

Today, any desktop publishing system should have a minimum of 20 megabytes of disk storage. Twice that much would not be too much for a busy shop with relatively high work volumes. Additional capacity can be added easily and inexpensively with units like the one shown in Figure 14-4.

Remember earlier advice about backing up files. All of your application files should be written off to diskettes at least once each day. One diskette drive should be considered mandatory for each desktop publishing system. If you decide to save to diskette routinely, as you create files, you may want to add a second, external diskette drive.

Figure 14-7. A track-ball attachment is an optional way to control a desktop system. The track ball replaces the functions of a mouse without requiring the space for a pad on which to roll the mouse. Courtesy of Disc Instruments.

Printer

For publishable output, you should have, at minimum, a laser printer. It is possible to output desktop publishing pages on a dot matrix printer. The results are good enough to use as rough proofs. But they are not acceptable commercially. Some people start with inexpensive dot-matrix printers and take their diskettes to service centers for printout. This is a minimum-cost way to get into desktop publishing. However, if you are going to be outputting 250 pages per month or more, you will want a laser printer of your own. Having your own laser printer is particularly important if you feel you have to control the quality of your work. The quality factor centers around the fact that you have no way of knowing what shape the service center printer is in. The cartridge of a publicly used printer may be new or almost empty. The images you get may or may not be of reproducible quality.

Shop carefully for your laser printer. Bear in mind that a 300 DPI capacity generally is adequate for anything but the highest-quality publications. As you shop, be aware that some laser printers advertised as having a 300 DPI capacity may not deliver 300 DPI over full 8.5-by-11-inch sheets. Read the fine print. One popular make of printer that advertises a 300 DPI capacity does so only for half-page-size printouts. If you use the full sheet, the capacity comes down to 150 DPI. This can be quite a comedown.

As a rule, a 300 DPI laser printer will cost two or three times as much as the computer itself. A laser printer of this type is shown in **Figure 14-8.** It pays to spend the time needed to check out the features and to watch demonstrations. Laser printers with higher-density dot patterns have come on the market recently. Models have been released that offer 1,000 and 1,200 DPI capabilities. As reliability is proven, and as prices begin to drop, these higher quality laser printers should see increasing use. For the present, the extremely high costs of these units place them beyond the budgets—and needs—of most desktop publishing shops.

Publishing Software

The major cost for any software package will be for the time required to master it. Proficiency takes time with any software package. This is true even if you buy a package similar to one you already know well, such as a word processor. It can take a week or two to master the new package fully. Invariably, the learning time of the user costs many times more than the selling price of the package.

The point: Buy only the software you feel you really need. Then, before you buy anything else,

---

Figure 14-8. An Apple LaserWriter can provide full-page, 300 DPI output that can be used for final pasteup.
Courtesy of Apple Computer, Inc.

Figure 14-9. Operator comfort and convenience should be designed into the work area where any desktop publishing operations are performed.
Photo by Benedict Kruse.

think about the time it took to master what you have. Then decide whether you have time to learn another application. Also bear in mind that the software can represent a major investment. The time of people who operate computers, as in **Figure 14-9,** is valuable. The learning/training time for mastery of software tools usually is the greatest single investment in desktop publishing. Also, the cost of software itself can add up. Individual packages may seem reasonable. But, when you add the costs of all the packages in a typical installation, the investment is greater than for the computer itself.

The current versions of popular page makeup software have modules that let you do almost everything necessary to create a publication. There are modules that enable you to capture text, format text into a variety of typefaces, create graphics, and make up pages. To illustrate, **Figure 14-10** is a screen display of a PageMaker 3.0 menu.

For low-volume shops, a single-page makeup package, such as PageMaker, may be all that is

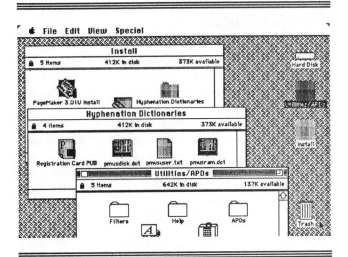

Figure 14-10. This screen display identifies some of the major features available under PageMaker 3.0 software. The software provides a powerful tool but also demands a lot of storage space.

needed. However, if you want more than minimal capabilities, you probably will want to buy a word processing program with sophisticated typesetting capabilities. In addition, you probably will want packages that provide drawing and painting capabilities.

If you go this far, you probably will want a *switcher,* or manager-type, program. This software keeps track automatically of the packages in use and enables you to move back and forth rapidly between different programs. As you do this, the switcher software closes out and saves the work you did.

At the very minimum, you will need the operating system for the computer you purchase. You also should get a word processing program with typesetting capabilities. For some applications, this minimal software will enable you to do desktop publishing. A graphics development package would be another early option. A page makeup package would add the capability to assemble type and illustrations to create complete pages.

You also will have decisions to make about the type fonts you want. Generally, a selection of fonts will be available with a word processing program such as Microsoft Word. In addition, some type fonts may be available with the purchase of page makeup software. For most shops, this selection is more than enough to get started. However, additional fonts can be purchased separately from a growing group of suppliers.

Electronic Typesetting

If a desktop publishing facility is expected to turn out top-quality work, you may want to consider Linotronic or similar equipment. Electronic typesetters can be adapted to accept input directly from desktop publishing diskettes. Outputs are photographic prints or film of commercial reproduction quality. Linotronic machines can output type at 1,250 or 2,500 DPI. Therefore, the type is shaped and reproduced more precisely than can be done from a desktop computer and laser printer.

One problem is that electronic typesetting takes desktop publishing out of the realm of a low-cost alternative. These machines cost $30,000 to $50,000 each. In addition, attachments are needed to accommodate desktop publishing diskettes. To justify this kind of expense,

a shop should have extremely high volumes of high-quality work. Bear in mind also, that bit-mapped graphics are processed at extremely slow speeds on these machines. Output times of an hour or more per page are not unusual if all of the copy is bit-mapped.

Finally, care and feeding of a typesetter requires special attention. The outputs, either paper or film, require "wet processing" in photographic solutions. These solutions are subject to rapid depletion through use and exposure to air. From day to day, film processed in the same solution can have markedly different image values. The processing solutions must be maintained at full chemical strength. Temperatures must be controlled to within a few degrees of specified levels. If the processing varies, the type that is delivered will not match from day to day. Therefore, installation of electronic typesetting equipment requires assignment of people to monitor the photographic chemicals closely, on a day-to-day basis.

Networking

Many options are available for linking a desktop computer system to other devices. At the very least, local connections will be needed between a computer, its disk storage, and its printer. It also may be desirable to link two or more desktop computers and a central laser printer. When the computers are linked, it is possible for two or more systems to share disk files. Thus, software stored in one system may be transferred to another; it is not necessary to encumber both disk files by duplicating all software.

Another networking opportunity is to connect a PC like those used for word processing into the desktop publishing network. This supports rapid transfer of word processing text into the desktop publishing system. **Figure 14-11** is a block diagram that shows linkage for a system like the one used to prepare this book. The interconnected units include a PC clone, two Macintosh Plus computers, two 20-megabyte hard disks, and an Apple LaserWriter.

Broader opportunities also can exist. A desktop publishing system can be linked into a local area network (LAN). This could provide direct communication between a desktop system and a wide range of business computers or computer file facilities. Thus, for example, secretarial and word processing personnel could capture text in

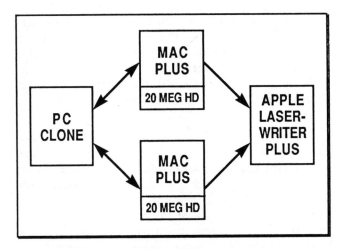

Figure 14-11. This block diagram shows the configuration of the networked devices used in producing this book.

their own offices. They could then dispatch this input for formatting and production on a word processing system— without setting type. A large-scale, corporate computer could **download** information for publication on desktop publishing equipment. Downloading is the term used for transferring information from a large, central computer to a microcomputer. When a microcomputer transmits information to a large system, this is called **uploading.**

PROVIDE FOR HUMAN FACTORS

A universal planning requirement is to set up each computer facility for the working comfort and efficiency of the people running it. Factors to be considered include lighting, seating, and desktop equipment other than the computer itself. The study of the effects upon people of their working conditions is known as **ergonomics.** The ergonomics of the computer-related workplace are, and should be, of great concern both for employers and workers.

In addition, all work facilities must meet government guidelines for safety. OSHA, the Occupational Safety and Hazards Administration, enforces a series of rules aimed at worker safety and protection. Most of OSHA's concerns deal with proper handling and disposal of hazardous materials. These generally do not apply to working areas for desktop computers. However, the electrical connections and the measures that protect against injury from improper wiring or housing of computers do apply. Employers are required to meet all applicable

OSHA standards, as well as those for local government agencies.

Ergonomic Factors

There has been great concern about strain and tension experienced by operators of computer terminals and microcomputers. A few counties have enacted legislation about rest periods for computer operations personnel. Also, under some laws, employers are required to pay for eye examinations. At this writing, a number of serious studies are under way to determine the effects of computer-related jobs.

Early studies led to widespread alarms. For example, the public press stressed adverse interpretations from a survey by Kaiser Permanente, the large health maintenance organization. This report indicated an increased rate of miscarriages for clerical personnel who work regularly at computers. This information received wide publicity. Less publicized was the fact that female managers and executives who used computer terminals had lower-than-average rates of miscarriage.

Radiation. There also have been concerns about radiation generated from video display terminals. Critics express fears that electron radiation from video devices may cause eye damage or other problems. Industry representatives point out that the video screen on a microcomputer is, basically, a TV display. They point out that many of today's computer operators were raised in front of TV screens.

 DESKTOP JARGON

switcher A program that controls access to application programs and enables the user to move quickly from one application to another.

download To transfer data from a large, central computer to a desktop computer.

upload To transfer data from a desktop computer to a central system.

ergonomics The study of the effects of the workplace upon humans and of measures to increase comfort and productivity of workers.

One characteristic of TV displays is encouraging. A video display does not emit ionizing radiation, the type that can lead to cancer. The radiation that does occur is electromechanical. This radiation results from the electron beams that form the video image. Because of the brightness of images generated, eyestrain is a definite possibility.

Other possible effects result from on-job tension and from the fact that some operators sit in one position for long periods.

Tension. Computers are installed at many companies as productivity tools. The idea is to get more work done. The emphasis on productivity has led to tensions for many workers. Clerical personnel commonly find themselves answering continuous streams of phone calls to take orders or answer questions. Other workers find themselves with large piles of source documents or forms from which they are to enter data.

In these and other similar situations, the work is always backlogged. Callers expect immediate service. Accuracy is essential. Delays in gaining access to computer files can be frustrating. Though it may be argued that computers are not to blame, tensions do increase. Worker stress definitely can become a factor. The problems are real. But they are human problems. Workers and managers should establish realistic goals. Performance expectations should reflect those realities. It also does not hurt when employers show real concern about the well-being of workers.

Physical fatigue. Sitting in one place for long periods can tire a person. Also, the individual can develop stiff, cramped muscles. Airline passengers and people who drive long distances know this feeling well. The same distress can afflict persons who are seated at work for long periods. Computer terminals can contribute to the fatigue problems because they attract and hold worker interest.

People who work at computers must learn, on their own, to stretch and exercise periodically. As you go through life, you will possess only one body. At work or at play, it is up to you to take care of it. Regular breaks are recommended for people who work at computers. Most employers arrange for these breaks. It is up to the individual workers to use these periods to get the stretching and exercising their bodies need.

Glare and eyestrain. Room lighting in a computer facility should balance the intensity of the images on the monitors. If room light is low, the screen will represent glare and can lead to eyestrain for the user. If the room light and screen image are balanced, the effect of glare is lessened.

Another factor is that reflections of room lights on the face of a display screen can be distracting and can add to fatigue. This problem can be eliminated with glare screens. These are easy to install, as shown in **Figure 14-12**. Control of glare also may be possible with monitor mount-ing devices that permit the user to tilt or swivel the screen for easy viewing.

Eyestrain can be a major problem. One way to avoid the problem is to recognize how the eye deals with the process of reading. When you read a book, you form an unconscious habit of blinking your eyes frequently. Most people blink, without even being aware, when they reach the end of one line of reading and before they begin another.

Keyboarding on a computer terminal doesn't lead to the same blinking patterns. Many people form a habit, subconsciously, of staring at the screen for long periods without blinking. This increases the effects of glare and can lead to eyestrain. To deal with this potential problem, start by being aware that your eyes have to be closed periodically. Try to form a habit of blinking between lines as you make keyboard entries. Also, form a habit of periodically—perhaps between paragraphs—closing your eyes for a few moments at a time.

Relief from exposure to light is necessary to avoid eyestrain. You can provide this relief. Just be aware of the problem and form the habits that will give you the relief you need.

Seating. The seating provided for computer operators should support the back and help the individual to maintain a good, comfortable posture. People seated at keyboards for long periods can develop backaches. Chairs that are adjusted properly can minimize these problems.

Desktop requirements. The work station for a desktop publishing operation should recognize the needs of the operator. For one thing, space must be provided for the mouse pad. The operator should be able to reach and manipulate the mouse with ease.

Figure 14-12. Glare screens, such as the one being installed in this photo, can help prevent eye strain.
Courtesy of Sentinel Bio-Tech Products.

The height at which the keyboard is positioned also can affect comfort and productivity. The keyboard should be at a level that provides comfort for long work sessions. A keyboard that is too high or too low can be a major factor in causing operator fatigue.

It may be desirable to provide special copy stands for operators who enter long sections of text from typed or printed documents. The idea: A copy stand holds the source documents in a position that eases neck strain on the operator. The copy holder should make it unnecessary for the operator to bend or twist his or her neck into an uncomfortable position. **Figure 14-13** shows a copy stand in use.

Since the people are the most valuable asset of a desktop publishing facility, attention to human factors is vital. **Figure 14-14** diagrams the elements that affect the comfort and productivity of a computer work station.

DESKTOP PUBLISHING TRENDS

The considerations just reviewed were applicable at the time this book was written. Planning for a publishing facility also should provide for trends or developments that are expected in the foreseeable future. Some of these projected developments, reviewed below, include:

- Increased hardware capabilities
- More sophisticated software
- Coordination between desktop and larger publishing systems
- Advances in printing technology.

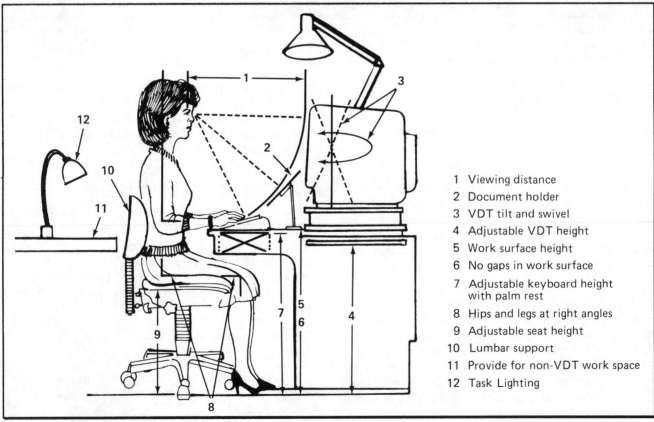

1 Viewing distance

2 Document holder

3 VDT tilt and swivel

4 Adjustable VDT height

5 Work surface height

6 No gaps in work surface

7 Adjustable keyboard height
   with palm rest

8 Hips and legs at right angles

9 Adjustable seat height

10 Lumbar support

11 Provide for non-VDT work space

12 Task Lighting

Increased Hardware Capabilities

Most microcomputers in present use have memories based upon 256K (256,000-bit) integrated circuit chips. In 1980, the standard memory chip had a 64K capacity. Currently, deliveries of sample chips with one megabit capacities have begun. Further, chip makers have announced that their laboratories are well along toward development of four-megabit chips.

As these developments take place, expect to see more memory available on microcomputers. In the future, memories of eight or 16 megabytes seem to be reasonable expectations.

Increased memory capacities, in turn, will make it possible to produce larger monitor screens with even better image definition than is available today. Also, printed and typeset film output can be generated faster and with better quality as more memory becomes available. The bigger the memory, the better the image definition can be.

Chip makers also are expected to deliver a continuing stream of more powerful processors. The microcomputer industry started with processor chips that handled 8-bit binary words. In 1981, the standard moved to 16-bit words. By 1988, chips that processed 32-bit words were coming to market. The future probably will see even larger processing capacities. Greater processor capacities will, in turn, mean faster handling and processing for graphics.

Still another factor will be greatly increased capacities for disk storage as new technologies, such as laser disk units, come on the market. Laser disks that hold a gigabyte (one billion bytes) of data already are in use. However, present models are limited to read-only operation. When read/write laser disks are introduced (they already are well along in development), available storage capacities can be expected to multiply.

More Sophisticated Software

With larger memories and faster processors, it will become possible to add sophistication to desktop publishing software. Already, page makeup software has jumped from 16- to 128-page capacities. As more storage becomes available, software capacities can continue to increase.

Also, the number of available type fonts will grow to rival traditional electronic typesetting capabilities. Word processing programs of the future will enable users to imbed typesetting codes so that fonts and sizes are selected automatically. They will not have to be specified by an operator. In short, capabilities of desktop systems will move closer to those of large-scale systems which started the trend toward electronic publishing.

Added memory will be a factor in making *voice activated transcription* available. This is a capability under which computers will be able to translate human speech into text outputs. Authors or executives will be able, literally, to talk to computers. The computers will translate sounds into text. The text files will be ready for editing. If the dictated material is to be published, the desktop publishing production cycle will be shortened considerably.

Coordination Between Desktop and Larger Publishing Systems

Desktop publishing systems, in effect, are scaled-down versions of full-scale computer composition techniques. These large-scale techniques were pioneered by newspapers, news magazines, and other large publishing organizations. Desktop publishing systems have fewer features and capabilities because they run on smaller computers with lower capacities.

As microcomputers gain processing, memory, and storage capacities, desktop publishing systems will be more like large, full-scale publishing systems. Eventually, it would make

Figure 14-13. A copy stand can be helpful for capturing or correcting text from paper documents.
Photo by Benedict Kruse.

Figure 14-14. This drawing identifies and illustrates the key elements of an ergonomically efficient work area.

 DESKTOP JARGON

voice activated transcription A technique under which a computer recognizes and transcribes human speech into text files.

sense for users to build bridges between desktop and larger systems. Desktop publishing systems could, in effect, become "smart" work stations at which users capture text and illustrations and format pages. These files could be incorporated into larger computer systems that handle, for example, catalogs with more than 1,000 full-color pages.

The point: If you want to preview the capabilities of tomorrow's desktop publishing systems, look at today's minicomputer-based systems. These systems currently have price tags in the range of $50,000 to $75,000. In the future, microcomputers will gain capacities to run the same software and produce the same caliber of results.

Figure 14-15. This laser printing system features PC-based user interface for full-line editing and control functions. It prints merged text and graphics at speeds up to 120 pages per minute. Courtesy of Xerox Corporation.

Advances in Printing Technology

The printing production techniques described throughout this book are based on a need to create lithographic film from which plates are produced. Some segments of the graphics industry already are experimenting with direct platemaking. That is, instead of creating film from computer files, the same laser scanning capability is applied to light-sensitive plates. Expensive film, which uses silver as one of its ingredients, may eventually be eliminated. Desktop publishing facilities of the future may be able to create offset plates directly on laser printers or with similar devices. This kind of breakthrough will cut production times and also should reduce printing costs.

Another type of breakthrough is expected for laser printing itself. Large scale laser printers already on the market are able to generate book-length outputs directly from computer files. One such printer is shown in **Figure 14-15.** Pages are printed at the rate of more than 7,000 per hour. Impressions are made on both sides of sheets of paper. Complete publications can be assembled

and stapled within a machine like the one shown in **Figure 14-16.**

As electronic imaging techniques improve, output quality should be enhanced even further. Higher capacities also are anticipated. A new electronic reproduction process is known as *ion deposition* printing. This method eliminates the need for plasticized toner that uses heat to affix images to paper. Ion deposition integrates images into the fiber of the paper. Image quality is

DESKTOP JARGON

ion deposition printing A reproduction method by which image-forming materials are integrated into the fabric of the paper.

Figure 14-16. Large-scale laser printers can be tools of publishing production. Systems like the one shown can generate more than 7,000 impressions per hour. They print on both sides of pages and can collate documents ready for binding.
Courtesy of Eastman Kodak Company.

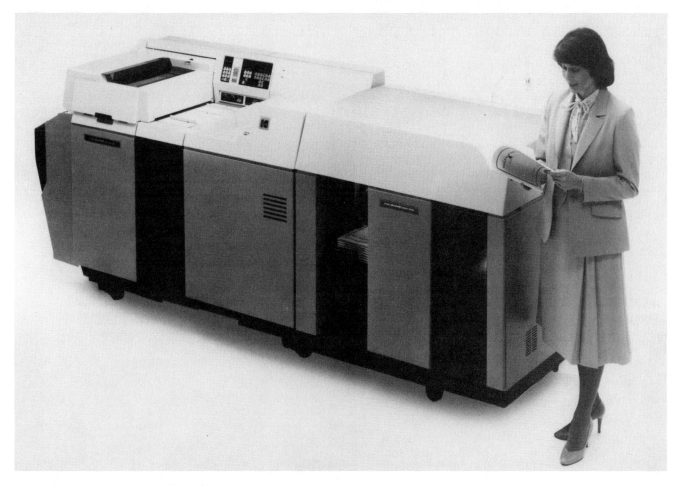

enhanced. Also, one of the longstanding objections to xerographic images is eliminated. When toner-imprinted pages are subjected to heat, their images transfer to other pages. The result is that pages tend to stick together. This doesn't happen with ion deposition copying.

The expected result: In the future, it may become unnecessary to plan press runs. Printing on presses requires long production runs for economy. In turn, publishers have to warehouse and control large inventories. Electronic imaging from computer storage should make it possible to run a few copies at a time—economically. Inventory maintenance and warehousing costs can be reduced drastically.

The future certainly is bright and holds promises for continuing, dynamic change. But, desktop publishing is a here-and-now reality that can deliver improvements, cost savings, and faster service. The promise of future enhancements means that now is a good time to become involved in desktop publishing.

THE MAKEUP DESK

1. As your final design/layout assignment, define and develop a design for any publication you choose. This is a final assignment. By now, you should be able to identify a problem or opportunity and define your own solution.

THE COMPOSING ROOM

1. Develop an on-line framework for producing the publication you have designed. You can use text from any available source. The purpose of this exercise is to execute a design from scratch.

Guide to Desktop Publishing Software

About This Appendix

The following is a listing of some of the software available for word processing, graphics, and page-makeup applications on the Apple Macintosh and the IBM PC. Although it does not include all the programs on the market, this guide should provide a good overview of the software that can be useful for desktop publishing. For information on prices, as well as further information on features, contact the publisher of the program in which you are interested. Before buying a software package, you always should shop around to find the one that best suits your individual needs.

WORD PROCESSING
Macintosh

FullWrite Professional

Description: Advanced word-processing package that integrates limited graphics and page-layout capabilities.

Publisher: Ashton-Tate Corp., 20101 Hamilton Ave., Torrance, CA 90502.

Laser Author

Description: Word processor with capabilities for importing and sizing graphics and blocks of text and creating master style formats for page layout.

Publisher: Firebird Licenses, Inc., P.O. Box 49, Ramsey, NJ 07446.

MacWrite

Description: Basic Macintosh word processor with global search and replace and LaserWriter compatibility.

Publisher: Claris, 440 Clyde Ave., Mountain View, CA 94043.

Microsoft Word

Description: Advanced word processor with style sheets, spelling checker, outlining, table of contents generation, page previewing, and graphics importation.

Publisher: Microsoft Corp., 16011 N.E. 36th Way, P.O. Box 97017, Redmond, WA 98073.

Microsoft Write

Description: Simplified version of Microsoft Word (see above).

Publisher: Microsoft Corp., 16011 N.E. 36th Way, P.O. Box 97017, Redmond, WA 98073.

MindWrite

Description: Word processor with outlining, table of contents generation, and graphics insertion capabilities.

Publisher: Access Technology, 555C Heritage Harbor, Monterey, CA 93940.

WordPerfect

Description: Word processor with footnoting, mail merge, graphics integration, dictionary, and thesaurus.

Publisher: WordPerfect Corp., 288 W. Center St., Orem, UT 84057.

WriteNow

Description: Basic word processor with footnoting and spell checker.

Publisher: T/Maker Co., 1973 Landings Dr., Mountain View, CA 94043.

WORD PROCESSING
IBM PC

DisplayWrite

Description: Advanced word processor with spell checker, thesaurus, page previewing, and multiple-column capability.

Publisher: IBM, Old Orchard Rd., Armonk, NY 10504.

GEM 1st Word Plus

Description: Word processor with spell checker, mail merge, hyphenation, and GEM Paint integration.

Publisher: Digital Research, Inc., 60 Garden Ct., P.O. Box DRI, Monterey, CA 93942.

Microsoft Word

Description: Advanced word processor with style sheets, spelling checker, outlining, table of contents generation, page previewing, and graphics importation.

Publisher: Microsoft Corp., 16011 N.E. 36th Way, P.O. Box 97017, Redmond, WA 98073.

MultiMate

Description: Word processor with spell checker, mail merge, and external copying capability.

Publisher: Ashton-Tate Corp., 20101 Hamilton Ave., Torrance, CA 90502.

Nota Bene

Description: Word processor with spell checker, indexing capability, and foreign-language modules. Originally designed for research papers and academic publications.

Publisher: Dragonfly Software, 285 W. Broadway #500, New York, NY 10013.

Professional Write

Description: Word processor with font selection and conversion from different file formats, including Microsoft Word, WordPerfect, MultiMate, and WordStar.

Publisher: Software Publishing Corp., P.O. Box 7210, 1901 Landings Dr., Mountain View, CA 94039.

Q&A Write

Description: Basic word processor with spell checker and graphics importation.

Publisher: Symantec Corp., 10201 Torre Ave., Cupertino, CA 95014.

WordPerfect

Description: Word processor with footnoting, mail merge, graphics integration, dictionary, and thesaurus.

Publisher: WordPerfect Corp., 288 W. Center St., Orem, UT 84057.

WordStar

Description: Command-driven word processor with mail merge, spell check, and global search and replace.

Publisher: MicroPro International Corp., 33 San Pablo Ave., San Rafael, CA 94903.

WordStar 2000

Description: Upgraded version of WordStar (see above), with thesaurus, page previewing, and graphics importation.

Publisher: MicroPro International Corp., 33 San Pablo Ave., San Rafael, CA 94903.

XyWrite III Plus

Description: Word processor with spell check, thesaurus, search and replace, and graphics importation.

Publisher: XyQuest, Inc., 44 Manning Rd., Billerica, MA 01821.

GRAPHICS
Macintosh

Adobe Illustrator 88

Description: Advanced drawing program.

Publisher: Adobe Systems, Inc., 1585 Charleston Rd., Mountain View, CA 94043.

Aldus FreeHand

Description: Advanced drawing program with free-form drawing ability, multiple layers, and color.

Publisher: Aldus Corp., 411 1st Ave. South, Suite 200, Seattle, WA 98104.

Canvas

Description: Integrated drawing/paint program with ability to import graphics from other programs.

Publisher: Deneba Software, 7855 N.W. 12th St., Suite 202, Miami, FL 33126.

Cricket Draw

Description: Object-oriented drawing program with graduated gray fills and text rotation/skewing.

Publisher: Cricket Software, 30 Valley Stream Parkway, Great Valley Corporate Center, Malvern, PA 19355.

CheapPaint

Description: Basic paint program for simple illustrations.

Publisher: Spinnaker/Hayden Software, One Kendall Square, Cambridge, MA 02139. Available as part of Macromind Utility Disk.

FullPaint

Description: Advanced paint program for complex graphics applications.

Publisher: Ashton-Tate Corp., 20101 Hamilton Ave., Torrance, CA 90502.

GraphicWorks

Description: Advanced paint program for complex illustrations.

Publisher: MindScape, Inc., 3444 Dundee Rd., Northbrook, IL 60062.

LaserPaint

Description: Advanced paint program with integrated drawing, text, and page-layout capabilities.

Publisher: LaserWare, Inc., P.O. Box 668, San Rafael, CA 94915.

MacBillboard

Description: Basic paint program with reduction/enlargement capability.

Publisher: CE Software, 801 73rd St., Des Moines, IA 50312.

MacDraft

Description: Object-oriented graphics program with variable scaling, single-degree rotation, and a magnification mode.

Publisher: Innovative Data Design, 2280 Bates Ave., Concord, CA 94520.

MacDraw

Description: Basic drawing program for simple illustrations.

Publisher: Claris, 440 Clyde Ave., Mountain View, CA 94043.

MacPaint

Description: Paint program with intermediate level of sophistication.

Publisher: Claris, 440 Clyde Ave., Mountain View, CA 94043.

Pict-O-Graph

Description: Graphics program that transforms database and spreadsheet information into pictorial graphs.

Publisher: Cricket Software, 30 Valley Stream Parkway, Great Valley Corporate Center, Malvern, PA 19355.

SuperPaint

Description: Advanced paint/drawing program with multiple layers and color capability.

Publisher: Silicon Beach Software, 9580 Black Mountain Rd., Suite E, P.O. Box 261430, San Diego, CA 92126.

GRAPHICS
IBM PC

Design

Description: Program for creation of flowcharts, organizational charts, and diagrams. Compatible with Ventura Publisher and PageMaker.

Publisher: Meta Software, 150 Cambridge Park Dr., Cambridge, MA 02140.

Designer

Description: Object-oriented graphics program for technical illustrations.

Publisher: Micrografx, 1820 N. Greenville Ave., Richardson, TX 75081.

Diagraph Windows

Description: Business graphics program integrating graphics objects and text.

Publisher: Computer Support Corp., 2215 Midway Rd., Carrollton, TX 75006.

GEM Paint

Description: Basic paint program.

Publisher: Digital Research, Inc., 60 Garden Ct., P.O. Box DRI, Monterey, CA 93942.

Publisher's Paintbrush

Description: Advanced paint program with gray-scale scanning ability.

Publisher: Z-Soft Corp., 1950 Spectrum Circle #A-495, Marietta, GA 30067.

VP-Graphics

Description: Object-oriented drawing program for charts, illustrations, and presentation graphics.

Publisher: Paperback Software, 2830 Ninth St., Berkeley, CA 94710.

PAGE MAKEUP
Macintosh

Aldus PageMaker

Description: Page-layout program with style sheets, automatic text flow, text wraparound ability, and spot color.

Publisher: Aldus Corp., 411 1st Ave. South, Suite 200, Seattle, WA 98104.

Command Typographer

Description: Page-layout program with justification, spell checker, manual kerning, and Linotronic 100 and 300 phototypesetter compatibility.

Publisher: Laser Text Publishing Systems, Inc., 487 Washington St., New York, NY 10013.

Fastforms Construction Kit

Description: Interactive program for creating forms, letterhead, and other documents.

Publisher: New Directions Software, #205 2915 19th St. N.E., Calgary, Alberta, T2E 7A2 Canada.

MacPublisher III

Description: Page-layout program with ability to save documents in MacPaint format.

Publisher: Boston Publishing Systems, Inc., 1260 Boylston St., Boston, MA 02215.

QuarkXPress

Description: High quality desktop publishing program using block format.

Publisher: Quark, 200 South Jackson, Denver, CO 80209.

Ragtime

Description: Integrated desktop publishing package that incorporates page-layout, word-processing, graphics, and spreadsheet capabilities.

Publisher: Orange Micro, Inc., 1400 N. Lakeview Ave., Anaheim, CA 92807.

Ready, Set, Go!

Description: Page-layout program with grid format, text wraparound ability, and word-processing features.

Publisher: Letraset, 40 Eisenhower Dr., Paramus, NJ 07652.

Scoop

Description: Page-layout program with graphics editors, diagonal margin capability, and special text effects.

Publisher: Target Software, 14206 S.W. 136th St., Miami, FL 33186.

PAGE MAKEUP
IBM PC

Aldus PageMaker

Description: Page-layout program with style sheets, automatic text flow, text wraparound ability, and spot color.

Publisher: Aldus Corp., 411 1st Ave. South, Suite 200, Seattle, WA 98104.

Byline

Description: Basic, keyboard-driven page-layout program with word-processing features, designed for creating newsletters and other simple documents.

Publisher: Ashton-Tate Corp., 20101 Hamilton Ave., Torrance, CA 90502.

First Impression

Description: Menu-driven page-layout program with style sheets and integration of graphics and spreadsheets.

Publisher: Megahaus Corp., 5703 Oberlin Dr., San Diego, CA 92121.

First Publisher

Description: Basic page-layout program with support for dot-matrix and laser printer output.

Publisher: Software Publishing Corp., P.O. Box 7210, 1901 Landings Dr., Mountain View, CA 94039.

GEM Desktop Publisher

Description: Basic page-layout program with style sheets and built-in text editor.

Publisher: Digital Research, Inc., 60 Garden Ct., P.O. Box DRI, Monterey, CA 93942.

Harvard Professional Publisher

Description: Advanced page-layout program with style sheets, text wraparound ability, and automatic continuation messages.

Publisher: Software Publishing Corp., P.O. Box 7210, 1901 Landings Dr., Mountain View, CA 94039.

PagePerfect

Description: Page-layout program with word-processing features and support for graphics and scanned art.

Publisher: International Microcomputer Software, Inc., 1299 Fourth St., San Rafael, CA 94901.

PowerText Formatter

Description: Inexpensive page-layout program suitable for long and/or graphically simple documents (books, letters, flyers, etc.).

Publisher: Beaman Porter, Inc., 417 Halstead Ave., Harrison, NY 10528.

Publish It!

Description: Page-layout program with word-processing features, text wraparound ability, and built-in graphic tool box.

Publisher: Timeworks Platinum Series, 444 Lake Cook Rd., Deerfield, IL 60015.

Ventura Publisher

Description: Advanced page-layout program for short, graphics-oriented documents (ads/flyers, complex newsletters, etc.).

Publisher: Xerox Corp., 101 Continental Blvd., El Segundo, CA 90245.

Layout Forms

An important, early activity in producing a desktop publication is to devise a layout. A practical method for layout development is to sketch the type and graphic elements in place on a layout form. Typically, the layout form is based on a grid that helps you to position the copy and other elements. This Appendix provides a series of grids that should be helpful as you prepare your own publication layouts. The pages that follow contain layout forms for a number of the types of publications for which production methods are described in this book.

Full-Sized Newspaper, Six-Column Format

Tabloid Newspaper, Five-Column Format

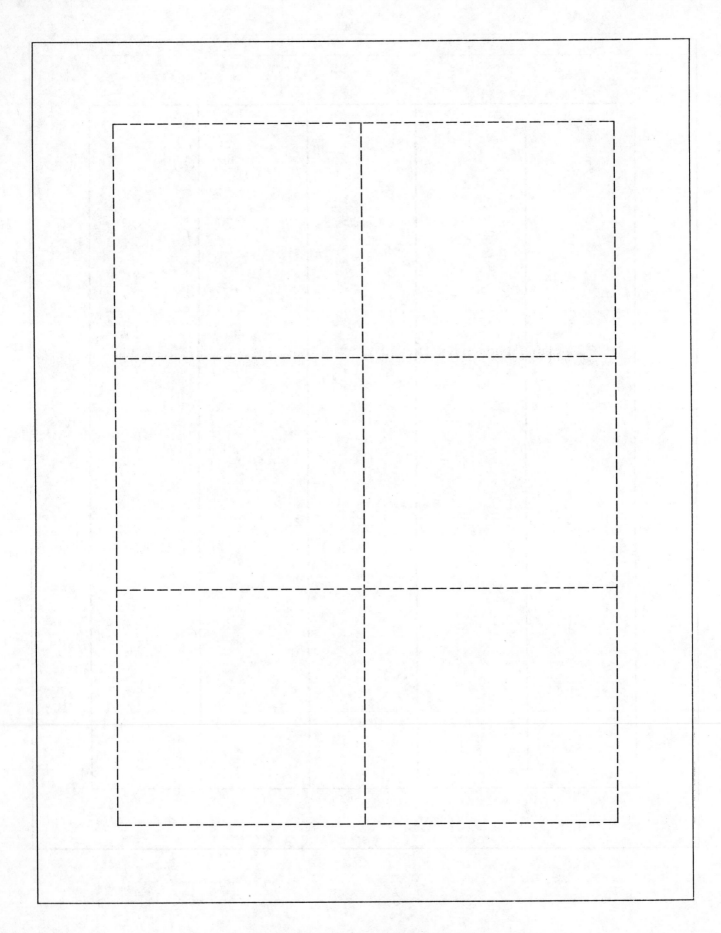

Grid for Report Cover

Newsletter Layout Sheet, Single Column

Newsletter Layout Sheet, Two-Column Format

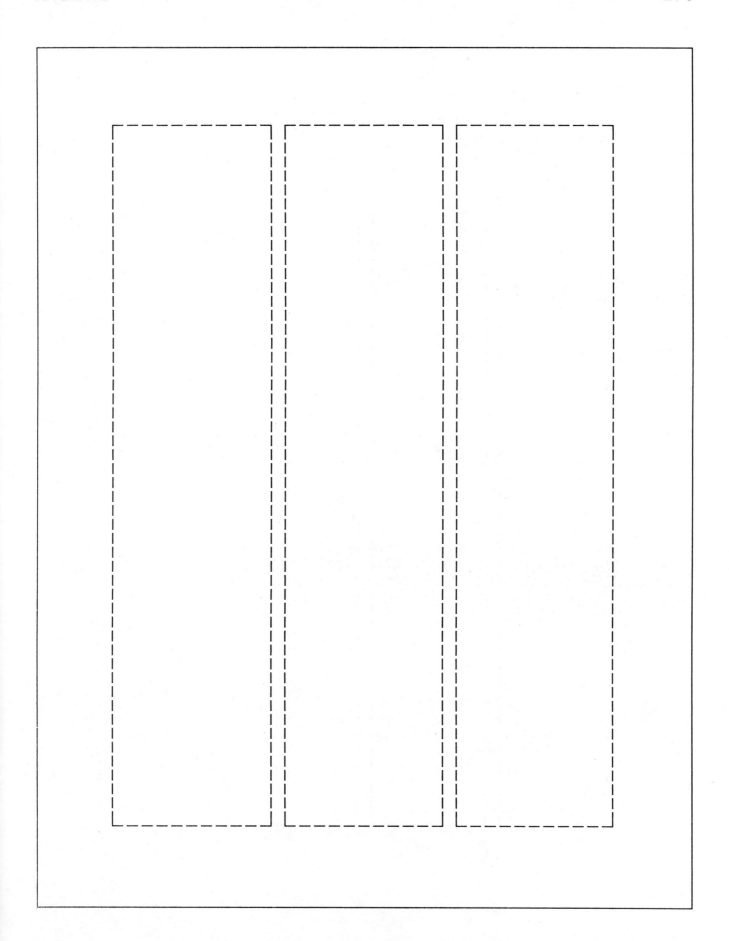

Newsletter Layout Sheet, Three-Column Format

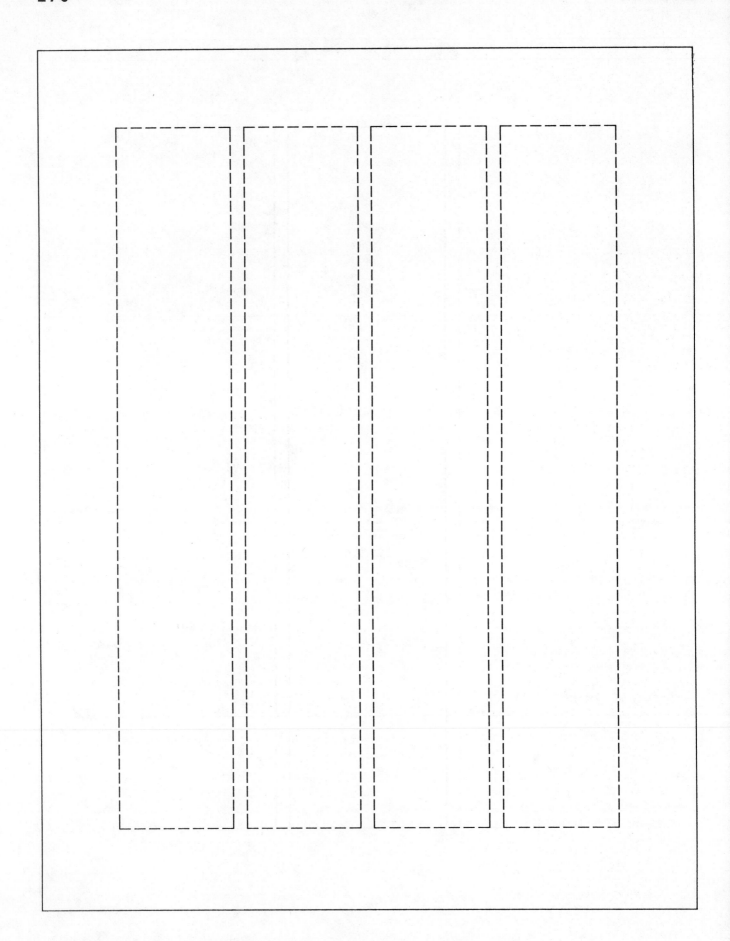

Newsletter Layout Sheet, Four-Column Format

Glossary

A

abstract A short summary of the content of a document.

acquisition editor A person who contacts prospective authors, defines products, and carries negotiations through to a contract.

additive primaries Basic components of white light: red, green, and blue.

amberlith Acetate sheets with removable layers of colored film; used for overlays to indicate positions of color elements.

American Standard Code for Information Interchange (ASCII) A binary coding format; standard in data communication and for many microcomputers.

annual report A document issued at year-end to describe the financial condition and operating achievements of a company.

application software Programs that process user applications.

arithmetic logic unit (ALU) A device within the central processing unit that performs arithmetic and logical operations.

author contract An agreement between an author and publisher to develop, publish, and market a defined work.

B

bar chart A graphic diagram that shows relationships of values in terms of lengths of bars or lines.

bid A document that offers to sell products or services. Like a proposal, except that a bid usually stresses price quotations.

binding The assembly of signatures into a finished publication, including the affixing of covers if necessary.

bit A single binary position used to establish value or meaning for information handled by a computer.

bit map A method of image formation through pixel values. Bit mapping assigns value to each bit, or point, in an image area.

blanket The image transfer unit in offset printing.

block *See* modular layout.

board Carrier sheet used in pasteup.

body The portion of a publication that contains informational text.

bold Typeface with dark image.

booting A procedure that prepares computer for service from a "cold," or unused, start.

bootstrapping *See* booting.

briefing A meeting at which people receive information needed for their jobs.

brochure A multi-page (four or more) publication that presents information on products, product lines, services, or companies.

budget meeting An editorial meeting that assigns priorities to stories to be used in a newspaper.

bulk mailing A special postal service for volume customers.

bureau An outlying office that provides news coverage for a paper or wire service.

burn Exposure of light-sensitive lithographic plates through negative images.

byte A group of eight binary bits that represents a letter, number, or symbol within a computer code.

C

camera-ready mechanicals *See* mechanical.

capture Process for entry of text into a computer in machine-readable format.

case bound A hard-cover publication formed by encasing cardboard within a printed exterior material.

cast-off *See* copy fitting.

catalog A publication that illustrates and describes a number of products or services.

cathode ray tube (CRT) A display device used within a computer work station.

central processing unit (CPU) A device within a computer that performs processing and control functions.

chase A device used to lock up metal type.

circulation blotter A listing of the number of papers needed for distribution.

city room The newsroom of a newspaper.

click Use of mouse to select text or a program function.

cold-type composition Typesetting directly onto paper through strike-on or photographic methods.

column-inch A depth of one inch on a single column of text.

command driven Reference to software that responds to coded instructions entered by a user.

compositor A person who makes up pages of type and illustrations for printing.

computer An electronic device that processes and stores information. Many can also set type.

continuous tone Type of art presented through tonal values, rather than lines.

control unit A device within a central processing unit that controls input, output, and internal communication for execution of program instructions.

controlled circulation Description of a publication that does not charge for subscriptions but does check on the interests of its readers.

coprocessor An auxiliary device that enhances a computer's processing capacity.

copy Term for text or manuscript.

copy checking A procedure to make sure units of text are complete and in proper sequence.

copy editing Review of manuscript to correct errors and language usage.

copy fitting Procedure for estimating space requirements for text and illustrations.

correspondent A reporter who covers an area distant from the home office of a news organization.

cropping Marking illustrations to indicate the areas to be used in a publication.

cursor A blinking line or block that indicates the point on a screen at which the next keyboard entry is to be made.

cut A metal plate for letterpress printing of pictures.

D

daily A newspaper that is issued every day.

database A group of files that are to be used in coordination and permit access to individual data items.

database management system (DBMS) Software package used to coordinate management of multiple files and to collect and access data at the item level.

default A setting or value applied automatically by a system if an operator does not enter other specifications.

delimit An entry that marks a block of text in move, copy, or delete functions.

demibold Typeface with medium-dark image.

demodulate Conversion of transmitted signals from communication code back to computer code.

design The specifications covering use of type, illustrations, and other elements in a publication.

developmental editor A person who works with an author to monitor and assist in development of a manuscript.

dialog box A display within a desktop publishing program in which a user can enter service requests or formatting and operating specifications.

direct-image printing Letterpress; printing from metal type.

disk A platter used for secondary storage of programs and information. May be coated for magnetic or laser recording.

diskette A recording medium used with microcomputers; small acetate disk with magnetic coating.

display A temporary form of computer ouput, such as a video tube or scoreboard.

display advertising Advertisements that appear on a paper's news pages.

dot matrix printer An output device that imprints images in a matrix format.

dots per inch (DPI) Measure of the number of halftone dots per linear inch.

download To transfer data from a large, central computer to a desktop computer.

drag A technique for use of a mouse in which a button is held down while the cursor is moved across the display screen.

draft An initial or interim version of a manuscript.

drafting software Program packages that support preparation of line drawings.

drop folio A page number placed at the bottom of a page.

dummy A layout that designates placement of elements in a publication.

E

electronic manuscript Text or manuscript stored on computer media.

electronic spreadsheet Software package for creation of spreadsheet reports on computers.

element A unit of type or an illustration to be included in a publication.

em Unit of measure equal to letter m in a font being used.

end matter Elements of a textbook that appear at the end of a chapter and/or at the back of the book.

ergonomics The study of the effects of the workplace upon humans and of measures to increase comfort and productivity of workers.

establishing photo In a picture story, the photo that sets the scene.

etching Processing of lithographic plates to remove unused light-sensitive coating.

F

face See typeface.

file A set of related records processed as a unit.

file server A central storage device that serves multiple users on a computer network.

filter A device that permits only selected portions of a beam of light to pass.

financial report A statement on condition or status of a company.

flat A carrier sheet into which platemaking film elements have been positioned.

flip chart Large pad used for information written during a presentation or prepared in advance.

floppy disk See diskette.

folder A set of programs joined for coordinated storage on a Macintosh system.

folding The operation that folds press sheets into signatures.

folio A sequential page number.

folio count The number of pages included in a publication.

font A typeface. Set of characters that conforms to a specific design.

format A function that prepares magnetic media for use.

format line A displayed line at the top of a screen used in word processing. Identifies line width, tab positions, and line spacing.

free circulation Description of a periodical that is given away.

G

galley Trial impression, or proof, from type.

gather Bringing together signatures during binding.

generation Reference to the number of times a photo image has been copied.

gigabyte One billion bytes.

Gothic A style of type with no serifs.

graphics card Circuit card added to a microcomputer to process and display images.

graphics processor *See* graphics card.

graphics tablet A device that permits a user to input images by drawing on a metal surface.

gray scale A series of tonal values that apply to reproduction of continuous-tone art.

grid Set of lines that guides the positioning of text and illustrations in a layout.

gutter The space at the inside margins of two facing pages.

H

halftone Dot pattern used to reproduce photos and other continuous-tone illustrations.

hard copy Any manuscript that is typed or printed on paper.

hard cover A rigid cover for a publication, usually formed by encasing heavy cardboard.

hard disk A recording platter with a rigid metal or plastic base.

hardware All units of computer equipment.

headline Unit of type that titles a story or article.

headline schedule Set of standard headlines designated for use in a newspaper's makeup.

hell box Container for discarded type.

hierarchy A top-down plan of an organization. Describes the methods for organizing and accessing multiple levels of programs.

hot-metal printing Letterpress printing. Done from metal type.

house organ A publication that promotes the internal or market interests of the organization that acts as publisher.

human interest story A story that is based on an emotional appeal rather than the importance of the event.

I

imposition The placement of pages within signatures for printing.

indicia The area of a publication set aside for mailing information.

input Entry of data or instructions into a computer.

input/output (I/O) port A computer communications channel.

instruction set A set of primitive instructions that can be executed by a computer.

ion deposition printing A reproduction method by which image-forming materials are integrated into the fabric of the paper.

italic Typeface with characters that slant from left to right.

J

journal A periodical that deals mainly with current events, as opposed to human-interest stories or articles. *See also* magazine.

jump Continuation to a later page of a story that is interrupted on one page.

K

key line A box that indicates where an illustration will be placed in a publication.

kill sheet A page of classified ads marked to indicate those to be dropped.

L

laptop computer A portable, battery operated computer.

laser printer Xerographic printer that uses a beam of light to register images on a xerographic drum.

layout Placement of publication elements to conform to design.

lead story The main, or most important, story on the front page of a newspaper.

leading Spacing inserted between lines of type.

letter size A page format that measures 8.5 by11 inches.

letterpress Method of printing from metal type.

light table A work station with a back-lighted glass surface; used for pasteup.

line art Images formed with solid lines.

line graph A graphic diagram that shows trends by linking points on a grid with connecting lines.

lines per inch Refers to the number of lines, or dots, per inch on a halftone screen; each line is a row of halftone dots. Also, the measurement of the resolution of an output device. *See also* dots per inch.

lithography Offset printing through transfer of images.

local area network (LAN) A group of connected computing devices located on a single floor or in a single building.

logic Computer capability; compares two items and acts on results of the comparison.

logo A design element that contains the name of a publication.

M

magazine A periodical issued on a regular schedule, but less frequently than daily, that presents news or human-interest editorial content.

makeup The function that places stories in newspaper layouts.

main memory Part of central processing unit that stores and retrieves program segments and data to support processing.

manual A publication that describes care and use of products or provides instructions for job performance.

manuscript The text of a publication in an initial, or intermediate, state.

market-support publication A publication that promotes products or services.

mass market book A book sold in supermarkets and high-volume outlets other than book stores.

masthead The information box within a publication that identifies its purpose and publisher.

mat Mold for casting of metal type on a Linotype machine.

matrix A display formed by highlighting a series of positioned dots or point values.

mechanical Finished pasteup from which plate-making film can be shot.

megabyte One million bytes.

memory *See* main memory.

menu Display that presents or lists options for user selection.

million instructions per second (MIPS) Measure of computer processing speed.

modem A device that enables computers to communicate over telephone lines.

modular layout A newspaper makeup approach that assigns modules, or areas, to individual news stories.

modulate Conversion from computer code to communication code for transmission over telephone lines.

module A portion of a program or a unit within a set of programs.

monitor Computer display device. Also, a function of system software that checks the computer's operating status.

monochrome Reference to a computer display that presents information in a single color.

mouse A device that permits use and control of a computer.

N

negative Photographic image in which black and white values are reversed.

newsletter A periodical that delivers information to a specialized audience.

newsprint The paper on which newspapers are printed; a coarse, uncoated paper made from wood pulp.

nonprofit A type of organization that serves a special function and does not develop income that exceeds expenses.

number Identifier for the number of times a publication has been issued during the current year, or volume.

O

offset printing Method of printing through the transfer of an image to a rubber blanket, then to paper.

on-line Direct operation of a computer by a user to create or modify files.

operating system (O/S) software A set of programs that controls operation of a computer; a unit of system software.

optical character recognition (OCR) Method of reading printed text directly into a computer through use of special equipment.

orphan A short line at the top of a page.

output Results delivered by computers for use by people or machines.

overhead transparency An acetate sheet for use on an overhead projector.

overlay An art element that is laid over the basic mechanical, usually to indicate the position of a color element.

P

page makeup software Program packages that support on-line assembly of text and illustrations into finished pages.

page oriented A type of word processing software that organizes and stores files in page segments.

paid subscription A confirmed order from a reader who pays to receive a publication.

paint software Program packages that support preparation of art with tone values.

palette A specialized tone and line selection menu provided with paint software.

pasteup Placement of publication elements on a carrier sheet from which platemaking film will be shot.

pedagogical material A textbook element designed to help students to review and remember what they have learned.

perfect binding Method of joining signatures through use of a plastic coating material.

periodical Publication produced on a regular schedule.

photo offset Offset printing using photographic platemaking.

photo resist Photographic material used to make offset plates.

photocomposition Typesetting by means of photographic methods.

photojournalism The journalistic technique of telling stories with photos.

pica Unit of measure equal to one-sixth of an inch.

pie To break up a form of metal type.

pie chart A graphic diagram that shows relationships of parts to a whole, represented as slices of a pie.

pin register A method of registering film elements for preparation of lithographic plates. Also, a technique for positioning publication elements accurately through use of metal pins that locate pasteup boards on work surfaces.

pixel A point on a display screen at which image-forming data can be presented.

plotter An output device that draws pictures through use of a stylus.

point Unit of measure equal to one seventy-second of an inch.

poster A large sign that conveys a message; may be printed and illustrated.

presentation graphics Pictorial materials used in meetings and instructional sessions.

press A printing device.

price list A document that gives pricing, packing, shipping, and other information needed to order identified products.

primary storage Another name for main memory.

primitive A basic instruction that can be executed by a computer.

printer A device that imprints character impressions on paper under computer control.

printer's devil An apprentice in charge of a hell box.

printout A document generated by a device connected to a computer.

process Series of steps followed in sequence to produce a planned result.

processor Another term for central processing unit (CPU).

product information sheet A document, usually a single page, that describes an individual product, a single family of products, or a service.

production editing Final review and correction of manuscript in preparation for production.

professional book A book sold directly to attorneys, doctors, businesspeople, and others who purchase books to help them do their jobs.

program Set of instructions that directs computer operation.

project report Document that describes the status of experiments or product development efforts.

proofreading Quality control procedure for correcting errors in typesetting.

proportional wheel A rotary slide rule used to determine the percentage of enlargement or reduction needed to reproduce an illustration at the size specified in a layout.

proposal A document that offers to sell products or services, usually in response to a request for proposal.

protocol A standard procedure, or system, for computer use.

Q

quadrant One-fourth of an equally divided item. In layout, a grid that divides a page into quarters with mid-point vertical and horizontal lines.

quotation box An area enclosed by a ruled box in which a quotation from text is used in large type.

R

rag right Description of type column with an unjustified right margin.

read-only memory (ROM) A device that stores data that can be read only; computer cannot alter content of this memory unit.

read/write head A device that records and retrieves data from magnetic media, including tapes and disks.

recto Term for a right-hand page.

referee A person who judges the quality of articles submitted for publication in a scientific or professional journal.

reference book A book designed for looking up information rather than for continuous reading.

reflective primaries See subtractive primaries.

registration The positioning of image elements to close tolerance for preparation of lithographic plates.

registration mark A symbol used to match the impressions of multiple colors.

report Any document that conveys information.

request for proposal (RFP) A document that asks potential suppliers to submit proposals to sell required goods or services.

reverse reading Backwards image, such as metal type for transfer to paper.

rewrite The writing of news copy from notes received over the telephone.

right-justify To set type with even right margins.

right reading Type or printing master with type that reads correctly.

Roman A style of type that uses serifs.

rubdown art Illustration elements affixed to a sheet that is rubbed to transfer the image.

rubdown type Type elements supplied on waxed sheets. Characters are applied to pasteup sheets by positioning and rubbing them to complete the transfer.

rubylith See amberlith.

run of publication (ROP) Description of the ability to place specific types of content or color on any page of a publication.

runaround type Type that varies in column width to accommodate illustrations.

running head A descriptive heading at the top of a publication page.

S

saddle The point on a signature where the pages are folded.

saddle stitching The joining of signatures by driving staples into the folded edge of the signatures.

sales literature Publications that support the sale of products or services; another term for market-support publications.

san serif A style of type with no serifs.

SAVE A software command that causes the system to write a file to disk.

scanner A device that reads text or images from paper directly into a computer.

scrivener An artisan who created handwritten documents.

scroll User function that causes a displayed image to move up, down, left, or right on the screen.

secondary storage Reference to a device that stores and retrieves information for support of a computer system. Storage is long term or permanent.

select An operation in which a mouse is used to identify type or an art element to be acted upon by a desktop publishing system.

self-covered Description of a publication on which the cover content is printed on the same paper as the body pages.

Send to Back A drafting software command that moves an art element from foreground to background.

separate For color reproduction, the preparation of separate lithographic film and plates for each color to be printed.

serif Horizontal lines added to type characters for design and readability.

side stitching The joining of printed signatures through use of staples or stitches at the edges of signatures.

signature A printed unit that has been folded for use in a publication.

size To indicate the size at which an illustration is to be used in a publication.

slide Image on transparent color film, usually 35mm, prepared for projection.

slug Working name for a publication element. Derived from a slug of linecast type.

soft cover A cover printed in flexible material.

soft hyphen A hyphen placed temporarily at the end of a line to support automatic spacing and justification of text. The soft hyphen is eliminated if the text is altered.

software All of the programs that enable you to use a computer, including those that operate the system and control individual jobs.

spine The edge of a publication at which signatures are joined.

spooling software Programs that permit a computer to operate a printer while a user is working on other materials.

spread Two facing pages in a publication.

spreadsheet Columnar document, usually used for financial reporting.

standalone computer A computer that is self-sufficient, with its own processing, storage, input, and output capabilities.

standard A size and category of newspapers. Trim size usually is 15 by 22.5 inches.

standoff The distance between the outside edge of an art element and the closest copy element.

status report A document that describes the condition of a company.

stitch Any method of joining signatures during binding.

stock art Drawings that can be purchased on disk files for import to desktop publications.

stone Work surface for making up hot metal forms.

storage Computer capability to record and retrieve information.

stripping The organization and positioning of film for platemaking.

style A standard for use of language.

style sheet A set of type specifications entered through a dialog box and used to format type.

stylus A device for drawing. Can input graphic images from a tablet. Also, a pen-like device used for drawing output images on a plotter.

subtractive primaries The basic colors that result when white light is passed through red, green, and blue filters. The subtractive primaries are magenta, cyan, and yellow.

supervisor A function of system software that directs computer operations.

switcher A program that controls access to application programs and enables the user to move quickly from one application to another.

syndicate An organization that provides news and feature materials to subscribing papers. The syndicate sells specific items and is different from a wire service that provides general news coverage.

system, computer The combination of equipment and programs to process, store, and retrieve information.

system software Sets of programs that operate the computer and make processing available to users and their applications.

systems analysis A discipline that specializes in designing procedures and determining hardware and software needs for computer operations.

T

tabloid A size and category of newspapers. Trim size usually is 11.5 by 15.5 inches.

tape storage A method of secondary storage using magnetic tape.

telephone and transient (T and T) Describes a classified ad received over the telephone from advertisers who are not regular customers.

template A guide used in placement of film during stripping. Also, a guide used to position type on dummies and pasteup boards.

text Series of words that presents information.

three-fold A six-page publication folded so that the pages overlap.

tombstone A layout flaw in which headings are lined up in rows so they are said to resemble tombstones in a cemetary.

tone Image value that can be represented by shades of gray or shaded color values.

toner An image-forming substance used in xerographic printing.

track A circular path around the surface of a disk platter that is used for recording and reading data.

track ball A cursor movement and option selection device that can be substituted for a mouse.

trade In the book business, the portion of the industry that prepares books for the general public.

transfer type *See* rubdown type.

transform To convert data to information through processing.

trend line Another name for line graph.

trim The cutting away of uneven edges of a publication on press or during binding.

trim size Measurements for the size of a publication page.

typeface Images that present letters, numbers, and symbols.

U

ultrabold Typeface with extra-dark image.

unispacing Display and print formats in which all characters occupy the same, uniform line widths.

upload To transfer data from a desktop computer to a central system.

user friendly Term that indicates relative ease of use for a computer.

users Persons who use computers or the information they generate.

utilities System software routines that provide standard support functions, such as sorting, copying files, etc.

V

vector A line or a shape whose position and size can be determined mathematically.

vector graphics Lines or shapes that can be defined through identification of points on a display screen.

verso Term for a left-hand page.

video display terminal (VDT) *See* cathode ray tube.

visible light White light viewed by the human eye.

visual aids Pictorial materials used to support oral presentations.

voice activated transcription A technique under which a computer recognizes and transcribes human speech into text files.

volume Value that identifies the number of years a publication has been issued.

W

weekly A newspaper issued once a week.

widow A short line at the bottom of a paragraph or page.

Winchester disk A type of hermetically sealed hard disk used with microcomputers.

wire service A news agency that delivers copy via telecommunications channels.

word processing Use of computer hardware and software to generate text.

word wrap Feature of word processing software that ends entry lines and starts new lines automatically.

WYSIWYG (what you see is what you get) A word processing display in the same format as the printed text to be developed.

X

xerography Electrostatic method of image reproduction.

Index

Page numbers in *italics* refer to Figures in text.

A

Abstracts, 133–134, 135
Access, 37
Accuracy, 200, 256
  of newsletters, 198
  of price lists, 170
Acquisition editors, 237
Additive primary colors, 160, *160*, 161
Adobe Systems, Inc., 54
Advertisements/advertising
  classified, 221
  display, 220–221
  four-color, 206
  Gothic type for, 14
  in magazines, 205, 206, *207*
  newsletters, 185, *186*
  in newspapers, 220–222
  placement of, 206, *207*, 229
  quality of, 207
  sale of, 185
  telephone and transient (T and T), 221
Aldus Corporation, 141
Aldus PageMaker. *See* PageMaker
  headings
Amberlith, 178
American Standard Code for Information
    Interchange (ASCII), 67
  TAB code, 238
Annual reports, 132, *133*
Anti-glare shield, 58, *58*, 256, *257*

Appearance
  of market-support publications, 166, 170, 172
  professional, 78
  of proposals and bids, 80
  of reports, 79
  in RFP preparation, 80
  white space and, 87
  widows and orphans and, 99, 104
Apple LaserWriter, *252*
  PostScript used with, 54
Apple Macintosh Plus, 25, 64, 74, 244, 254
  cost of, 65, 247
  displays, 54
  supplementary memory cards, 58
Apple Macintosh SE, 65
Apple Macintosh 2, 65
Application software, 26, 37, *52*
  defined, 52, 53
  packages, 54
Architectural drawing, 122–123
  symbols, *124*
Arithmetic, 15
Arithmetic logic unit (ALU), 44, 45
Arrowheads, 121–122, *123*
ASCII (American Standard Code for
    Information Interchange), 67, 238
Associated Press (AP), 218
Audio-visual presentations, 153–155, *154*, 163
Author contracts, 237
Authors, 231, 234–235, 237
  coordination with publishers, 63
  external, 63

identifying, 244
in-house, 63
relationships with, 231
word processing software and, 63

B

Background patterns/tones, 107
Backup copies, 50, 51, *51*, 251
Balance
  headlines and subheads, 99
  of illustrations and text, *116*, 240
  across spread, 99
Bar charts, 116, 117, *118*
Batelle Memorial Institute, 8
Bids, defined, 80, 81
Binding, 19, 33—35
  defined, 33
  of newsletters, 182, 198—199
Bit, defined, 44, 45
Bit map/bit-mapping, 46, 47, 142
Blank space. *See* White space
Blanket, defined, 7
Blinking patterns, 256
Block layout, 227
Boards. *See also* Mechanicals
  defined, 29
  line art illustrations on, 108
Body, defined, 15
Bold italic type. *See* Boldface italic
Bold type, 14, *14*, 15
  typesetting codes for, 71, *71*
Boldface italic, 14, *14*, 238—239
  typesetting codes for, 238—239, *239*
Book depositories, 236
Book development, 236—240
Book production, 234—235, 237—240
  scheduling challenges, 235
Book publishing, 232—240
  control in, 234—235
  desktop publishing systems and, 238—240
  marketing challenges, 235—236
Books, 231—241
  copy editing, 237
  design and layout, 237—238
  full-text, 83, 87
  hand-printed, 3

movable type and, 3
page makeup, 239—240
pasteup of, 239—240
trim size, 237
typeface selection, 89
typesetting, 238—239
Bookstores, 233, 234
Booting, 44, 45, 52
Bootstrapping. *See* Booting
Borders, 78
  bottom, 99
  minimum, *87*
  taste and, 89
  top, 99
Bottom alignment, 99, 104
Bottom of page, 104
Boxes/boxing, 116, 133, *133*, 176
Briefings, 153—154
Brochures, 167, *167. See also* Market-support publications
  defined, 167
  three-fold, *200*
Budget meetings, 227
Budgeting, 78, 104—105
Bulk mailing, 194
Bulletins, 81
Bundle sheets, 230
Bureaus, defined, 218, 219
Burn, 32, 33
Business magazines, 203
  layout, 205
Byte, defined, 44, 45

C

Cameras, lithographic process, *30*
Capabilities descriptions, 170, 172
Capture, 21, 61. *See also* Text capture
  defined, 25
Carlson, Chester F., 8
Case bound, defined, 35
Cast off, 131
  defined, 137
  priorities in, 137, 138
  procedure, 137—138
Catalogs, 167—168, *168. See also* Market-support publications
  complexity of, 168

defined, 167
design of, 172
grid formats, 172—174, *173, 174*
grid technique for, 170—172
mail-order, 167
page makeup software for, 174—176
runaround type for, 173, *174*
typeface selection, 172
Cathode ray tube (CRT). *See* Video display terminal (VDT)
Central processing unit (CPU), 42—44, *43*
Change, resistance to, 247
Chapter titles, as running heads, 104
Character display, imaging points, 46
Chase, defined, 5
Checklists, for monitoring magazine production, 210
Circuit boards, 44, *45*, 248, *249*
Circulation
controlled, 205, 216
of magazines and journals, 203, 205
of newspapers, 213, 216
Circulation blotter, 217, 230
Circulation records, of newspapers, 229—230
City room, defined, 220, *221*
Classified advertising, 221
"Clean" copy, 74
Click, 57
Coding for type formats, 23. *See also* Typesetting codes
Coding searches, 74
Cold-type composition, 8, 9, 11
Color
designing in, 160—163
magazines and, 205—206
popularity of, 205
Color coprocessors, 156, *157*
Color elements, identification techniques for, 177—180
Color filters, 161, *161*, 162
Color monitors, 156
Color reproduction, 160—163
balance and control of, 162—163
four-color, 176
photographs, 162—163
preparing for, 176—180
two-color, 176
type elements, 163
Color separation, 165
Color separation scanning machines, *177*
Color-marked tissues, 177, 178, *179*

Column formats
books, 238
for catalogs, 172—174
layout grids for, 172—174
for newsletters, 172, 174, *175,* 188, *189—193*
single-column, 188, *189*
three-column, 188, *191—193*
two-column, 188, *190,* 238
Column inch, defined, 137
Column width
of newsletters, 89—90, *91—95*
rag right lines and, 96
readability and, 89
right-justified type and, 96
Comb binding, 34, *34,* 35
COMMAND module, 52—53
Command-driven software, 67—68
Commands, 67
defined, 56
Communication, 9, 48—49
Communication capabilities, 17, 63—65
Communication links, 25
text input through, 39—40
Compatibility, 245
authorship and, 63
defined, 22
Completion date, 105
Compositor, defined, 5
Computer separation, 177, 178—180
Computers/computer systems, 17, 37. *See also* Desktop computer work stations; Desktop publishing; Microcomputers
components, 38—51
defined, 15
functions, 38
laptop, 219
large-scale, 206, 216—217, *217,* 228, 247
role in desktop publishing, 15—16
standalone, 220, 221
type composition by, 11
Computer work stations, *22,* 228, 256—257, *258*
Computerized typesetting, 12, 26, 239
early, 11
microcomputers and, 12—13
Continuous tone, 108, 109
Contracts, 80—81
Control unit, 43—44
Controlled circulation, defined, 184—185
"Cool" images, 163
Coordination, author-publisher, tips for, 63—68

Copiers. *See* Xerographic reproduction

Coprocessors, 45
  auxiliary, 59
  defined, 45
  for graphics, 46–47
  hypercard, 59

Copy
  defined, 23
  sources of, 213

Copy boxes, 133, *133*

Copy checking, 182, 200
  defined, 199
  newsletters, 198

Copy desks, 220, *221*

Copy editing, 23, *24*
  of books, 235
  defined, 19, 23
  of newspapers, 213, 220
  production editing and, 24

Copy editors, 74, 220, 237

Copy fitting, 131
  defined, 137
  for newsletters, 197
  priorities in, 137, 138
  procedure, 137–138

Copy operation, 73

Copy stands, 257, *258*

Correction(s), 76
  of newsletters, 197

Correspondents, 218–219

Cost-benefit comparisons, 65

Cost-effectiveness, 59

Costs, 26
  desktop publishing and, 105
  of desktop publishing systems, 247–248
  of electronic typesetting machines, 254
  of error-correction, 74
  of IBM PC clones, 65
  of IBM Personal System/2, 65
  of Linotronic outputs, 207
  of Macintosh systems, 65
  for market-support publications, 166
  of microcomputer systems, 247
  of minicomputer-based systems, 260
  monitoring, 105
  overruns, 105
  of plotters, 157
  of publishing software, 253
  of storage capacity, 247
  of transparency preparation, 155

Covers, 34–35
  hard, 35

  of journals and magazines, 205
  soft, 35

Cropping/crop marks, 208–209, *209*

CRT. *See* Video display terminal (VDT)

Cursor, defined, 38, 39

Cuts, defined, 2

D

Data files, 54

Database, defined, 53

Database management system (DBMS),
    defined, 53

Decision making, 248

Decorative boxes, 116

Default, defined, 144–145

Deleting text, 72–73

Delimit, 73, *73*

Delivery date, 105

Demibold typeface, defined, 14

Demodulation, defined, 40, 41

Design/designing, 19
  checklist, *86*, 87, 89–90, 96, 99, 104
  in color, 160–163
  defined, 27
  of magazines, 206–210
  of manuals and reports, 136–137
  of market-support publications, 165, 170, 172
  of newsletters, 182
  readability and, 13–15
  steps in, 27–28
  techniques of, 172–174

Design patterns, for line art, 111, *112*

"Desktop" area, 108

Desktop computer workstations, 22, 228,
    256–257, *258*

Desktop publishing, 1
  computer operations and, 15–16
  introduction of, 12

Desktop publishing systems
  advertisements and, 207
  for book publishing, 231, 234, 238–240
  color capabilities, 206
  coordination with large-scale systems, 260
  cost of, 247–248
  decision criteria for development of, 248
  files, 56
  hardware selection, 248–252

limitations of, 121—122
for market-support publications, 166
networking, 228
for newspaper publishing, 216
newspapers and, 227—228, 229—230
for presentation graphics, 155
setting up, 242—257
"smart," 260
software selection, 252—254
trends, 257, 259—262
typesetting and, 238—239
Developmental editors, 235, 237
Dialog box, 74, *75*
defined, 75
as style sheet, 75
Dictionary, PageMaker, 142
DIF format, 67
Direct-image printing, 6. *See also* Letterpress
Direct-mail catalogs, 167
Diskettes, *50*
capacities, 51
defined, 51
for in-house authorship, 63
input on, 244—245
loading with, 69
for typesetting input, 63
Disks, *50*, 51. *See also* Diskettes; Hard disks
Display advertising, defined, 220, 221
Display(s), 44—45. *See also* Character
display; Graphics displays
colored, 58
defined, 47
drafting software, *55*
graphic, 37, 46—47
large-screen, 58, *59*
page makeup, 56
painting software, 55
for presentations, 153, 155, *156*
versus printer output, 121
projection of, 155, *156*
word processing, *55, 68,* 68—69
Distribution, 19, 35—36
list maintenance, 183
of newsletters, 182, 183, 200
of newspapers, 230
Dot matrix printers, 47—48
Dot patterns, and line art, 108
Dots per inch (DPI), 30, 33
Download, defined, 255
Draft/drafting, defined, 23
Drafting software, 55, 107, 142
defined, 55

screen display, *55*
tool kit, 107
Drag, defined, 109
Drop folio, defined, 96
Dummy, 131, 139—140, *141*
defined, 28, 29

E

EBCDIC (Extended Binary Coded Decimal
Interchange Code), 67
Editing, 21. *See also* Copy editing; Production
editing
electronic, 22
errors in, 74
by hand, 23, *24*, 72
on-line, 23, 72
Editors
acquisition, 237
copy, 74, 220, 237
developmental, 235, 237
of magazines, 210
makeup, 223
of newspapers, 220
production, 23, 237
Educational books, 231, 233, *233*
in depositories, 236
design elements, 234
marketing, 234, 235—236
production scheduling, 235
Efficiency, 74
Electrical circuit diagrams
line art, 122
symbols, *123*
Electronic imaging techniques, 261—262
Electronic manuscripts. *See* Manuscripts,
electronic
Electronic spreadsheets, 116, 117, *117*
Electronic typesetting, 11, 259
Elements, 28
defined, 29
separate files for, 143
Em, defined, 5
End matter, defined, 234, 235
Equations, 80
special treatment for, 133, *133*
Ergonomics, 255—257
defined, 255

Errors
    in correcting errors, 74
    detecting, 26–27
Establishing photographs, defined, 135
Etching, 32, 33
Eyestrain, 13, 256

F

Facilities descriptions, 170
Fatigue, physical, 256
File management software, 53, 56
File servers, defined, 220, 221
Files
    creating, 70–71
    defined, 53, 54
    length of, 240
    names of, 176, *176*
    storage needs, 246–247
    updating, 76
Filters, 161, *161*, 162
Financial reports, defined, 132, 133
Financial statements, abstracts of, 134
First line of page, 99
Flatbed printing, defined, 6
Flats, defined, 32, 33
Flexibility, of page makeup software, 150
Flip charts, defined, 153
Floor plans, as line art example, 122–123, *125*
Floppy disks. *See* Diskettes
Flowcharts, 245, *245*
    development of, 120–122, *121–122*
Folders, 56, 57
Folding
    defined, 199
    machines for, 198
Folio count, defined, 183
Folios
    defined, 87, 96
    position of, 96, 99
Fonts, defined, 26, 27
Format. *See also* Column formats
    of magazines and journals, 204, *204*
    of newsletters, 187–188
    of newspapers, 215
    of periodicals, 27–28

Format line, defined, 68, 69
Formatting
    dialog box and, 74–76
    with PageMaker 3.0, 141–150
    software for, 74
Formatting (disks), 53
Four-color design, 176
Front page layout, of newspapers, 223, *224*, *225*, *226*, 227
Furniture, 57

G

Galleys, *12*, 76, 139
    copy checking, 198
Gathering, 34, 35
Generation, 8, 9
Gigabyte, defined, 220, 221
Glare, 256
Glare screens, 58, *58*, 256, *257*
Gothic typefaces, 14, *14*, 89
Graphics, presentation, 153, 155, 163
Graphics application packages
    for line art, 108–114
Graphics capabilities, 45
    color coprocessors and, 156, *157*
    defined, 12, 43
    early uses of, 12
    function, 45
Graphics card. *See* Graphics processor
Graphics displays
    generation of, 37
    imaging points, 46
Graphics input, 38–42
    with graphics tablet, 40–41
    with mouse, 40, *41*
    through scanner, 42
Graphics outputs, 47–49
Graphics processor, 43, 44–46
Graphics tablet, 40–41
Gray scale, 108, 109
Grayness, 87
Grid, 131, *139*
    defined, 138
Grid technique, 172–174
    multicolumn formats, 172–174
    for newsletters, 173, *173*, *175*

Gutenberg, Johann, 3– 4
Gutenberg Bible, 3, *3*
Gutter, defined, 104, 105

H

Half-life, defined, 154
Halftone, 30, *31*, 33, 108
  defined, 33
Handwriting speed, 10
Hard cover, defined, 35
Hard disks, 50– 51, *246*, 247, 249– 251
  backing up, 50, 51
  defined, 50, 51
  memory requirements, 247
  need for, 69
  purging inactive files on, 54
Hardware
  defined, 38, 39
  trends, 258
Headings, 71, 87
  near bottom of page, 104
Headline schedules, 222– 223, *223*
Headlines, 13
  balancing, 99
  defined, 15
  of newsletters, 197
  positioning of, 99, 240
  size of, 222– 223, 227
  tombstoning of, 240
  typefaces for, 14
Hell box, defined, 3
Hierarchy, defined, 56, 57
High-resolution output, 207– 208
Horizontal images, 158– 159
Hot-metal printing, *2*, 2– 4
House organs, 204
  defined, 187
Human factors, 255– 257
Human interest photographs, 135, *135*
Human interest stories, 227
Hypercard, 59
Hyphenation/hyphens, 96
  automatic, 96
  page-ending, 99
  with PageMaker 3.0, 142

I

IBM, 166
IBM Magnetic Tape/Selectric Typewriter, 217
IBM PC, 22, 247
  clones, 65
  F4 key, 238
  MacLink and, 64– 65, *65*
IBM Personal System/2, 65
Icons, defined, 56, 57
Illustrations, 107, 131. *See also* Graphics
    headings
  coding for identifying descriptions of, 239
  computers for preparation of, 128
  copy fitting, 137– 138
  identifying inputs for, 244– 245
  method of identifying, 24, *25*
  placement of, 107
  positioning, 116, *116*, 138
  preparation of, 19
  preparation costs, 26
  storage capacity and, 246
  subject matter of, 116
  techniques used, 26
  types of, 132– 136
  using, 128
Image area, and laser printers, 87
Imaging software, 54
Imposition, defined, 198, 199
Indentation, 238
Index, 28
Indexing, 240
  automatic, 240
  computer-assisted, 240– 241
Indicia, 182, 194, *196*
  affixing labels to, 200
Information sessions, 154– 155
Initial letters, large, 117
Input function
  components, 38– 42
  defined, 16, 17
  tools, 37
Input/output (I/O) ports
  defined, 48, 49
Inputs, defining, 244– 245
Inserting text, 72, *72*
Instruction sessions, 154– 155, *155*
Instruction set, 43
Instructor's guides, 87
Ion deposition printing, defined, 261

Italic type, 14, *14*, 15
    coding for, 71, *71*, 239

J

Jobs
    complex, 20
    scope of, 104
Journals, 203–204. *See also* Magazines
    covers of, 205
    defined, 203
    layout of, 205
Jumps, 205, 207
    defined, 205
Justification, with PageMaker 3.0, 142

K

Kennedy, John F., 20
Key line, 127, *129*
Keyboard input, 38–40
Keyboards, 38, 39, *39*
Kill sheet, defined, 223

L

Labels, 200
    newspaper, 229–230
Landscape mode, 158
Laptop computers, 219, *219*
Laser disks, 51
Laser printers, *9*, 252
    color cartridges in, 157–158
    costs of, 247–248
    defined, 9
    image area, 87
    large-scale, *260*, 261, *261*
    outputs, 47, 54
    overhead transparencies and, 157–158
    programs stored in, 54
    versus screen displays, 121

selection of, 252
technical requirements, 87
300 DPI capacity, 252, *252*
Layout, 19, 27–28, 78, *91. See also* Makeup; Page
        makeup, electronic
    file names and, 176, *176*
    defined, 27
    of display advertising, 220–221
    front page, of newspapers, 223, *224*
    grid technique, 172–174
    guides for, 138–139
    of line art, 116, *116*
    of magazines and journals, 205, 206–210
    of newsletters, *100–103*, 183
    of newspapers, 213
    overall, 99
    planning of, 138–139
    with PageMaker 3.0, 145–150, *145–150*
    sketching, 138–139
    steps in, 27–28
    structure of, 99
    for text-only publications, 99, *100–103*
Layout forms, 138–139, *139*
Layout grids. *See* Grid
Lead story, defined, 227
Leading, *74*, 75, 96
Legal documents, 80–81
Letter size format, defined, 187, 188
Letterpress, 1, 6–7, *7*
Libraries, 232, *232*
Light tables, 139
Lighting, 57
Line art, 107, 131
    defined, 46, 47, 108, 109
    electrical circuit diagrams, 122, *123*, *124*
    entering with scanning devices, 126–127
    floor plan example, 122–124, *125*
    flowchart development example, 120–122,
        121–122
    generated, 107, 116–118
    layout of, 116
    logo example, 125–126, *125–126*
    mixing with type, 113
    organization chart example, 118–120,
        119–120
    placement of, 138
    preparation with MacDraw II, 108–115,
        108–115
    role of, 108
    scanning devices for entering, 126–127
    software tools for preparation of, 108–114
    special elements, 132–134
    uses of, 108

Line graphs, 116, 117, *118*

Line negatives, 108

Line width, 78. *See also* Column width
   for books, 89
   for newsletters, 89
   for newspapers, 89
   readability and, 89, 90

Linecasting machine, 4, *5*

Lines per inch, 30, 33

Linotronic machines, 207, *208*, 239, 240, 254

Linotype, 4, *5*, 62, 81
   keyboard, *83*
   printing process with, 5

Literacy, 3, 232

Lithography, *7*, 7–8, *8*. *See also* Offset
   printing
   defined, 7
   methods, 29–33
   for printmaking, 7

Loading, 69

Local area networks (LANs), 220, 221, 254–255

Logic, defined, 15

Logos
   Aldus, 142
   alternative, 126
   creating, 124–126
   defined, 124, 125
   line art example, *125, 126*
   newsletters, 194, *195*

Luther, Martin, 4

M

MacDraw format, 175–176

MacDraw II application package
   changing or duplicating shapes with,
      110–111, *111*
   Fill menu, 111, *111*, 112
   line art preparation with, 108–115, *108–115*
   MacDraw format option, 175–176
   main menu, *108*
   organization chart development, 118–120
   PICT format option, 175
   Send to Back function, 112, 113, *113*
   toolbox, *109*

Macintosh. *See* Apple Macintosh *headings*

MacLink, 74

MacLink Plus, 25, 64, 67

Magazines, 4. *See also* Journals
   advertisements in, 206, *207*
   checklists for monitoring production of, 210
   circulation volumes, 203
   covers, 205
   defined, 202, 203
   feature-oriented, 203
   formats, 204, *204*
   high-resolution outputs, 207–208
   layout of, 205
   limitations of desktop publishing
      techniques for, 206–207
   news, 203
   organization of, 205
   photographs in, 206, 208–210
   production concerns, 210–211
   professional, 203–204
   readability of, 13–14
   size of, 204, *204*
   sponsored, 204
   types of, 202, 203–204
   weekly, 203

Magnetic disk devices, 16, *16*, 37, 50–51

Magnetic tape, 37, 51

Mail order catalogs, 167

Mailing, 194

Mailing indicia. *See* Indicia

Mailing lists, newsletters, 187

Main memory. *See* Memory

Makeup. *See also* Layout
   defined, 223
   of display advertising, *222*
   newspapers, 222–223, 228
   typography and, 229

Makeup editors, 223

Management. *See* Project management

Manuals, *85*, 131
   defined, 83, 132, 133
   design of, 136–137

Manuscript development, 22, 61, 237
   steps in, 69–78, *69*

Manuscripts. *See also* Manuscripts,
   electronic
   defined, 19, 21
   length of, 235
   review of, 238
   revision of, 22

Manuscripts, electronic, 22, 235
   capturing of (*see* Text capture)
   defined, 21
   on diskette, 235
   release to typesetting, 74

Market-support publications, 165—180
    appearance of, 170, 172
    deadlines and, 166—167
    design principles, 170, 172
    desktop publishing systems and, 166
    production considerations, 174—180
    types of, 165, 167—170
Marketing, 19, 35—36
Mass market books, defined, 233
Masthead
    defined, 124, 125, 194
    newsletter, *195*
Mat, defined, 5
Matrix displays, defined, 47
Measuring system, for printing, 5, 6
Mechanicals, 238
    camera-ready, 29
    for color reproduction, 176
    defined, 29
Megabyte, defined, 50, 51
Memory, 44
    adding, 248
    defined, 45
    function of, 44
    size of, 246
    supplementary, 58
    temporary, 70
Menus, 26, 67, *67*
    defined, 56, 57
    hierarchy of, 56
    selection from, 74—76
Merganthaler, Ottmar, 4
Metal type, 2, *2*
Microcomputers, *13*, 247. *See also* Desktop
        publishing systems
    configuration, *16*
    costs of, 247
    for input, 245
    memory capacities, 12
    selection of, 248—249
    trends, 259
    typesetting and, 12—13
Microsoft Word, 74, 142, 254
    PageMaker 3.0 and, 142, 143
    style sheets and, 178—179
    version 3.0, 143, 240
Million instructions per second (MIPS), 43
Minicomputer-base systems, 260
MIPS (million instructions per second), 43
Modems, 219—220
    defined, 39—40
Modulation, defined, 40, 41

Modules, defined, 56, 57
Molds, for letterpress printing, 6
Monitors. *See also* Video display terminal
    auxiliary, 58
    defined, 47, 52, 53
    monochrome, 47, 58
Monochrome displays, 47, 58
Monochrome systems, and color cartridges in
        laser printers, 157
Mouse, 26, *40*, 46, 74
    defined, 17
    for graphics input, 40, *41*
    with MacDraw II, 108—111
    selection with, 56—57
    use of, 57, 155
    use of pad with, *57*
Movable type, 1, 3—4
Move operation, 73, *73*
MS DOS, 247
Multicolumn formats, 89—90, *94—95*
MultiMate, 74

N

Negatives, 8, 30
    defined, 7
    halftone, 108
Networking, 254—255
Newsletters, 81, *84*, 182—200, *184*
    accuracy of, 197, 198
    advertising space, 185, *186*
    binding, 198—199
    characteristics of, 183
    classifications for, 182
    column formats, 188, *189*
    column widths, 89—90, *91—95*
    copy checking, 198
    copy fitting, 197
    correction of, 197
    defined, 182, 183
    design and layout considerations, 187—188,
        194
    distribution of, 200
    formats for, 182
    function of, 183
    grid layout for, 173, *175*
    headlines, 197
    layout of, *100—103*, 139, *139*, 183,
        187—188, 194, 197

logos, 124–126, 194, *195*
mailing, 194
mailing lists, 187
masthead, 194, *195*
nonprofit, 185, 187
priority classification system for, 197
profit-making, 183–185
proofreading, 197, 198
scheduling, 200
sponsored, 187
text capture for, 195
three-fold design, 198, *200*
trimming, 198
typesetting, 197
Newspaper composing rooms, 228, *228*
Newspapers, 4, 11, 21, 213–230
advertisements in, 220–222
characteristics of, 214–216
circulation documentation, 213, 229–230
circulation volume, 216
column-oriented layout, 223, *225*
computer work stations in, *12*, 228
copy desk, *23*
copy editing, 213, 220
copy sources, 213, 218–220
daily, 215
defined, 213
design, 222, 223
desktop publishing systems and, 229–230
distribution of, 230
editors, 220
information storage, 220
large-scale computer for, 216–217
layout of, 213
makeup function, 213, 222–223, 228
modular layout, *226*, 227
page size, 215, *215*
paper stock, 214
procedures, former versus current, 62
production concerns, 227–230
publication schedule, 215–216
quality of, 229
readability of, 13–14
standard size, 215, *215*, 223, *224*
typeface selection, 89
weekly, 215
Newsprint, defined, 214, 215
Nonprofit newsletters, 185–186, 187
Nonprofit organizations, defined, 185
Number (of periodical), defined, 194

O

Occupational Safety and Hazards Administration (OSHA), 255
OCR. *See* Optical character recognition
Offset plates, creating, 32
Offset printing, 1. *See also* Lithography
computer outputs for, 16
On-line, defined, 23
Operating (O/S) systems, 52–53, 56, 254
defined, 53
loading, 69
modules, 56
Optical character recognition (OCR), 25
font, *25*
Optical readers, 65–66
Orphans
defined, 99
eliminating, 104
OSHA (Occupational Safety and Hazards Administration), 255
Outline shadows, 112–113, *112–113*
Outputs, 47–51, 207–208
defined, 16, 17, 47
forms of, 16
generation of, 37
graphic, 47–49
high-resolution, 207–208
Overhead transparencies
color, 153
costs of, 155
defined, 153
horizontal outputs, 158–159
laser printers for generation of, 157–158
masters, 155
plotters and, 157
for training sessions, 154–155
writing on, 154–155
Overlays, 177
cutting, 178, *178*
defined, 177

P

Page layout. *See* Layout; Page makeup, electronic
Page makeup, electronic. *See also* PageMaker *headings*

of books, 231, 239–240
with PageMaker 3.0, 143–150, *147–150*
Page makeup software, 28–29, 56, 74, 131,
     140–150, 253–254. *See also* PageMaker
     headings
  for catalogs, 174–176
  defined, 29, 57
  flexibility of, 150
  word processing software in, 63
Page numbering, continuity of, between text
     files, 104
Page-oriented software, 70–71
PageMaker 1.0, 142
PageMaker 2.0, 142
PageMaker 3.0, 253, *253*
  advanced capabilities of, 142
  Autoflow option, 148, *148*
  color separation and, 157, 165, 178–180, 206
  Column Guides option, 144
  default setting, 144–145
  Define Colors option, 179, *180*
  Define Styles option, 179, *180*
  Edit Color option, 179, *180*
  Edit Style dialog box, 179, *180*
  File menu, 143, 145
  file names for layout, *176*
  File pulldown menu, *144*
  Finder menu, 143, *143*
  Fit the Window mode, 150
  flexibility of, 150, *150*
  formatting report with, 143–150
  as formatting tool, 142
  importing copy into, 143, 146–147
  main menu, *143*
  master created with, 138
  menu, *176*
  Microsoft Word and, 142, 143
  opening new file, 143–144
  Options menu, 144, *144*, 148
  Orientation option, 159, *159*
  output for color reproduction, 180
  page makeup with, 143–150, *147–150*, 231,
     239, *239*
  Page Setup dialog box, *144*
  Place option, 145–146, *150*
  processing speed, 143
  standoff specification, 149–150
  storage needs, 142–143
  success of, 141–142
  text flow options, 149
  Text Wrap option, 148–149, *149*, 150
  Toolbox option, 147, *150*
  using, 143

working grids and, 145
  Wrap option, 149, *149*
Paid subscriptions, 184, 185, 187
Painting software, 55
  screen display, *55*
Palette, defined, 55
Paper, newsprint, 214, 215
"Paper trail," 72
Pasteup, 139–140. *See also* Boards;
     Mechanicals
  of books, 239–240
  defined, 28, 29
  desktop publishing and, 29
  of newspapers, *228*, 228–229, *229*
  traditional, 141, 142
Pedagogical materials, defined, 234, 235
Perfect binding, defined, 34, 35
Periodicals. *See also* Journals; Magazines;
     Newsletters; Newspapers
  deadline pressure of, 81
  defined, 4
  formats of, 27–28
  production editing, 24
Photo offset techniques, 7–8
Photo resist, defined, 8, 9
Photocomposition, 8
Photographs, 131
  color, 162–163
  cropping, 208–209, *209*
  "day in the life of," 136
  establishing, 135
  halftone reproductions, 127, 128
  human-interest, 135, *135*
  instructional sequences, 136, *136*
  lithography and, 7
  in magazines, 208–210
  portrait, 138
  positioning, 127–128, 138, *210*
  reproduction of, 30
  role of, 134–136
  selection of, 208
  series of, 134
  sizing of, 209
  sources of, 208
  story-telling, 134–136
  tagging, 209, *210*
Photojournalism, 134–136, *135*
Phototypesetting, 11, 47
Pica, defined, 5–6
Pica ruler, *6*
PICT format, 175

Pie, defined, 3
Pie charts, 116, 117, *118*
Pin register, 32
    defined, 33, 141
    using, 140
Pixel, defined, 45– 46, 47
Pixel graphics, 46– 47
Placement
    of advertisements, 229
    of headlines, 240
    of illustrations, 240
    of photographs, 127– 128, 138, *210*
Platemaking, 32, *33*
Platemaking film, 176, 177
Plotters, *48*
    costs of, 157
    defined, 48, 49
    for transparency generation, 157
Point, *6*
    defined, 6, 7
Positioning. *See* Placement
Postage meters, 194
Posters, defined, 153
PostScript, 54, 142
Presentation graphics. *See also* Graphics
    headings
    defined, 153
    forms of, 153
    in information transfer, 163
    time to output, 155
Press(es)
    defined, 5
    first, 4, *4*
    origin of use of word, 4
    web, 33, *33*, 214, *214*
Press checks, 210– 211
Press runs, and electronic imaging techniques,
    261– 262
Price lists, 170, *171*
Prices. *See* Costs
Primary colors, additive, 160, *160*, 161
Primary storage, defined, 45. *See also* Memory
Primitives, 43
Printer's devil, 3
Printers, 47– 48
    defined, 47
    dot-matrix, 252
    laser (*see* Laser printers)
Printing, 19, 29– 33
    as trade, 2– 3
    trends in, 261

Printing presses. *See* Press(es)
Printing processes, 4– 5
Printouts, defined, 47
Priorities
    in copy fitting, 137
    establishing, 197
Process, defined, 4, 5, 20
Process approach, 20– 21, *20*
Processing
    analyzing needs, 245– 246
    capabilities, trends in, 258
    computer components, 42– 47
    speed of, 43, 246
    tools, 37
Processors, 42– 44
Product information sheets, 168, *169*, 170, 172.
    See also Market-support publications
Production
    of magazines, 210– 211
    of market-support publications, 174– 180
    of newsletters, 182, 197– 200
Production editing, 19, 23– 24, 237
Production editors, 23, 237
Production management, 19
Production techniques, 78
    special, 104
Productivity
    formatting and, 71
    tension and, 256
Professional appearance, 78
Professional books, 231
    defined, 235
    marketing, 234
Profit-making newsletters, 183– 185
Programs, 15, 16
Project management, 104– 105
Project reports, defined, 132, 133
Projection devices, 155, 156, *156*
Promotion, of trade books, 236
Proofreading, 26– 27, 61, 76, 200
    corrections in, *27*
    defined, 26, 27
    newsletters, 197, 198
    reasons for, 76
    tasks, 27
Proportional spacing, 71– 72
Proportional wheel, 210, 211, *211*
Proposals, defined, 81, 82
Prospectus documents, 81, *82*
Protocols, 67

Publication, frequency of, 215

Publication management, of newsletters, 183—185

Publishers, coordination with authors, 63—68

Publishing process, 20—21
    flowchart, *21*
    steps in, 21—35, 166

Purchasing process, 79—80, *80*

Purging, 54

Q

Quadrants, 174, 175, *175*

Quality
    laser printers and, 9
    of magazines, 207, 210—211
    of newspapers, 214, 229
    offset presses and, 8

Quality control
    of magazines, 207
    production editing and, 23
    proofreading and, 26

Quality master, preparation of, 160

"Quick and dirty," 132

Quotation boxes, defined, 99

R

Radiation, 255—256

Rag right lines, 6, 96, *97*, *98*

Read-only memory (ROM), 44, 45, 52

Read/write head, defined, 50, 51

Readability, 13—14
    color and, 162—163
    design and, 13—15
    line width and, 89, 90
    of text-only publications, 89
    type size and, 96

Rectangle, drawing with MacDraw II, 110

Recto, defined, 104, 105

Referees, 203—204

Reference books, 234, 235

Reflective primaries, defined, 161

Registration, defined, 32, 33

Registration marks, defined, 180

Release
    for makeup, 76
    to typesetting, 74

Reports, 131
    case situation, 79
    defined, 79, 132, 133
    design of, 136—137
    examples of, 79
    formatting with PageMaker, 141—150
    layout and production of, 137—140
    "quick and dirty," 132
    special situations, 132
    text-only, 79
    typeface selection, 89
    types of, 132

Requests for proposal (RFP), 79—80

Reverse reading
    defined, 4, 5
    etching and, 7

Review, of manuscripts, 72—74, 238

Review copies, 235—236

Revision, 22, 24, 54, 61, 72—74

Rewrite, defined, 220, 221

Right reading, defined, 5

Right-justified type, 96

ROM. *See* Read-only memory

Roman typefaces
    defined, 14, 15
    example, *14*
    newspapers and, 89
    uses, 14

Rotary presses, *6*, 6—7

Rubdown art, 122, *123*

Rubdown type, 160, *161*

Rubylith, 178

Ruler, printer's, *6*

Run of publication (ROP), 206, 207

Runaround type, 136, 137, *137*
    for catalog layout, 173, *174*

Running heads, 96
    chapter titles printed as, 104
    defined, 87, 96
    space around, 96
    typeface, 96

S

Saddle, defined, 198, 199

Saddle stitching, 34
    defined, 35
    machine for, *199*
    with staples, 198, *199*

Sales literature, 166, 167. *See also* Market-support publications

San-serif typeface, 1, 14, *14*, 15
Saturation, indicating with PageMaker, 179
Save operation, 70—71
Scan pattern, 16, *17*, 45—46
Scanners. *See* Scanning devices
Scanning, 65—67, 244
Scanning devices, 25, *42*, 65—67, *66*, *127*, *128*
    defined, 43
    for graphics input, 42
    high-quality, 207
    input, 42, 126—127
    use of, 127
Scheduling, 105
    book production, 231, 235
    market-support publications and, 166—167
    newsletters, 200
    newspapers, 215—216
    "tight," 105
Scope of job, 104
Scratchpad function, 44
Scrivener, defined, 9—10
Scrolling, 75
Seating, 256, *258*
Secondary storage, 48, 49
Securities and Exchange Commission (SEC),
    80—81
Selection of computer, 248—249
Selection operation, 15, 74, 75
Selenium, 8
Self-covered publications, 34—35, *35*
    trimming, 35
Send to Back function, 112, 113, *113*
Separation, 176—177
Sequencing, 15
Serif, 1, *14*
    defined, 14, 15
Setting type. *See* Typesetting
Setting up production facility, 243—257
    steps in, 243—257, *244*
Shakespeare, William, 4
Shapes
    changing or duplicating with MacDraw II,
        110—111
    combining, 114, *114*
Shortcuts, 132
Side stitching, 34
Signatures, defined, 32, 33
Size
    of headlines, 222—223, 227

of magazines, *204*
of newspapers, 215, *215*, 222
Sizing
    defined, 209
    instructions for, 209, *210*
    tools for, 210, *211*
Slides
    color, 153
    defined, 153
    production of, 156—157, *158*
Slugs, 223, 229
    defined, 139, 220
Soft cover publications
    defined, 35
    trimming, 35
Soft hyphens, 96
Software. *See also* Application software;
        System software
    defined, 38, 39
    storage capacities and, 49
    trends in, 259
Spine, defined, 34, 35
Split-screen, 74—75, *75*
Sponsored newsletters, 187
    internal versus external, 187
Spooling software, defined, 240
Spread, defined, 99
Spreadsheets, 116, 117
Standalone computers, 220, 221
Standard type, *14*
Standoff
    defined, 149
    specification with PageMaker 3.0, 149—150
Stapling, 34
Status reports, defined, 132, 133
Steam engines, 4
Stitching, 34, 35
Stock art, 107, 115, *115*
Stone, defined, 5
Storage, 54
    costs of, 247
    defined, 15
    determining needs for, 246—247, 250—251
    minimum needs, 250—251
    at newspapers, 220
    trends, 259
Storage devices, 15
    defined, 49
Stress, 256
Strippers, 32, *32*, 176, 178

Stripping, defined, 32, 33
Study guides, 87
Style, defined, 23
Style sheets
    books, 239, *239*
    defined, 75
    support of, 142
Stylus, 40–41
Subheads, 89
    balancing, 99
    near bottom of page, 104
    space above and below, 96
Subject matter, of illustrations, 116
Subscription sales, of newsletters, 184–185
Subtractive primaries, 161, 162, *162*
Supercomputers, 15, 43
Superscripts, 133
Supervisor, defined, 52, 53
Switcher, defined, 254, 255
Symbols, 80
    architectural drawing, *124*
    electrical circuit diagrams, *123*
    flowchart, *121*
Syndicates, defined, 218, 219
System software, *52*
    defined, 52, 53
    storage space for, 246–247
    types of, 52–54
System, computer, defined, 17
Systems analysis, defined, 243

T

Table of contents, 28
Tables, 134, *134*
Tabloids
    defined, 215
    makeup patterns, 223, *224*
    size of, 215, *215*
Tape storage. *See* Magnetic tape
Tasks, 20
    dividing job into, 104
    time for, 105
Telephone and transient (T and T)
        advertisements, 221
Telephone lines, 49
Teletypewriters, 62

Television technology, 16–17
Templates, 32, 140, *140*
    defined, 33, 139
Tension, 256
Text
    defined, 15
    illustration guidelines, 116
    typefaces for (*see* Typeface)
Text capture, 19, 21, 69–72. *See also* Capture
    for newsletters, 195
    typesetting codes and, 71
Text files, 54
Textbooks. *See* Educational books
Text-only publications, 78–105
    types of, 79–81, 83, 85
Three-column format, 188, *191–193*
Three-fold design, 199, *200*
Tombstoning, defined, 240
Tone, 46
    defined, 47
Toner, 8, 261
    defined, 9
    opaque images and, 158
    quality output and, 240
Top alignment, 99, 104
Top of page, 99
Track, 50, 51
Track ball, 58, 59, *251*
Tracks, 50
Trade books, 231
    defined, 233
    marketing, 234, 236
    production scheduling, 235
    profit potential, 236
Training sessions, 154–155, *155*
Transfer type, 160, *161*
Transform, defined, 44, 45
Translation capabilities, 64–65
    general purpose programs, 67
Transmission, 39–40
    screen display, *40*
Transparencies. *See* Overhead transparencies;
        Slides
Transparency masters, 155
    monochrome, 158
Trend line, 118, 119. *See also* Line graphs
Trends, 257, 259–262
Trim/trimming, 198
    defined, 35

Trim size
    books, 237
    defined, 183
Two-color design, 176
Two-column format, 188, *190*, 238
Type elements, manipulation of, 104
Typeface, 74– 75, *76*, 78, 89, 187
    for catalogs, 172
    color, 163
    condensation of text by, 80
    defined, 1, 14
    formatting categories, 14– 15
    readability and, 13, 89
    for running heads, 96
    san-serif, 14
    scanning devices and, 66– 67
    selection of, 71, 74– 75, *76*, 78
    serif, 14
    size of, 96
    specification of, 71, *86*, 87
    variety of, *90*
Typesetting, 61
    computerized, 11, 12– 13, 26, 239
    cost savings, 26
    with desktop publishing systems, 231
    detecting errors in, 27
    electronic, 11, 254, 259
    impact-printing, 217
    Linotype and, 5
    for newsletters, 197
    release to, 74
    traditional versus desktop publishing, 24
Typesetting codes, 24, 71, 231, 238– 239, 259
Typewriters, 10, *10*, 54
    with computer-type memories, 10
    electronic, 10
    tape-operated, 10, *11*
Typography, and makeup, 224

U

Ultrabold typefaces, 14, 15
Unispacing, defined, 72
United Press International (UPI), 218
U.S. Postal Service, 194
    permits, 194
Updating, 76
Upload, defined, 255

User friendly, defined, 53
User guides, 132
Users, defined, 39
Utilities, defined, 53

V

VDT. *See* Video display terminal
Vector, defined, 46, 47
Vector graphics, 46, *46*, 47
Ventura Publisher, 63, 247
Verso, defined, 104, 105
Vertical images, 158
Video display terminal (VDT), 16, 47, 68, 248.
    See also Displays; Monitors
    color, 156
    large-screen, 248– 249, *250*
    radiation from, 255– 256
    scan pattern, 16, *17*
Videotype presentations, 153
Visible light, defined, 160, 161
Vision, 13, 256
Visual aids. *See* Presentation graphics
Visual interest, 116
    boxing for, 133
    large initial letters for, *117*
Voice activated transcription, defined, 259
Volume, defined, 194

W

"Warm" images, 162– 163
Watson, Thomas, Jr., 166
Web presses, 33, *33*, 214, *214*
Wet processing, 254
White space, 78, 87, 89
    breaking gray area with, 89
    guidelines for, 87
    between lines, 96
    between paragraphs, 89
    at side, 89
    above and below subheads, 96
    at top, 89

Widows
  avoiding, 104
  defined, 99
Winchester disk drives, 51, *51*
Wire services, 218, *218*, 219
Word. *See* Microsoft Word
Word processing, 26
  newspaper operations and, 62—63
Word processing software, 54—55, 78
  display capabilities, *55, 68*, 68—69
  loading, 69
  menu versus command driven, 67—68
  packages, 54—55
  page-oriented, 70—71
  selecting, 63
  with typesetting capabilities, 254
Word wrap, 70, *70*, 71
WordPerfect, translation programs, 67
WordStar, 247

Work stations, 228
  ergonomically efficient, 256—257, *258*
Workbooks, 87
Writing on computers, 1, 22. *See also* Word
  processing
WYSIWYG (what you see is what you get), 68, 69

X

Xerographic reproduction, 1, 8—9, *9*
  color, 160
  defined, 9
  development of, 8
  laser printers and, 9
  objection to, 262
  for overhead transparencies, 159—160
Xerox Corporation, 8, 247